THE CHILDREN'S BOOK OF
QUESTIONS
&ANSWERS

THE CHILDREN'S BOOK OF

QUESTIONS

Edited by
Anthony Addison

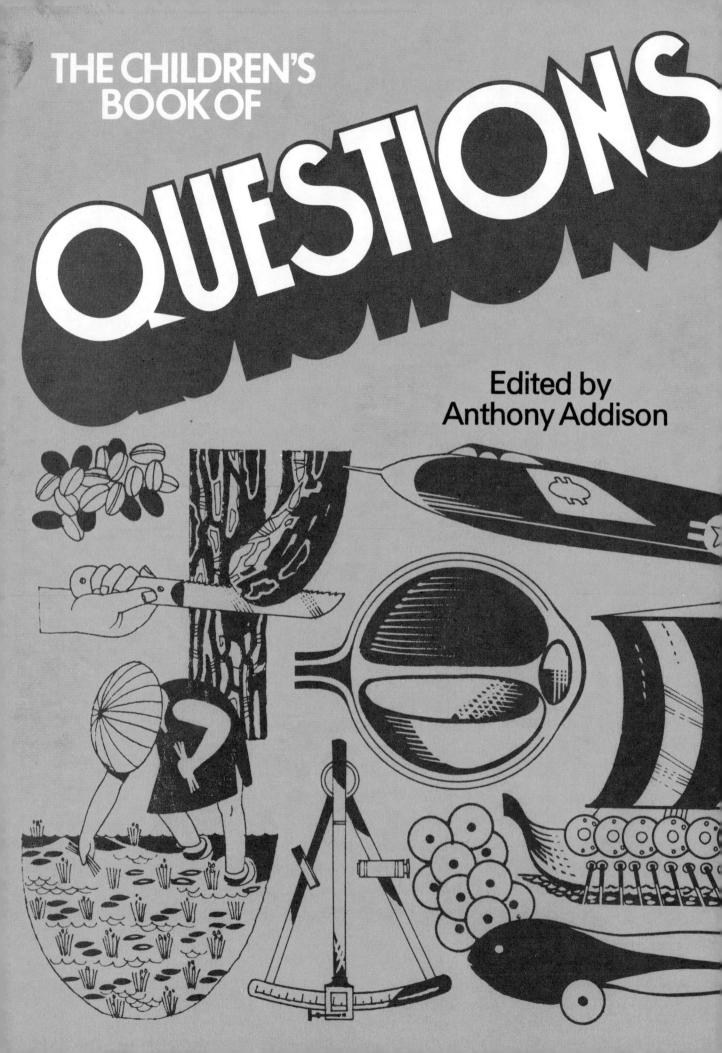

&ANSWERS

TREASURE PRESS

Contents

ABOUT THIS BOOK

Life consists of asking questions. We start from the moment we learn
to string words together and most of us go on asking them for
the rest of our lives. Alas, we don't always find the answers. This book
presents a random array of questions most commonly
asked by children and parents alike.

When a question springs to mind, ferreting out
the answer can be a difficult business. Often the
answer lies buried in a mass of information we don't need.

This book goes straight to the heart of the matter and answers simple
(and not so simple) questions in a down-to-earth manner.

What is a loofah? When does an atom split? Where do
teeth come from? Why do rabbits have large ears?

The questions are divided into six main categories. There is no attempt

**First published in Great Britain in 1974 by
Octopus Books Limited**

**This edition published in 1987 by
Treasure Press
Michelin House
81 Fulham Road
London SW3 6RB
Under licence from Lynx Press Limited**

Reprinted 1988, 1989

© 1974 Lynx Press

ISBN 1 85051 215 9

**Printed in Czechoslovakia
50344/19**

to be definitive, for millions of questions could be posed. With the help of a team of teachers and students, we've picked out the ones most commonly asked—and some that simply appeal to us. If you know what makes a pencil seem to "bend" when you put it in a tumbler of water, if you can instantly explain the nature of a vacuum then go to the top of the question class. If you can't then welcome aboard. Our family book of questions will be your perfect guide and companion.

And when you've exhausted *our* questions, try dreaming up some of your own—and find out the answers for yourself!

8

WHEN does the male stickleback turn red? WHEN do birds

Natural History

MALE STICKLEBACK

The male stickleback's belly turns red at the start of the breeding season in spring. Normally the belly of this small fish is silver-coloured, the rest of it varying from brown to green. But when the time comes for him to mate he becomes very active in attracting females with his bright new colour.

In building the home and rearing the family the male stickleback performs many of the functions usually associated with a female fish. He chooses the place for the nest, collects the stems of various aquatic plants and binds them together using a threadlike web secreted from his kidney.

Once the female has been enticed into his nest, she will lay her eggs and depart, leaving him on guard. He watches over the eggs with great care and even looks after the baby fish.

MIGRATION

Millions of birds of many different varieties migrate at the end of summer. With unfailing regularity they leave the regions where they were born to fly to warmer climates for the winter. The following spring they return to their breeding grounds.

Each year these migratory birds travel as much as 20,000 miles, finding their way back on time with extraordinary precision. Some travel as individuals.

Migration is triggered off by the length of daylight, which apparently affects the birds' nervous systems. When the days get shorter the birds receive the signal to leave for their warmer winter grounds, and, when the daylight increases to a certain level, they receive another signal to return home.

The swallows pictured above are European swallows wintering in Africa.

migrate? WHEN does a chameleon change colour?

CHAMELEON

A chameleon will change colour when it senses danger. This remarkable member of the lizard family can change colour to match its background or, at least, to become almost unrecognizable.

The ranges of colours and patterns of the various species differ widely, but most chameleons can become yellow or cream, green or dark brown. They can also adapt spots either dark or light depending on the colour of the ground.

Apart from its response to danger, the chameleon will change colour according to the light and temperature. This mechanism is controlled from the nervous system and involves the dispersion or concentration of colour pigments in the creature's skin.

10

WHERE did all the dodos go? WHERE would you find the

THE DODO

The dodo was rather a stupid bird. Indeed, it was so stupid that it was named dodo by the Portuguese when they discovered Mauritius—its home—in 1507. The Portuguese word *doudo* means stupid.

Mauritius is an island, 720 square miles in area and lying 500 miles to the east of Madagascar in the Indian Ocean. Until the arrival of man, with his attendant creatures such as the cat and dog, the dodo had been able to live in peace. It had no enemies, which was fortunate because it was big and clumsy and was completely unsuited to fleeing from danger. Its short legs were almost incapable of supporting the weight of the fat, round body (about the size of a swan's), and the ridiculously inadequate, stubby wings were of no use for flying.

Within 180 years of its discovery by the Portuguese, the dodo was extinct. Over the intervening years several were brought to Europe alive, and one was to be seen in London in 1638. By 1680 the dodo had succumbed.

With the help of drawings and by the collection of bones gathered in Mauritius, an almost complete reconstruction has been made of the poor bird. It can be seen at the Natural History Museum in London.

Mauritius is the only place in the world where the bird is known to have existed. A similar bird once lived on the neighbouring island of Rodriguez, but this also has become extinct.

The phrase "as dead as the dodo" is used to mean that something is very dead indeed.

The illustration shows how a man is dwarfed by the vast size of the blue whale.

LARGEST ANIMAL

Blue whales are the largest living animals. They are cosmopolitan creatures and are found in most of the seas, from the polar caps to the equator. Normally those which inhabit the colder seas will migrate to warmer waters in winter.

Their dimensions are almost beyond belief. Although figures can never be quite accurate, a blue whale can weigh more than 200 tons and many have been found measuring over 100 feet in length. The tongue alone, of a female whale found in Antarctica, weighed well over four tons.

It has been estimated that in the 1930s there were nearly 40,000

world's largest animal? **WHERE** does a bee keep its sting? **WHERE** would you find truffles?

BEE STING

A bee keeps its sting at the end of its abdomen. At the tip of a bee's abdomen is a shaft where its stinging thorn is to be found. It can sting several times, but once it leaves the thorn in its victim's flesh it will not be able to sting again.

It is not true to say that a bee will automatically die once it loses its thorn. Only female bees can sting. Male bees, or drones, lack this means of protecting themselves.

There is a species of which even the female cannot sting. But these bees which live mainly in Africa and South America are not defenceless. If disturbed, they will fly at the intruder in great numbers, crawl into his eyes, ears and hair and smear him with a sticky substance, causing him to retreat in great discomfort.

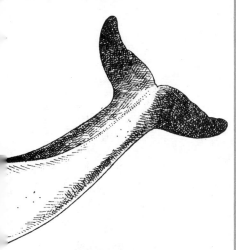

Approx 5′ 8″

blue whales in the world. But by the end of the 1960s there were fewer than 1,000 alive. This was because they became popular victims for the misdirected efforts of over-zealous hunters.

TRUFFLES

If you want to sound extremely clever you can confuse your friends by telling them that the real name for truffles is Ascomycetes. That's what the botanists call them. But you're most likely to come across truffles in the very best French pâtés—for example, in the famous pâtés of the Perigord region of France.

The Perigord truffles became famous for culinary purposes as long ago as the 15th Century and ever since that time they have been regarded as essential to the production of the very finest pâtés.

These Perigord truffles have a distinct smell, but this is by no means unpleasant. Some truffle hunters can actually smell out the truffle in the woodlands but in France specially trained hounds with a keenly developed sense of smell are used.

Truffles look rather like large spongy walnuts and they grow under the soil. Pigs adore them. In early days pigs were turned loose in the woodlands to root for the truffles buried beneath the soil and leaves. Even today pigs are used to sniff out truffles but they certainly are not allowed to eat them, since truffles fetch high prices as a food delicacy.

The best truffles are considered to be those in the forest regions of the Dordogne area of France, where the climate is warm and moist, and there is plenty of limestone in the earth. This is one reason why Perigord, in the heart of the Dordogne, has achieved such a great reputation for fine pâtés. The most famous pâté of all —the very expensive *pâté de foie gras*—comes from Perigord.

Truffles are also found in the southern counties of France's neighbour, England. The commonest English truffle has the botanical name of *Tuber Aestivam*. It is found on chalky soil and in beech woods. In the county of Wiltshire these truffles are cropped commercially.

WHAT is a flying fox? WHAT is a greenshank?

FLYING FOX

A flying fox is a kind of bat and is so called because its head somewhat resembles that of the fox. Most bats are small and look like winged mice. But flying foxes can be as big as little dogs and have a wing span of up to six feet.

Their habits are rather similar to those of ordinary bats, except that they are fond of fruit, a peculiarity which makes them great pests in orchards. Flying foxes of different species are found in Malaysia, India and other parts of Asia, islands of the Pacific and Indian Oceans. Flying foxes rely on sight instead of sound for finding their way.

GREENSHANK

A greenshank is a little bird with a long beak and olive-green legs—a member of a group of birds known as sandpipers.

The greenshank breeds in Scotland, Norway, Sweden and Finland. It builds its nest on the ground, being content usually to settle in a small hollow, lined with heather or dry grass. The eggs are pale buff or stone colour, blotched with purplish-grey and spotted with dark brown.

Worms, insects and tiny fish provide the bird's food. In winter the greenshank migrates, sometimes as far south as Australia or South Africa.

WHY do bats make a high-pitched sound as they fly? WHY

WHY is the ichneumon fly known

SOUND OF BATS

Bats use high-pitched sounds to find their way about. They are nocturnal animals. That is they move about by night. So they have developed their hearing to such an extent that they can find their way by a method known as echolocation.

The blind-flying abilities of bats were first studied by Lazzaro Spallanzani (1729–1799). He surgically removed the eyeballs from several bats to prove that they did not need to see to fly.

In the 20th Century, biologists, using electronic instruments, have carried out experiments with bats. They have discovered that bats find out where to go by emitting high-frequency sounds and receiving the echoes as they bounce off objects. Most of the sounds have too high a frequency to be heard by the human ear.

Bats commonly fly together in groups, but apparently they are not confused by the sounds and echoes produced by each other. When hunting in woods and in the rain they are able to discriminate between the faint echoes bouncing off insects and those bouncing off the ground, tree-trunks, branches, twigs and raindrops.

These tiny flying mammals have been using the equivalent of our modern sonar device for millions of years.

SENSE OF SMELL

Dogs have a better sense of smell than we do because the physical structure of a dog is better adapted for scenting odours. In dogs this sense has remained keen, while in man it has become comparatively dull. Dogs use scent in feeding, detecting enemies, recognizing mates and offspring and in rivalry.

The chemical sense of smell is called chemoreception and the sense organs chemoreceptors. But there is little in the structure of the

ICHNEUMON FLY

The Ichneumon fly is known as the farmer's friend because it controls a great many plant pests. Species have even been transported by man to colonize areas where artificial pest controls have not been successful.

Ichneumon flies, of which there are thousands of species spread throughout the world, are parasitic and their larvae feed on caterpillars, pupae and larvae of other insects.

Larva (plural, larvae) is the name given to an insect from the time it leaves the egg till it is transformed into the pupa or grub. The pupa (plural, pupae) is the name given to the chrysalis.

The female fly lays her eggs in or on the larvae or pupae of the host species. When the maggotlike parasitic larvae hatch out, they feed on the body fats and fluids of the host until they are fully grown. Then the parasitic larvae spin cocoons within which they pupate and from whence the adult fly emerges. In the case of parasitic larvae breeding inside the host, the latter behaves normally until shortly before the uninvited guest larva has fully developed.

There are some ichneumon flies which live on other ichneumon flies and these are called hyperparasitic. The different species of ichneumon vary greatly in size and the range extends from $\frac{1}{8}$" up to $1\frac{1}{2}$–2" in length.

do dogs have a better sense of smell than we do?
as the farmer's friend?　WHY are birds' eggs so shaped?

nose to provide clues about its mechanism, and relatively little is known about how smell works. There are no accessory structures in the nose, and the receptors and nerve fibres leading to the brain are so fine that they are difficult to study. The chemoreceptors of human beings, dogs and other mammals lie in a cleft in each nostril.

During quiet breathing the main flow of air by-passes the cleft. But when a mammal sniffs, air is drawn into the clefts and over about half a square inch of yellowish tissue in which are embedded several million chemoreceptors. They are long thin cells with hair-like crowns making a web lying on the surface of the tissue which is bathed in mucus. These are connected to a part of the brain called the olfactory bulb, the size of which is a fair indication of the keeness of the sense of smell.

The olfactory bulb of a dog is much larger than that of a man. The moist nose of a dog also aids his sense of smell.

Smells are immensely important to dogs as we see from the way they refuse to by-pass a scent without investigating it and, very often, adding to it. They mark their home range and investigate passers-by. Their keen sense has been used by man as a help in hunting and tracking for many thousands of years.

BIRDS' EGGS

The roundness of an egg allows pressure to be applied from the outside which would break it if applied from the inside. Thus a helpless chick is protected until the moment it needs to break out from its shell. It can then do this with the gentlest of tapping.

Eggs are hatched by an adult bird sitting on them, and the best container for round objects is a cup-shaped nest which prevents them rolling about. So the best shape for eggs is for one end to be smaller than the other. The normal position for eggs in a nest is to have the smaller ends pointing inwards. This means the eggs take up the minimum of room and make it easier for the sitting bird to cover them.

Birds with scanty nests, as in the case of most sea birds, have more elongated eggs. If such eggs are caught by the wind while lying on some cliff-face or rocky ledge, they will spin round instead of rolling over the edge.

BUTTERFLY

A caterpillar starts to become a butterfly as soon as it enters the chrysalis stage, by wrapping itself in a cocoon. During this phase, known as pupation, the insect gradually develops all the butterfly characteristics, including wings. For some butterflies the transformation may be complete in one or two weeks. But others need many months before they are ready to leave the cocoon and fly away.

From the time it is hatched to the time it starts the pupation stage, a caterpillar or larva does little more than eat, grow larger and moult several times. This larval stage varies according to the species. Small caterpillars will complete their development in a week, but some large varieties will take up to two years or more.

When this period is over the caterpillar spins a cocoon under a leaf or even underground, and enters it to begin the transformation. Many cocoons are of silk.

pollution kill a river?

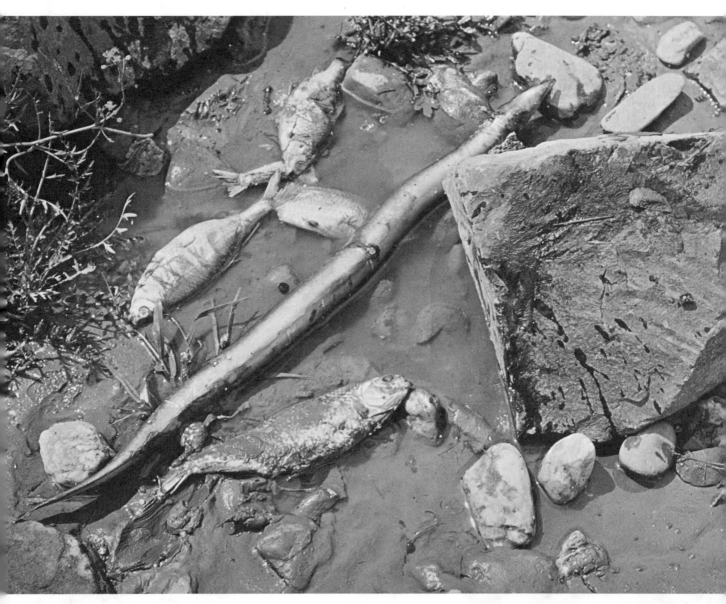

DYING RIVER

A river will die when pollution reaches such a level that all the available oxygen is absorbed.

This can happen if the oxygen is used up by the presence in the water of an excessive number of waste organisms.

Large amounts of nitrogen or phosphorus make a river's oxygen-producing plants grow so rapidly that they become overcrowded and die of exhaustion. Then the fish also die because they are deprived of plant food. Finally various forms of bacteria decay and the water becomes putrefied.

All human industrial waste produces pollution. Excessive quantities of chemicals and minerals deposited in rivers will kill the water by destroying its oxygen content.

Some rivers flowing through industrial areas have been so changed that it is possible to set fire to them. This happened to the Cuyahoga River in Ohio in 1969.

Above: dead fish in a stagnant pond.
Below: detergent foam covers the surface of a river in Pennsylvania, U.S.A. The foam will gradually kill the river.

WHERE do whelks lay their eggs? WHERE does caviare

WHELKS

A whelk is a kind of sea-snail. It eats clams, worms, barnacles and smaller snails. The female lays her eggs in hard capsules. These are arranged in clusters of strings and attached to rock, wood, and shells.

Fishermen use whelks as bait. They catch the whelks by setting traps and baiting them with crabs.

Whelks are eaten by cod and starfish, the kind of fish that find their food at or near the bottom of the sea bed.

CAVIARE

Caviare is the roe of the female members of the sturgeon family. These fish are found in northern and central Asia, Europe and North America.

The best quality black caviare comes from sturgeon caught during the winter months in the estuaries of rivers which flow into the Baltic Sea. It is regarded as a great delicacy and has been known in western Europe since the sixteenth century. Shakespeare mentions it in his play *Hamlet*. In the Soviet Union and eastern Europe, the coarser quality caviare is a staple food and is traditionally accompanied by gulps of vodka.

When caviare is prepared, the roe is carefully strained to remove fibres and fat. It is then salted and packed into small barrels, jars or tins. Its salty flavour and grainy texture are an acquired taste. But like all expensive foods, it is a taste thought by many people to be worth acquiring. Caviare is usually served as an *hors d'oeuvre* with bread or toast, or on small biscuits with drinks.

As well as the grey and black caviare, there is also a red caviare. This is prepared from the roe of salmon and is considered by experts in these matters to be of inferior quality.

come from? **WHERE** do butterflies go when it rains?

BUTTERFLIES

When it rains butterflies settle on the stems of flowers or stalks of grass. They hang head downwards with their wings folded together over their backs. Most butterflies are difficult to see when their wings are closed, because the undersides have only pale colours and faint patterns.

There are about 10,000 known species of butterfly. They range in size from less than an inch to the swallow-tails which live in north Australia and the Pacific Islands and have a wing span of 10 inches. Most female butterflies have less colourful wings than the males of the same species. They lay between 100 and 3,000 eggs, according to the species, placing them on a plant which will provide suitable food for the caterpillars which develop from the eggs.

The caterpillar becomes a chrysalis from which, eventually, the fully grown butterfly emerges. Adult life may last for only a few weeks, but some butterflies hibernate.

Butterflies feed on the nectar of plants and on sweet juices, particularly those of over-ripe or rotting fruit. This food provides them with the energy to fly but is not used for body-building. All growth takes place at the caterpillar stage of a butterfly's life.

A silver-studded blue butterfly

WHAT is a salamander? WHAT is a fossil?

SALAMANDER

A salamander is amphibian—an animal that lives both on land and in the water. It is a lizard-like member of a group of back-boned creatures between fish and reptiles. This class includes frogs and toads. Like fish and reptiles, the salamander is cold-blooded.

It was anciently believed that the first salamander was born out of the heart of a fire and that the so-called fire salamanders were unaffected by heat. In fact, the salamander is active usually only in the cool of the night, when it hunts worms, slugs and insects.

The salamander, which grows up to about 11 inches long, is attacked by few enemies, as its skin glands are poisonous. But the European water snake is not affected by the venom and frequently makes the salamander its prey.

FOSSIL

Fossils are the remains, moulds, traces or impressions of prehistoric animals and plants found in the ground. The word comes from the Latin *fodere*, meaning "to dig", and originally meant any old, curious object dug out of the earth. But since about the middle of the 16th Century, fossils have been regarded specifically as hard objects showing evidence of earlier forms of life, often many millions of years old.

There are many kinds of fossils. Some are footprints which strange, prehistoric animals left behind in mud long since turned to rock. Others are stones which were once soft substances, but still preserve the outlines of extinct plants, or of seashells, or of the bodies of animals. Sometimes even the bones of creatures have survived.

The study of fossils, which is called palaeontology, has enabled scientists to fill many vital gaps in the history of the world and its inhabitants. For example, fossils have shown that rocks in great mountain ranges like the Alps or mountain ranges like the Alps or the Rocky Mountains were once below the surface of the sea. They have indicated that the United States and Europe were once covered by tropical forests. Also, they provide evidence of the common ancestry of animals which today differ widely in appearance.

The subject can be a rewarding hobby for amateurs. Many important contributions to the world's great collections have been made by people who looked for fossils in their spare time or even came across fossils by sheer accident.

WHY are crabs, lobsters and shrimps called crustaceans?

CRUSTACEANS

The word "crustacean" comes from the Latin *crusta* meaning a hard covering shell or crust. Apart from crabs, lobsters and shrimps, there are thousands of different crustaceans. They live in the sea, except for a few species such as the common woodlouse.

Crustaceans differ greatly in size and shape. Many of them pass through remarkable changes of form (metamorphoses) before reaching the adult stage. All of them, however, have bodies and limbs which are divided into segments. All, too, are covered with a tough, hard, lime-impregnated coat, or shell, which is pliable at the joints, so that the creature can move its limbs.

This coat, or cuticle, cannot grow to fit its wearer. As its owner grows, it is split and cast off. A new coat, still soft and pliable, has been forming underneath, and may take several days before it hardens into a truly protective shell. During this time the creature is defenceless and may fall an easy prey to any enemy.

Vast numbers of crustaceans live in the oceans. They provide food for many kinds of fish and also for the largest living mammals, the whales.

VAMPIRE BATS

Vampire bats are dangerous because they carry rabies and other diseases and infect their victims as they suck the blood which is their only food.

Vampire bats (Desmodontidae) are found only in South and Central America. They have extremely sharp teeth and pierce the skin of their prey so gently that the victim does not awaken. Blood is drawn into the mouth by the almost tubular tongue and the vampire bat's whole digestive system is specially adapted for his diet of blood.

WHY are vampire bats dangerous?
WHY do birds preen themselves?

PREENING

Birds preen themselves to clean and waterproof their feathers, to maintain their general health and to keep them lying smooth and neat. This preening or grooming starts as the nestling's feathers are breaking out of their sheaths. The young bird spends a great deal of time combing the feathers with its bill and freeing them from bits of sheath and other blemishes.

In adult life the bird continues this behaviour and also uses the preen glands or oil glands which are located on the back, just in front of the tail. The birds nibble at the glands and rub their heads against them, spreading the secretion on their feathers. This oil waterproofs the plumage, keeps it supple and maintains its insulating qualities. The oil may also be useful as a source of Vitamin D if swallowed accidentally by the bird.

Many kinds of birds have preen glands. They often combine preening with dust or water bathing. Ducks may be seen dipping their heads under water, flicking their wings and wriggling their bodies while preening. This seems to give them great pleasure and fun.

HERMIT CRAB

A hermit crab changes its shell when it has grown large enough to need a bigger home. This type of crab has a soft abdomen or "tail", which is folded up under the body, but it is not protected by a shell of its own as are most other crabs. Instead, the hermit uses empty snail shells as portable shelters, often having to fight with another crab for possession of an attractive home. Sometimes the homeseeker pulls out the original occupier, eats it and then takes over the shell.

One of the claws of the hermit is larger than the other. The crab uses this to stop up the entrance after withdrawing into the shell. The last two legs on its abdomen have roughened pads which grip the inside of the shell and hold the body in position. The crab has a spiral-shaped abdomen and moves in and out of its shell with a spiral movement.

One kind of hermit occupies a sponge which conveniently grows at the same pace as the crab. Sometimes sea-anemones enter into partnership with hermit crabs and take up residence on top of the shells. The crab provides the sea-anemone with transport and in return, receives an extra shield against attack.

swarm? **WHEN** did the pterodactyl live?

BEES SWARM

Bees swarm in late spring in search of a new home. During the winter the queen bee begins to lay her eggs and the colony sets about rearing its young. As the weather becomes warmer and the early flowers appear, the raising of young bees increases rapidly.

By the end of spring the colony has become so overcrowded that a large number of the bees, including the old queen, leave the hive and establish a new colony. In the old colony a new queen emerges who will experience the same swarming instincts the following year. And so the cycle of activity goes on.

PTERODACTYL

Pterodactyls (or pterosaurs) lived between 150 million and 70 million years ago. These extraordinary reptiles were able to fly. Some had a wing-span of over 25 feet, making them by far the largest flying animals known to man. Their skulls were often longer than four feet.

Unlike the birds, their descendants, pterodactyls must have been unable to perch upright. They probably hung upside down like bats when sleeping or at rest.

Since most remains of pterodactyls have been discovered among marine sediments, it seems likely that these flying dinosaurs found their food in the sea, like seagulls, by diving for fish.

26

WHERE do ostriches nest? WHERE do salmon go to breed?

OSTRICH NESTS

We all know that birds build nests. Some find trees the most convenient. Others prefer hedges, the eaves of roofs, chimney pots, rocky ledges or holes in trees. But what does a bird do that can neither fly nor swim?

Living on the dry, open plains of eastern and southern Africa, the ostrich takes no pains to hide its nest. It merely finds a suitable shallow depression in the ground, which it may scoop out further with its feet. The hole may be up to three yards across. In it are laid six to eight eggs, each one by a different female. Then one hen and one cock take turns guarding the two and a half pound eggs until they are ready to hatch.

However, the ostrich does not sit on its eggs to incubate them. Rather, it squats between them, spreading its wings to provide shade and keep them from cooking in the hot desert sun. With one bird squatting and the other standing guard, there is little chance that any smaller egg-eating mammal or bird will find a meal.

WHERE would you look for a trap-door spider?

SALMON

Atlantic salmon, called the "greatest game fish in the world" by sportsmen, spawn in the freshwater streams of Europe, from Portugal to northern Russia, and in the streams of the eastern seaboard of North America, from Maine up to northern Canada. They are found also in the streams of Greenland and Iceland.

Pacific salmon, of which there are several kinds, spawn in the streams of southern Alaska, British Columbia and the states of Washington and Oregon on the Pacific coast. There is also one kind which breeds in the streams of Russia's east coast.

The females spawn their thousands of eggs and the males fertilize them. Once the Pacific female salmon have spawned they die. The eggs hatch in about 19 weeks. The tiny salmon called an "alevin" hides in the gravelly bed of the stream, living at first on a large yolk-sac under its body. When about a year old it is called a "parr" and looks like a young trout. Six months later when it has a more salmony look it is called a "smolt". On reaching the sea it becomes a "grilse" until it reaches maturity.

The instinct of the salmon to head for the sea after a couple of years in fresh water is one of the great mysteries of nature. So too is its instinct, after ranging the Atlantic and Pacific Oceans and travelling up to 4,000 miles, to return to spawn in the stream where its own life began.

TRAP-DOOR SPIDER

Trap-door spiders are to be found just under the surface of the earth. They belong to the class of spiders called *mygalomorphae* which includes the bird-eating spiders of the tropics. All these spiders tend to be rather large. They have four lungs instead of two, and their jaws work vertically instead of sideways.

The trap-door spider has perfected the art of burrowing underground. Its jaws are provided with a special row of teeth with which to dig out its home. It lines its burrow with silk and makes a trap-door consisting of layers of silk and earth. The outside of this door is coated with moss or some other form of camouflage. The spider lies in wait behind its trap-door, darting out to seize its prey.

Trap-door spiders are widespread throughout the hottest regions of the world, with comparatively few in the temperate zones. Specimens of up to four and a half inches have been found. It is estimated that some may live up to 20 years.

WHAT are birds of prey? **WHAT** makes a glow-worm glow?

BIRDS OF PREY

Birds of prey are those that feed wholly or mainly on meat taken by hunting. They catch other birds, and small animals, for their food.

There are two chief families, the hawks and the falcons. The hawks include eagles, such as the bald eagle (symbol of the United States) and the golden eagle. The falcons are smaller but share the same general characteristics— hooked beaks, keen vision and outstanding powers of flight. Owls, also, feed on flesh.

Besides being fast flyers, many birds of prey are expert at gliding and hovering. Their principal strategy of attack is the "stoop", when from a great height they sight their prey, close their wings and swoop upon the victim. This manoeuvre calls for a combination of speed and last-second braking unique to this type of bird.

In advanced countries birds of prey have suffered severely from the effects of poisonous agricultural sprays which have polluted their food sources. This has threatened their survival. But the danger has now been recognized, and in many areas their numbers are slowly recovering.

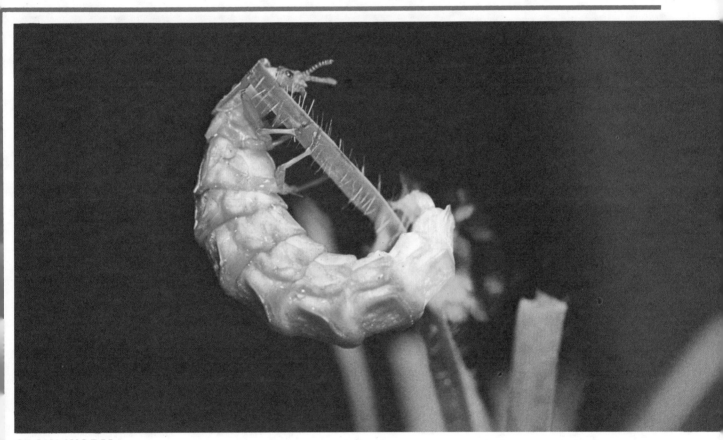

GLOW-WORM

The female glow-worm is equipped with one of the most marvellous lighting systems in the world. A wingless beetle, she crawls about at night eating small insects. But on the lower side of her abdomen she possesses a "lantern" which she uses to signal to her winged mate flying above.

This "lantern" has a transparent layer of skin, like the lens of a lamp. Behind this is an oily layer of tissue which produces the light by a chemical process, and a second layer which acts as a reflector.

The glow-worm is able to control this remarkably bright light, using it only at certain times to attract a mate. In fact, the light is a sex-call, and the male has particularly large eyes to enable him to see the signal. An abundant supply of water and oxygen is needed by the glow-worm to maintain the chemical activity producing the light. For a time, even the insect's eggs are luminous.

Glow-worms, which are about half an inch long, are natives of Europe. Other beetles with built-in lighting systems are called fireflies. Both male and female fireflies have wings and use lanterns to signal to each other and to warn off night birds who seem to find them unpalatable. The most famous are the large and brilliant cucujos of tropical America. On special occasions young women fasten them to their dresses where they shine like glowing gems.

HONEYCOMBED BONES

Birds fly so well because they have developed skeletons which are especially light and strong. Most of their bones are hollow, with the interior webbed or honeycombed across by fine girders of bone to give added strength. They are sometimes called "pneumatic" or air-filled bones.

A bird's skull is made of thin bone in remarkable contrast to the solid, heavy skull of the mammal. The bones of its spine are flexibly connected in the neck, strongly bound together in the front part of the body and united at the rear into a solid, rigid mass. Powerful muscles attached to the breast-bone move the wings.

The bones in the wings have been reduced in number to provide greater strength. Wings can be used also as propellers. They can be shortened or lengthened by flexing, the feathers at the tips can be spread or closed, and the angle of the wings or their parts can be altered. All these adjustments make the aerodynamics of a bird's wings much more complicated than those of an aircraft. Consequently, the flight of a bird is more varied and adaptable.

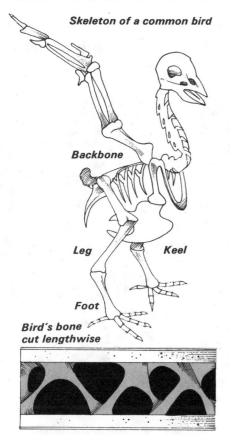

Skeleton of a common bird

Backbone

Leg Keel

Foot

Bird's bone cut lengthwise

JAPANESE TREES

Many Japanese trees are small because they are dwarfed by the Japanese art of bonsai. This art consists in training and growing dwarf trees as symbols of the Japanese ideal of the immersion of the self in nature. This ideal also finds expression in their poetry, the tea ceremony and flower arranging.

The tiny trees express quietness, beauty of shape and line, and the changes brought about by the seasons. They must look old, with a sturdy yet shapely trunk which has bark of an interesting colour and texture, and well-exposed roots. There must also be a proper feeling of scale. This means short needles on conifers, tiny leaves on deciduous trees, and small flowers or fruit. Lastly, there must be open space between branches and between masses of foliage.

The word "bonsai" means tray-

nany Japanese trees small?

imes of the year? WHY don't trees grow on mountain tops?

PLANTS IN FLOWER

The flowers appear at the times most suited to the production of seed for the continuation of the species. Before seed can develop the flower must be pollinated. This means that the dust-like pollen produced by the stamen of the flower must be transferred to the stigma of the ovary.

Pollination is brought about by various means. Most plants are pollinated by insects and, therefore, flower at a time when the insects are active. The flowers may have evolved a particular colour and scent to attract particular varieties of insects.

Five classes of insects visit flowers—Hamiptera (bugs), Coleoptera (beetles), Dipters (flies), Hymenoptera (bees) and Lepidoptera (moths and butterflies). Pollination by birds is widespread throughout the tropics and some animals, such as bats, also play a part.

Wind-pollinated plants include all the conifers, grasses, sedges and rushes, and many forest trees which tend to flower either early or late in the season when the chance of wind is greater.

If pollination by some other agent has failed, self-pollination will often take place at the end of a flower's life. This is usually brought about by movements of the stamens.

planted. The art goes back more than 1,000 years. It originated in China and spread to Japan in the 12th Century. During the 19th Century many Westerners came to admire bonsai. But it was not until the end of the Second World War that it became really popular in the western world. Bonsai societies were established in many countries, and many Japanese families now maintain a flourishing overseas trade.

TREES ON MOUNTAINS

Trees do not grow on mountain tops either because the situation is too exposed, or because the soil is too thin or too frozen to allow their roots to draw nourishment from the ground.

In most mountainous areas there is usually a clearly marked timberline, a boundary above which there is no tree growth. Sometimes the height of the timberline is dictated by local climatic or soil conditions, but as a general rule the boundary gets lower as the distance from the Equator increases. In the far north and south the cold is so intense that it is quite impossible for any trees to grow, and the timberline is therefore at sea level.

A range of mountains on or near the Equator, like the Ruwenzori range in Africa, can be divided into different belts of vegetation according to the types of trees growing at its base and at various heights up its slopes.

Similarly the belts of vegetation change according to the distance from the Equator. The first belt is the tropical or rain-forest region where it is hot and trees grow rapidly. Next comes a hot dry belt where few trees grow because there is so little rain. This is followed by the deciduous or warm and temperate belt, and by the coniferous belt, with very cold winters but fairly warm summers. Then comes the timberline, beyond which trees cannot grow, and finally the regions of permanent ice and snow, where no vegetation at all can live.

WHEN does a tadpole become a frog?

WHEN were the American bison almost wiped

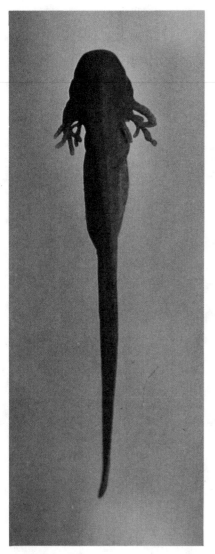

TADPOLES

Frogs' eggs become tadpoles within two weeks of being laid in the water, but tadpoles may take anything from two months to three years to change completely into frogs.

The time taken seems to depend on the environment. Tadpoles will generally develop faster in warmer waters. Also the more advanced species of frog have simplified and shortened the process of transformation.

Tadpoles, like fish, breathe through gills. They develop lungs during the change-over, gain legs and lose their tails. The menu changes, too—from plants to very small insects.

AMERICAN BISON

The American bison were near to extinction by 1900, although they numbered more than 60 million when the white man first arrived in their feeding grounds.

Buffalo, as the bison were commonly called, were the prime essential of the Plains Indian's economy. The powerful animal's meat, bones, and hide provided the Indians with food, medicine, clothing and shelter.

At first the white man, too, killed the buffalo for meat and hides. But after 1850, as the American–Indian war neared its climax, United States soldiers began to slaughter the animals indiscriminately to force the Indians to leave their homelands. With the advent of the railroad the killing of the bison became a sport. Travellers would shoot from railroad carriages, leaving the carcases to rot by the tracks. In less than 50 years about 50 million buffalo had been exterminated.

The voices of those who wished to save the animal from extinction were heeded just in time. From the few survivors, new herds were reared. Today buffalo are increasing in numbers, with herds totalling several thousand.

TUATARA

The tuatara is the only survivor of the beak-headed order of reptiles, called Rhynchocephalia, that goes back to the time of the dinosaurs. It hunts by night and its prey are insects. Like the coelecanth, a prehistoric fish that still survives, the tuatara is almost a living fossil.

It can now be found only on some of the small islets off the coast of New Zealand, having been exterminated from the mainland. It basks in the sun during the day and burrows into the soil for safety. It is covered in scales and grows to about 30 ins.

out? WHEN does the tuatara hunt?

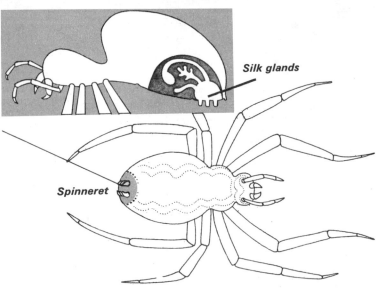

Silk glands

Spinneret

SPIDER'S WEB

A spider does not have a ready-made web. She spins one. If you are lucky, you may be able to watch the female spider doing this.

The material that makes the thread for the spider's web is a liquid which she produces from tiny spinning tubes. These spinning tubes are to be found on small lumps on her body, known as spinnerets. As soon as the liquid comes into the air, it hardens and changes into thread.

When a spider sets out to spin a web she first uses a tough thread to build an outer frame in which she fits spokes, as in a wheel. Next she starts from the hub to weave a spiral crossing the spokes about five times, just to keep them in position. Then she begins again at the outside rim to spin a complete spiral with finer silk, cutting away the "scaffolding" as she nears the centre. Finally she constructs new support-lines for the finished web.

When the spiders move they spin out lines behind them. These are known as the "draglines", and spiders use them as anchors. They do this by pressing their spinnerets against small objects like pebbles or plants. These are the most important threads of all.

Spiders use their webs for trapping flies and other insects to eat. So, besides being beautiful to look at, spiders' webs are vital to them as food providers.

FIRST ZOO

The first zoo was formed in China in the 12th Century B.C. But it was not called a zoo. Wen, the ancient Chinese king who started it, wanted to collect different types of animals from all over his empire. He kept them in what he called a "garden of intelligence", near his palace.

Some of the largest zoos are in North America. There are big ones in the Bronx, New York City, and in Washington and San Diego.

zoo? WHERE does a swallow nest?

SWALLOW'S NEST

A swallow builds its nest inside farm buildings and on ledges in old chimneys. The nest is made of mud, straw and saliva, with feathers and wool to line the inside. It takes a pair of swallows up to several weeks to make the saucer-shaped nest in the rafters of a barn.

Swallows start arriving in Europe at the end of March, a little earlier than their close relatives, the house martins. They spend the winter in South Africa and usually return to the same district—and even the same nest—where they settled before. The female lays four or five eggs, white with reddish-brown speckles. She sits on them for about 15 days before they hatch out. Both parents then feed the nestlings with insects which they catch while flying. Swallows usually lay two sets of eggs.

They leave for their winter quarters in September, gathering in large flocks and often perching on telephone wires, before setting off. The young birds of the first brood leave before their parents and, by an inborn knowledge, know which way to go.

An old country proverb says: "One swallow does not make a summer". This means that when the first one or two swallows arrive, summer has not yet come. It is not until large flocks are seen that countrymen know they can expect the warmer weather.

36

WHAT are fish scales? WHAT is reindeer moss? WHAT

FISH SCALES

Scales are the remnants of the bony armour which enveloped the very earliest fish.

Fish have scales as a protective coating for the skin. In fact, not all fish have them. But we usually think of a fish as a cold-blooded, aquatic animal that swims by means of fins, breathes by means of gills, and is covered with scales. Scales may be of four different kinds—placoid, ganoid, cycloid and ctenoid.

Placoid scales are long, spiny and toothlike, and are made of enamel and dentine. These are found on fishes which have a backbone made of gristle, such as sharks and rays.

Ganoid scales are rather like placoid scales but are mainly bony and covered with a kind of enamel called ganoin. These thick scales are found especially in garfish.

Cycloid scales are thin, large, round or oval scales arranged in an overlapping pattern. They are found in carps and similar fishes.

REINDEER MOSS

Reindeer moss is a species of lichen so called because it is the staple winter food of reindeer (and caribou) in Arctic and sub-Arctic regions. The animals reach the plant by scraping away the snow with their feet. But plant growth in those cold northern lands is so slow that the lichen can take more than 30 years to recover after the reindeer have grazed. These domesticated herds therefore have to travel long distances in search of food, and the Laplanders of northern Scandinavia, who depend on the animals for their livelihood, must travel with them.

Fortunately, reindeer moss is especially abundant in Lapland, although it also grows extensively in much of northern Europe, the tundra (or treeless plains) of Siberia and the barren expanses of Arctic America.

During the short summer the reindeer are able to feed on herbage and shoots then accessible in the valleys. These versatile animals provide the Laplanders with meat, milk, cheese and the raw materials for clothing, shoes and tents. They are also a means of transport.

Reindeer moss is sometimes eaten by human beings, after being powdered and mixed with other food. But it leaves a slightly burning sensation on the human palate. This bluish-grey plant grows erect in tufts, and is remarkable for its many branches, which, strangely, resemble a deer's antlers.

BEE-LINE

To make a bee-line is to follow the example of bees in taking the shortest route from one place to another. The expression comes from the belief that bees return to the hive by the shortest possible way after they have gathered their food. And the shortest distance between two points is, of course, a straight line.

But on their return home, the bees sometimes make lines which are far from straight. These are dancing movements in the air to inform other members of the colony about their source of supply. They indicate whether the food is pollen or nectar, the direction and distance from the hive and even the colours of the flowers.

This bee code was discovered by the German naturalist Professor K. von Frisch. He found, for example, that a circular dance says the food source is close to the hive and that a waggle dance indicates longer distances.

LEMMINGS

The strange thing about lemmings is the way they, apparently, commit mass suicide. These grey or reddish-brown rodents look like mice, but are slightly larger. They live in large areas of the northern world, including Alaska, northwest Canada and Scandinavia.

But, in fact, only the Scandinavian lemmings stampede in such a suicidal manner. Now and then thousands of them travel miles over land in panic to the sea. Many die on the way, but those that arrive leap immediately over the cliffs into the sea, and swim until they become exhausted and drown.

No one is certain what makes the lemmings behave so strangely. It may be because the weather becomes too warm for them, or because their food supply changes, or simply because they feel they are getting overcrowded.

does bee-line mean? **WHAT** is unusual about lemmings?

38

WHY do some animals hibernate? WHY are frogs, toads

AMPHIBIA

The word amphibia comes from two Greek words: *amphi* meaning "of both kinds" and *bios* meaning "life". Amphibia are a class of vertebrate (back-boned) animals that can live both in water and on land. They are descended from fishes that lived more than 300 million years ago.

The first amphibia to crawl out of the water were heavily built, and slow and clumsy on land, but more active in water. They had long bodies and tails, and some developed into the highly efficient class of reptiles.

About 160 million years ago many amphibia became extinct. But a few survived to develop into the present-day frogs, toads, newts, salamanders and the worm-like caecilians.

Modern amphibia usually have moist, tough skins. They breathe partly through their skins, although they also have lungs. They usually lay their eggs in water. Here the young live, breathing chiefly through gills, until they change into their adult forms.

They eat insects, snails, worms and similar food, and are eaten by fish, snakes and birds. They are usually small. But the Giant Salamander of the Far East is 5½ feet long and the Giant Frog of west Africa grows to a mature length of almost one foot.

HIBERNATION

Some animals in cold climates escape the severest weather by hibernating. That is, they spend the winter months in a very long deep sleep. The word "hibernate" comes from the Latin *hibernare*, which means "to winter". Many animals find sheltered places underground or at the base of trees and hedges in which to hibernate.

Hibernating animals include frogs, newts, toads, lizards, dormice, bats, snails, tortoises, hedgehogs and squirrels. During hibernation the animal appears to be lifeless. Breathing almost stops and the heartbeat is slow. The feet, tails and snouts of warm-blooded animals are much colder than usual, although the blood in their hearts remains at a high temperature. The animals are nourished by sugars stored in the liver and by fat that has been built up during the summer.

Mild winters are bad for hibernating animals, because they wake up during warm spells, and use energy in moving about. But they do not feed normally and, by the end of the winter, are very thin.

Creatures which cannot burrow find cracks and holes in which to shelter. Some have been known to return to the same place year after year. Just as animals in cold climates escape winter by hibernating, so some in the tropics avoid hot, dry spells by sleeping underground. This is known as aestivation, from the Latin word meaning heat.

and newts called amphibia? **WHY** do cats purr?
WHY do some trees lose their leaves in winter?

CATS PURR

Most people think that cats purr to show pleasure or contentment. Purring is a kind of low continous rattling hum, but it is nothing to do with a cat's real voice, for the vibration frequency is far lower than that of the vocal chords. In fact, a mother cat uses purring to call her kittens to feed. At birth kittens cannot see, hear or smell but they can feel the purring of their mother as a vibratory movement and so come towards it to nurse. Once the kittens are feeding, the mother stops purring. So it would seem that purring began as a kind of homing device and your cat may simply be reminding you that he is there so that you will continue to stroke him. On the other hand he is quite likely to give a sudden playful bite even when he is purring!

TREES IN WINTER

Some trees with broad-bladed leaves lose their leaves in the winter because the tree has a rest period during the cold weather, and the leaves are not needed for the production of food. These trees are called deciduous trees—from the Latin *decidere* which means to fall. They drop their leaves in temperate or cold climates, but remain evergreen in the tropics.

Most of these trees grow in the deciduous belt of the earth. This is a mild, temperate region where the summers are warm and the winters cool, and rain falls throughout the year. Some also grow in tropical regions, and a few survive in sheltered places in the belt of the coniferous trees.

The fall of the leaves is brought about by the formation of a weak area, called the abscission layer, at the base of the leaf stalk or petiole. Before the leaves fall, the tree takes back some of the food in the leaves. Chemical changes take place. The result is the brilliant autumn colours of the leaves.

Scientists think that the shortening days in autumn have something to do with the formation of the abscission layer. As the hours of daylight lessen a zone of cells across the base of a leaf stalk softens until the leaf falls. A healing layer then forms on the stem and closes the wound. A leaf scar remains, which may be easily noticeable on winter twigs and help in identifying a tree.

In the spring the trees put forth their leaves and the cycle of nourishment begins again.

WHEN do stags fight ? **WHEN** does a forest become petrified ?

WHEN do snakes shed their skins?

STAGS

Stags, the red deer of Europe, fight in autumn and winter for possession of the females or does. Most stags are polygamous and collect harems. A stag wishing to add to its harem at the expense of another's will challenge its rival to a duel.

At other times stags are prone to solitary wandering. But when the breeding season arrives, their fighting instincts are aroused. Occasionally the stags' antlers become so firmly interlocked in combat that they cannot free themselves. In such cases the battle ends with the deaths of both contestants from starvation.

SNAKE SKINS

Snakes shed their skins when they outgrow them. This happens continually, because snakes keep growing throughout their lives, although more slowly as they get older.

The skins are discarded at regular intervals of one to three months, according to the variety of snake. During this process, which is known as sloughing, the old skin is turned back on itself, beginning at the lips and gradually revealing the new skin underneath. When sloughing has ended, the old skin will have been turned completely inside out and left in one piece.

PETRIFIED FOREST

A forest becomes petrified or turned to stone under certain conditions, through the action over the centuries of water containing large quantities of minerals.

Tree trunks buried ages ago under mud, sand or volcanic ash have been gradually transformed as water seeped into the empty cells of the decaying wood, filling them with mineral matter and preserving every detail of the original structure.

Petrified forests have been found in many parts of North and South America, dating from different geological periods and containing stone replicas of the trees that grew in those eras. The most famous of these forests is the Petrified Forest National Park in north Arizona, in the United States. There thousands of stone trunks and logs have been exposed to view through the rain washing away the soil in which they were buried. Although now composed of a mineral called silica, the original details of the trees can be studied through a microscope. Some of the trunks are up to 80 feet long and three to four feet in diameter. They are the fossils of cone-bearing trees belonging to Triassic times, the age of the dinosaurs, and are more than 150 million years old.

WHAT is a camel's hump for? WHAT is photosynthesis?

CAMEL'S HUMP

A camel uses its hump as a portable storehouse of fat from which to draw nourishment when food is scarce. A chemical process enables the camel to covert some of this fat into water, an advantage which enables it to survive for up to 17 days in the desert without drinking.

The Arabian camel or dromedary, found in Arab countries of the Mediterranean, has only one hump. But the Bactrian camel of western Asia has two, giving it greater powers of endurance. A camel has a special way of running called "pacing", which looks like a slow run and saves energy. Yet another advantage which enables the camel to survive in regions where food is scarce is its ability to eat twigs and thorny plants which other animals would not touch.

As is the case with all animals, including human beings, the greater part of a camel's body weight consists of water. But, unlike us, this "ship of the desert" can lose up to a quarter of the water through dehydration and live to make another journey. When it does get a chance to replenish supplies, it can put all that weight back in 10 minutes by drinking 25 gallons of water at a time. The Bactrian camel is slower than the Arabian, but has more stamina.

PHOTOSYNTHESIS

Photosynthesis is the process by which green plants make food for themselves—and, indirectly, for all animals, including human beings. Without it, life as we know it on this earth would be impossible.

In photosynthesis plants combine water and salts in the soil, and carbon dioxide in the air to build up organic compounds, such as sugar starch and proteins. To do this they use the energy of sunlight, which is absorbed with the help of the green dye in their leaves called chlorophyll.

This process of manufacturing food from what they absorb through their roots and leaves makes green plants the primary food producers in the world. All animals draw their nourishment from them, either by feeding on the plants themselves or by eating other animals that do so. During photosynthesis, which takes place only in daylight, excess oxygen is produced and released into the atmosphere for animals to breathe.

After the Second World War, the American scientist Melvin Calvin wrote a book about how plants capture the carbon dioxide in the atmosphere. In 1961 he received the Nobel Prize in chemistry in recognition of his work.

WHAT is a praying mantis? WHAT are termites?
WHAT is a Manx cat?

PRAYING MANTIS

The praying mantis is an insect belonging to the family Mantoidea. The name "mantis" means "a diviner" and the insect has always been surrounded by superstition and legend because of its habit of remaining motionless or swaying gently backwards and forwards with its head raised and front legs outstretched as if in prayer.

In fact it is a ferocious killer and could more aptly be described as a "preying mantis". Most mantids are camouflaged and look very like the vegetation amongst which they live. The front legs are shaped like clasp knives to grasp the mantis's victim in an inexorable grip while it is torn apart by its captor's mandibles. The mantis even devours poisonous insects as well as its own kind. A male mantis may often be eaten by the female after mating.

Most species of mantids are tropical or sub-tropical, but about 20 species occur in Europe.

TERMITES

Termites are soft-bodied insects belonging to the family Isoptera. They are sometimes called "white ants" but they are like ants only in that both species live in social colonies. They live in the tropics and temperate countries and make various kinds of nests. Some make galleries in decaying tree trunks, some make nests below the ground, but the most spectacular are large structures built above ground called "termitaria". They are built from earth excavated below ground and cemented together by saliva. Some of these nests are 20 feet high and almost too hard to break open even with a pickaxe.

The termite community is divided into four groups, but only two can breed. Each colony is founded by a "royal pair" and the queen's life is devoted to laying eggs.

MANX CAT

The Manx cat is a tail-less cat found principally upon the Isle of Man, a lozenge-shaped island about 30 miles long and 20 miles wide, which is situated in the Irish Sea, at roughly the same distance from England, Ireland, Scotland and Wales.

The Manx cat is a common household pet on the Isle of Man and is easily recognized by its lack of tail, the pronounced hollow at the end of its backbone, and its very thick, or double, coat. Its back legs are longer than those in front and it therefore runs with a peculiar and very characteristic hopping motion.

A Manx cat may be of any colour and its fur is short. It has the reputation of being an excellent mouser. The only other tail-less breed is found in Japan.

44

WHY does wood have a grain? WHY is there usually a yew

WOOD GRAIN

The grain in a piece of wood is the pattern produced by the annual bands or rings which grow in the trunk of the tree during its lifetime.

The tree's rate of growth varies with the seasons. In the spring soft porous wood is needed to carry sap. In the summer, stronger cells of hard wood develop to support the growing weight of new leaves and branches. The number of these alternate bands of soft and hard wood gives the age of the tree.

In close-grained wood, which has grown slowly, the annual rings are narrow and packed closely together. If the coarse-grained wood has grown more quickly, the rings are broader and spaced more widely apart. Sometimes the rings are irregular, and the grain may be straight, spiral, interlocked or wavy.

Skilful sawing is necessary to make the most of the grain and enhance the beauty of furniture made from the wood.

YEW IN CHURCHYARD

Yews have long been associated with religious worship. So it is likely that churches were originally built near the sacred trees rather than the other way round.

These trees live longer than any other species in Europe and can grow to an enormous size. Many are thought to be well over 1,000 years old. Yews were revered by the druids of ancient Britain, France and Ireland and no doubt early Christian missionaries preached in the shelter of the trees before their first churches were built. Hywel Dda—Howell the Good—a Welsh king who reigned in the 10th Century, set a special value on "consecrated yews".

Some yews are even older than the ancient churches beside them, suggesting that the church was built on a spot already devoted to worship. The association continued, and it became traditional for yews to be planted in churchyards.

Also the great age to which yews live caused them to be regarded as a symbol of immortality and, therefore, associated with death, as man only becomes immortal after he dies.

Another theory is that yews were planted in churchyards so that they might provide wood for the longbows of medieval archers.

OWLS

The night vision of owls is 100 times as keen as that of human beings, because their eyes are especially adapted for seeing in the dark. But most are almost colour-blind and the pictures they receive are slightly blurred. This is because their eyes contain more rod-shaped receptor cells than cone-shaped ones.

Operating in bright light, cone cells sharpen details and react to colour. Rod cells gather light and owls have 10 times as many of these as do human beings. Each cell contains "visual purple", a substance capable of transforming the slightest glimmer of light into a sight impression.

Owls have exceptionally large eyes and can control the amount of light entering by expanding or contracting the pupil. Each pupil can act independently of the other so that owls can see objects in the shadows and in bright light at the same time. Owls' eyes are so large that they are supported by thin, bony, tubular structures called sclerotic rings. Because of this the eyes are almost immovable and nature has compensated for this by giving owls extremely flexible necks, which enable them to turn their heads through an arc of 270 degrees.

These birds have excellent binocular vision as their eyes are in the front of their heads. This gives them a tremendous advantage in swooping on small lively prey, because distance judgment depends on binocular vision. To add to their advantages at night, the owls have outstanding hearing, keener than that of any other carnivorous bird.

But owls can also see well in the daytime. Although most species hunt by night, others are active at dusk or in full daylight.

WHEN does a lizard shed its tail? WHEN does a drone die?

LIZARD'S TAIL

A lizard is capable of shedding its tail at any time. If a lizard is attacked it may sacrifice its tail in an attempt to surprise and confuse the enemy.

When a lizard's tail is caught by an assailant or a trap, it will simply snap off and enable the reptile to escape.

Although some lizards' tails can be four times as long as the rest of their bodies, the loss is only temporary. A new tail can be grown quickly from the old stump.

RUBBER

Although the remarkable properties of the rubber tree were known to the Aztecs and other South American Indians, for perhaps a thousand years, rubber was unknown in Europe until the discovery of the New World.

Pietro Martyre d'Anghiera, chaplain to the court of Ferdinand of Aragon, Castile and Léon, gave the first written account of the elastic gum in his book *De Orbo Novo*. In it he described a game played by Aztec children using rubber balls. He was particularly amazed by the balls' ability to bounce back into the air after being thrown to the ground.

In 1615, about 100 years later, another Spaniard, Juan de Torquemada, described how the Indians made incisions into rubber trees and collected the milk or sap which oozed out. When dried, this rubber milk was used for making bottles and soles for footwear.

LAND ANIMALS

Animals first appeared on earth about 430 million years ago, but did not begin to resemble the ones we know today until 360 million years later. Sharks, however, were already abundant about 340 million years ago.

It seems that the first land animals were insects such as scorpions and millipedes. But they were greatly different from today's insects. Next to develop were reptiles, the ancestors of lizards and crocodiles.

About 180 million years ago the first mammals began to develop on land along with primitive birds. During this period the forerunners of apes began to appear. The earliest species lived both on the land and in the water. It took about 20 million years for animals to develop the art of breathing air and so to live on land.

DRONE

The male bee, or drone, dies when there is no more nectar available from the fields. The reason for this is that, when the worker bees can no longer collect nectar for the hive, the production of honey stops. Deprived of their food the drones rapidly grow weak and are

Workers and drone on honeycomb. The drone has the bigger eyes.

carried from the hive by the workers to die.

The drone takes 24 days to develop from the egg to a fully grown male and may live as an adult for several months. Its only function in the bee's community is as a potential mate for the queen.

WHEN was rubber discovered?

WHEN were the first land animals?

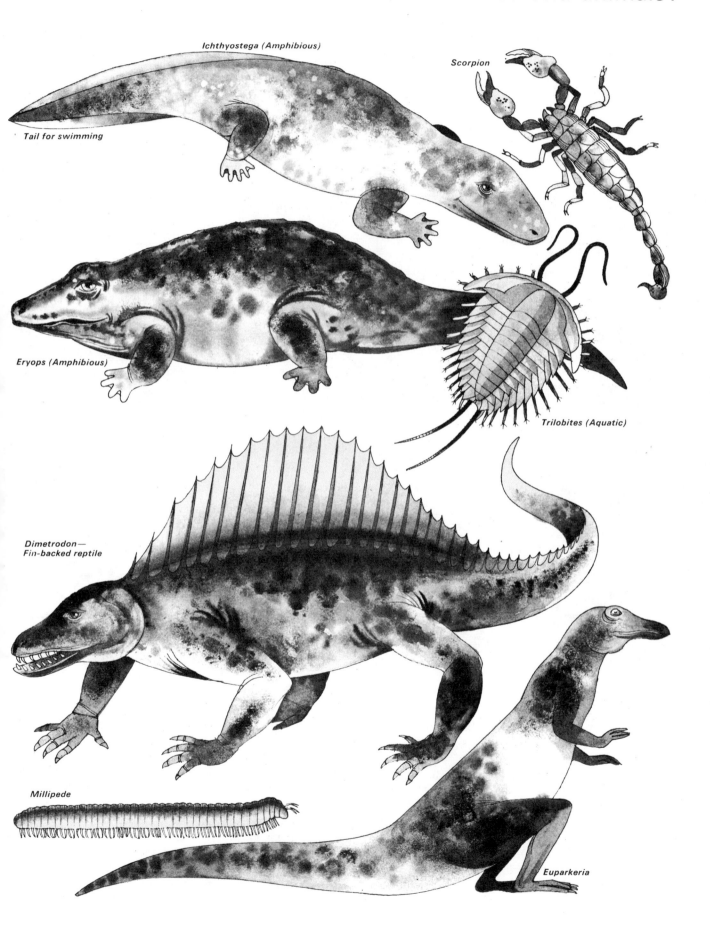

Ichthyostega (Amphibious)

Scorpion

Tail for swimming

Eryops (Amphibious)

Trilobites (Aquatic)

Dimetrodon—
Fin-backed reptile

Millipede

Euparkeria

WHERE would you find a live prehistoric fish? WHERE do
WHERE does the word 'ambergris'

PREHISTORIC FISH

Numerous fossil remains have been found of coelacanth fish which died over 70 million years ago. In fact the coelacanth is said to have first appeared some 350 million years ago.

But to the amazement of experts the first living coelacanth was found in 1938 off the coast of South Africa. In 1952 a second one was caught on a line by a fisherman from the Comoro Islands, between Mozambique and Madagascar. Since then many more coelacanths have been taken around the Comoros.

Modern coelacanths are bigger than most of the fossil forms. They average about five feet in length and can weigh more than 100 pounds.

Usually they live among reefs, from which they will dart out on their prey. They are strong and powerful flesh eaters. The heart of a coelacanth is an S-shaped tube and is probably the most primitive of its kind in existence today.

FLIES

During winter flies will hibernate, sometimes in large groups, in any available dry and warm space such as an attic.

The reason there are so few houseflies in winter is that their eggs will hatch only at temperatures between 24° Centigrade and 35° Centigrade (75° Fahrenheit and 95° Fahrenheit). Meanwhile their numbers steadily diminish owing to insecticides and natural causes. This is a good thing since flies often carry diseases.

AMBERGRIS

The French words *ambre gris* mean grey amber, but amber bears no relation to ambergris. The first is derived from plants and the second from animals.

Amber is a yellowish, translucent fossil resin. Millions of years ago large heaps of resin which oozed from pine trees were buried by soil, and hardened into amber. Insects now extinct have been found preserved in these amber lumps. Amber is found chiefly along the southern shores of the Baltic Sea. It has long been used for making into beads and ornaments.

The Greeks and Romans believed that amber had special and mysterious powers because, when rubbed, it attracts light objects. The Greeks called it *elektron* from which the word electricity is derived.

Grey amber or ambergris is a secretion from the intestines of the spermaceti or sperm whale. It is a light, fatty substance, grey in colour and flecked like marble. It is sometimes found floating in large masses weighing as much as 200 pounds in tropical seas.

In ancient times ambergris was used as a scent. It is still used by modern scent manufacturers as a fixative in the making of perfumes.

flies go in the winter?

come from? **WHERE** would you find a Red Giant?

RED GIANTS

You would find a Red Giant on the Sierra Nevada mountains of California in North America. It is a huge redwood tree, called a giant sequoia. These trees, members of the conifer family, are the largest in the world and grow to a height of 300 feet. They have a very hard, reddish brown wood and a thick, very rough bark. The giant sequoias were believed to be the oldest living things in the world. The ring marks on the stumps of the oldest trunks have been carefully counted and it is now known that some of the biggest are about 4,000 years old.

Many of these trees were cut down for their timber, which is resistant to attacks by fungus, and termites and other insects. To preserve the remaining groves of these huge redwoods, a reservation called the Sequoia National Park was set up in 1890. The largest tree there is 272 feet high and has a circumference at the base of its trunk of $101\frac{1}{2}$ feet. Its weight has been estimated to be over 6,000 tons.

Some of the other trees are taller but do not have such large trunks. A tunnel has been cut through the base of one of these giant trees which is big enough to drive a car through.

50

WHAT is a loofah? WHAT makes grass green? WHAT did

LOOFAH

A loofah is a fibrous, cylinder-shaped vegetable product often used in bathrooms as a kind of rough sponge or gentle brush. It is the dried interior of the fruit of a plant known to botanists as *Luffa aegyptiaca*. Less dignified, though more descriptive, names for this tropical climbing or trailing herb are dishcloth gourd and vegetable gourd.

The luffa belongs to the great gourd family of plants, and its 800 relations include the cucumber, the melon and the pumpkin. In spite of having an unpleasant smell, the luffa is cultivated in Egypt (hence the second part of its Latin name) and in Arabia, India and China. The yellow-flowered climbers can sometimes be seen adorning the trunks of palm trees. Besides being used to make loofahs, the luffa's fruit is eaten in curry.

The development of man-made materials has led to a decline in the loofah's popularity, but many people still use its slightly abrasive qualities to stimulate the skin.

MAMMOTH

The mammoth fed entirely on plants. In other words, it was a herbivore—like its smaller relative, the elephant of today. These colossal animals, whose name has become another word for hugeness, must have needed a great amount of vegetation to keep themselves alive.

In a broad sense, the name

GRASS

The green colour in grass—and in most other plants—comes from chloroplast within the cells, each of which contains four different colours or pigments. These are: chlorophyll a, which is the strongest and is blue-green; chlorophyll b, which is yellow-green; xantophyll, which is yellow; and carotene, which is orange and gives carrots their bright colour.

Grass goes from light green in early spring to dark green and brown in summer and autumn because the amount of each pigment changes, like the paint on a palette, to mix new colours.

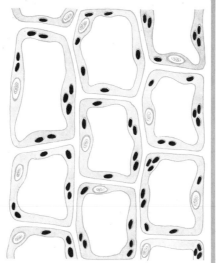

Cross section of a blade of grass.
A Nucleus
B Chloroplast
C Cytoplasmic lining
D Cellulose cell wall
E Vacuole

a mammoth eat?

mammoth has come to be applied to any extinct members of the elephant family. Their fossils have been found in every continent except Australia and South America.

Although similar to present-day elephants in their general skeletal formation, mammoths differed from them and from each other in the shape of their skulls and tusks, and the structure of their teeth.

By far the best-known mammoths are the woolly, northern or Siberian giants. Not only skeletons but even well-preserved carcasses of these beasts have been discovered in the permanently frozen north of the Soviet Union.

Elsewhere their appearance is preserved by the cave paintings, drawings and carvings left by Stone Age men of the beasts they hunted. In these pictures the mammoths are shown as shaggy animals, completely covered with hair and with large tusks growing upwards and inwards. They had a shoulder height of about nine and a half feet.

52

WHY do birds eat grit? WHY do butterflies and moths have
WHY are some

BIRDS EAT GRIT

Birds which peck grain and other seeds also peck grit to help them to digest these hard foods. Because birds have no teeth, the work of chewing, which would require muscles and strong jaw bones, is done by the gizzard. This makes it possible for the skull to be delicate in structure and therefore light in weight.

Grit is taken into the gizzard, or ventriculus, which has thick and often very muscular walls and the combined action of the two grinds down the hard food. The ventriculus is the back part of a bird's stomach, the fore part is glandular and secretes digestive juices and is called the proventriculus. Food passes from the ventriculus to be absorbed by the intestines.

BUTTERFLY WINGS

The "powder" on the wings of moths and butterflies is really a layer of tiny, coloured scales which overlap each other almost like the tiles on a roof. If you touch the wing with a finger the "powder" is rubbed off, leaving the wing more or less transparent and colourless.

The scales are generally like the shape of a hand tapered off at the wrist, and the whole surface is often grooved or cross-grooved. They are really hollow bags growing from tiny cup joints formed in the outer skin of the wing membranes.

They are either filled with colouring materials, or so minutely grooved and surfaced that they refract light to give off an irridescent colour, even though they contain no pigment. The brown, red, yellow, white or black scales are pigmented. The blues and greens are irridescent.

Many male butterflies and moths have specially shaped "scent-scales" (androconia). These are long and feather-like or broad and bat-shaped. They contain glands for making scents which attract the females.

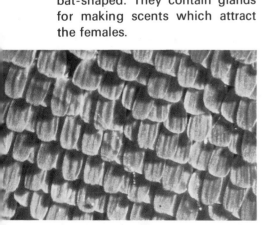

MOTHS AND LIGHT

Moths are attracted to lights at night because they mistake them for the light of the moon which they use as a means of navigation. These other lights confuse the moths and make them lose their sense of direction.

In trying to keep the artificial light at the same angle as the moon's they circle it and come closer. Collectors use this behaviour to trap moths with a special electric bulb which gives off light rich in ultra-violet rays.

The insects are extremely responsive to these rays. But they cannot see red or yellow. So by using a red light you can watch them feeding at night without disturbing them.

'powder'' on their wings?

moths attracted by lights? **WHY** do rabbits have large ears?

RABBITS' EARS

Rabbits are timid animals with many enemies and rely on their large ears to warn them of the sound of approaching danger. Their ears act like old-fashioned ear-trumpets. The large area catches a great many sound waves and channels them into the rabbit's inner ear.

Wild rabbits spend most of the day underground, usually coming out to feed between dusk and dawn. They are continually on the alert, their long ears twitching and moving round to pick up the faintest sound from an enemy. They also have a keen sense of smell.

Long back legs give rabbits speed. But they are virtually defenceless and, in fact, often seem to be hypnotized by approaching predators. When this happens, they crouch squealing and make no attempt to run away. Only their extraordinary fertility has enabled them to survive the onslaughts of foxes, badgers, wild cats, martens, stoats, weasels, polecats, dogs, man and disease.

The rabbit's close relative, the hare, has even longer ears. It, too, relies upon its acute hearing and sense of smell for warning. But it stands a good chance of escaping an enemy because its powerful hindquarters and unusually long back legs enable it to travel at an estimated speed of 40 miles an hour. A racing greyhound will gain on it eventually, but only after a long run, when the hare begins to tire.

54

WHEN does a tree have to be pruned? WHEN was tea first

PRUNING

Trees have to be pruned to protect their health, improve their appearance or remove danger to people or property. Sometimes it is necessary to remove broken, dead or diseased branches, to restore vigour to an ageing tree by cutting back and to admit more air and light by thinning out the centre.

One of the most obvious reasons for pruning trees is to control their growth within the space available for them to flourish. In this type of pruning, live-pruning as it is called, branches are lopped from the trees to control their size and to maintain a pleasing shape.

Sometimes trees are "topped" by removing some of the upper trunk. Pollard pruning involves cutting the trees back to a point at which strong branches are to be allowed to grow. As shoots grow from these points they are cut back each year. This method makes a very ugly tree shape. The lightest method of pruning is known as drop-crotching, which trims only the upper and outer branches.

Another type of pruning is orchard pruning, for stimulating the production of flowers and fruit on fruit trees. Here the farmer tries to maintain a framework of branches which will best allow the sunlight to penetrate to the middle of the tree's crown.

Most deciduous trees may be pruned at any time of the year. The pruning of evergreen trees with needle-like leaves should normally be limited to the removal of dead wood.

Dead-pruning, or brashing, is the cutting away of dead or dying side branches, most often used with conifers growing in plantations.

The last type of pruning is side-shoot pruning or shrouding, which means the removal of small side branches on such trees as pollards or limes to provide a knot-free

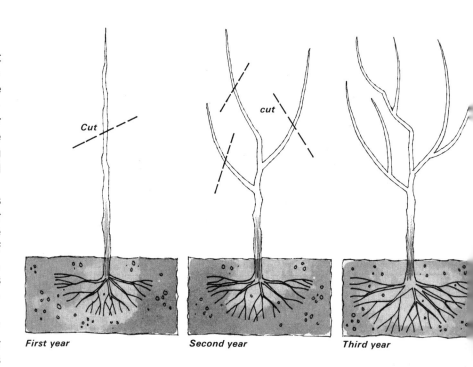

First year   Second year   Third year

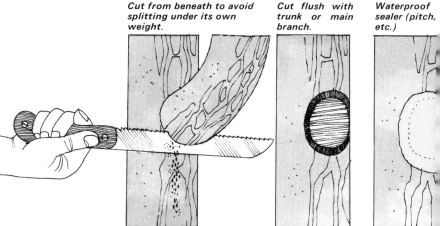

Cut from beneath to avoid splitting under its own weight.

Cut flush with trunk or main branch.

Waterproof sealer (pitch, etc.)

In pruning, leave a lateral A growing right at the base of the fruiting shoot. Leave second shoot B and third shoot C. The idea is that A will produce next year's flower bud, B is retained to produce leaves and C will pull the sap upwards as the weeks proceed. B and C are cut back in the middle of July about half-way down. A is not touched but if sub-laterals grow out at points D then these must be pinched out in July. In winter the fruited branch is cut at F.

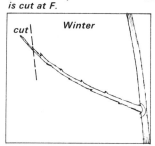

Winter

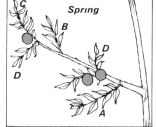

Spring

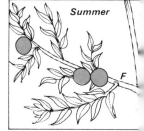

Summer

bottom length of timber.

Pruning means causing wounds and these may cause disease. Special dressings available at most garden supply stores should be applied to cuts more than an inch in diameter to protect the trees from fungi.

grown? WHEN do plants breathe?

WHEN are cats said to be in season?

TEA

We do not know when the tea plant was first cultivated, but the earliest mention of it occurs in a Chinese dictionary, the *Erh Ya*, about the year 350.

The cultivation of tea is believed to have begun in the province of Szechwan in central China. From there its cultivation and use as a beverage spread throughout China and Japan under the patronage of Buddhist priests. Perhaps it was this religious connection which gave rise to the Japanese legend about the discovery of tea. According to this story, tea first grew in China at a spot where the Buddhist saint Bodhidharma, who is said to have spent nine years in meditation before a wall, once fell asleep. He was said to have been so annoyed with himself when he awoke that he cut off his eyelids and threw them on the ground, where they took root and grew into a tea plant.

Tea was brought to Europe by the Dutch via Java in 1610 and became increasingly fashionable from the middle of the 17th Century. In England tea (pronounced tay) eventually began to oust coffee with the encouragement of the British East India Company who enjoyed a tea trade monopoly. India's tea industry was founded in 1834 after Major Robert Bruce had found the plant growing in the north.

While Britain began to change from coffee to tea, America did the reverse after the Boston Tea Party of 1773 when the East India Company's tea was thrown into the harbour as a protest against British taxation.

Tea is drunk by about half the world's population, but is second to coffee in commercial importance.

PLANTS

Plants breathe oxygen and carbon dioxide. In daylight they produce their own food at the same time by a process known as photosynthesis. During this process the plants release more oxygen into the atmosphere than they breathe in.

The effect of the plants' feeding and breathing system is that they exhale oxygen during the day and carbon dioxide during the night. This is the reason for the old custom in hospitals of removing plants and flowers from the wards at night and bringing them back in the morning. Without enough plants, the world's atmosphere would not be replenished with sufficient oxygen for the human race to survive.

Generally plants breathe more slowly the colder it becomes. Some plants, including many trees, go into a form of hibernation during the winter, with their breathing reduced to a minimum.

CATS IN SEASON

A female cat can be in season five times a year. It is only during these periods, which last about five days each, that the cat is fertile. Her mating call is a shrill caterwauling.

The domestic cat, as a rule, goes in season for the first time between the ages of seven and twelve months. Her pregnancy generally lasts two months. A few hours before she delivers her litter she stops eating. A normal litter of kittens is four.

WHERE do you find frogs that live in trees? WHERE would

TREE-FROGS

Tree-frogs are found in Europe, North and South America, New Guinea, North Africa, and warm parts of Asia. They have small sticky discs on the tops of their fingers and toes which help them cling to the branches of trees.

The best-known European tree-frog is less than two inches long. Its Latin name is *Hyla arborea*. Its colour is usually bright green. But tree-frogs can change colour even as you watch them. They can become yellow, brown or black.

In North America there are two main types of tree-frog. One is called the spring peeper. It has a shrill piping voice. The other one is known as *Hyla versicolor*. Versicolor is a Latin word meaning "various colours". This frog can be grey, green or brown. It has a loud croaking voice.

PEARLS

Pearls come from molluscs—a group of animals which includes squids, clams, and oysters.

Under its shell the mollusc has a mantle, or outer-skin. When a particle of dirt, or tiny marine creature gets stuck in this mantle, a hard substance forms around it. This makes the pearl. It is formed of the same material as the mollusc shell—nacre or mother-of-pearl.

Pearls come in many different shapes and colours. The most valuable ones are completely smooth, spherical and usually white. But there is a black pearl from the Gulf of Mexico, which is also extremely valuable.

The people who first discovered how to stimulate the production of pearls were the Chinese. They put the mollusc into a shallow pond, inserted a speck of mud into the mantle, and waited for the pearl to form. After a couple of months they would detach the pearl from the mollusc's mantle—and eat the mollusc.

you find pearls? **WHERE** does lichen grow?

LICHEN

Lichens are found throughout the world, often occupying areas where no other plant can become established. They are found in their greatest numbers in the Alpine and Arctic regions, where they are the dominant form of vegetation.

Lichens are the products of two distinct groups of plants. Together fungi and algae (seaweed is an algae) combine to produce lichens. Most rocks you will come across have an abundance of these plants. Lichens are almost the only plants able to survive the severe conditions at high altitudes.

In Antarctica, where there are very few flowering plants, more than 400 species of lichens have been found. In warmer climates lichens are common in old fields and forests, on rotting logs and on tree trunks. However, few species survive near large cities. Unfortunately, lichens are very sensitive to industrial smoke and gases.

JUMPING BEANS

Jumping beans are made to jump by the action of little insects inside them. The beans are the long seed of certain Mexican shrubs and contain the larvae or caterpillars of a small species of moth with the large scientific name of *Carpocapsa saltitans*. The second of these two Latin words means jumping.

The larvae are stirred into movement by warmth, and it is this activity that makes the beans jump.

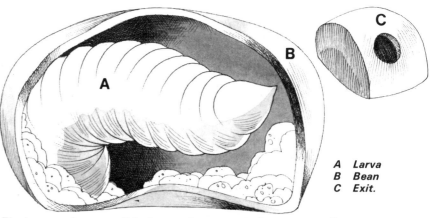

A Larva
B Bean
C Exit.

The larva pushes open this door and emerges to become a moth.

FRUIT AND VEGETABLE

In 1893 the United States Supreme Court tried to clarify the difference between a fruit and a vegetable by saying that vegetables are eaten as part of the main course of a meal, but fruit is eaten as an appetizer or dessert, or for a snack.

But, as with so many words, there is one definition which is correct according to the dictionary and another one which people use in everyday life. Sweet corn, for instance, is eaten as an appetizer, but most people would consider it a vegetable.

In botany, a fruit is the ripened ovary of a plant. (The ovary is the part of the plant where the seeds are kept.) So, strictly speaking, an acorn is as much a fruit as an apple. But, if you went into a store and asked for fruit, the store-owner would not offer you acorns. When we talk about fruit in everyday life, we mean the juicy fruits like apples, grapes, oranges and melons.

"Vegetable" has even more meanings than "fruit". The word covers any kind of plant life, even including trees. But, again, in everyday life vegetables mean food like lettuce, carrots, cabbage and sprouts.

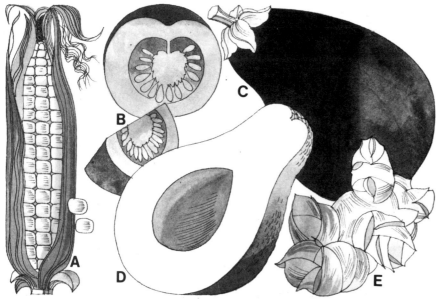

A Sweetcorn (vegetable)
B Tomato (fruit)
C Aubergine or egg-plant (vegetable)
D Avocado (fruit and or vegetable)
E Jerusalem artichoke (vegetable)

CORAL

The hard, dry corals seen in stores and museums are made up of the combined skeletons of tiny creatures which once lived joined together as a colony in the sea. The coral animal, or polyp, measures only about a fifteenth of an inch in diameter. It is a primitive type of plant-like creature closely related to the sea anemone. But, unlike the sea anemone, the polyp has a stony skeleton and, once it has made its home, cannot move.

Each polyp is like a tiny tube, closed at one end and with a mouth, fringed with tentacles, at the other. The tentacles have a sting and capture minute sea creatures for food. Most polyps multiply by budding. A small bud grows from the animal's body and finally becomes as big as the parent with a mouth and tentacles of its own. Gradually the corals build up into colonies of many millions.

Coral animals inhabit shallow water in warm seas. In tropical waters colonies form reefs round islands which can be dangerous to ships. Eventually new islands are formed by the accumulated skeletons of billions of dead polyps.

But the romantic coral islands and reefs of the South Seas do not supply the precious material used for beads and brooches. These are made from the red and pink coral found in the Mediterranean off the coasts of Africa and Italy.

between a fruit and a vegetable? WHAT is coral?
WHAT are teasels used for? WHAT is a mudskipper?

Soft coral polyps extended.

TEASELS

Teasels are used in the making of woollen cloth. The common teasel grows wild in England and Wales and southern parts of Scotland. It is also found in Europe, Asia and North Africa.

The teasel has large prickly flower heads which remain on the dead stems throughout the winter. The actual flowers are tiny deep lilac clorets and round the base of the flowerhead there is a ring of spines. The stem and leaves are prickly and the leaves are joined at the stem to collect rain-water.

The teasel belongs to the scabious family and many people collect them in autumn for decoration throughout the winter.

There is also a garden teasel called fuller's teasel, which has little hooks at the end of the spines, or bracts, surrounding the base of the flowerhead. This is the teasel that is used in the making of woollen cloth. The cloth is brushed up with the teasels so that the fibres of wool become separated from each other. This is known as "teasing".

MUDSKIPPER

Mudskippers are small tropical fish of the eastern Atlantic, the Indian Ocean and the western Pacific from Australia to Japan. They live in estuaries with mud-banks and also in mangrove swamps. Their eyes protrude from their heads and can be moved independently of each other. When the mud is exposed by the ebbing of the tide the mudskippers come out of the water and hunt for crustaceans and other small invertebrates. They crawl and hop about rapidly with the help of their powerful muscular pectoral fins which they use as forelegs. Their gill openings are small and they can live on land for hours at a time, providing the air is humid.

60

WHY do some plants capture insects?   WHY do African

INSECTIVOROUS PLANTS

Some plants capture insects and other tiny animals and use them as food. They do not devour their prey by chewing but decompose them in a mixture of enzymes. The pitcher plant attracts an insect to its large showy leaf by means of sweet-smelling nectar. The leaf has a treacherous lip which precipitates the unwary victim into a deep hollow pitcher full of a digestive 'broth', which soon decomposes its body. Other plants, like the Venus's flytrap, snap their leaves shut on their prey as it prowls about the trigger hairs glistening with drops of nectar. The sundews secrete a sticky fluid.

ELEPHANTS

African elephants have larger ears than Indian, or Asiatic, elephants because they live in hotter conditions and are bigger and more aggressive and active. The huge ears of the African elephant, sometimes three and a half feet wide, enable it to hear more acutely. When the animal charges it fans out its ears, augmenting its terrible appearance and striking fear into the heart of any enemy.

The ears also present a large surface for losing body-heat. African elephants, who are at a disadvantage in the heat because of their large size, wave their ears to keep cool and to chase away flies.

The African elephant is the biggest and noblest of land animals, reaching a height of 11 feet and a weight of nearly six tons.

The Asiatic elephant is smaller. It inhabits the forests of south-east Asia from India to Ceylon and Borneo. It does not like heat and seeks the deep shade of the forest. The Asiatic elephant likes bathing, and showers itself with water sprayed over its back from its flexible trunk. For hundreds of years this elephant has been domesticated and used as a beast of burden, and its relationship with man can be close. Elephants are said to have excellent memories.

elephants have bigger ears than Indian elephants?

TREE GROWTH

A tree never permanently stops growing as long as it lives. But in most countries each year's growth is ended during the cold and dry seasons. The annual period of growth depends on the climate. In moist tropical regions a tree may grow continuously.

Every period of growth is marked by an annual ring. This ring takes the form of a new layer of wood added to the width of the tree. So the age of a tree may be calculated. Some trees, notably the Redwood trees of California, are said to live for 4,000 years.

COW'S MILK

A cow starts to give milk between the ages of two and two-and-a-half years, after the birth of its first calf. For the first few days the milk is unfit for human consumption and is fed to the calf which is afterwards reared separately. During the milking or lactation period that follows the cow's yield usually reaches a maximum after four to six weeks and continues in decreasing quantities for nine to ten months.

To ensure a steady supply of milk, farmers arrange for their cows to calve every 12 months.

Attention to breeding has led to steady improvements in yields. A good cow may produce up to 2,000 gallons during the lactation period.

Cows are normally milked twice a day, morning and evening. Except for the smallest herds, milking in advanced countries is usually done by machines which suck the milk from the cows' udders and transfer it to covered containers. But there are still many countries where milking is largely done by hand, in the traditional way.

WORM

If the earthworm detects an unfamiliar object next to its skin, the muscles will contract immediately and the body will turn to avoid the object. The worm will also turn in response to heat and, in a lesser degree, to light and sound.

Even the heat given out by an ordinary match some inches away, will cause a worm to retreat. Sound waves will also lead the earthworm to change direction rather than approach what, to human ears, may seem only a slight noise. Light, on the other hand, usually attracts the worm. It turns inquisitively to inspect the brighter patch, even although, of course, earthworms can live underground for long periods.

The phrase "even a worm will turn" is used in the sense that even the humblest of creatures will eventually rebel if goaded or pushed too hard. But the phrase has no real relationship to the activities of worms as such.

to give milk? WHEN does a worm turn?

WHEN were breakfast cereals first used?

Above: *Barley.* Below: *Rice growing in Japan.*

BREAKFAST CEREALS

Cereals, of course, in the general sense, including wheat, rice, maize (known as corn in Canada and the United States), rye, oats and barley were among the earliest plants grown by man. But packaged or processed cereals are a modern development.

Breakfast cereals owe their origin to the vegetarians of the last century and health fanatics who believed they could save souls by preaching the virtues of a non-meat diet.

Granula, which was the beginning of Grape-Nuts, was launched in 1863 by a man called James C. Jackson, of Danville, New York. Henry D. Perkey brought out Shredded Wheat in 1893 and Puffed Wheat was developed by Alexander Anderson in 1902.

The religious sect, the Seventh Day Adventists, made Battle Creek, Michigan, the cereal headquarters of the world when the sect formed the Western Health Reform Institute at Battle Creek in 1866, later called the Battle Creek Sanatorium. John Harvey Kellogg, who was a doctor and a writer, took over control of the Sanatorium in 1876 and his advocacy of cereals helped to develop what was to become a vast new food industry. His brother, W. K. Kellogg, started a cereal producing company in 1906.

C. W. Post was another cereal pioneer and his Postum Cereal Company formed in 1897 later developed into General Foods Corporation.

The basic idea behind packaged cereals has remained largely unchanged.

64

WHERE is nectar produced?   WHERE do you find

NECTAR

The sweet scent of flowers is designed to attract insects who seek food in the shape of pollen and the fragrant-smelling nectar. This nectar is a solution of sugars produced in little sacs called nectaries at the base of the flower petal.

The insects have a part in the process of fertilization. Almost all plants perpetuate themselves by means of sexual reproduction, during which a male reproductive cell or sperm fuses with the female reproductive cell or egg.

When bees or other insects visit flowers in search of the sweet-smelling nectar, parts of their hairy bodies become dusted with pollen which contains the male reproductive cells. This rubs off on the flower's carpels which contain the egg or ovule.

Insects seem to be strongly attracted by sweet scents. In fact, some flowers, such as the Meadow Sweet, are so highly scented that insects are attracted to them although they have no nectar to offer.

COWRIE SHELLS

Cowrie shells are widely distributed and possibly the favourites among shell collectors because of their polished enamel-like surfaces and their beautiful coloured patterns. The cowrie appears in all the warmer seas of the globe. But the great cowries, the tiger cowrie and the orange cowrie are natives of tropical regions. They crawl slowly, browsing on weeds, and are shy creatures remaining hidden during the day in crevices or under rocks.

The best-known and most popular is the tiger cowrie. The shell grows about four inches long and is covered with spots. It was used by 18th Century silversmiths to make shell snuff-boxes and in Italy for burnishing paper and ironing lace. The shells were often distributed in Europe by sailors and gypsies.

Orange cowries at one time sold for large sums on the market. In Fiji and the New Hebrides in the Pacific they are still worn as badges of rank by the chiefs.

The money cowrie is a small oval shell, flat and white underneath with thick yellowish-white edges and a pale lemon upper surface. It is found in enormous quantities in the Pacific, from the Moluccas eastward. Large fortunes were at one time made by European traders who transported shells to the west coast of Africa and exchanged them for ivory,

cowrie shells? WHERE would you find a breadfruit tree?

gold and slaves. A slave would be worth anything from 20,000 to 50,000 shells. In 1849 money cowries weighing 240 tons were imported into the English port of Liverpool.

A man at Cuttack in Orissa, India, paid for the erection of his bungalow entirely in cowries. The building cost him £400, which in cowries amounted to 16,000,000 shells. The common method of handling the cowries was by threading them on a string, 40 cowries to one string.

Among the cowries the rarest is *Cypreae leucedon*. Only two known examples of this pale brown, creamy-spotted shell exist. One is in the British Museum, the other in the Harvard University Museum. More than 190 species of cowrie shell are known to collectors. Some species are used as charms against evil spirits.

BREADFRUIT TREE

The breadfruit tree is found in the South Pacific islands and, to a lesser degree, in other parts of the tropics. It is an extremely handsome tree, growing up to 60 feet high. The oval leaves are a pleasant, glossy green and quite large.

There are two distinct forms of breadfruit, one seedless and the other containing many seeds which, when boiled or roasted, taste much like chestnuts.

The breadfruit, which contains a considerable amount of starch, is not really a fruit in the popular sense and is rarely eaten raw. It can be boiled or baked, served with salt, butter or syrup, and even sliced and fried like potatoes.

The tree has been cultivated in Malaya since remote antiquity. It can also be found in the West Indies where Captain Bligh, of H.M.S. Bounty, introduced it on a later voyage.

ARACHNIDA

Ages ago, people believed there was magic in the weaving of a spider's web and the Greeks told a story about a girl, Arachne, who was to give all spiders the name of Arachnida.

One day, Arachne, who was skilled in the art of weaving, challenged the goddess to a contest. She proved herself better than Athene at the craft and that immortal goddess, jealous and enraged that a mere mortal should defeat her, changed Arachne into a spider, eternally doomed to weave her web with the thread spun from her own body.

It is interesting to see how scientists have classified animals in order to bring out their natural evolutionary relationship. There are other creatures in the class of Arachnida, including scorpions, mites and king-crabs. Arachnida is grouped under Arthropoda, the class of animals with an outer skeleton made of chitin—a horny substance, the body divided into segments with jointed limbs. Arthropoda in turn comes under Metozoa—animals with bodies made up of many cells. Metozoa is one of the two main groupings of animals, the other is Protozoa which consists of very small, usually microscopic, animals found in fresh water or in the sea and having only one cell.

SEPALS

The sepals of a flower protect it while it is in bud. The flower is really a kind of shoot, in which the leaves have been altered so that they can take on the task of producing seeds.

In a simple flower these leaves are arranged in circles, called whorls. The outermost are five green, leaf-shaped sepals. Inside these are five petals, usually heart-shaped, each with a small flap at its base where nectar is produced to attract bees and other insects.

Both the sepals and the petals are attached at their bases to the "receptacle", the swollen end of the flower-stalk, which looks like a cone in the middle of the flower.

Above the sepals and petals are the parts of the flower used in reproduction. These are the stamens, which contain the yellow pollen, and the carpels, which contain the ovules.

Most flowers are built on this plan but there are wide variations in size, shape and colour, and in the numbers of the different parts of the flowers.

PENGUINS

Nearly all birds use their wings for flight, but penguins use theirs as paddles for swimming. They spend most of their lives in the sea and find their food there.

Although many birds can both swim and fly, no other bird can swim as well as the flightless penguins.

Penguins have muscles, bones and organs very much like those of flying birds, so we assume that their ancestors must have been able to fly. Probably they slowly lost the power of flight while learning to swim faster and dive deeper in search of food. This must have happened millions of years ago, for by Miocene times— 25,000,000 years ago—there were penguins very much like those alive today.

The feathers of penguins are short and grow all over their bodies, leaving no bare spots unprotected

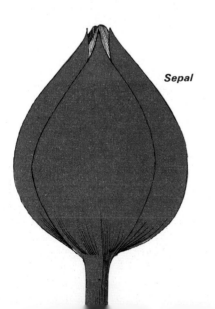

Sepal

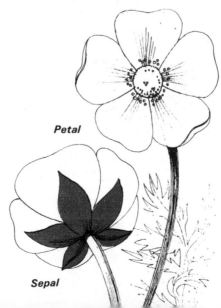

Petal

Sepal

do flowers have sepals?
small flipper-like wings? **WHY** do we have a dawn chorus?

DAWN CHORUS

The song of the birds at dawn has given pleasure to millions of people and has been celebrated in poetry and prose for many years. The most usual explanation given in the Middle Ages was that the birds sang each day in praise of God and the beauty with which He had clothed the world. More recently, there was the feeling that the birds sang joyously to welcome the rising of the sun, which meant food, warmth and activity.

However, scientists now think that the dawn chorus is made up of the warning signals of each bird as he re-establishes his territory. The establishment of a territory for courtship, nesting and food getting is the first step in the breeding cycle and the area is defended against competing birds of the same species by a warning song, although seldom by actual fighting. A robin, incidentally, has a particularly strong sense of territory.

from cold air and water. The feathers of the paddle-like wing are small and stiff, with broad flat shafts. On the rear edge of the wing are rows of many short feathers with strong shafts.

The bones of the wing are flattened. This allows the whole wing to be thin and streamlined, but yet strong enough to push the bird through the water. Its shape is much like that of the flipper of a seal. Some of the bones have grown together, so that the penguin paddle is stiffer, though thinner, than the wing of a flying bird.

The breast muscles, which work the wings, are as large and powerful as those of any bird, but the muscles in the wings are small. Many of them are largely made up of slender bands of strong tendon. This, too, helps in making the paddle wing flat and thin.

WHERE are crocodiles born?   WHERE would you look for

CROCODILES

A newly-hatched crocodile is about eight inches long and can be found on the mud near the water's edge of marshes, rivers, estuaries and lakes around the tropical regions of the world. For it is here that the female lays her eggs and buries them—30 to 70 at a time—in holes in the warm mud.

Each of the hard-shelled eggs is about the size of a goose's egg. After being covered by vegetation which, as it rots, supplements the warmth of the sun, the batch is guarded by the female until the eggs are about to hatch. Then the crocodile digs down to free them from the mud.

Adult crocodiles vary in size from the three-feet-long dwarf ones of West Africa to those in the estuaries of tropical Asia and Australia which can attain a length of 20 feet.

These salt-water estuary crocodiles, including those that live in the tidal part of the River Nile in North Africa, are occasionally man-eaters and will attack and eat almost any living creature that comes within their reach. They were once thought to weep as they snapped up their victim. That is why in popular speech we often describe a false display of sorrow as "crocodile tears".

a baobab tree?   WHERE does a leech feed?

LEECH

Leeches, which are rather slimy worms and vary in length from an inch to several inches, have two suckers, a big one at the rear and a smaller one at the mouth end. They have powerful muscles which enable them to expand and contract their bodies.

This makes them excellent swimmers. They can also use their suckers to crawl on the land. In tropical Asia, the islands of the Pacific and the Indian ocean, there is a particularly vicious and dreaded species of land leech which enters the breathing passages of animals, gorges on the animal's blood and swells so that it cannot escape.

Aquatic or water leeches cling to fishes, turtles and shell fish. Some leeches feed on earthworms and frogs' eggs. Others live on the larvae of insects and even on the microscopic life on the floor of the pond.

Leeches have been used in medicine from early times until quite recently to draw blood from a patient. They also serve as fish bait. In parts of the United States they are regarded as useful in controlling the snail population in lakes and ponds.

BAOBAB TREE

The baobab tree is to be found in tropical Africa. It is a most strange-looking tree. Its barrel-like trunk can reach 30 feet or more in diameter, although its height is not proportionately great.

It has a large gourd-like, woody, fruit containing a pleasant, cool tasting juice. A strong fibre obtained from the bark is used in Africa to make ropes and cloth. The wood is soft and light and so easy to work that the trunks of living trees are often excavated to form houses.

So peculiar is the baobab in appearance that an Arabian legend says: "The devil plucked up the baobab, thrust its branches into the earth, and left its roots in the air".

A related species is found in Australia, where it is also known as the bottle tree.

WHY do laurel and holly trees have shiny waxy leaves?

LAUREL AND HOLLY

Laurel and holly trees have developed special kinds of leaves to seal the water inside them during the winter months.

Both trees are evergreen. Instead of dropping all their leaves in autumn, they shed old ones and grow new ones throughout the year. In winter the soil is too cold for the trees to draw water from it through their roots. Normal leaves would continue to transpire and to give off moisture until the trees died of drought. But the special leaves of the holly and laurel hold the water. Their waxy surface and leathery texture make certain that the water is contained safely within the green tissues.

Some of the holly leaves have a further modification. On the lower branches which are within reach of browsing animals, each leaf has a series of sharp points along its edge. The higher leaves have only a single point.

The leaves of the cherry laurel, if crushed, give out a faint but unmistakable smell of almonds because of the weak fumes of hydrocyanic (prussic) acid found in them. These fumes are poisonous. Scientists who want undamaged specimens of dead insects sometimes kill them by putting them with crushed laurel leaves in a closed glass tube.

MENACE OF RABBITS

Rabbits became a menace in Australia because they breed so quickly and eat almost any vegetable. Three pairs of rabbits were introduced into Australia in the 18th Century. They multiplied so rapidly that, with the addition of others which were brought over, they spread over most of the continent and caused a tremendous amount of damage.

The female rabbit, or doe, produces four to eight litters of five to eight young in a year. They are blind, helpless and nearly naked at birth, but in two weeks are able to run, and in a month can fend for themselves. At the age of six months they are able to breed. It is reckoned that a pair of rabbits, given ideal conditions, could in three years have 13,718,000 descendants.

Many costly attempts to control the rabbits failed in Australia, but, in the early 1950s a virus disease called myxamatosis was introduced. The virus is a specific parasite of the rabbit and is transmitted by the mosquito and the rabbit flea. It is so lethal that 80 per cent of the rabbit population had died within three years. However, by 1960, a strain of rabbits resistant to the disease was again becoming a serious pest.

They cause an enormous amount of damage to Australian farmland. But the export of their skins has proved profitable, and Australia is a principal source of the rabbit fur used commercially.

WHY were rabbits such a menace in Australia?
WHY is the manchineel tree dangerous?

MANCHINEEL

The manchineel tree is dangerous because its sap and fruit contain poison. Its other name is *Hippomane*, which comes from the Greek and means "causing horses to run mad".

The tree is a member of the Euphorbiaceae family and grows in tropical America, producing a crop of acrid, bitter apple-like fruits which drop spontaneously and carpet the ground beneath it. The sap is white and highly caustic, so that a drop on the skin produces a burning sensation and raises a blister. It used to be believed by many that to sleep beneath the tree meant certain death. But the great 18th Century naturalist Nicolas von Jacquin "reposed under it for hours at a time without inconvenience."

The wood has often been used for furniture as it is beautifully patterned in brown and white. Before felling the tree by hand, workmen light a fire round the trunk, so that the sap thickens and does not run down the handles of their axes.

ELEPHANTS

Groups of elephants have been found buried together both in Africa and Asia. The nearness of the animals to each other may be no more than a coincidence. The areas may be no more than sites, since elevated and dried, where elephants have been drowned in bogs or while crossing rivers.

However, many people will argue that old elephants, when their end is near, resort to their legendary "graveyards". The discovery of the remains of a solitary elephant is rare. On the other hand a body in elephant country would usually soon disappear owing to the activities of natural scavengers.

Most experts will accept that there is much truth in the old saying "an elephant never forgets". It does have a retentive memory. Also, when an elephant is dying it is not uncommon for members of the herd to gather round and try to revive it. When all hope is lost they encircle their relation as if in mourning at a funeral.

LONGEST SNAKE

The longest snake in the world— the python—is found in the tropics, in and around the Malay region. It is the reticulated or regal python, which can sometimes be as much as 30 feet long. It kills its prey by coiling itself round the animal and hugging it, so that it cannot breathe. Then it swallows the victim whole.

The python is strong enough to kill an ox, but chooses smaller animals which it can swallow. If a python is disturbed soon after a meal, it is likely to vomit the animal up again, still whole. It rarely attacks man and is not poisonous.

Most pythons live in trees. They also like lying in water where it is cool.

The python lays oval eggs with leathery shells, sometimes as many as 100 at a time. It guards the eggs by coiling itself round them.

The anaconda, which inhabits the rivers and swamps of Brazil, Peru and the Guianas is the largest American snake; it rivals and sometimes exceeds the python in size.

SPONGES

The soft, absorbent, natural sponges used in baths are the skeletal remains of a marine animal. Biologists once thought sponges were plants. This seemed natural as sponges have no special shape and attach themselves to one spot on the sea-bed like plants. Also, they have no limbs, mouths or internal organs. Today, however, they are classified as animals.

The familiar commercial sponges are gathered by divers or by dredging ships. They are prised from the sea floor and dried in the sun. After any impurities have been washed out of the sponge, it is ready to be sold in the market. Some of the best sponges are found off the coasts of Turkey, Greece and Egypt.

WHERE is the longest snake in the world?

WHEN will sharks attack a human being? WHEN does apple

SHARKS

Some sharks may attack human beings if attracted by underwater noises, erratic swimming, the presence of a large number of bathers, or the glint of jewellery or some other article. But probably the greatest provocation to a shark is the presence of blood, for instance from a speared fish or live bait.

Sharks are most likely to attack during the daytime, the areas of greatest danger being those where the sea temperature is between 16°

and 21° Centigrade (60° and 70° Fahrenheit). Most attacks seem to occur about 200 to 300 feet from the shore where the water is shallow—or no more than two or three feet in depth.

Among the kinds of sharks known to attack human beings are the tiger and the blue and grey nurse sharks. The most feared and the largest of all the shark family is the great white shark, a powerful and aggressive creature.

APPLE SCAB

Apple scab occurs when an apple tree falls victim to a fungus called *Venturia Inaequalis*, a malignant growth which slowly eats away at the leaves and fruit.

It is a widespread and serious disease affecting apple trees all over the world, but is more powerful in warm climates.

Farmers control the fungus by spraying the trees with sulphur. That is one reason why apples should be washed before eating.

scab occur? WHEN does a snake "dance"?
WHEN do animals become mutants?

SNAKE'S "DANCE"

There are two occasions when a snake will "dance"—both connected with the mating season. In the first case the dancing partners are both male and their performance appears to be a form of aggression designed to impress the female.

The second occasion is a nuptial dance between male and female. First the snakes pursue each other and coil together. Then the couple raise their necks and heads as if forming the shape of the letter U. During the dance, which may last an hour, the male rubs its chin against the female's neck.

The nuptial dance occurs mainly among European snakes, but the males' dance of aggression is to be seen all over the world especially among rattlesnakes, adders and cobras.

MUTANTS

Animals are said to be mutants when they show characteristics different from the rest of their species. Mutations are processes by which the hereditary properties of some of the reproductive cells in animals are altered.

In nature these changes can take place spontaneously and unpredictably. But they are rare, and little is known about this cause, beyond the fact that the longer an animal takes to breed, the less likely it is to give birth to a mutant.

Nowadays, the most common causes of animals producing mutants are chemical substances and radiation. Indeed, radiation is a rapidly increasing hazard.

Animals born from parents who have suffered the effects of more than normal radiation are invariably mutants. Cows have been known to grow a fifth leg. In the Pacific Islands, where nuclear tests have been conducted, there are fish which have forgotten how to swim and have been found on land. Birds have lost the power to fly, and some may have only one wing. Turtle mutants are unable to find the sea and consequently die.

Animal mutants have long intrigued and frightened people. In Greek mythology, mutants such as dogs and horses with two heads were believed to possess magical powers.

76

WHY was Louis XIV known as the Sun King? WHY did the

People and Events

SUN KING

Louis XIV was the King of France from 1643 to 1715 and was known as the Sun King because of the general style and magnificence of his reign. Although he became king when he was four, he did not assume his full powers until 1661, after the death of the famous Cardinal Mazarin. Louis then became his own "first minister" and embarked upon years of personalized government.

Louis thoroughly enjoyed being king. He desired to shine in his role and a prime aim of his government was to foster any project that added to the king's glory.

He became a great patron of the arts and gave personal encouragement to writers who were to become some of the greatest names in French literature, including Molière and Racine.

Architecture, of course, was one of the most obvious ways of adding to the grandeur of his reign. The Palace of Versailles also took shape under his direction. He constantly changed his mind and frequently altered the plans for the palace. In 1685 Versailles, by then one of Europe's most beautiful palaces, became the Sun King's permanent seat of government. Louis entertained on an appropri-ately lavish scale and the grace, elegance and excesses of his Court became a by-word through-out the civilized world. But he did have excellent taste. The de-lightful château of Marly-le-Roi is another example of this. Life at Court was governed by careful and meticulous rules, although the Sun King's love affairs were greatly resented by the nobility since his various mistresses were given high rank and exercised a considerable influence on policy. But despite Louis' very dubious private life he revelled in the title of "most Christian king" and did his best to protect the Catholic religion. This resulted in him making life for his Protestant sub-jects thoroughly uncomfortable. Indeed, in 1685 he issued an edict under which Protestantism was no longer tolerated in France. It is easy to smile at some of the Sun King's excesses but even Voltaire, the great French satirist, extolled his reign for the glory it added to the fame of France and French civilisation.

Louis encouraged good administration, promoted industry and attended diligently to his duties as "first minister" and steered France through the long war of the Spanish Succession.

CIVIL WAR

The American Civil War (1861–65) arose chiefly over the question of Negro slavery. In the 15th Century the Portuguese found a ready market for Negro slaves, which they captured during their expeditions along the African coasts.

As the American continent developed, these slaves were eagerly sought to labour on the cotton and tobacco plantations, in mines, or in general farm work. Between 1680 and 1786 more than 2,000,000 slaves were transported and it was not until 1833 that the United Kingdom Parliament passed

American Civil War start?

an Act that set free all slaves in its territories.

In the United States the struggle between the slave-owning southern states and those of the North, where there was no slavery, was long and bitter. As the frontier moved westward, new states were seeking admission to the Union. Some had slaves and some did not.

In the north a growing party demanded immediate abolition of slavery, while in the south were some who threatened to leave the Union rather than give up their slaves. In 1860, Abraham Lincoln (1809—65) who favoured the gradual abolition of slavery, was elected President of the United States. **Next year seven southern states left the Union and formed the Confederate States, with Jefferson Davis as president. On April 12, the officer in charge of Port Sumter, Charleston, South Carolina, refused to surrender it to Confederate soldiers, who opened fire and thus began the Civil War.**

Although the North had greater numbers, the South had better generals and the war dragged on for four years, with no fewer than 2,260 battles and skirmishes. In 1863, there were great victories for the North at Gettysburg and Vicksburg. It was at Gettysburg that Lincoln delivered his famous address promising freedom for all.

General Lee, commander of the Confederate armies, surrendered on April 9 at Appomatox Court House, Virginia.

Detail from a painting of the Battle of Missionary Ridge, fought between November 23 and 25, 1863.

WHERE did the American War of Independence start?
WHERE was the Klondike

WAR OF INDEPENDENCE

The American War of Independence started at Lexington, near Boston, Massachusetts, in 1775. The military governor of Massachusetts had sent troops from Boston to Concord to seize a store of illegal weapons. On the way back, at Lexington, the troops were attacked by angry farmers and 273 of the 800 soldiers were killed. When the news of this battle reached Britain, war was declared on the rebellious colonists.

Although this was the first open conflict, the colonists' resentment against Britain had been growing for several years. This was mainly caused by the taxes imposed by the British government on certain goods imported into America. The taxes were intended to help pay for the Seven Years' War which Britain had fought against France

to defend the American states. The Americans considered these taxes to be unjust and refused to pay them. Eventually all these taxes were abolished, except for the tax on imported tea.

When war was declared, the Americans had no regular army. But one was soon formed under the command of a Virginian, George Washington. This army was badly equipped and lacked training. But it was fighting over vast territories against a British army 3,000 miles from home. Many times in the following six years the American army was nearly defeated by the superior training and numbers of the British troops, but gradually the tide turned. As the war continued, France and Spain sent help, declaring war on Britain.

On July 4, 1776, Congress, the American parliament, drew up the formal Declaration of Independence in Philadelphia. This stated that America would no longer obey the British government and that the United States would be an independent republic.

In 1781 at Yorktown in Virginia, the British forces were forced to surrender to a combined American and French army, and it became clear that the United States had won. For a time George III and the British government refused to accept defeat. But at the Treaty of Versailles in 1783 the independence of the colonies was recognized and peace was made between Britain, America, France and Spain. The war was over and the United States had gained her independence.

This is the first draft of the Declaration of Independence in Jefferson's own handwriting, with his corrections.

WHERE did the Light Brigade charge?
WHERE was Napoleon banished to after Waterloo?

THE LIGHT BRIGADE

The famous Charge of the Light Brigade took place eight miles south of the great port of Sebastopol on the west coast of the Crimean peninsula, near the small harbour of Balaclava. During the Crimean War (1854-56), when the forces of France, Britain and Turkey fought the Russian Army, Balaclava was the Allied base. It was defended by lines of earthworks on the hills around the harbour.

On October 25, 1854, Russian forces attempted to break these lines. Over-running some Turks on the heights and seizing their guns, the Russians then descended to the plains and attacked the British forces. The British Heavy Brigade drove them back over a low ridge of hills crossing the plain.

Then occured one of the most famous feats in the chronicles of the British Army, the Charge of the Light Brigade. Led by Lord Cardigan, 673 horsemen rode up a valley under heavy Russian fire. They charged a mile and a half up the valley to capture some Russian guns. They achieved their objective, but only 195 men returned. Among them was Lord Cardigan, who behaved as if the charge had been of no special significance.

Boarding his yacht, where he was living during the campaign, he bathed, dined and went to bed.

This most gallant action would have never taken place if a mistake had not been made in the giving of orders by the High Command. The 673 men of the Light Brigade had charged straight at the wrong guns!

Alfred, Lord Tennyson, a famous Victorian poet, immortalized the charge of the Brigade in the poem he wrote to celebrate it.

NAPOLEON'S EXILE

On July 15, 1815, after his defeat at Waterloo, Napoleon surrendered to the British and was exiled to the remote island of St Helena in the South Atlantic, 1,200 miles off the African coast.

The actual surrender was made to Captain Maitland of the British frigate Bellerophon. Napoleon was transferred to the Northumberland and then taken to St Helena.

This island is only $10\frac{1}{2}$ miles long and $6\frac{1}{2}$ miles wide. Napoleon had no force at his disposal, as he did on the Mediterranean island of Elba, where he was given sovereignty during his first exile.

He was to spend six years on the island before his death. He frequently quarrelled with Sir Hudson Lowe, the Governor, who was very conscientious at thwarting all Napoleon's hopes of escape. He never gave up these attempts, but he also found time to write his memoirs.

He died on May 5, 1821. There were rumours that he had been poisoned, but modern historians and doctors believe it is far more likely that he had cancer of the stomach.

THE KLONDIKE

The Klondike was—and still is—in remote north-western Canada on the borders of Alaska. This area is now part of the Yukon Territory. Dawson, once the capital of the Klondike, lies on the bank of the Yukon river.

For a time Dawson was a bustling town of 10,000 people. Now the population has dwindled to less than 1,000. But there is much less gold than there was at the beginning of the century, and it was only the promise of gold that persuaded people to live so far north in such frozen wastes. For in the streams and creeks of the area the gravel was rich in gold.

At the peak of the Gold Rush in the Klondike more than 30,000 newcomers arrived in four years. In 1900 gold worth more than $22 million was found in the region. Only six years later little more than $5 million in gold was found. By 1910 most of the people had left. A few had made fortunes but the rest were simply cold and disappointed.

Gold production still continues there. But since the remaining gold is underground and almost all the ground is frozen, mining is today a most expensive and very difficult operation. The glorious days of the Klondike are only a memory.

WHEN was Jesus born? WHEN did Hamlet live? WHEN were

This richly coloured painting of the Nativity is by Domenico Ghirlandaio.

BIRTH OF JESUS

Although the Christian calendar is nominally dated from the year of Christ's birth, modern researchers have placed the actual year between 4 and 7 B.C. When the calendar was changed the monk Dionysius Exiguus (500–600) set the date of "the incarnation of the Lord" as the year 753 after the founding of the city of Rome. But his arithmetic was inaccurate.

The Gospels say that Jesus was born while Herod was on the throne, and Herod died about 749, according to the Roman calendar, or about 4 B.C. Also the census mentioned by St Luke as the reason why Joseph and Mary travelled to Bethlehem seems to have been held in the Roman year 747, or 6 B.C.

the Crusades?

HAMLET

Hamlet, the hero of Shakespeare's great tragedy, seems to correspond to a figure called Amleth, who appears in a history of Denmark, written by Saxo Grammaticus late in the 12th Century.

However, it is impossible to say whether he did in fact exist. The figure of the young man whose father was murdered by a brother who later married his victim's widow appears in many legends. In all of them the son pretends to be mad in order to revenge his father's death. Such stories are found as far back as the Icelandic saga of Amlöoi, mentioned by the 10th Century poet, Snaebjörn.

The story of Hamlet is told in the fifth volume of *Histoires Tragiques* (1570) by François de Belleforest and an English version of this, *The Hystorie of Hamblet* was published in London in 1608. Shakespeare's tragedy was written about 1601, but a play about Hamlet believed to have been written by Thomas Kyd was performed in about 1509.

Kronborg Castle—Hamlet's Elsinore.

As he often did, Shakespeare borrowed the plot from others and transformed it by his genius into a great work of art.

CRUSADES

The Crusades were a series of holy wars authorized by successive Popes and waged by the Christians of western Europe from 1095 to the end of the 13th Century. Their purpose was the recovery of the Holy Sepulchre in Jerusalem and other sacred places from the Mohammedans. The word comes from the Spanish *cruzada*, meaning "marked with a cross".

There were three basic causes for the Crusades: first, the threat to pilgrims journeying to the Holy Sepulchre from the Seljuk Turks who had overrun Anatolia, Syria and Palestine; secondly, a great surge of energy in Christianized western Europe and a desire to expand territory and control trade routes; thirdly, the determination of the Church to make its authority universal.

The First Crusade, summoned by Pope Urban II in 1095, took Jerusalem by storm on July 15, 1099 and set up Christian governments in the city and in the three "Latin states" of Edessa, Antioch and Tripoli. When Edessa was captured by the Mohammedans in 1144, Pope Eugenius III called the Second Crusade (1147–1149), but this was so mismanaged that it accomplished nothing.

The recapture of Jerusalem in 1187 by the wise, brave and chivalrous Mohammedan leader Saladin gave rise to the Third Crusade (1189–1191) led by Philip the Fair of France and Richard the Lion-Hearted of England. In the Holy Land Acre was captured but the two kings quarrelled and first Philip and then Richard abandoned the struggle. The Fourth Crusade (1202–1204) never reached Palestine but instead attacked and captured the Christian city of Constantinople. The Fifth Crusade (1221) was a complete failure but on the Sixth Crusade (1228–1229) Jerusalem was obtained from the Mohammedans by negotiation. The city's capture by the Turks in 1244 brought the Seventh Crusade (1249) in which the leader King Louis IX of France was taken prisoner and ransomed. Louis also led the Eighth Crusade, this time to Tunis where he died of the plague in 1270. The knights held out in Acre until 1291 when they surrendered. Attempts to revive the Holy Wars in the 14th Century failed.

WHITNEY'S GIN

Whitney's cotton gin was exceedingly important as it more than trebled the amount of cotton which could be picked free of seeds in a day. This stimulated the extension of the cotton plantations and the growth of Negro slavery in the south of the United States. In that way the cotton gin was indirectly responsible for the American Civil War.

Eli Whitney (1765–1825) was born in Westboro, Massachusetts. After graduating from Yale College in 1792, he became aware of the need for a machine which would separate cotton from its seeds. The Industrial Revolution was in full flood and inventions such as John Kay's flying shuttle (1733) and James Hargreaves's spinning jenny (1769) had created a growing demand for raw cotton as the production of finished goods was now so much faster and easier.

Whitney produced, in only a few weeks, a hand-operated machine or gin, and by April 1793 had built a machine that could clean 50 pounds of cotton fibres a day. It consisted of a wooden cylinder encircled by rows of slender spikes, set half an inch apart, which extended between the bars of a grid set so closely together that the seeds could not pass, although the lint was pulled through by the revolving spikes. A revolving brush cleaned the spikes and the seeds fell into another compartment.

The gin was immediately in great demand. Country blacksmiths helped to fulfil the orders when the factory Whitney set up at New Haven, Connecticut, was unable to cope with all the orders. In the South, almost the whole region was given over to cotton growing, increasing the value of slaves and reinforcing the slave system, which had been declining.

SLAVES

Negro slaves were taken to the West Indies because the original population had almost become extinct.

While Christopher Columbus explored all parts of the West Indies, his successors colonized only those islands which were peopled by the Ciboney and Arawak Indians. They avoided the Carib islands of the Lesser Antilles because they had no gold and the Carib Indians were fierce and difficult to subdue. As the Spaniards conquered each island, they rounded up its Indians and put

slaves taken to the West Indies?

An interior view of a House of Correction in Jamaica in the 1830s. The whipping of female slaves was a commonplace cruelty. This contemporary print illustrated an anti-slavery pamphlet.

them to work in mines or on plantations.

Many were worked to death, some starved, others died from diseases introduced from Europe and still others were killed when they tried to rebel. By 1550, the Ciboney were extinct and only a few Arawak remained.

In the 16th Century, the Spaniards introduced Negro slaves to replace the dwindling supply of labour. They did not bring in many, for their mines were exhausted, and they owned cattle ranches which did not require much labour.

The main shipments of Negro slaves came in the 18th Century, when sugar plantations were developed by the French in Haiti and the Lesser Antilles.

After the French Revolution, the slaves in Haiti revolted and set up an independent Negro republic. The French went to neighbouring British and Spanish islands, established new plantations and imported more slaves.

When slavery was abolished in the first half of the 19th Century the British imported Chinese and Indians from Asia who rapidly increased in numbers until, by the middle of the 20th Century, they comprised more than one third of the population of Trinidad. Throughout the Antilles the Negroes and Asians have assumed more and more prominence, so that they now dominate the area except in countries like Cuba and Puerto Rico.

A painting in the Tassili Plateau caves, Algeria.

FIRST MEN

Our early ancestors in all lands made their first homes in the natural shelter provided by caves. In these primitive dwellings the caveman stored all his worldly belongings, his tools, weapons, ornaments, and the bones of the animals he killed. Many caves were decorated with fine but simple paintings and engravings on the rock surfaces, usually depicting animals and hunting scenes. Man, at the beginning of history, was a good gatherer depending for his survival on hunting wild animals and birds, fishing and collecting wild fruits, nuts and berries.

Nobody can be sure when man first started to use caves as shelter. But our history begins about 600,000 or 700,000 years ago, when our ancestors first started to make and use tools. From the remnants of these tools archaeologists and historians have been able to piece together the caveman's way of life.

Originally cavemen lived just with their families, but soon tribes were formed and bigger caves sought to house them all together. In Switzerland the Holloch cave extends for 38 miles and near Grenoble in France caves as deep as 3,000 feet have been found.

JOAN OF ARC

Joan of Arc, the peasant girl who led the French to victory at Orleans and Charles VII to his coronation at Rheims, was burned to death as a heretic by the English on May 31, 1431, in the Place du Vieux Marché in Rouen. Her great heroism and leadership, which she claimed to be inspired by the voices of three saints, played a decisive part in the revival of France at the crisis of the Hundred Years War against the English invaders.

Joan was born in 1412 at Domrémy, a village between Champagne and Lorraine on the banks of the Meuse. She led cattle to pasture and sang and danced with the other village girls until, at the age of 13, she began to hear voices and see visions. Later these voices urged her to go to Orleans and raise the siege of the city. With the approval of the Church she entered Orleans and defeated the besieging English.

After a famous battle at Patay in June, 1429, in which Joan led the French to a great victory, she persuaded Charles the Dauphin to go to Rheims where he was crowned king. Joan, the Maid of Orleans, stood near the altar during the ceremony, holding her banner aloft.

The Maid was captured by the Burgundians in a skirmish on May 30, 1430, and handed over to the Bishop of Beauvais. After an inquisition by the Church she was delivered to the English. To the very last moment of her ordeal she claimed that her voices were sent to her by God. The executioner later said that her heart would not burn and that he had found it intact in the ashes. This story became part of her legend.

THE BUDDHA

Buddha's full name was Gautama Buddha, and he lived in north-east India. He was born into a warrior tribe called the Sakyas in the 6th Century B.C. and became the founder of the religion called Buddhism.

Although he was of noble birth, Buddha was not proud and fond of luxury. Even when young, he was serious and thought a great deal. He decided it was better to lead a humble, religious life.

When he was 29, he left his home and became a monk. He found strength in quiet meditation. He saw that the world was full of suffering, and wanted to help people. So he became a wandering teacher.

Buddha gave his first sermon at Benares on the River Ganges. Here, he outlined the beliefs which have guided Buddhists ever since. Buddha said first of all that worldly life cannot give final happiness. You should not be either completely self-indulgent or too strict with yourself. You should try to follow a middle path, maintaining inner peace and discipline. A Buddhist's final spiritual goal is a blissful state called Nirvana, in which he is completely calm and free from any pain or anxiety.

The name Buddha means "The Enlightened One". He died near Benares when he was 80. By then he had organized a community of monks, called the Sangha, to carry on his teachings.

The main countries where Buddhism is practised are Burma, Thailand, Ceylon and Japan. There are about 177,000 Buddhists in North America.

This magnificent gilt bronze figure of a seated Buddha comes from Nepal. It was made in the 15th Century. The position of the seated figure is typical of many statues of Buddha, of which there are a huge number.

WHEN was Pearl Harbor? WHEN was Persepolis destroyed WHEN does war escalate?

PEARL HARBOR

The Japanese bombing raids on Pearl Harbor, Hawaii, which led to the entry of the United States into the Second World War, were made about breakfast time on December 7, 1941. In a little over an hour and without even a declaration of war, Japan crippled the American Pacific fleet and made possible the conquest or domination of large areas of land and sea.

Relations between the United States and Japan had been strained for at least 10 years. Although neither country had yet taken an active part in the great conflict, their sympathies were on opposite sides. Japan had signed an agreement with Germany and Italy, while the United States was supplying Britain.

America's Pacific fleet of nearly 100 vessels, including eight battleships, had been stationed at Pearl Harbor since April 1940, and the commanders there had been warned of the possibility of war. However, when the attack came, it took the Americans almost completely by surprise.

At 7.55 am local time their warships and protective airfields were attacked by 200 Japanese aircraft, including torpedo planes, bombers

and fighters. At 8.50 am a second attack began and lasted just over 10 minutes.

When it was all over the Americans counted their losses; more than 2,000 sailors and 200 Army personnel killed; three battleships destroyed, a fourth capsized, a fifth heavily damaged and the remaining three lightly damaged; two light cruisers and three destroyers among other ships also damaged; 42 aircraft destroyed and 41 damaged.

The Japanese had lost 29 aircraft and five midget submarines.

PERSEPOLIS

Persepolis, the ancient capital of Darius the Great, king of the Persians, was partly destroyed by Alexander the Great, the celebrated king of Macedonia who overthrew the Persian empire and conquered large sections of India.

The great palace of Darius was by all accounts a marvellous building and the surviving ruins are a tribute to its vast size. Situated some thirty miles northeast of Shirez in southwest Iran, the ruins consist of retaining walls up to more than forty feet in height and a truly splendid double stair of 111 stone steps ascending to a terrace.

There are the remains of a number of once enormous buildings on this terrace. The buildings are built from huge slabs of highly polished grey stone beautifully cut and laid together without the aid of mortar. The remains of Darius's great audience hall can still be seen, with its huge stone columns. Thirteen of these are still standing.

Alexander had long vowed to destroy the might of Darius and the burning of Persepolis was a symbol of Greek revenge against the Persians. Some sources say that the burning of the great palace was encouraged by a courtesan

at a drunken celebration. But undoubtedly it was symbolic of the triumph of the Greeks.

Alexander was one of the greatest generals in history. He was a pupil of Aristotle, the great Greek philosopher, and was keenly interested in scientific exploration. Indeed, his invasion of India was largely inspired by his desire to explore. His achievements—and he was only 32 when he died—were truly enormous. He spread the influence of Greek thought and civilization from Gibraltar to India and he created the city of Alexandria in Egypt.

WHEN did West Point start?
WHEN was the Battle of Agincourt?

WEST POINT

West Point, the United States military academy for the training of regular army officers was established on March 16, 1802 at West Point on the Hudson River about 50 miles north of the city of New York. The place was already famous as the scene, 22 years earlier, of a dramatic incident in the War of Independence, when the traitor Benedict Arnold failed in an attempt to betray the strategically important position to the British.

Three chief reasons for the formation of the academy were: first, the fact that in the War of Independence the United States had been forced to rely on foreign military technicians; second, the belief of army leaders, including George Washington, that military techniques must be studied and not acquired solely through experience; third, the desire of some reformers for a new approach to the education of officers.

In 1812 the academy, which had been training only engineers, was reorganized and given more scope. In 1866 an Act of Congress was passed to allow the selection of an academy superintendent who was not an engineer.

West Point is under the direct control of the army and the four-year course of instruction leads to a science degree and a commission of second lieutenant in the regular army. Studies are balanced between mathematics and engineering sciences (55 per cent) and the humanities and social sciences (45 per cent). The 3,100 cadets must be between 17 and 22 years old and unmarried, with a high school education. Aptitude tests and a medical examination must be passed before admission.

ESCALATION

War is said to escalate when it increases rapidly in scale or intensity. The word was added to the military vocabulary by the Americans during the Vietnam War to denote the increasing degrees of United States involvement in the fighting. It has also been used by military writers to describe the development of a possible war between two powers through successive stages from the use of conventional weapons to the localized employment of atomic weapons and, finally, an all-out exchange of annihilating nuclear missiles.

It is a far cry from the use of the word escalator by the American Jesse W. Reno to describe the moving staircase he invented in 1891. Both words come from the Spanish *escalada*, meaning the scaling of the walls of a fortress by means of ladders. A staircase moving inevitably upwards provides a more fitting image than a scaling ladder of the horrifying expansion of which war today is capable.

BATTLE OF AGINCOURT

The Battle of Agincourt took place on October 25, 1415, near the village of Agincourt in the Pas-de-Calais, France. The battle was one of the most notable in history and is particularly famous for the havoc wrought on the French by the longbowmen of England.

The English army was led by King Henry V. He had already taken Harfleur in Normandy and his plan was to return to England via Calais. However, this plan was thwarted when he discovered that his road to the port was blocked by the French army.

Henry's men had marched and fought for many days. They were tired and short of food. The king knew he must give battle.

Although the English were outnumbered by three to one, the French had sandwiched themselves in between two areas of woodland which made it difficult for them to deploy their troops in the narrow space of open land. Henry cleverly stationed his force of some 5,000 archers towards one end of the woods and other archers protected groups of men-at-arms.

The French were greatly hampered on the soggy land by their heavy armour. After a devastating archery assault—the air was said to be dark with English arrows—the archers were ordered to move in for the kill and to attack with axe and sword. The French lost about 10,000 men and were completely routed. English casualties were light—about 1,500 men. It was at Agincourt that the power of the longbow reached its supreme point.

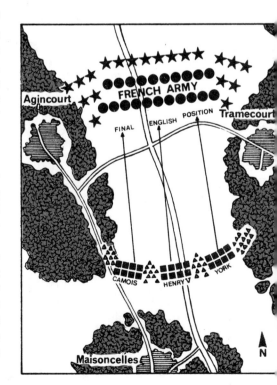

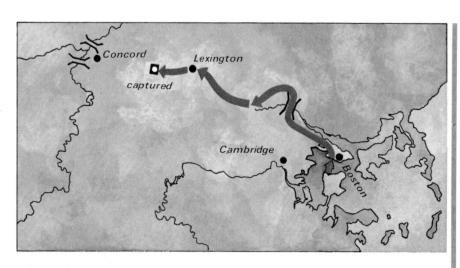

PAUL REVERE

Paul Revere (1735–1818) is famous for his ride on horseback during the American Revolution to warn Massachusetts colonists of the approach of British troops.

Paul Revere's father, a Huguenot refugee, who had settled in Boston, Massachusetts, taught his son the art of silversmithing. Revere became a great artist in silver but, in his need to support his family he also sold spectacles, replaced missing teeth and made surgical instruments.

He was a fervent patriot, cut many copper plates for anti-British propaganda and was a leader of the Boston Tea Party in 1773, when a group of citizens disguised as Indians threw a cargo of tea into the sea as a protest against the British tax on it.

In 1775, when the American Revolution broke out, Revere constructed a powder mill to supply the colonial troops. He enlisted in the army and in 1776 was a lieutenant-colonel, in command of Castle William, at Boston.

But his most famous exploit took place the year before when, as principal express rider for Boston's Committee of Safety, he warned Middlesex County, on April 18, that British troops were leaving Boston to seize military stores at Lexington and Concord. His exploit has been immortalized in the poem *Paul Revere's Ride* by Henry Wadsworth Longfellow (1807–1882).

After the colonists' victory, Revere set up a rolling mill for the manufacture of sheet copper in Massachusetts, and became rich.

BRITISH EMPIRE

It is possible to list at least four basic forces which brought about the dissolution of the British Empire. First, both Britain and her colonies recognized that some kind of self-government was necessary in territories which were separated by thousands of miles from Britain. Administration centred in London was increasingly difficult and expensive.

Secondly, the colonies themselves began to chafe against British rule and to demand to manage their own affairs. A note of aggressive nationalism entered into the appeals for self-government.

In the third place, individual British colonies and other nations began to forge economic, social and political links. Two world wars also greatly reduced Britain's power in the world and made some colonies look elsewhere for leadership.

Finally, many Britons themselves realized that the Empire had

MING VASE

Ming porcelain is admired and distinguished for its use of colour. It was the most important development of China's Ming Dynasty (1368–1644) in the realms of art. A completely new style arose in which the emphasis was on the decorative element as opposed to form and glaze with which the potters of the Sung (960–1279) and Yüan (1280–1368) dynasties had been concerned.

During the Ming dynasty production of Chinese porcelain reached a very high standard. This was especially so in the case of the imperial porcelain factory at Ching-tê Chên which had ample deposits of the finest white clay to draw upon. Chinese fashion at this period turned towards richness of colouring and to striking effects in decoration. The full-bodied sturdy shapes and the gorgeous colouring of Ming porcelain reflected the prosperous community which produced it.

There were three methods employed by the potters to create the colourful decorations. One, used in the T'ang dynasty (618–906), was to scratch a line which, as well as strengthening the design, form-

become unwieldy and that relationships within it were a handicap rather than a gain.

Nevertheless, there was not a complete break up but the growth of an association of independent nations called the Commonwealth. There were three bonds which united the association. The close economic relationship of trade, labour and capital; the acceptance of many Commonwealth countries of British social, economic, educational, political, military and legal institutions and customs; and the savings that could be made in the member countries by acceptance of British military and diplomatic services.

break up?   WHY is a Ming vase so admired?

ed a ditch to separate the various fields of colour. A second method was to separate these areas by putting down tiny raised borders to these fields by means of threads of clay. Then a third way was to create the design in relief, so that it was easy to separate the colours for the raised decoration from those for the background.

Towards the close of the Ming period, the standard of pottery declined through a loss of vitality, and it was not until K'ang Hsi came to the throne early in the succeeding Ch'ing dynasty (1674–1912) that Chinese porcelain once again flourished.

This magnificent vase was found in a tomb of the Ming period.

WHEN was gas first used in war?   WHEN does Modern
WHEN was keelhauling used as a method of punishment?

GAS IN WAR

Gas was, perhaps, first used in battle in the Peloponnesian War between Sparta and Athens (431–404 B.C.) when burning pitch and sulphur were used to produce suffocating gases. But poison gas as a modern weapon was introduced in the First World War on April 22, 1915. The Germans then launched a cylinder attack with chlorine against the British and French at Ypres.

Later many varieties of war gas were introduced. In July 1917 the Germans began using mustard gas, which caused severe, slow-healing burns on the skin and damage to the lungs. Many casualties resulted from gas bombardment, but relatively few people died. Both sides were ready to use increased gas attacks when the war ended in 1918.

During the Second World War and the Korean War gas was not used, but preparations were carried out by both sides. Perhaps the most terrifying discovery was made by the Germans. This was a new series of chemical agents called nerve gases which rapidly result in convulsions, coma and—unless promptly treated—death.

Tear gas, which causes intense smarting and watering of the eyes is used in many countries to control rioting crowds, but its effects are only temporary.

German soldiers advance in gas masks.

MODERN HISTORY

Most historians date the beginning of modern history from about the year 1500. "Modern" comes from a Latin adverb meaning "just now", and the word was applied to history as early as Elizabethan days. It meant an awareness of newness, of living in times different from those of one's ancestors.

The Renaissance, with its great revival in art and learning, the great geographical discoveries, the invention of printing, and the Reformation, with the rise of Protestantism, combined to make the start of the 16th Century a convenient time from which to date modern history.

However, it is a convenient, rather than an accurate, date.

Modern times should not be seen as a sunrise ending the medieval night. The last few centuries of the Middle Ages saw much scientific advancement, growth of trade and the establishment of a money economy. Also, many medieval ways persisted in western Europe as late as the 17th Century, including the legal system in England and the land-holding system in France.

Even today, pockets of culture can be found in out-of-the-way places which are mediaeval or pre-medieval in structure. The Middle Ages grows into the Modern Age and the 15th, 16th and 17th Centuries are perhaps best seen as centuries of transition.

KEELHAULING

Keelhauling was first referred to as a punishment for offenders in a Dutch naval ordinance of 1560. It was carried out in the British Navy at least as early as the first half of the 17th Century.

The punishment consisted of lowering the victim down one side of the ship and dragging him under the keel to the other side.

It was never 'official' in the British Navy but the Dutch retained it until 1853.

History begin?
WHEN was the Battle of Britain?

BATTLE OF BRITAIN

The Battle of Britain in the Second World War began with skirmishes in June and July 1940, reached a climax in August and September and ended in the ferocity of the Blitz during the following winter. It laid the foundations for the survival of Britain and the eventual destruction of Nazi Germany.

Soon after the fall of France in the middle of June, the Germans began to prepare for a possible invasion of Britain by setting out first to destroy the Royal Air Force. There was a long series of air battles and bombardments.

The Germans seemed to have no systematic plan of action. On the other hand, Britain had developed a radar early warning system and a superb fighting aircraft, the Spitfire. Thus, although outnumbered, the British were able to defend with superior equipment and undivided aim against an enemy whose fleets of bombers, the Dornier 17, the Heinkel III and the Junkers 88, proved vulnerable to attacks by Spitfires and Hurricanes. The best German fighter, the Messerschmitt 109, was on a par with the Spitfire but, over England, was at the limit of its range.

After waves of attacks had failed to put the R.A.F. out of action, the Germans switched their offensive from Fighter Command airfields and installations to London and other cities, causing terrible damage. But the raiders also suffered heavy casualties. On September 15 the British destroyed 185 enemy aircraft, demonstrating to the Luftwaffe, the German air force, that it had lost the battle. Attacks on cities with explosive and fire bombs continued but lost their impetus by the end of April 1941.

Bombs dropping near St. Paul's Cathedral, London, in 1940.

WHERE do the stars and stripes come from? WHERE did

WHERE did the Dalai Lama live?

Delaware	Dec. 7, 1787	Michigan	Jan. 26, 1837
Pennsylvania	Dec. 12, 1787	Florida	Mar. 3, 1845
New Jersey	Dec. 18, 1787	Texas	Dec. 29, 1845
Georgia	Jan. 2, 1788	Iowa	Dec. 28, 1846
Connecticut	Jan. 9, 1788	Wisconsin	May 29, 1848
Massachusetts	Feb. 6, 1788	California	Sept. 9, 1850
Maryland	Apr. 28, 1788	Minnesota	May 11, 1858
South Carolina	May 23, 1788	Oregon	Feb. 14, 1859
New Hampshire	June 21, 1788	Kansas	Jan. 29, 1861
Virginia	June 25, 1788	West Virginia	June 20, 1863
New York	July 26, 1788	Nevada	Oct. 31, 1864
North Carolina	Nov. 21, 1789	Nebraska	Mar. 1, 1867
Rhode Island	May 29, 1790	Colorado	Aug. 1, 1876
Vermont	Mar. 4, 1791	North Dakota	Nov. 2, 1889
Kentucky	June 1, 1792	South Dakota	Nov. 2, 1889
Tennessee	June 1, 1796	Montana	Nov. 8, 1889
Ohio	Mar. 1, 1803	Washington	Nov. 11, 1889
Louisiana	Apr. 30, 1812	Idaho	July 3, 1890
Indiana	Dec. 11, 1816	Wyoming	July 10, 1890
Mississippi	Dec. 10, 1817	Utah	Jan. 4, 1896
Illinois	Dec. 3, 1818	Oklahoma	Nov. 16, 1907
Alabama	Dec. 14, 1819	New Mexico	Jan. 6, 1912
Maine	Mar. 15, 1820	Arizona	Feb. 14, 1912
Missouri	Aug. 10, 1821	Alaska	Jan. 3, 1959
Arkansas	June 15, 1836	Hawaii	Aug 21, 1959

STARS & STRIPES

In the early days of the American War of Independence each state adopted a flag of its own. South Carolina had a flag of red and blue stripes adorned with rattlesnakes. That of Massachusetts bore a pine tree. Even the colours carried by different regiments differed according to the taste of their commanders. This was confusing, especially at sea, where one ship might well end up firing on her own ally!

The Rhodes Island flag was the first to contain any stars. There were 13 stars representing the 13 colonies which later were to become the first members of the United States.

In 1776 Washington's new continental army displayed its flag. This time there were no stars. Still in the top left-hand corner was the British Grand Union flag, with its crosses of St George and St Andrew—a sign, one supposes, that independence was not yet the Americans' intention. But around the British emblem appeared the stripes: six white horizontal stripes and seven red ones, again giving the total of 13.

It was not until 1777, almost a year after the adoption of the Declaration of Independence, that Congress adopted a design for the national flag. This consisted of 13 stars (in place of the Grand Union flag) and 13 stripes, alternately red and white.

Every time a new state was accepted in the Union a new star and a new stripe would be added to the flag. By 1795 the flag was getting a little cramped; there was no room for any more stripes. So Congress decided that the flag should contain only 13 stripes representing the original states, and that a star for each new state should be added on the July 4 following its admission to the Union.

In 1959 Alaska became the 49th state and in the same year Hawaii became the 50th and most recent.

Lady Godiva ride naked through the town?
WHERE is Golgotha?

LADY GODIVA

Since 1678 Lady Godiva's legendary ride naked through the streets of Coventry, England, has been reenacted every seven or eight years. But today the lady wears a body stocking. The famous ride, if it took place, happened around the year 1057, according to the chronicler Roger of Wendover (d. 1236). Godiva, her long hair falling loosely round her body, rode through the market place accompanied by two soldiers.

Legend has it that Lady Godiva pleaded with Leofric, Earl of Mercia, to lessen the townspeople's tax burden. Exasperated, the earl declared he would do as she asked, if she rode naked through the town. Lady Godiva did so and the earl cut the townspeople's taxes. Over the years the legend became embellished. The soldiers disappeared and, in the 17th Century, the legend of Peeping Tom crept into the story. Tom is said to have been struck blind because he could not resist peeping at Lady Godiva through a window as she rode by.

The true facts record that Coventry's early fame rested on the foundation of a Benedictine monastery by Leofric and his wife Godgifu (the real name of Godiva) in 1043.

The phrase "to send to Coventry" (to refuse to speak with someone) might well have been the fate of Peeping Tom. But although the origin of the phrase is uncertain it seems more likely to have originated during the Civil War. Captured supporters of King Charles were sent by Cromwell's forces to Coventry for imprisonment.

GOLGOTHA

Golgotha is just outside the walls of the old city of Jerusalem in Israel. It is named in the New Testament as the place where Jesus was crucified.

Jesus was brought before the Roman governor of the province, Pontius Pilate, and accused of blasphemy. Pilate could find nothing to support the charge and offered to release Jesus. But the chief priests and elders persuaded the people to demand his death. Jesus was beaten by the Roman soldiers, dressed in a scarlet cloak and crowned with thorns to mock him as "King of the Jews". Afterwards he was forced to carry his own cross through the streets of Jerusalem to Golgotha.

The name Golgotha, meaning the place of a skull, is derived from the Aramaic language spoken in that part of Palestine. The word Calvary comes from "calvaria", which is the Latin translation of Golgotha. No one knows why Golgotha was so called, but a very ancient story says that Adam's skull was buried there.

This beautiful 15th Century mural was painted by Philip Goul.

THE DALAI LAMA

The first Dalai Lama, head of an order of Buddhist Monks in Tibet, lived in the Tashilhumpo monastery, which he founded. He died in 1474, and was called Dge-'dun-grub-pa.

Since then, there have been many Dalai Lamas. Most of them have had both political and religious power. The fifth Dalai Lama moved his residence to Lhasa, where he had an enormous palace built, called the Potala. From there Tibet was governed by him and his descendants.

In 1959, the Dalai Lama had to flee to India, because he was thrown out of Tibet by the Chinese Communists.

94

WHEN did the Incas live? WHEN were ducking stools in use

DUCKING STOOLS

Ducking stools first came into use as a punishment for women at the beginning of the 17th Century and were used in England as late as the beginning of the 19th. A ducking stool was a wooden armchair fastened to the end of a long wooden beam fixed like a seesaw on the edge of a river or pond. Sometimes it was mounted on wheels so that it could be pushed through the streets.

The stool was used to punish nagging wives, witches and prostitutes. An iron band kept the victim from falling out of the chair when it was plunged under the water. It was the duty of magistrates to order the number of duckings a woman should be given.

Another type of ducking stool was a chair on two wheels with two long shafts fixed to the axles. When the stool was pushed into the pond and the shafts were released the seat was tipped up backwards, but, in this case, the woman was not fastened in.

INCAS

The Incas, a race of South American Indians, are believed to have started their rise to power in Peru about five hundred years before the arrival of the Spanish conquerors in the 16th Century. They are said to have climbed into the Andes mountains from the eastern forests calling themselves "children of the Sun".

According to their favourite legend, Manco Capac, the founder of the race, came out of Lake Titicaca in Peru with his sister who was also his wife. The sun god was said to have given him a staff and told him to build a city at a spot where it sank into the ground—in other words, where the ground was fertile. This city was given the name Cuzco, meaning navel, because the Incas regarded it as the centre of the earth.

It was not long before the Incas began to conquer or absorb the neighbouring tribes. By 1460 their empire extended from the Amazon forests to the Pacific Ocean, from the borders of what is now Ecuador, deep into Chile. This 2,000-mile territory was governed by a mild form of despotism. The term Inca properly applied only to the upper caste of the nobility and those of royal blood.

Property was held in common, money was not used and the products of labour were divided in three equal portions between the church, the governing classes and the people. Inca skills included the spinning of woollen clothes, mining, engineering with tin and copper tools, the fashioning of gold and silver ornaments, irrigation and the use of fertilizers.

They used a system of writing by means of knots tied in lengths of string.

The doom of this thriving and industrious civilization was sealed when the Spanish adventurer Francisco Pizarro sailed from the Isthmus of Panama with fewer than 200 men in 1531 to conquer and loot the country. Pizarro seized the Inca ruler Atahualpa and had him put to death after accepting a vast gold and silver ransom for his life. With their leader executed and their chiefs slain, the people were forced into submission. Slaughter, plunder and oppression followed. But today the remains of massive stone temples and palaces survive as reminders of the high state of Inca culture. Like the mask above, ornaments have also survived.

WHEN were submarines first used?

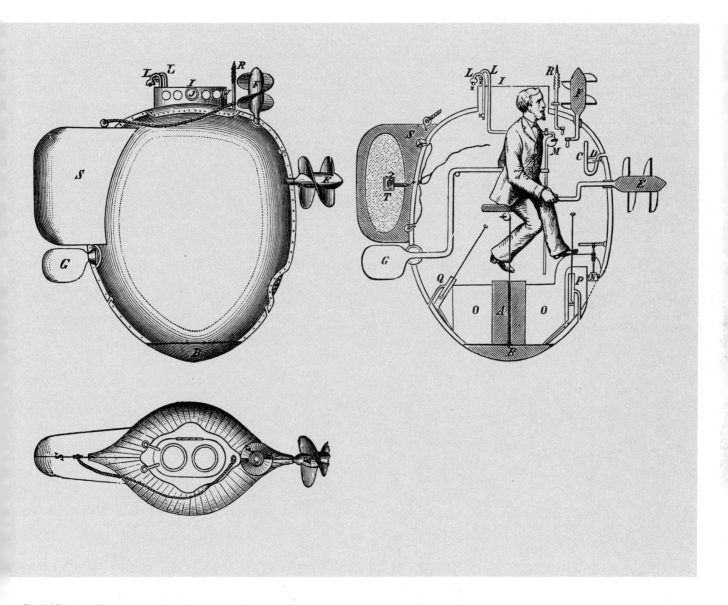

David Bushnell's remarkable submarine "Turtle". I Entry hatch O Water ballast N Water inlet P,Q Water outlets and pumps E Screw propeller for forward movement F Screw propeller for vertical movement G Rudder C,D Indicator for angle of dive L Breathing snorkel M Ventilator S Mine T Trigger charge R Screw for fixing mine to ship's bottom A,B Ballast

SUBMARINES

The first submarine which we know to have been used was built by a Dutchman, Cornelius van Drebel, in 1620. It was constructed of greased leather stretched over a wooden frame and was propelled by oars extended through the sides and sealed with tight-fitting leather flaps. Hand vices were employed to contract the sides of the vessel and reduce its volume, thus causing it to submerge. King James I of England is said to have gone for a ride in it, 12 to 15 feet below the surface of the River Thames.

But the first use of a submarine as a weapon occurred during the American War of Independence. In 1776 the Turtle, a one-man wooden submarine with a screw propeller, invented by an American, David Bushnell, tried unsuccessfully to sink a British man-of-war in New York harbour.

Attempts to build an underwater craft were made as far back as the days of ancient Greece. But practical designs had to wait for the invention of the internal combustion engine and the electric motor at the end of the 19th Century. The first truly successful submarine to travel under the sea in rough weather was the Argonaught, a 36-foot, cigar-shaped vessel built by an American, Simon Lake, in 1897. It was driven by a 30 horse-power engine.

WHY was the Great Wall of China built? WHY did the

GREAT WALL

The Great Wall of China was built in the Third Century BC to keep out the raiding Tartars of Mongolia. It is 20 to 30 feet high and 15 to 25 feet wide at the top, with towers 60 feet high every few hundred yards.

The Wall stretches from Shanhaikwan on the Yellow Sea to the borders of Kansu and Sinkiang in the west, crossing high mountains and deep valleys. Probably over 500,000 workers were employed to build it. Even today, the Wall is in a wonderful state of preservation.

This marvellous structure is constructed of brick and stone. The sides have battlements—parapets with openings or embrasures through which weapons could be discharged.

All large cities of China were provided with similar walls, and the gates were closed at night to give the citizens protection against surprise attack. For China has been envied by her neighbours throughout history. Many times these neighbours have invaded the country, seized the capital and begun a new dynasty.

Probably man's greatest-ever constructional achievement. More than 500,000 workers were employed to build it.

Roman Civilization fall?

ROMAN CIVILIZATION

Rome's conquest of the Near East, mainly in the last century B.C. probably sowed the seeds of decay which led to the fall of one of the mightiest empires ever known.

Beginning as a tiny settlement on the Palatine Hill, about 17 miles from the mouth of the Tiber in central Italy, Rome had become the conqueror and leader of the Western world.

But then the ancient and sturdy simplicity of the Roman character gave way to Oriental luxury and bitter hostility developed between the wealthy aristocracy and the poverty stricken majority.

The death of Tiberius Gracchus in 133 B.C. marked the beginning of a century of revolution and civil war which ended in the downfall of the republic and the establishment of an empire. Julius Caesar

(102–44 B.C.), the great warrior-statesman, welded the tottering structure together and two centuries of peace followed. They included periods of great splendour, such as the wise rule of Hadrian (A.D. 117–138), when the empire reached its greatest extent.

The Christian religion spread until, in the reign of Constantine (280–337), it become the official faith of the Roman Empire. Rome was prosperous and her influence in art and letters reigned throughout the known world, but prosperity brought corruption and self-indulgence completed the ruin.

Diocletian (284–305) took the first step which led to the division of the empire, entrusting an associate with the government of the west, while he ruled the east. Then Constantine the Great in 330 moved the capital to the Greek city of Byzantium, renaming it Constantinople.

The story of the Byzantine Empire is long and glorious but that of the western empire is one of weakness and decline. Northern barbarians invaded Italy and in 410 the Visigoth King Alaric conquered Rome. The western empire from that time became the prey of successive waves of fierce barbarians.

In 476 Romulus Augustus, the last of the imperial line in the west, was deposed by the barbarian leader Odoacer, and the Roman Empire was formally ended.

However, in reading the history of France, Italy and Spain, you will see that the end of the Roman Empire was in a way only its beginning. These new kingdoms governed themselves mainly by Roman law, spoke forms of Latin and professed the Christian religion. Thus even though a great empire decayed and fell, Rome had won a dominion which persists to this day.

WHERE was Akbar's empire?   WHERE did Julius Caesar

AKBAR'S EMPIRE

Jalal-ud-Din Mohammed Akbar (1542–1605), the greatest of the Mogul emperors of India, was a ruler only in name when he came to the throne in 1556. His Mongolian grandfather, Baber, had established a Mohammedan empire in northern India through a combination of daring, luck and military skill. But his father had been driven from the capital, Delhi, by a usurper.

With able generalship, Akbar overthrew all his rivals and embarked upon a career of conquest which, by 1562, gave him domain over the Punjab and Multan, the basin of the Ganges and Jumna Rivers, Gwalior to the south and Kabul in Afghanistan in the northwest. Subsequently he crossed the Narbada River into the Deccan and extended his dominion southward. By 1605, his empire contained 15 provinces, or *subahs*, and stretched from the Hindu Kush mountains to the Godocari River and from Bengal across to Gujarat.

JULIUS CAESAR

Julius Caesar landed in Britain on a low, shelving beach somewhere between the modern towns of Deal and Walmer in Kent.

Caesar decided to invade Britain when he was Proconsul in Gaul. Only vague ideas prevailed about the British islands, but they were known to be rich in tin. So, late in August 55 B.C., Caesar sailed across the channel with 80 transports and two legions. After a short, ferocious fight amid the waves, his men reached the shore and put the Britons to flight.

But Caesar's troubles had only just begun. His cavalry, in 18 transports, was caught in a sudden gale and driven back to Gaul, while the high tide battered the ships that lay at anchor. The Britons again attacked, were once more driven back and finally submitted. Caesar made no attempt to penetrate further inland and never even pretended that his expedition had been a success.

The following year he returned with five legions and some cavalry in 800 ships. He spent 10 days having all his ships hauled ashore. Then he crossed the River Thames near Brentford. The British had found a leader, Cassivelaunus, who harassed the Roman troops severely. Caesar was glad to negotiate with the British chieftain, to accept some hostages and tribute and then to quit the island.

For nearly 100 years no invading army landed again in Britain.

Julius Caesar (102-44 B.C.) was a member of a noble family but also became a favourite with the people of Rome. As Overseer of the Public Games in 65 B.C., he organized magnificent spectacles to win popularity, for he felt himself to be the man who would save Rome from decay. In 59 B.C. he was elected Consul and a year later was sent as Proconsul to Transalpine Gaul (now France).

land in Britain? WHERE is Karl Marx buried?
WHERE are the Heights of Abraham?

KARL MARX

Karl Marx was buried in Highgate Cemetery in North London on 17 March, 1883. On his gravestone are carved these sentences from his works:

"The philosophers have only interpreted the world in various ways; the point, however, is to change it."

"Workers of all lands, unite."

Karl Marx had German-Jewish parents. He started work as a journalist, after attending university in Bonn, Berlin and Jena where he studied law, philosophy and history. When he was 25 his newspaper was closed down, and he left Germany in search of freedom. After being expelled from France he went to Brussels where with Frederick Engels he wrote *The Communist Manifesto*.

He eventually settled in England, where he lived with his family in poverty in Soho, London. It was here that he wrote his classic work *Das Kapital*, which describes in an historical setting the working of the capitalist system and what Marx felt would be its ultimate evolution into control of all the means of production and supply by the workers.

HEIGHTS OF ABRAHAM

These cliffs are one of the outstanding natural features of the city of Quebec in Canada and were the scene of a famous battle.

Major-General James Wolfe (1727-59) was only 32 years old when commanded by the British Prime Minister, William Pitt, to capture Quebec from the French during the Seven Years' War (1756-63). The capture of the city lying on the banks of the St Lawrence River in eastern Canada, would open the way for the overthrow of the French forces in North America.

For three months in the summer of 1759, Wolfe attempted to overcome the French by frontal attack from across the river, but the defenders held an almost impregnable position. Wolfe decided to make an attack from the rear. In the early, dark hours of September 13, he led his army across the river above the town and surprised the French soldiers guarding the small cove which now bears his name.

Then came the highly dangerous task of scaling the cliffs—the Heights of Abraham. By sunrise Wolfe and his army of 4,000 had achieved their goal and were on the Plains of Abraham, drawn up in battle array and ready for battle.

Before Wolfe's audacious plan had been carried to its successful conclusion, both Wolfe and the great French commander, Montcalm, lay dying on the battlefield. Knowing that success was his, Wolfe whispered, "I die contented". On the other hand, when told that he was fatally wounded, Montcalm cried out: "Thank God! I shall not live to see the surrender of Quebec."

KINGS AS GODS

Throughout history, kings have often been supposed to enjoy a special relationship with the gods of their people, and in many cases, have been regarded as gods themselves.

In ancient Egypt, the king or pharaoh was believed to be divine and the Hittite kings were deified after their deaths. The Minoan kings of Crete were identified with the bull-headed sun god. In many primitive tribes in Asia and Africa, the king was identified with the sacred and divine animal of his tribe. The Swedes and Prussians of pagan Europe had divine kings, and the rulers of the Aztecs in Mexico and the Incas in Peru were, if not gods themselves, considered to be direct descendants.

Alexander the Great (356–323 B.C.), who had himself declared a god in the last year of his life, was followed by a number of god-kings throughout the Near East. In the Roman Empire the practice of making the emperor a god originated when Julius Caesar was pronounced *divus Julius* after his death. The Byzantine emperors were venerated as God's representative on earth.

The Japanese emperor was thought of as supernatural in some degree, but their term "kami", usually translated as "god", does not have such an all-embracing meaning as in the West. In China kings interceded with the gods for their people.

The statue of Amenophis II of Egypt, at Karnak. His wife is at his feet.

GUNPOWDER PLOT

"Remember, remember the fifth of November, gunpowder, treason and plot"—so goes the old English chant associated with the yearly burning on thousands of village greens and in millions of private gardens throughout England every fifth of November of the effigy of Guy Fawkes. For November 5th celebrates the discovery of the famous plot to blow up the English House of Commons.

Guy Fawkes was a Catholic gentleman who played a major role in Robert Catesby's plot to blow up King James I and his Parliament for failing to honour James's pledge to extend more toleration to the Catholics.

Catesby apparently had vague ideas of a Catholic take-over of the country.

There were five main conspirators, including Fawkes. In May 1604 they rented a house near the Parliament building and started to dig a passage which was designed to reach a point just below the House of Lords.

But in 1605 the conspirators were able to rent a neighbouring cellar which was directly beneath the Palace of Westminster. They linked their passageway to this cellar and Fawkes was allotted the task of preparing the explosion. He gathered together at least twenty barrels of gunpowder in the cellar and covered them up with wood and coal.

All seemed set for the great day, which was the November opening of Parliament. By this time the number of conspirators had risen to thirteen, one of whom, Francis Tresham, had a brother, Lord Monteagle, in the House of Lords. Tresham sent a secret letter warning his brother that a "terrible blow" was to be delivered against Parliament and adding "yet they shall not see who hurts them".

Monteagle took the letter to the King's ministers. On November 4th they had the cellars at Westminster searched and Guy Fawkes was discovered there with his gunpowder.

Gunpowder Plot?

COLONIES

Some countries still have colonies and dependencies because these are usually small territories, often with few inhabitants, which do not have the capacity to carry out all those aspects of administration and government necessary to an independent state.

Nowadays, the possession of colonies is an embarrassment rather than an advantage to the country having them, and few are retained against the wishes of their people. Before the great decolonising years which followed the Second World War, having colonies seemed a natural part of being a great power.

France had many overseas territories such as Algeria, French Morocco and those of French West Africa, but all of these are now self-governing republics. Italy had Eritrea, now federated with Ethiopia, and Italian Somaliland, now the Somali Democratic Republic. Holland's old Dutch East Indies is mostly the present-day Republic of Indonesia.

As in the case of the British Empire the breaking up of these empires left many small territories who were not big enough for independence or who preferred to wait. These saw advantages in remaining under the protective umbrella of a greater power.

Such protection means that defence, external affairs, internal security, and the safeguarding of the terms and conditions of public officers is the responsibility of the colonizing power through its appointed governor.

In some cases the governor is also responsible for the financial and economic stability of the territory. But internal affairs are normally in the hands of the locals.

LONE STAR STATE

Texas is called the 'Lone Star State' because for almost ten years, from 1836 until its annexation by the United States in 1845, the country was independent.

For three centuries up to 1821, Texas and Mexico had belonged to Spain. In all that time, Spain had shown hardly any interest in this vast territory which is equal in size to the total area of France, Belgium, the Netherlands and Denmark combined. When Mexico gained her independence, Texas was peopled by no more than 7,000 and with only three settle- ments large enough to be called towns. Beset with her own problems of administration and revolts, Mexico allowed American families to colonize land in Texas.

By 1835 there were around 30,000 Americans settled in Texas, outnumbering the Mexicans by four to one. Too late for her own interests, Mexico tried to discipline the American Texans by abolishing slavery, levying duties and establishing military garrisons. Fighting broke out when martial law was declared by the Mexicans who tried to disarm the Texans. On October 2, 1835, the Texans won the first battle of the Texas revolution at Gonzales. San Antonio was captured in December and the Mexicans withdrew to Mexico.

The Texans were weakened by arguments and lack of unity which allowed the Mexicans to recapture San Antonio on March 2, 1836, but while the Mexicans closed in on the Alamo, Texas declared her independence. The new nation found this independence difficult to manage and was relieved to be annexed in 1845 by a rather unwilling United States of America.

called "the Lone Star State"?

WHY did the Vietnam War occur?

VIETNAM WAR

The Vietnam War had its roots firmly established in the authoritarian colonial rule of the French which was formally recognized at the Convention of Tientsin in May 1885. The name Vietnam came into Western use in 1946 to designate the eastern part of Indochina stretching from the borders of China in the north to the delta of the Mekong River in the south. French colonial rule generated a deep dissatisfaction among the Vietnamese, and the Indochinese Communist Party, formed by Ho Chi Minh, arose in 1930.

During the Second World War, the Japanese worked with the French to suppress rebellion. But, in 1941 Ho Chi Minh established the Vietnam League for Independence, generally known as the Viet Minh, which, after Japan's surrender, seized control of Hanoi, in the North, and proclaimed Vietnam's independence.

The French attempted to reassert their rule in the Franco-Vietnamese War (1946–54) but were unsuccessful, even with generous financial help from the United States. An international conference at Geneva in 1954 under the co-chairmanship of Brittain and Russia, with China and United States playing major roles, divided the country into two at the 17th parallel, with the Communist Viet Minh in the North and French forces in the South.

After the settlement, the United States undertook to build a separate anti-Communist state in the South, with Ngo Dinh Diem as Prime Minister at Saigon. However, his rule became increasingly unpopular and a Communist People's Revolutionary Party (Viet Cong) was established in 1962, pledged to bring communism to South Vietnam.

Diem was overthrown and killed, and after three other short-lived governments, President Nguyen Van Thieu assumed control. Viet Cong estimated military strength rose rapidly and the United States began to move military advisers into the country. In 1965 America began bombing raids on the north and introduced the first contingent of United States marines.

The country was locked in a bitter struggle in which the Viet Minh and Viet Cong maintained their offensive despite the vast number of men, money and resources poured into Vietnam by the United States of America.

WHERE is Tutankhamun's tomb?
WHERE is Wounded Knee?   WHERE is

WOUNDED KNEE

Wounded Knee is a narrow creek in north-western South Dakota in the United States. One night in 1890 some 400 Sioux Indians, led by Big Foot, camped in a hollow near the creek. The Sioux were on their way back to the reservation after a "ghost dance" ceremony, farther south in the Badlands.

In the morning the Seventh Cavalry lined up their Hotchkiss guns on the hill and the troopers took up positions round the Indian camp.

The Indians were ordered to hand over their weapons. Suspicious and fearful, they refused. In the subsequent search a shot was fired. At once the machine guns opened up, and in a short time most of the Indians were dead. Survivors, including women and children, were pursued up the creek and gunned down. Heavy snow began to fall, and the bodies were left to freeze grotesquely where they lay. Several days later the dead were heaped on wagons and thrown into a mass grave.

The Seventh Cavalry were awarded 26 Congressional Medals of Honour for their part in the action. The Battle of Wounded Knee, or, more accurately, the Massacre of the Big Foot Band, was the last battle to be fought in America's longest undeclared war.

TUTANKHAMUN

Tutankhamun's tomb is in Egypt, in a place called the Valley of the Kings. Tutankhamun was a pharaoh, who died in 1352 B.C. His name was familiar only to scholars until his tomb was discovered in 1922 by Howard Carter. The tomb was filled with precious jewels, ornaments, vases, furniture, clothes, ornamented coffins, chariots, and the mummified body of the young king himself, wearing a gold mask.

When the Egyptians buried a pharaoh, they took trouble to surround him with beautiful and useful things. They did not believe he was really dead. They thought he would go on living if he were provided with enough things to protect him in his journey through the underworlds, and afterwards.

Most of the kings' tombs were robbed, frequently by local people, of their jewels and gold.

There are several chambers in the tomb—the Antechamber, the Burial Chamber, the Treasury, and the Store Room. In the Antechamber was a beautiful alabaster wishing-cup and a painted wooden casket with brilliant designs. At the doorway of the Treasury was a figure of a God called Anubis, a sort of jackal-like dog, who was supposed to keep watch over the dead. Round his neck he wore a scarf decorated with lotus and cornflowers.

William Penn buried? WHERE was Custer's last stand?

WILLIAM PENN

William Penn (1644-1718), who gave his name to the state of Pennsylvania in the United States, is buried in the graveyard of an early Quaker meeting house in Jordans, in the English county of Buckinghamshire.

He was the son of Admiral Sir William Penn (1621-70) and became a convert to Quakerism in 1661. These peaceful people were persecuted and despised. William Penn was expelled from Oxford University because he joined the sect, and was later imprisoned in the Tower of London.

In 1681 Charles II granted Penn a domain of some 50,000 square miles of English Crown land in America in payment of a debt owed by the Crown to his father. Persecuted in England, the Quakers were not allowed to enter any of the established American colonies. To found a haven for people of all religions, and in the hope of converting the warlike Red Indians, Penn sent out the first settlers to his newly-aquired colony which he named Pennsylvania (Penn's forestland). He, too, went out a year later.

He gave the settlers democratic government and made friends with the Delaware Indians who agreed to "live in love with William Penn and his children as long as the sun and moon gave light". Penn lived at Philadelphia, the capital of his colony, but after two years was called back to England on business and was absent for 15 years.

After a period of trouble he revisited Pennsylvania in 1899 and granted a charter to its 20,000 inhabitants which remained in force for 75 years until the American War of Independence.

In 1701 Penn returned to England to find that his unscrupulous steward had robbed him of his fortune. He was imprisoned for debt and the conditions of the jail affected his health. His friends secured his release, and he lived quietly until his death on May 30, 1718. The fine old building in whose graveyard he is buried has been preserved and is open to the public.

"GENERAL" CUSTER

"General" Custer made his famous last stand on the banks of the Little Big Horn river near what is now the interchange for United States Highways 87 and 212, in the State of Montana. Today the Custer Battlefield National Monument marks the scene of the battle.

George Armstrong Custer, born in 1839, was called "General" by the men of the 7th Cavalry Brigade under his command. He had shown his brilliance as a cavalry officer in the American Civil War (1861-65) reaching the rank of major-general.

In 1876 when Sioux and Cheyennes were on the warpath with Chief Sitting Bull as their leader, Custer and his 7th Cavalry Brigade were under the command of General Terry. The brigade of 655 men was ordered by Terry to advance towards the Indians, but not to attack until the rest of the army—composed of three columns under General Crook, Gibbon and Terry—had moved into position.

Custer reached the Little Big Horn to see the large Indian camp on the opposite side of the river. For a reason that will never be known, Custer decided to disobey orders and attack. Dividing his brigade into three, he sent Major Reno and Captain Benteen, each with three companies, to attack the flanks. At the same time he led 264 troopers on a frontal approach across the river.

His force stood no chance when the Indians attacked. The troopers dismounted from their horses to seek cover, but there was none. When the Indians drove off their horses, the troopers' fate was sealed.

Believing that Reno and Benteen would soon come to their aid, they fought bravely, but the flank attacks had been foiled and the cavalry put to flight. Custer and 264 men fought to the last man.

AT WAR

American and England were last at war with each other from June 1812 to December 1814. War broke out for two reasons: first, America's expanding trade was threatened because the British were maintaining a blockade to prevent supplies reaching the French, with whom they were at war; secondly, there was a growing sense of nationalism in America, a feeling that she must fight to preserve her independence, sovereignty and honour.

When war was declared by President Madison, the Americans immediately invaded Canada, but were driven back. In 1813, after talk of an armistice came to nothing, more skirmishes broke out on the Canadian border and British sailors began to raid the American coast. By October 1814 it became clear that the Americans could not successfully invade Canada, while the British Navy could do no more than harry the coasts of America.

The chief sufferers were the merchants of New England. Also the financial state of the American government was so bad that it had no money to pay its bills abroad. Governor Strong of Massachusetts openly spoke against the war, and was suspected of planning to take his state over to the British.

However, no one in Britain wanted to fight the War of Independence all over again. The desire was to trade with and not to fight against the United States. On December 24, 1814 the Treaty of Ghent was signed and the war was over. Neither side gained.

HUMAN SACRIFICES

Human sacrifices have been made throughout history. But seldom have they been so terrible as the ceremonies associated with the barbarous religion of the Aztecs who began to establish their civilization in present-day Mexico in about 1168.

The Aztecs, who in many other respects were a comparatively enlightened people, believed that human bloodshed was the way to make sure that the sun would rise each day. At one of their biggest sacrificial ceremonies about 20,000 people were slaughtered.

The chief places for sacrifice were two great pyramid temples, 100 feet high, in the capital city of Tenochtitlan, which was built on an island in the middle of a lake.

An Aztec warrior's chief aim in battle was to take his enemy prisoner and hand him over for sacrifice to his war-god. On the day chosen for the ceremony the war drums were sounded and the prisoners were taken, one by one, up the winding stairs round the outside of the temple to the altar. Here their chests were cut open and their hearts torn out as offerings to the sun. Afterwards some of their bodies were eaten at ritual feasts.

The great empire of the Aztecs, stretching from the deserts of northern Mexico to the tropical forests of Guatemala, seemed to be at the height of its splendour when the Spanish conqueror Hernando Cortez landed with a tiny army from Cuba in March, 1519. After being treated as gods, the invaders were attacked and nearly destroyed. But within two years the Aztec ruler Montezuma was slain by his people and his empire overthrown by Cortez.

human sacrifices made?   WHEN was slavery abolished?
WHEN was the auto-da-fé?

SLAVERY

The first big step to rid the world of slavery was taken in 1811 when Britain abolished slave-trading. In 1833 an Act of Parliament was passed emancipating all slaves in the British colonies, thus setting an example which was followed by other European countries.

In the United States a number of conflicting interests led in 1861 to a civil war between the Northern states who wished to abolish slavery and the seceded Southern states who wanted to retain it on the plantations. In 1863 President Lincoln issued his famous Emancipation Proclamation, and two years later the victory of the North led to a constitutional amendment which prohibited slavery in the United States for ever.

In South America, a kind of agricultural slavery of the Indians continued under the name of peonage, and laws prohibiting the system did not succeed immediately in stamping it out. Even today conditions of slavery, sometimes disguised as forced labour in payment of debt, exist in some countries.

Until people's consciences began to be stirred by the efforts of humanitarians like William Wilberforce (1759–1833), slavery had generally been regarded as an inevitable part of the natural order of things. From earliest times men had forced their captured enemies to work for them. Slaves were a vital part of most ancient civilizations, providing food and services for their masters and the labour to build such man-made marvels as the pyramids. In Greece and Rome many slaves became skilled workers and held responsible positions.

After the discovery of the New World large fortunes were made by the transport of Negroes from Africa and their exploitation in the Americas.

AUTO-DA-FÉ

The auto-da-fé (act of faith) was the name of the public ceremony which followed the secret trials of the Spanish Inquisition established in 1478 during the reign of King Ferdinand of Aragon and Queen Isabella of Castile.

These two Christian monarchs, having united most of Spain by their marriage, were about to complete the age-old battle to free the country from "the infidels" by the conquest of Granada from the Moors. The time was ripe for them to seek to encourage national unity and strengthen the authority both of themselves and of the Church.

So it was a mixture of motives that led Ferdinand and Isabella to persuade Pope Sixtus IV to set up the Spanish Inquisition, with the declared purpose of disciplining the flourishing and influential Jewish community, whose wealth aroused envy and whose presence seemed to offer the greatest obstacle to unity. Soon the powers of the Inquisition (from the Latin *inquiro*, to inquire into) were directed not only against Jews but also against Moors, Christian Protestants and even Catholics whose behaviour was deemed to threaten the solidarity of the Church on which the royal authority also rested.

After secret interrogations, sometimes aided by torture, the auto-da-fé was celebrated. First came a procession of priests, officials and accused persons who had confessed their guilt and declared themselves penitent. This was followed by a solemn mass, an oath of obedience to the Inquisition and the reading of sentences whether of punishment or acquittal. Those condemned to death were handed over to the civil power to emphasize the fact that the Church did not itself shed blood.

But the severity of the first Grand Inquisitor, Tomás de Torquemada (1420–1498) is thought to have led to 2,000 burnings at the stake and unsuccessful attempts at mediation by the Pope.

After the reigns of Ferdinand's successors, Charles I (1516–56) and Philip II (1556–98), the Inquisition gradually dwindled in influence and was finally suppressed in 1834.

TAJ MAHAL

The Taj Mahal was built by the Mogul emperor Shah Jehan (1614–66) as a tomb for his favourite wife, Mumtaz Mahal. It is situated at Agra in northern India and is one of the most beautiful buildings in the world. When the Moguls arrived in India early in the 16th Century, they brought Persian civilization with them. The tomb is a perfect example of the Persian style of architecture.

The name of the tomb means "Crown of the Palace", one of the titles given to the Empress Mumtaz. It is built of white marble, inlaid with precious stones, and is eight-sided, 130 feet across at its widest points and nearly 200 feet high to the top of the huge dome. It is flanked on each side by two slender minarets and stands on a vast marble terrace overlooking the River Jumna and surrounded by Persian gardens.

Inside, under the dome, are the marble cenotaphs or monuments of Shah Jehan and his empress, on which the sun flickers through marble screens as delicate and intricate as lace. The walls are covered in floral designs and inscriptions from the Koran, picked out in onyx, jasper, cornelian and other semi-precious stones. The tombs which hold the royal bodies are in a vaulted chamber below and, in contrast to the chamber itself, are quite plain.

According to a legend the marvellous building appeared to Mumtaz in a dream and the Shah searched the whole of India for an architect. The plans were said to have been drawn up only after the architect had been given a drug which enabled him to see a vision of the monument in all its splendour and glory.

DICTATORS

We call a dictator "benevolent" if he uses his powers for the good of the people, not simply for his own. The word "benevolent" is derived from the Latin and means "well-wishing", but though many dictators have promised to defend the rights of the populace, most of them have failed to do so.

A dictator is a ruler who, usually because of some emergency, is given extraordinary powers of government. The office was first instituted in ancient Rome in 501 B.C. to deal with serious military, civil or criminal disturbances. The dictator was described as the "administrative dictator" (*rei gerundae causa*) and held office for six months. The time limit was intended to ensure that some of these dictators were benevolent.

Modern dictators, like the ancient ones, have taken over the reins of government in times of crisis, but they have used their powers to establish a permanent and often tyrannical rule. Both Benito Mussolini and Adolph Hitler eventually became heads of government formally, in accordance with the constitution. Present day dictatorships include the long established figure of Spain's General Franco and more recently Uganda's President Amin.

Perhaps the best example of a benevolent dictator is Napoleon Bonaparte (1769–1821), Napoleon I of France from 1804 to 1814 and again for the "Hundred Days" in 1815. He seized absolute power in France, but his ambitions were for his country and his people rather than for himself. Under his rule industry expanded and the universities flourished, while he left enduring legacies in the shape of the Code Napoleon (the codification of French civil law), the reorganization of the judicial system, the Bank of France and the establishment of the military academies such as St. Cyr.

called ''benevolent''?

WHAT is the Ku-Klux-Klan? **WHAT** was the Great Trek?

KU-KLUX-KLAN

This was an underground organization started in the South after the American Civil War to keep down the negro population and resist the expected exploitation by the North.

It sprang from a Tennessee social club, which based its name on the Greek *kyklos*, a circle. The young members used to ride about on horses at night, dressed in flowing white gowns, to frighten the newly-freed slaves and to amuse themselves.

Fanatics turned this amusement into "the invisible Empire of the South", a secret society of terror, indulging in murder and kidnapping. Laws were passed to suppress it, and Klansmen were imprisoned, to be greeted as heroes on their release.

The KKK was revived in 1915 as a general ragbag for all manner of intolerance, but it faded with the Depression of the 1930s, though it is still active today.

THE GREAT TREK

The Great Trek is the name given to the mass exodus of Afrikaner settlers from South Africa's Cape Colony between 1835 and 1843.

In those years 12,000 "voortrekkers"—men, women and children—with their cattle, sheep and ox-waggons moved out from the Cape towards the High Veld area around the Vaal River in protest against British rule and what they regarded as the spread of "liberal" ideas.

Originally the Cape was colonized by the Dutch under the control of the Dutch East India Company. By the 1660s there were roughly 2,000 settlers in the Colony, employing more than 1,000 slaves. These settlers were mainly Dutch and German.

By the end of the 18th Century the white population numbered about 15,000 people, who by that time had developed their own language—Afrikaans, a variety of

Dutch—and their own customs. Of this white, Afrikaner, population about half were known as voortrekkers. These people lived a semi-nomadic life. They farmed wherever they could find good grazing and moved from area to area, constantly pushing forward the frontiers of white expansion.

The Cape was conquered by the British in 1795 during the Napoleonic wars. British settlers were introduced to the Colony and soon these settlers began to agitate for a more liberal administration. English became the official language and by 1838 slavery was abolished.

To the Boers this was the final straw. Declaring that the British had "placed their slaves on an equal footing with Christians, contrary to the laws of God", they decided to shake off British influence and commenced their exodus. Thousands of families

moved off in their covered waggons, taking their coloured servants with them.

During their journey, the trekkers encountered fierce resistance from the native Zulu warriors. Their waggons were constantly ambushed and their leader, Piet Retief, was killed. The trekkers, however, had the advantages of rifles and superior military techniques and in 1838 defeated the Zulu at the Battle of Blood River.

The trekkers settled in the territory previously occupied by the Zulu and established a new state of their own, the Republic of Natal. But in 1842 the British took over Natal, whereupon the voortrekkers took to their waggons again and moved back north of the Vaal River. The British decided to recognize the independence of the voortrekkers who established a series of republics, including the Orange Free State.

WHAT is hara-kiri?

HARA-KIRI

Ceremonial suicide, or hara-kiri, was undertaken by members of the samurai (warrior) class in old Japan. Voluntary hara-kiri dated back to the 12th Century, and was committed to wipe out the dishonour of defeat in battle, as a protest at the behaviour of a superior, and for similar reasons.

The word means "belly-cutting". If carried out according to the rules, it was a slow and extremely painful means of suicide, meant to demonstrate the military virtues of great courage and extreme self-control.

Another version of hara-kiri was observed when a samurai was sentenced to be beheaded for a crime. To escape the shame of the common executioner, he was allowed to stab himself with a short sword. Immediately afterwards the sentenced samurai would be decapitated by a friend or relative waiting behind him.

A recent case of hara-kiri occurred on November 26, 1970, after the well-known Japanese author, Yukio Mishima, failed to incite a regiment of Japanese soldiers to join his "Association of Shields" and stage a coup d'etat. Mishima, who was once mentioned as a possible Nobel Prize winner, is shown on the right in full Samurai warrior's uniform.

When the soldiers ignored his appeal, Mishima entered a room at their military headquarters, together with four supporters, and, in front of the commanding general, who had been tied to a chair, Mishima slit his own stomach in the Samurai hara-kiri fashion. He was then decapitated by his "Chief of Staff", Hissho Morita, in the traditional way. Morita himself then committed hara-kiri and was subsequently decapitated in turn by another of Mishima's supporters.

WHERE did Robin Hood live? WHERE is Pompeii?

ROBIN HOOD

Robin Hood lived in Sherwood Forest, near Nottingham in the centre of England. In those 12th Century days a vast region of open tracts, woodland glades and great oaks used to stretch for many miles from the city northwards. This region was called Sherwood Forest.

Until the time of the Normans the forest was used for hunting by the people of that region, or shire, and thereby acquired its earlier name of Shire Wood. The common people's right to hunt ceased when the Norman kings took over the forest for their own use. Strict laws were passed and special courts were set up to preserve them.

Whether Robin Hood and his merry band of followers, which included Little John, Friar Tuck, Will Scarlet and Maid Marian, ever exsisted is difficult to establish.

Certainly by the end of the 12th Century, with control of royal Sherwood in the hands of feudal barons, the common people deeply resented the harsh and oppressive rule under which they lived. The time was ripe for stories about a man who robbed the rich to feed the poor.

The character of Robin Hood represented the ideals of the common people of the late Middle Ages. Ballads about his exploits have been preserved and may date from the 14th and 15th Centuries. In 1795 Joseph Ritson first published a collection of these in book form.

Over the years stories of the carefree folk-hero and his band of happy followers, living an idyllic life in the woodland glades of Sherwood during the days of the Plantagenet kings, have become the subject of many books.

This statue of Robin Hood is at Nottingham.

POMPEII

For nearly 1,700 years Pompeii in southern Italy was a dead and buried city, forgotten by all except historians. But for more than 600 years before disaster overtook it, Pompeii was a proud city and port of the Roman Empire in the shadow of Mount Vesuvius on the Bay of Naples.

On the morning of August 24, in the year A.D. 79 an event occured that was to preserve for us the story of Roman everyday life. Sixteen years previously an earthquake had damaged Pompeii, a city where wealthy Romans had their country villas, and the damage had been repaired. Now, Vesuvius once again erupted violently. For three days the sky was darkened, and a deadly hail of volcanic ash and pumice rained down upon the doomed city.

By the time the eruption settled down, Pompeii lay under a blanket of pumice eight to ten feet thick. The outlines of the land had been so altered that the sea was now nearly two miles away. Two thousand of the city's 20,000 inhabitants died in the disaster, suffocated by the sulphurous fumes or crushed by falling roofs. Pompeii, it seemed, had been wiped off the face of the earth.

So it was until, in 1748, a peasant digging in his vineyard unearthed some statues. This led to a remarkable record of a Roman city in its heyday being brought to light.

Excavation has revealed rows of shops and houses, the forum or market-place, with temples adjoining business houses, an open air theatre, and public baths. In the museum at Naples are many thousands of objects recovered from Pompeii—statues and paintings, pens and ink-bottles, coins, looking-glasses and even charred food served on the day of the eruption nearly 1,900 years ago.

WHERE do Mormons live? WHERE did Mohammed live?

A view of the excavated Roman city of Pompeii.

THE MORMONS

Most Mormons live in the state of Utah in the United States. There are Mormons elsewhere in the world, but Utah has been their chief home since 1846, when a picked company of 150 Mormons under their leader Brigham Young, came to the valley of the Great Salt Lake in the Rocky Mountains with their horses and livestock, their covered wagons filled with provisions, implements and seed grain.

Sixteen years earlier the Church of Jesus Christ of Latter-Day Saints had been founded by Joseph Smith (1805-44) at Fayette in New York State. Joseph Smith claimed to have obtained the Book of Mormon, through a number of revelations, in 1827. This book is regarded by followers of the sect as of equal authority with the Old and New Testaments.

In spite of persecution, the Mormons increased in numbers and sent missionaries to European countries. Converts were encouraged to emigrate to the United States and to join the "Gathering of Israel". Persecution in America increased and the Mormons were driven from one state to another.

Joseph Smith and other leaders were arrested in 1844, and he and his brother were murdered in the jail at Carthage, Missouri. The leadership passed to Brigham Young, and the Mormons left Missouri for Illinois.

When in 1846 the Mormons were expelled from Illinois, they decided to move beyond the frontier of the United States, at that time the Missouri River, and settle in undeveloped land in the far west where no one would molest them. So it was that Brigham Young, now recognized as one of the great pioneers of American history, led the Mormons on their trek across the great plains. It was mostly desert country in the valley of the Great Salt Lake, but, joined by bigger parties, the Mormons succeeded by tremendous effort in turning it into a fertile land.

Churches and schools were built and industries started. So successful were the Mormons in establishing a thriving community that, after only four years, the Territory of Utah was recognized by the Government and Young was appointed its first governor.

MOHAMMED

The Prophet Mohammed lived most of the time in Mecca, where he was born in A.D. 570. The holy city of Mecca is situated in what is now Saudi Arabia. It is the greatest place of pilgrimage for members of the Mohammedan religion which the Prophet founded. Hundreds of thousands of Mohammedans make the sacred journey to Mecca every year.

After his father's death, Mohammed was a poor shepherd boy in the mountains near Mecca. As he grew older he often used to go alone into the mountains to pray. He did not begin preaching until he was 40, a few years after he thought he heard the archangel Gabriel speaking to him on Mount Hira.

Mohammed taught simply that there was one all-powerful God, and that men should try to serve him through prayer, helping one another and trying to lead a good life.

In 622, persecution from men, who disagreed with his teaching, led to the flight or "hegira" of Mohammed from Mecca to the neighbouring city of Medina. This is the year from which the whole Mohammedan world reckons time. In Medina, Mohammed developed a more formal and organized religion. But he wanted Mecca to become the chief centre for Mohammedans. Already they faced Mecca when they prayed, because they believed it was a holy place.

In 630, the Mohammedans advanced on Mecca, and took the city easily. The people who lived there then accepted the Mohammedan religion which today has hundreds of millions of followers throughout the world, especially in Africa, Asia and eastern Europe.

It is now one of the most influential and widespread religious systems in the world.

WHEN did the Vikings reach America?
WHEN was Charlemagne crowned Holy Roman

VIKINGS

The Vikings discovered America about the year 1000, more than four centuries before Christopher Columbus was born. They were sea adventurers from Scandinavia who left their homes in search of conquest and plunder.

Information about the Viking discoveries comes from two sagas, or narrative ballads, the *Saga of Eric the Red* and the *Saga of the Greenlanders*. These differ considerably, but it seems possible that Bjarni Herjolfsson discovered North America in 986, when driven off course on a voyage from Iceland to Greenland. About 1000, Leif Ericsson sailed west from Greenland and gave the names Helluland, Markland and Vinland to sections of the American coast as he moved south. A few years later Thorfinn Karlsefni sailed for Vinland with three ships, with a party of settlers and domestic animals. But they stayed only three years.

The so-called Vinland Map, discovered and published in 1965, dates from 1431–1449 and supports the theory that Herjolfsson originally discovered America. In 1961 a Viking-style settlement was discovered at L'Anse au Meadow, Newfoundland. The Vinland Map itself is now held by some experts to be a clever fake.

CHARLEMAGNE

Charlemagne (Charles the Great) was crowned Holy Roman Emperor at St Peter's Basilica in Rome on Christmas Day in the year 800.

It is one of the most important dates in the Middle Ages, the beginning of a new era in European history. The man thus charged with the task of restoring order and unity out of the chaos which had followed the downfall of Christian Rome was already an emperor in fact, though not in name.

When his ally Pope Leo III placed the crown on Charles's head—unexpectedly, it was said, while he knelt in prayer—this heir to the Caesars already ruled lands stretching from Denmark to Rome and from the Atlantic to the Danube.

Charlemagne was born in 742, the grandson of Charles Martel who, 10 years before, had saved Christendom from the Saracens at the Battle of Tours in France. At the age of 26 he inherited the kingdom of the Franks and set out to bring order to western Europe and Christianity to heathen tribes. At the time of his death in 814 he had extended his rule from the Baltic Sea to the Pyrenees and from the coast of Brittany eastwards across Germany and Italy to the lower valley of the Danube.

Although he never learned to write, Charlemagne did much to encourage education and the arts. After his death the Frankish empire broke into pieces. About 130 years later the Holy Roman Empire was again revived and lasted with dwindling power until its extinction in 1806. But the fragmentation of western Europe persisted through the centuries with continual outbreaks of warfare up to the end of the Second World War.

The picture at the top was done by Albrecht Durer in 1510. It shows Charlemagne dressed as a German emperor.

RENAISSANCE

The name "renaissance" means rebirth. It was given to the revival of learning that began among the educated classes of northern Italy in the early 14th Century, developed and spread in 15th and 16th Centuries to the rest of Europe.

One important feature of the Renaissance set it apart from the period that had gone before. This was an amazing rebirth of interest in the thought, literature, sculpture and architecture of Greece and Rome. Two of the greatest names associated with the arts at this time are those of Leonardo da Vinci (1452–1519) and Michelangelo (1475–1564).

Men began to look about them in a more questioning way, politics assumed a new importance, and the way was opened for the great scientific discoveries of later years.

In Mainz, Germany, about the middle of the 15th Century, Johann Gutenberg invented a printing process using movable type which made possible the widespread distribution of books. It was a Christian Renaissance, summed up in the life and work of Desiderius Erasmus (1466–1536) of Holland. Among the literary giants of the later Renaissance were William Shakespeare (1564–1616) in England and Miguel de Cervantes (1547–1616) in Spain.

The Renaissance inspired the curiosity of hundreds of explorers who took part in the Great Age of Discovery. Christopher Columbus, Vasco da Gama, Ferdinand Magellan and others voyaged across the seas to discover the New World and to open up the longed-for trading routes to Asia. Trade prospered and powerful banking houses stimulated the growth of capitalism.

Detail from a drawing by Michelangelo, one of the greatest artists and sculptors of the Renaissance.

Emperor? WHEN was the Renaissance?

WHY were the pyramids built?

PYRAMIDS

Pyramids are found both in the old world and the new. We associate the name pyramid with the colossal tombs in Egypt, but there are many more in central America which were erected by the Aztecs as altars to their gods.

The royal tombs of ancient Egypt are situated on the west bank of the Nile, near Memphis. The best examples are the three great pyramids of Gizeh, probably built between 2690 and 2560 BC. The largest, the Great Pyramid, was erected by King Khufu (Cheops) and its base covers an area of 13 acres.

Great skill was displayed in planning and laying out the pyramids. Stones were transported across the Nile from quarries on the east side. The sides of the pyramid were faced to the cardinal points (the four points of the compass), and the base was nearly a perfect square.

An immense amount of slave labour was needed to raise the vast structures, with the blocks being hauled along sloping ramps.

Stonecutters and masons used saws up to nine feet long.

The pyramids were designed to protect the mummies of kings and queens and the vast treasure buried with them. The polished granite and limestone slabs which once encased their sides have been removed, but the complicated interior passages and chambers, composed of rough-hewn blocks of stone or brickwork still remain. However, tomb-robbers were busy even in the time of the pharaohs, and no pyramid has preserved its treasures intact.

The Aztec pyramids were the scenes of human sacrifice, the victims being led one by one up the steep steps of the pyramid and stretched out on a humped stone by four black-robed priests. A fifth priest ripped open their chests with a stone knife and tore out their hearts. These were burnt in a stone vessel, as nourishment for the gods. The bodies were thrown down the pyramid, near the base of which was a great rack full of the skulls of previous victims.

MONTEZUMA

Montezuma was an emperor of the 16th Century ruling over the Aztec empire from one of the greatest capitals in the world at that time—Tenochtitlan in what is now Mexico.

"It was like an enchantment . . . on account of the great towers and temples rising from the water . . . things never heard of, nor seen, nor even dreamed". So wrote the Spanish chronicler Bernal Diaz of the city of some 200,000 people. Montezuma's capital was on an island in Lake Texcoco which had been enlarged by a system of drainage canals, and was joined to the shore by causeways.

Across these causeways Hermán Cortés in 1519 led a force of 400 Spaniards, to be greeted by Montezuma as a god. The Spaniards were shown over the shrine-topped pyramids where human sacrifices were made to the Aztecs' stern war god, Huitzilopochtli.

"The figure . . . had a very broad face and monstrous and terrible eyes, and the whole of his body was covered with precious stones, and gold and pearls . . . There were some braziers and in them were burning the hearts of three Indians they had sacrificed that day." Diaz wrote, describing the scene he witnessed with Cortés. The Aztecs held the Spaniards in awe, but suspicion took over and they realized that Cortés was no god. In this atmosphere, Cortés took Montezuma as a hostage. Hostilities flared, and Montezuma was injured and died.

In the Noche Triste or Night of Sadness which followed, the Spaniards were all but annihilated by the Aztecs. Cortés and some of his men escaped. A year later they captured Tenochtitlan and razed it to the ground. The Spaniards built a town upon the ruins. It is still the capital of a nation—Mexico City.

IRON BATTLESHIPS

The first battle involving "ironclads" was between the Monitor and the Merrimack in March, 1862.

The Monitor was built by the Federals in the North during the Civil War. She had a displacement of only 987 tons. Meanwhile, the Confederates in the South also built an ironclad, the C.S.S. Virginia, better known by her former name Merrimack. She had been a wooden frigate, but was burned down to the waterline by enemy action and rebuilt as an ironclad, sheathed in two inches of metal. Her displacement was 4,636 tons.

In 1862 the ships of the North were maintaining a blockade to prevent supplies reaching the South and the opposing vessels met in battle at Hampton Roads off the south-east coast of Virginia. Thousands of people lined the shores to watch the fight as the ships passed on opposite courses, turned and passed again.

Both crews lacked training and their shooting was ineffective. The Merrimack had more guns, but was heavy and slow. The Monitor was lightly armed, but much faster. The battle was indecisive—the Monitor sheered off and the Merrimack returned to the navy yard.

On the previous day the Merrimack had achieved spectacular success by ramming and sinking the sailing sloop Cumberland and then destroying the Federal sailing frigate Congress by gunfire. Her prowess convinced the public that the day of the wooden man-of-war was ended.

The first ironclad, or armoured warship, had been completed in France in 1858. Next year the British Admiralty ordered two ironclads, the Warrior and the Black Prince. Completed in October 1861 and September 1862 respectively, they each displaced 9,210 tons, could attain a speed of 14 knots and had a complement of 707 offficers and men. These two ships, with the French Gloire and Couronne, were the first battleships, although the name was not then applied to them.

The Monitor, with its round turret, is in the foreground.

iron battleships fight?   WHERE did Columbus land?

First journey

Santa Maria

COLUMBUS

Christopher Columbus, on his famous voyage of 1492, made landfall after nine weeks at sea on an island he named San Salvador — now also known as Watling Island — in the Bahamas.

Columbus, a Genoese, set sail with three ships, the Santa Maria, the Pinta and the Nina, under the patronage of King Ferdinand and Queen Isabella of Spain. This voyage was the first of his attempts to find a sea route to Asia.

After leaving San Salvador, Columbus discovered the island of Cuba and then Haiti, where he left some members of his crews garrisoning a fort called La Navidad. His flagship had been wrecked and there was not enough room on the remaining two ships to take all the men home.

Believing that he had reached Asia, Columbus returned to Spain where he was given a great reception. He came back with some "Indians" to show at court and evidence of the existence of gold in the New World.

On his second voyage Columbus founded the city of Isabella on Haiti. Calling at La Navidad he found that his "colony" had been killed by the natives. The Spaniards had treated them with such cruelty, it seems, that the formerly mild-natured people had sought revenge. Columbus pushed on westwards and explored more of the Caribbean Sea, although he still believed Cuba to be the mainland of Asia. He returned to Isabella, but increasing difficulties and trouble with his own subordinates exhausted him, and he was ill for many months.

The Spanish general Ojeda and Columbus's brother, Bartholomew, were responsible for the crushing of a so-called rebellion of the natives, and in 1495 five ship-loads of captured men were sent to Spain as slaves. Eventually Columbus fell from favour at the Spanish court. Although he was fitted out for another voyage during which he discovered Trinidad, the king and queen sent out a new governor to the new territories.

This man, Bobadilla, became so infuriated with the behaviour of Columbus and his brother that he sent them back to Spain in irons. Insisting on wearing these irons in the presence of Ferdinand and Isabella, Columbus was forgiven.

On his last voyage in 1502, Columbus reached Honduras. After much hardship, he returned to Spain in 1504 and died in 1506, an impoverished and broken man.

COLOSSEUM

The great Flavian Amphitheatre, or Colosseum, was built between A.D. 69 and 81 by the Emperors Vespasian and Titus on the site of an artificial lake in the grounds of Nero's palace, the Golden House. The name Colosseum was bestowed on it, because of its colossal size, some time after the 8th Century.

In its full magnificence the Colosseum must have been one of the most imposing buildings in the Roman Empire, a gigantic oval measuring 620 feet by 513 feet with a height of 160 feet. Round the actual arena—287 feet by 180 feet—tiers of marble seats pro-

vided accommodation for 50,000 spectators.

The building was constructed to house gigantic spectacles organized by the authorities for the entertainment—and distraction—of the public. It became a scene of much bloodshed. Here were staged gladiatorial combats

Depression?

DEPRESSION

The American Depression began in September 1929 with a great collapse of the stock market in Wall Street, New York. During the money-making mania which accompanied the great prosperity of the 1920s, "paper" fortunes were made and the prices of shares soared to record high levels.

President Herbert Hoover tried unsuccessfully to abate the fever. On September 7 a reaction set in and on October 24 came the great Wall Street crash. On that Black Thursday, 13,000 million shares of stock were sold and prices plunged faster than ever before.

Huge fortunes were lost by many businessmen, and the savings of millions of small investors vanished. Factories were closed, the number of unemployed rocketed, foreign trade fell, banks failed, mortgages were foreclosed and, all the time, the prices of wheat, cotton, copper, oil and other commodities kept sinking. The buying power of the United States was paralysed.

These were the days of "Buddy, can you spare a dime?". All over the country people lined up at emergency "soup kitchens" Young men rode freight trains looking for work and old people died of starvation. By February 1932 a full third of the American workforce was idle. The rest of the world, too, was affected and international trade dwindled to a third of its 1928 volume.

In 1933 a new president, Franklin D. Roosevelt (1933–1945) was elected. He launched the New Deal and set up a vast system of public works paid for by the state. Contractors' orders for these schemes revived heavy industry, and workers' wages restored prosperity to the towns. Trade unions were encouraged, tariffs lowered and many laws passed which helped to save the economy.

(fights to the death between men) and contests between wild beasts or between men and animals. And here, too, many of the early Christians met martyrdom with a courage that helped greatly to spread their faith.

The highest tiers of seats and the fourth storey were rebuilt in the 3rd Century, and the building was seriously damaged by lightning and earthquakes during Roman times and the Middle Ages. For hundreds of years this symbol of Roman power was used as a quarry. But even today its ruins form one of the most famous buildings in the world.

WHY is America called America?   WHY are some murderers

AMERICA

America gets its name from the traditional family name Amerigo belonging to Amerigo Vespucci (1454–1512), who was an Italian navigator and merchant.

Vespucci began his career in the bank of Lorenzo and Giovanni Pier Francesco de' Medici. In 1491, he was sent to Seville, where he met Columbus. At the beginning of 1505 he was summoned to the court of Spain for a private consultation and was appointed chief navigator for the famous Casa de Contración de las Indias (Commercial House for the West Indies), a post of great responsibility, which he held until his death.

The period during which he made his voyages falls between 1497 and 1504. The first took place in 1499–1500 when, it is believed, he discovered the mouth of the Amazon and sailed as far as the Cape of La Consolación or São Agostinho (about 6° latitude South). On the way back he reached Trinidad and then made for Haiti, believing all the time that he was sailing along the coast of the extreme easterly peninsula of Asia.

At the end of 1500, under the auspices of the Portuguese government, he reached the coast of Brazil and discovered the Plate river. This voyage was of tremendous importance in that Vespucci became convinced, and convinced others, that the newly discovered lands were not part of Asia, but a New World.

In 1507, a humanist scholar named Waldseemüller suggested that the newly discovered world should be named America, after Amerigo. The extension of the name to North America came later. The first official use of the name United States of America was in the Declaration of Independence of 1776.

ASSASSINS

Some murderers are called assassins because this name was given in the 11th Century to a sect of Shi'ite Muslim fanatics who pledged themselves to murder those who did not believe in their religion.

The word assassin comes from the Arab *hashishi* or hashish eater, supposedly because the killers were alleged to take hashish to give ecstatic visions of paradise before setting out on a mission which might well end in their own deaths. We use the word now for one who kills a public figure.

The history of the Shi'ite Muslim sect began in 1090 in Persia, where it was founded by Hassan ibn al-Sabbah and where its endeavours were chiefly directed against the regime of the Seljuks, a Turkish family who had invaded western Asia and founded a powerful empire.

In the 12th Century the assassins extended their activities to Syria, where the expansion of Seljuk rule and the arrival of the Christian crusaders gave them ample scope. They seized a group of castles and waged a war of terror against rulers and crusaders. At one time, they made a pact with Saladin (1138–1193) and murdered Conrad de Montferrat, a crusader who had been made King of Jerusalem. The successive assassin chiefs in Syria were known as the "Old Man of the Mountain". The chief of the sect in Persia proclaimed himself as ruler or Imam.

The end of the power of the assassins came in the 13th Century. The last of their castles fell in 1272. There are still followers of the sect to be found in Syria, Iran and Pakistan, where they are known as Khojas.

Today they owe allegiance to the Aga Khan, as the spiritual leader of the Nizari Isma'ili sect of the Shi'ite Mohammedans.

called assassins? WHY are some soldiers called mercenaries?

A mercenary cleans his gun on the shores of the Congo River near Stanleyville.

MERCENARIES

Mercenaries are soldiers who give their services, and, if necessary, their lives, to anyone who will pay them enough to do so. They were common even in ancient times.

Sometimes they were slaves, as were the Nubians who served the first Pharaohs, or freebooters, such as the Philistines who were found in armies throughout the ancient Near East.

In mediaeval armies, professional soldiers often went to war instead of vassals who owed allegiance to a king or noble. The vassal had to furnish a certain number of armed men to fight in his lord's service for 40 days a year, but an alternative levy of gold was permitted which was used to hire mercenaries.

Mercenaries dominated the turbulent period from the Black Death of the mid-14th Century to the end of the wars of religion three centuries later. The bands which devastated France in the Hundred Years' War (1337–1453) were like those which ruined Germany in the Thirty Years' War (1618–48). The wealthy cities of Renaissance Italy gave them long-term contracts for they were tough, skilful men who could cope with any kind of disturbance.

There are still men whose love of adventure and action leads them to enlist with any army who will pay them enough. Many governments, especially those in developing nations, are anxious to pay for their daring and expertise.

Through the ages mercenaries have become heroes, murderers, and the inevitable face of war.

WHAT is the Bayeux Tapestry?   WHAT happened to the

Aborigines?

BAYEUX TAPESTRY

The Bayeux Tapestry, an ancestor of the strip cartoon, is an embroidery showing, on a continuous linen band over 230 feet long, details of the invasion of England by William the Conqueror in 1066.

Its manufacture was probably ordered by William's half-brother Odo, Bishop of Bayeux, who is pictured on it. The tapestry's existence is first recorded in 1476. It was produced once a year as a decora-tion in Bayeux Cathedral. The first reproduction dates from 1730.

There is general agreement that the tapestry, in worsted wool of eight colours, was made soon after the Conquest. Its description of events tallies well with what is known of the Battle of Hastings.

The tapestry is also noted for its decorative borders, which include figures from Aesop's fables, and farming and hunting scenes.

ABORIGINES

The original inhabitants of Australia, the Aborigines, met the usual fate of widely-scattered native peoples when the white settlers began to arrive and multiply. Their numbers fell drastically.

This was not due to any policy of cruelty or repression. From the start intentions towards them were good. But the vision of the white administrators was not equal to bridging the gulf between the intensely religious and ceremonial native culture, and the materialistic aims of the settlers.

By a natural process—perhaps the result of apathy or despair—the number of Aborigines fell from 350,000 in the 18th Century to some 40,000 in the 1930s. But since then, with more sympathy and understanding, their numbers have started to rise again.

The main effort is now being directed to stop them becoming a permanently underprivileged minority, and to develop their undoubted gifts.

WHERE was Nelson born? WHERE were the remains of

NELSON'S BIRTHPLACE

The great British naval hero, Horatio Nelson, who defeated the French at Trafalgar in 1805 in one of the most memorable of all sea battles, was born at Burnham Thorpe in Norfolk, England. His father was rector of that parish. Horatio's mother (née Suckling) was related to Sir Robert Walpole the British statesman and Prime Minister.

Nelson's uncle, Captain Maurice Suckling, who later became Comptroller of the Navy, gave Horatio his first taste of the sea. Horatio, who was educated in his home county of Norfolk by the North Sea, was entered in the ship Raisonnable by Captain Suckling in 1770 when there was an alarm of war with Spain. But the dispute with Spain was quickly settled, and Nelson was packed off in a merchant vessel to the West Indies to gain experience.

This was the beginning of a hard apprenticeship during which time Nelson visited such remote areas as the Arctic and the East Indies.

Five years after his first appointment at sea Nelson fell ill and was invalided home. It was not until two years later, having just passed his examination as lieutenant, that his remarkable career began in earnest.

NOAH'S ARK

After seven months afloat Noah came to rest, the Bible tells us, "upon the mountains of Ararat". Mount Ararat, an extinct volcanic massif 17,160 feet high consists of two peaks seven miles apart and separated by a saddle 8,800 feet above sea level. It stands in Turkish territory overlooking the point where the frontiers of Turkey, Iran and Soviet Armenia converge, and is about 25 miles in diameter.

The story of the Ark is still a living tradition among the Armen-ians, who believe themselves to be the first race of men to appear in the world after the Deluge. Local legend maintains that the remains of the Ark were long to be seen on top of the mountain. Near the foot of a mountain chasm stood the village of Aghuri, where, according to tradition, Noah built his altar and made sacrifice after his safe deliverance, and where he planted his vineyard. The village was destroyed by earthquake in 1840. A Persian legend refers to Ararat as the cradle of the human race; the Persian name for it is Koh-i-Nuh, meaning Noah's Mountain.

For centuries the Armenians believed that God forbade anyone to reach the top of Ararat and view the remains of the Ark. However, on September 7, 1829, Johann Hacob von Parrot (1792–1840), a German in the Russian service, made the first successful ascent known. Since then the mountain has been climbed many times. The ascent is said to be not difficult.

Noah's Ark discovered? WHERE is Dunkirk? WHERE did Prester John live?

DUNKIRK

Dunkirk is a seaport of Northern France lying between Calais and the Belgian coast, but for millions of people all over the world Dunkirk is one of the most evocative names of the Second World War. For it was from Dunkirk and its 10-mile stretch of beaches that the British evacuated some 338,200 soldiers after the collapse of Belgium and immediately before the collapse of France. Today, Dunkirk has become another name for the supreme heroism that can snatch a victory from defeat.

The troop evacuation took place between May 26 and June 3, 1940. The men were under constant German bombardment both from the land and from the air. At home in England, the British organized an immortal flotilla of small boats. Thames pleasure boats, cabin-cruisers, fishing smacks, even rowing boats were pressed into service —all, of course, on a volunteer basis. The "little ships" ferried the troops from the beaches to the waiting Navy ships.

Evacuation first began from the damaged harbour at Dunkirk, but by May 28 heavy German bombing had severely restricted the harbour's usefulness. By the end of June 1 the greater part of the British Expeditionary Force had been removed, although rescue operations continued until June 4.

The toll of ships was considerable. Out of 41 destroyers used by the British, 6 were sunk and 19 damaged. Most of the expeditionary force's supplies and materials were lost. The British were reduced to their weakest point. But Dunkirk was the great turning point in the war. Hitler's Germany had, it seemed, reached its greatest point of menace, and was never to seem so threatening again.

PRESTER JOHN

Nobody knows for certain and, indeed, nobody has ever succeeded in proving that Prester John ever lived. The legend of Prester John or John the Priest—Prester is a shortened form of Presbyter—dates from the Middle Ages. According to these early legends Prester John was a mighty Christian potentate, a sort of King Priest of the Indies, of fabulous wealth and power.

In the year 1165, the story goes, a letter was sent by Prester John, King of the Indies, to various European rulers, in which he claimed to be a "lord of lords" and hinted that he enjoyed a divine authority.

The land of John was apparently an earthly paradise flowing with milk and honey. Justice and peace ruled supreme. Envy, flattery, greed, theft—none of these evils existed in John's kingdom. Poverty, too, did not exist. So many people enjoyed high-sounding titles at John's court, the letter claimed, that John himself used the plain title of Presbyter or Priest. Apparently John's butler, in this fabled kingdom, was an archbishop and even his cook was a king.

The idea behind this alleged letter to the European princes was that they should feel humbled that one as mighty as John should use such a modest title. Really the letter was an ingenious forgery and a satire on the princes of Europe.

But the fable of a great Christian ruler lingered on. The crusaders loved the idea of this powerful Christian monarch ruling in the mysterious East. So the territories of Prester John were duly shown on medieval maps, although the boundaries were always vague.

In later centuries it was suggested that the land of John really lay in Ethiopia, and gradually this became the accepted version of the legend. John Buchan makes use of the story in his famous adventure novel, *Prester John*.

128

WHEN did Ghenghis Khan live? WHEN was the Black Death? WHEN was

GENGHIS KHAN

Genghis Khan was born in 1155, 1162 or—more likely—1167. We cannot date his birth with certainty, but we do know that he died in 1227. He was a Mongolian, a member of a small group of clans in Outer Mongolia (now the Mongolian People's Republic) north of China.

As a boy he was named Temujin, but he grew up to be such an able soldier that he was acclaimed by his followers in 1206 as "Genghis Khan". The new name probably meant Ocean Chief, using the word ocean as meaning wide or encompassing.

A series of conquests made him undisputed leader of all the nomad, or wandering, tribes of the district. He campaigned against the Kin dynasty of Manchuria and eastern North China in 1211–1214 and reached Peking.

Leaving further conquest in China to his generals, he turned his attention to the west, where his most distant and ambitious campaign, from 1219–1225, carried him through Turkestan into Persia, Afghanistan, Azerbaijan, the Caucasus and south Russia.

Genghis Khan's ferocity became a byword, for he used living citizens as shield walls for his troops and deliberately massacred thousands of prisoners to frighten cities into surrendering. His last campaign was to the kingdom of Tanggut, called by the Chinese Hsi-Hsia, which lay across the Yellow River in Kanon Province. In the course of it the Khan died, partly from the effects of a fall while hunting.

He was particularly clever at psychological warfare and made many secret alliances, which he was careful to break only when he had made sure that he could justify his action to the satisfaction of his more important allies.

WASHINGTON D.C.

Washington D.C. (District of Columbia), named after the first American president, George Washington, was made the capital of the United States when Congress, the American parliament, met there in the middle of November, 1800.

The United States was the first nation in the world to plan a capital city especially for its seat of government. Her example has been followed in this century by Australia, Pakistan and Brazil. Before 1800 Congress sat in eight cities—Philadelphia, Baltimore, Lancaster, York, Princeton, Trenton, Annapolis and New York— and competition was keen to secure the seat of government.

In 1790 it was decided that the capital city should be a district not exceeding 10 square miles on the Potomac River "at some place between the mouths of the Eastern Branch and the Connogocheague".

On September 18, 1793, George Washington laid the cornerstone of the presidential palace. It was built of Virginia freestone (limestone), a material so white that, as early as 1809, people began to speak of it as the White House.

The present day Washington covers an area of about 69 square miles.

BLACK DEATH

The Black Death was a plague that raged through Europe from 1347–1350. It was caused by fleas living on rats which were carried to Europe from Asia by Genoese trading ships. It is suggested that the Black Death was probably bubonic plague, that is to say the sufferers developed "buboes" or inflamed swellings.

About one in three Europeans died of the disease. The sudden decrease in population brought serious social problems. An acute labour shortage led to higher wages and there was a short-lived slump in trade. Many people became obsessed with the idea of death, for there were many recurrences of the plague, notably during the years 1361–3, 1369–71, 1374–5, 1390 and 1400.

On the other hand, the plague speeded changes that had already begun, changes which had their roots in growing trade and the increasing use of money. It became profitable to export wool and wheat. So land gained a new importance, and many nobles, who had lost labourers and were forced to pay much higher wages to those remaining, chose to sell their estates land to rich merchants. Thus arose a new class of landowners where wealth counted as much as birth.

The population of western Europe did not regain its pre-1348 level until the beginning of the 16th Century.

Washington D.C. made the capital of the United States?

The White House, Washington, at sunset with the Jefferson Memorial behind.

The march on Rome – Mussolini is the third from the left.

EVIL OF FASCISM

Fascism is considered evil by those nations who believe strongly in personal liberty, on the grounds that it disregards individual rights, as well as humanity, in its exclusive concern for the nation. Fascism is a political attitude which sees the authority of the nation, state or race as the centre of life. The Italian word *fascismo* comes from the Latin *fasces* (bundles) which described the bundle of rods with an axe which was the symbol of the law's authority in ancient Rome.

As founded in Italy in 1919 by Benito Mussolini (1883–1945), fascism proclaimed its intention to create order out of chaos and replace argument with decision. In fact, it established an authoritarian regime by violence, dictated unity and gave overall priority to military discipline, fighting spirit and ruthless action. Fascism insisted on the "iron logic of nature" that the weak would be conquered by the strong. War was regarded as inevitable. So the chief aim was to make the nation strong and resolute. Mussolini said: "War is to the man what maternity is to the woman".

In fascism service to the nation is the one supreme duty. Absolute devotion is instilled into all citizens by the use of all means of communication. Criticism of the government is not allowed. Cultural or intellectual exchange with other countries is closely regulated. During the 1930s the movement became world-wide with Germany quickly gaining the ascendancy, and Austria, Hungary, Poland, Romania, Bulgaria and Japan joining the ranks.

In Spain the civil war ended in 1939 with the victory of the fascist General Franco. The Second World War resulted in defeat for fascism, but fascist ideas succeeded in surviving in some countries and reviving in others.

largely Roman Catholic?

ROMAN CATHOLIC

South America is largely Roman Catholic because the continent was first discovered and opened up by explorers from the strongly Roman Catholic countries of Spain and Portugal.

Venezuela was the first of the South American countries to be colonized by the Spaniards. Christopher Columbus discovered it on his third voyage in 1498, and settlers soon followed in the early 16th Century. Uruguay, discovered by the Spanish explorer, Juan Diaz de Solis, in 1515, was claimed over the years—until its independence in 1830—by both the Portuguese in Brazil and the Spanish in Argentina. Brazil, although first discovered by a Spaniard in 1500, was declared a possession of the Portuguese crown in the same year by Pedro Alvares Cabral.

In the early 16th Century, Colombia and Ecuador were also conquered by the Spanish. In 1532, Francisco Pizarro added to the Spanish dominions by the conquest of Peru and its Inca empire, which at that time included much of what is now Bolivia, Chile, Columbia and Ecuador.

Paraguay was claimed for Spain by Sebastian Cabot in 1526. The Spanish captain, Pedro de Mendoza, established a settlement on the site of what is now Buenos Aires in 1536. Although this was soon burnt down by Indians, Juan de Garay and other Spanish settlers reestablished the settlement in 1580 and gave it the name Santos Trinidad y Puerto de Santa Maria de Buenos Aires. This long name which means Holy Trinity and Harbour of Our Lady of Kind Winds, was soon shortened to Buenos Aires.

This history of the Spanish and Portuguese control in South America is one of oppression and exploitation. In the early 19th Century, the colonies revolted and established republics. One of the strongest forces remaining from the centuries of colonial domination is the vital Roman Catholic faith of the conquistadores—the conquerors.

JEWISH DIASPORA

Diaspora is the name given to Jewish communities who over thousands of years established themselves in different parts of the world. It is a Greek word meaning scattering.

The history of diaspora goes back to the 8th Century B.C. when the people of Judah in northern Palestine were taken to captivity in Babylon on the River Euphrates in modern Iraq. When the exile ended after about 200 years a great number of their descendants remained behind and formed a community, or diaspora, which continued to be important until the middle of the 11th Century.

The next great diaspora period occurred after the death of Alexander the Great in 323 B.C. when attempts by his successors to impose Greek authority on Jewish customs in Palestine led to thousands of Jews choosing exile. This period saw the formation of the great diaspora in Alexandria, Egypt. Here in the first century B.C. more than 40 per cent of the population were Jews who had learned to combine Greek ideas with their own to produce a flourishing culture.

But the biggest dispersal from Palestine took place under the Roman Empire, especially after A.D. 70 when the army of Titus, later Roman emperor, crushed a nationalist revolt and destroyed the temple in Jerusalem. Although financial help from exiled patriots continued, Palestine gradually ceased to be a Jewish state. In the following centuries the "scattering" spread throughout the world.

In 1939 the estimated number of Jews in the world was 16 million, of whom about 475,000 were in Palestine. Horror and pity aroused by the systematic destruction of Jews by Nazi Germany led indirectly to the creation of the state of Israel in 1948.

CONVICTS

The last convicts were sent to Australia in 1849. They arrived in a ship called the Hashemy, the first convicts to arrive in the colony since 1840. The Hashemy docked in Melbourne, but public protests against the landing of the prisoners caused the authorities to move the ship on to Sydney. There the public outcry was even greater and the Hashemy sailed to Brisbane, where the convicts were put ashore.

The protests arose because many Australians, especially tradespeople and wage earners, were bitterly opposed to the continued flow of free labour to the colony. But transportation (the sending of convicts) was still favoured by sheep owners and farmers, who wanted the labour, and by the British Government, who found it a cheap way of getting rid of unwanted citizens.

After the convicts from the Hashemy had finally disembarked, anti-transportation leagues were formed and attracted so much public support that it was decided to send no more convicts to any part of the colony.

An early engraving of a convict chain gang in Australia.

MIDDLE AGES

The Middle Ages in Europe can be regarded as lasting roughly from about 800 to 1500, or from the times of Charlemagne to those of Columbus. The changes that came about in that period were largely due to the growth of towns and the increase in trade. The Mediterranean area, especially, was opened up by new routes over land, river and sea. Bartering, or the exchange of one kind of goods for another, gave way to the use of money.

Outside the towns, the social classes in Europe were mainly of three kinds: the church, the nobility or warrior class, and the peasants who worked the land. Feudalism was the pattern of

A monk at work—from a medieval illuminated manuscript.

society. The word comes from the Latin *feudum*, meaning a piece of land granted in return for services.

The nobles held the land and it was leased to freemen or worked by serfs (labourers "bound to the soil" who could not leave their master's estate). The feudal system began to weaken about the end of the 13th Century, and meanwhile the trading classes were growing in wealth and power.

The Roman Catholic Church became an international power, as missionaries followed in the footsteps of the traders, but its authority did not go unchallenged. By fighting the Church and one another, medieval kings awoke national feelings in their peoples and laid the foundation for the separate nation-states of Europe.

Nevertheless, during the Middle Ages, Europe—especially western Europe—felt a sense of unity which it did not again experience until the present time. This was due to a common religion and to a common use of Latin.

WHERE did General Lee surrender to General Grant?
WHERE was the Mutiny on the Bounty?

LEE'S SURRENDER

General Lee and his poorly equipped, outnumbered Confederate Army surrendered to General Ulysses S. Grant, commander of the Federal Army, on April 9, 1865 at the court house of the Virginian town of Appomattox.

"The very best soldier I ever saw in the field," said an American general of Robert E. Lee, shortly before Lee resigned his commission in the United States Army.

Lee had been offered the command of the Federal (Northern) Army by President Lincoln. But because he was a Southerner, born in the state of Virginia, he chose to fight on the opposite side.

This defeat by the North in the American Civil War (1861-65) was a bitter pill to take.

The Battle of Gettysburg in July, 1863, was the decisive turning point in the fortunes of General Lee and the Confederates. Before this most bloody battle, Lee had many victories. Among them were Cedar Run and Bull Run, and the outstanding triumph of Chancellorsville in May, 1863. Lee wanted to build on these achievements and carry the war to the North. Success there might have led to the seizure of the rich farmlands and industrial centres of Pennsylvania for the refurbishing of his

much depleted supplies, and eventually a negotiated settlement. But the victory at Gettysburg by the Federals under General George G. Meade meant that Lee failed to get his supplies.

In the spring of 1864, General Grant, now in command of the Federals, took the field in person against Lee. In the following spring he compelled the Confederate general to abandon Virginia's capital, Richmond, and chased him westward to defeat.

Lee died in 1870, Grant went on to be the 18th President. The court house at Appomattox is now preserved in a national park.

HMP

WHERE did David kill Goliath?
WHERE did the Queen of Sheba live?

DAVID AND GOLIATH

The famous fight in which the boy David slew the giant Goliath took place about 15 miles south-west of Jerusalem, in the Valley of Elah in Israel.

David was the youngest of eight brothers and looked after his father's sheep at Bethlehem while the Israelites under King Saul were at war with the Philistines. The First Book of Samuel in the Bible tells how David was sent by his father to take food to the Israelites' camp. Goliath had challenged the Israelites to send a man to do battle with him, the result to decide which array should have the fruits of victory.

No Israelite had dared to take up the challenge. But David persuaded Saul to let him fight Goliath, saying the giant was no more dangerous an adversary than the lion and bear he had slain while protecting his father's sheep.

The two contestants rushed to meet each other, the giant in full armour with sword, spear and shield, the boy with only a sling and five smooth stones from the river. David took a stone in his sling and aimed it at Goliath. The giant was hit on the forehead and stunned. David then killed him with his own sword. The Philistines fled, pursued by the victorious Israelites.

MUTINY ON THE BOUNTY

The famous Mutiny on the Bounty took place on a voyage to the South Seas. In 1787 Captain William Bligh (1754-1817) set sail in the British naval transport ship Bounty with a crew of 44 men for the island of Tahiti in the Pacific Ocean.

The Bounty was a small ship even by the standards of the second half of the 18th Century, displacing 250 tons and only 90 feet long.

Bligh's task was to collect cuttings of bread-fruit trees from the beautiful South Sea island, only recently discovered by Captain Cook, and carry them to the West Indies. There it was hoped the cuttings might thrive and provide food for the African slaves on the sugar plantations.

Captain Bligh was a stern disciplinarian and a bad-tempered man. His temper did not lessen the general discomfort of the voyage to Tahiti. The crew, staying for several months on the lovely island while the cuttings were being gathered, enjoyed the contrast to their cramped quarters and the ill-tempered captain.

So not long after the Bounty had set sail for the West Indies some of the crew demonstrated their renewed discontent. On April 28, 1789 Fletcher Christian, the master's mate, took control of the ship by force. The captain and those men loyal to him were put in a 23-foot open boat. With no chart and few provisions, Bligh and 18 men sailed 3,618 miles in seven weeks to the island of Timor. Whatever his faults, Bligh proved his seamanship. On reaching England, he reported the mutiny.

Christian and the mutineers returned with the Bounty to Tahiti where some of the men decided to settle. But Christian thought it best to move on and sailed to the remote Pacific island of Pitcairn with seven of the mutineers, their Tahitian wives and some male islanders. Some of their descendents still live on the island today.

The men who had elected to remain on Tahiti were later captured and returned to England for trial. Three were hanged. Captain Bligh continued to serve in the navy and eventually rose to the rank of vice-admiral.

QUEEN OF SHEBA

There is a legend in Ethiopia that her emperors are descended from the Queen of Sheba and Solomon, King of Israel, who died about 937 B.C. The story relates that Aksum, the once-splendid city on the high central plateau of Ethiopia, was formerly called Sheba. It is said Queen Makeda of Aksum visited King Solomon at Jerusalem, and that their son, Menelik, became the first Ethiopian emperor.

But Aksum in the time of Solomon was probably not large enough to have a ruler of such wealth and power as the queen of the story. However, there could have been such a Queen of Sheba in the Yemen, the southern part of the Arabian peninsula.

The kingdom of Saba, which may have been the Biblical Sheba, straddled the profitable incense routes that stretched from the Hadhramaut, on Arabia's south coast, to ports on the Mediterranean. It was a rich and powerful kingdom and its inhabitants built a great dam and irrigation system which made the land lush and fertile. Today only a few ruins of the old kingdom survive.

This old Greek amphora shows a story from the Iliad—Odysseus piercing the single eye of the giant Polyphemus.

ILIAD

According to ancient Greek tradition the Iliad was written by the poet Homer (8th–7th Century B.C.). He was said to have been the author of many epic or heroic poems, of which only the Iliad, the story of the siege of Troy, and the Odyssey, the story of Odysseus' wanderings, survive.

The "Homeric question", the attempt which has gone on ever since to find out whether Homer really existed, and, if he did, whether he wrote the poetry, began towards the end of the 6th Century B.C. The first to inquire into the matter was Theagenes of Rhegium. Two writers in the early 7th Century B.C. mention Homer as a poet, but the first person to name his poems was the historian Herodotus in the 5th Century B.C.

What little information is available about Homer suggests that he was born in Smyrna about 740 B.C., trained as a bard (a singer-poet) and travelled about the Greek world until he went blind. Then he settled on the island of Chios and gathered pupils about him. He is believed to have composed the Iliad and perhaps the Odyssey towards the end of his life and to have died about 670 B.C. while on a visit to the island of Ios.

The works credited to him were admired so much by later Greeks that they often referred to him simply as "the poet". The Iliad and the Odyssey are among the greatest works of world literature.

book written? WHEN was the French Revolution?

HISTORY BOOK

Herodotus, a Greek author, known as the "father of history" was born some time in the 5th Century B.C. His book *History*, describing the wars between Greece and Persia, is generally considered to be the first deliberate attempt to see the events of the time against a historical background.

"I am giving," he says in his opening words, "the results of my inquiries (*historiai*) so that the memory of what men have done shall not perish from the world nor their achievements, whether of Greeks or of foreigners, go unsung. They form my theme, and the cause why they went to war."

The *History* is told as a story, using conversation, tragedy and humour. Herodotus was a great traveller with an eye for detail and, on the whole, a good geographer. He was intensely interested in his fellow men and his lack of prejudices makes his book not only very readable but also enormously important historically. Herodotus was also the first European writer of straightforward prose.

FRENCH REVOLUTION

The French Revolution began on July 14, 1789 with the storming of the Bastille prison in Paris, popularly regarded as a symbol of oppression and injustice. Evidence that a revolution was at hand had been provided two months earlier when King Louis XVI, a well-meaning but irresolute man, tried to solve his desperate financial problems by calling a meeting of the Estates-General, the French parliament.

When this almost forgotten body met on May 5 for the first time in 175 years, the third estate, who represented the people, defied the nobles and clergy and declared themselves the National Assembly. On June 20 they took an oath not to disperse until they had given France a constitution which would defend the middle class and peasants against the feudal aristocracy.

Spurred on by the example of the United States, people everywhere were in revolt against absolute and obsolete authority. Two years after the fall of the Bastille, the National Assembly issued the Declaration of the Rights of Man, proclaiming liberty, equality and brotherhood. Then came the flight and recapture of the royal family, and the declaration of a republic in September, 1792.

Four months later Louis was beheaded by the newly invented guillotine. For 18 months France was ruled by an extreme group,

The storming of the Bastille, July 14, 1789.

the Jacobins, who instituted the "Reign of Terror" during which thousands of people were executed, including Queen Marie Antoinette, aristocrats, deposed revolutionaries, such as Danton and Hébert, and finally, on July 28, 1794, the terror leader Robespierre himself became a victim.

France turned with relief to the moderate rule of a committee known as the Directory of Five. At length on November 9, 1799, Napoleon Bonaparte seized power. The revolution was over, leaving Europe and the world a lasting legacy of violence in the cause of liberty and equality.

WHAT made Drake famous? WHAT is a ghetto? WHAT are WHAT are the Nobel Prizes?

SIR FRANCIS DRAKE

Francis Drake became the first Englishman to sail round the world in a voyage which lasted from 1577 to 1580. He left Plymouth on December 13 with his flagship the 100-ton Pelican, four other ships and 160 men on an expedition to the Pacific.

After sailing down the coast of South America, Drake passed through the Strait of Magellan. Then he encountered a fierce storm which drove him southward to Tierra del Fuego.

Drake's other ships had by now been lost or returned home. But the Pelican, renamed the Golden Hind, pushed on alone up the coasts of Chile and Peru, attacking towns and plundering Spanish vessels, notably the treasure-ship Cacafuego.

After continuing northwards and claiming the Californian coast in the name of Queen Elizabeth, he decided to avoid the outraged Spaniards by sailing home across the Pacific. Later he helped to defeat the Spanish Armada in 1588.

GHETTO

In times past a ghetto was a street or district of a town in which all Jews were ordered to live. Its meaning has widened to include any closed settlement of people who feel themselves at a disadvantage compared with the rest of the population.

During the Roman Empire and the early Middle Ages, the Jews of Europe were not segregated, but accorded equal citizenship. However, from about the 11th Century, Church leaders and commercial interests laid the beginnings of segregation. With the Counter Reformation, Pope Paul IV founded the first ghetto in Rome in 1556.

The end of the ghettos began with the French Revolution, but they were only slowly abolished. They lingered on in Russia until 1917, and were revived by the Nazis as the prelude to their notorious extermination camps in which many millions died.

NOBEL PRIZES

Alfred Nobel, the Swedish scientist who invented dynamite, bequeathed most of his £1,750,000 fortune to found these prizes when he died in 1896. A trust fund was established to provide for five annual awards to those who had made the greatest contributions to the common good in the realms of physics, chemistry, medicine, literature and peace.

The prizes, first given in 1901, are awarded on the recommendation of three Swedish learned institutions, and a Norwegian one. Each consists of a diploma, a gold medal, and a cash sum ranging from about £10,000 to £20,000. Five committees, one for each division, sit in secret to decide the prizewinners. Except for the peace prize, which can be won by a group, awards can be given only to individuals. They are open to men and women of all races.

The peace prize is publicly awarded in Oslo on December 10, the anniversary of Nobel's death. The others are given in Stockholm.

Polish Jews being escorted to a concentration camp by members of the Nazi Gestapo.

RUNES

Runes are a kind of alphabet used by the ancient tribes of Europe. The oldest known are Danish and date from the 3rd and 4th Centuries A.D. They are thought to be founded on Greek and Italian originals.

Britain is one country rich in runic remains.. About 50 inscriptions have been found there upon articles of domestic use and stone crosses. The Anglo-Saxons used runes for 500 years.

Runic alphabets were arranged in staves, or groups, of letters. They ranged from 16 characters to more than 30. Runes are sometimes thought to be specially connected with magic and spells. This is wrong. They were simply down-to-earth instruments for recording facts and events.

MAFIA

The Mafia, a criminal society, originated in Sicily when the large landowners put their estates into the hands of ruffianly "security men" during the disturbances which followed Napoleon's invasion of Italy. These men terrorized the peasantry, and finally turned on the landowners.

Their principles were never to appeal to the law and never to help in the detection of crime. By faithfully following their savage code, the Mafia soon became powerful not only in the country but in the towns. Successive Italian governments tried in vain to suppress it.

With European emigration to the United States during the last century, an organization similar to the Mafia came into being there, with the familiar set-up of ruling families, infiltration of society, protection rackets, and bloody acts of vendetta and revenge.

Its heyday was probably the Prohibition era. But it is still believed to exert considerable influence in American life.

MAGNA CARTA

Magna Carta is the great charter of English liberty granted by King John in 1215 at Runnymede, near Windsor. It was reissued with some alterations in 1216 and again with further changes in 1217. In 1225 King Henry III reissued it and it is this document that is the Magna Carta of English law and history.

King John had quarrelled with the Church, barons, merchants and eventually the whole nation. Magna Carta, produced by Stephen Langton, Archbishop of Canterbury, insisted that the King should obey that law.

The Charter asserted the right to personal liberty and to property; protested against punishment administered without trial; required that justice should be properly administered and that there should be a right to free trial.

Medicine and the Body

KIDNEYS

Our kidneys perform four functions, of which the most obvious is the ejection of waste materials containing nitrogen from the body. They also keep the acid-base balance of the blood constant, and regulate the volume of circulating blood and the fluid content of the body as a whole. Finally they regulate pressure relationships between the blood and the tissues.

The kidneys, bean-shaped and about four inches long, lie on the back wall of the abdomen just above the waist, one on each side of the spinal column.

Blood enters the kidney by the renal artery. Some of its plasma is filtered off and, after other processes, ends as urine. The rest leaves the kidney by the renal vein to return to the heart. The urine collects in the central cavity (pelvis) of the kidney, passes down to the bladder via a tube (ureter) and is finally expelled.

A human being can survive without kidneys for only two or three weeks. Nearly one-fifth of the blood pumped out of the heart goes through the kidneys. The kidneys thus regulate the body fluid—a fluid which Claude Bernard (1813–1878), the great French physiologist, called our "internal environment".

BRUISES

We bruise because the body has received a heavy blow which injures the bodily tissues without rupturing or tearing the outer covering of skin.

A bruise is a wound, and a wound may be defined as a breach in the continuity of any body tissue. Often the skin is cut or torn. But closed wounds, such as the rupturing of internal organs, may leave no visible external sign.

A bruise, or contusion of the skin, is caused by the rupture of the blood vessels in the deeper layers of the tissues under the skin. The blood escapes from the damaged vessels into the surrounding tissues and brings about discoloration of the skin, which at first goes red, and then "black and blue". As the blood pigments break down, the bruise changes to yellow and green, and eventually fades away. Usually bruises show in the area where the blow has fallen. But there are times when the blood will track along muscles and the planes of connective tissue, causing the bruise to appear some way away from the injury.

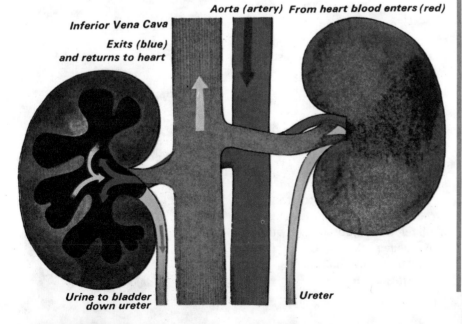

Aorta (artery) From heart blood enters (red)

Inferior Vena Cava
Exits (blue) and returns to heart

Urine to bladder down ureter

Ureter

the knee or ankle swell up if injured?
WHY do medicines come in different forms?

KNEES AND ANKLES

The swelling of an injured joint, like a knee or an ankle, is caused by the multiplication of normal cells to cushion the affected part. This sudden increase is called hyperplasia. There is also a certain amount of internal bleeding as a result of the injury.

Swellings are divided into two main groups, false tumours and true tumours. The inflammatory swellings that appear after joint injuries belong to the first group, which includes bruises, black eyes, sprains, fractures and infectious swellings such as boils and abscesses. Swollen joints can be eased by the application of cold compresses, or pads, and ice packs. Firm bandages are used to give support.

True tumours or swellings are composed of masses of tissue developed from body cells which already exist. They have a tendency to keep growing. Some of these tumours have normal cells and are said to be benign or harmless. In others the cells are slightly different from their parents and the tumours are generally malignant.

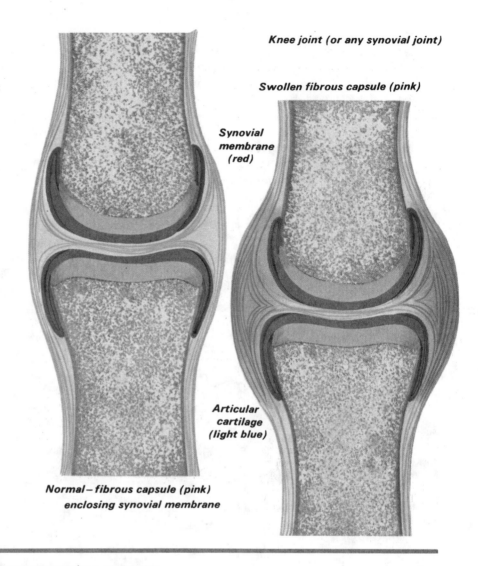

Knee joint (or any synovial joint)

Swollen fibrous capsule (pink)

Synovial membrane (red)

Articular cartilage (light blue)

Normal — fibrous capsule (pink) enclosing synovial membrane

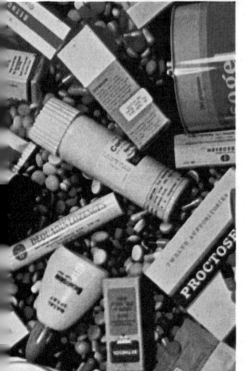

MEDICINAL FORMS

Medicine is given in different forms because of the necessity for convenience or for speed. It can be given by mouth (orally) in the form of tablets, capsules or draughts. It can be inhaled in the form of gases, fine aerosols or, very rarely, exceedingly fine powder. Injections of medicine are given subcutaneously (beneath the skin), intramuscularly or intravenously. Sometimes solid implants in the form of tablets may be placed subcutaneously. Injections may also be given in the spine or brain. Medicines can be given through the rectum as solids (suppositories) or enemas, or through the vagina as pessaries or douches. Finally, there are solutions, powders, creams and ointments which are placed locally on the skin.

Convenient medicines are those which can be taken or administered easily by the patient himself. Oral medicine and inhalations are convenient and a great deal of research is carried out to make these more palatable.

Manufacturers prefer oral preparations because they can be attractively coloured and flavoured and made impressively mysterious in size and shape. They can also be code-stamped or named for identification. Injections have to be sterile and kept in appropriate containers and are therefore relatively expensive.

CANCER

Cancer is what happens when the normal cells making up a part of a person's body start to grow faster than usual, take an odd shape, and stop their part of the body from doing its work.

If the cancer lump is found early enough, it can sometimes be removed by surgical operation or killed by treatment with X-rays or gamma rays. But if this is not done soon, stray cells break off from the cancerous part and float off in the blood to start trouble elsewhere.

Cancer can start in almost any part of the body—the lungs, the kidneys, the stomach, the bones, the blood and even the skin. No one really knows why cancer starts. But ideas are becoming clearer about what makes people likely to get cancer, and doctors are keen to stop people doing things—like smoking cigarettes—which they think may encourage the disease.

Magnified human cancer cells.

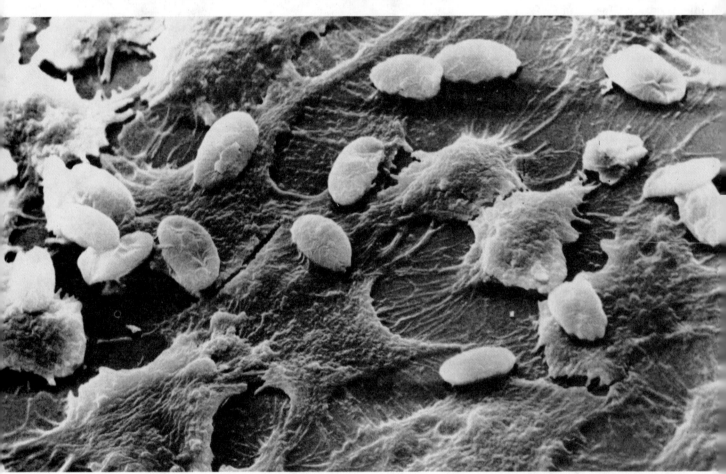

YAWN

When you yawn, or when you see somebody else do so, it is a sign of great need. That need is for more oxygen in your lungs. When you have been sitting in a room where the air has become stale your body cries out for oxygen to cleanse and purify your blood—and the quickest way to supply that need is to open the mouth wide and gulp air.

Better still, you should get out into the fresh air and breathe deeply. You will then find that the need to yawn will vanish, because you are getting a better supply of oxygen.

You must have noticed that you sometimes yawn when you are tired. This means your body-cells need renewal, and your blood needs help in its continual task of reaching and restoring the farthest parts of your body. It indicates oxygen-hunger. Going to sleep not only rests the body, but sets up deep rhythmic breathing which satisfies this hunger.

Why should you yawn when you are bored? You are probably not breathing deeply and feeding your lungs as you should. Of course, the ideal cure is to escape from what is boring you. If that is not possible, try breathing deeply. This will not get rid of the boredom, but it will tend to stop the yawning.

people faint? **WHAT** is pus? **WHAT** is the coccyx?

FAINT

The most urgent need of the body —more important even than food or drink—is oxygen, which is found in the air we breathe. When we breathe in, the oxygen is absorbed through our lungs into the blood which is carried round the body by the veins and arteries with the heart working as a pump. The most important place for the blood and oxygen to reach is the brain which controls the rest of the body through the nervous system. If the brain does not receive enough blood and oxygen, it can no longer control the limbs, and the person's legs give way under him in a faint.

There are all sorts of ways this could happen. It might be due to something blocking the blood flow, a tight collar or some more serious cause. But fainting is mostly due to stuffy atmospheres, lacking in oxygen.

If a person with you faints, get the victim into the fresh air, loosen the clothes and put the head between the knees, so that the weak blood supply does not have to climb upwards into the head, but can run downwards. Usually the circulation will get going again quickly and the person will soon come round, with no damage done.

PUS

The pus we see oozing out from a septic cut is made up of the dead bodies of white blood cells which have fought against the infection.

These white cells, or corpuscles, live in the blood and float around the body ready to fight infection. There are at least five kinds of white cells. The ones which fight the kind of infection that happens when a spot or a cut goes bad are called leucocytes. A speck of blood, the size of a pinhead, normally contains about 5,000 leucocytes. But it may have 30,000 in a really bad septic wound. This is because the leucocytes gather at a point of infection and multiply.

Antibodies in the blood help to fight bacteria. When these have killed the bacteria, the white cells move into destroy them. If a doctor suspects that the blood may not contain enough antibodies to counteract the infection, he prescribes extra antibiotics, like penicillin, which do the same job.

Often the infection is defeated even without help from injections and pills, but not before many of the white cells have been killed, and discarded as pus.

COCCYX

The coccyx is the lower end of the spinal column of man and consists of four nodules of bone, like tiny vertebrae, corresponding to the tail, which is found in lower animals. The bones are deeply buried in muscle tissue, but occasionally they jut backwards and are surrounded by a fold of skin, so as to form an actual tail.

The name coccyx was given by the Greek physician Galen (c.A.D. 130–200) and comes from the Greek word for "cuckoo", as the bone rather resembles a cuckoo's bill.

WHERE are tears made? WHERE do dreams go when
WHERE are the metatarsals?

TEARS

Tears are made of salt water, as you will know if you have ever licked a finger after wiping them away. They happen when the gland which provides moisture to keep the eyeball rotating properly produces more water than usual. The eye cannot drain all this water as it does normally, so a flood occurs.

The gland which makes tears is called the lachrymal gland (*Lacryma* is the Latin word for tear). It is about the size of an almond nut and is situated above the eye. It opens on to the surface of the eyeball by six or more little ducts. Every time we blink the water is spread over the eye. Any extra water is collected in two little canals at the inner corner of the eye where the upper and lower eyelids join, and carried away to the lachrymal sac near the nose.

The tear gland makes more water than usual when stimulated by a really pungent smell, like onions, or household ammonia, or by a situation of great emotional stress, be it happy or sad.

THE METATARSALS

The metatarsal bones are found in your feet. The foot is made up of the tarsus, or ankle, which consists of seven bones; the metatarsus, which consists of five bones, or metatarsals; and the five free digits or toes.

Metatarsals are short and irregularly cube-like in shape. Their surfaces are rough for the attachment of ligaments. In number and general form they are like the similarly positioned bones of the hand, which are known as the metacarpals.

Although the bones of the feet and hand move in a generally similar sort of way there are, of course, important differences. One of the most obvious differences is that in the bones of the hand the thumb has a far greater play of movement than the big toe in the foot. A joint at the base of the thumb allows many more movements than in the case of the big toe.

This "opposable finger and thumb" is one of the physical attributes that has enabled man to reach the peak of the animal "league" table. It is one of the keys to human development.

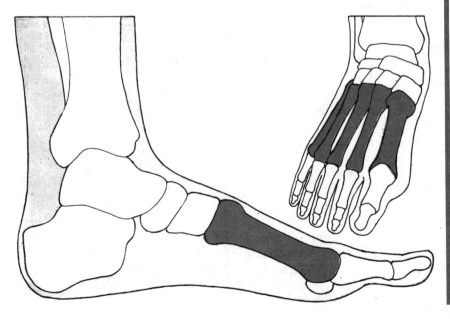

DREAMS

The simple answer is either they are stored in your memory or you forget them. But this question makes us ask a great number of other questions. What is the difference between day-dreaming and the dreams we have when we are asleep? Can dreams foretell the future? How long do they really last? Do we have dreams in

you wake up?

Charles Dickens dreams of the immortal characters in his famous books

colour or only in black and white? Why do we forget some dreams and remember others? Are dreams good for us, or bad? Why do some dreams wake us up at once and others not?

Some experts say that to be healthy in mind, we have to dream every night, whether we remember them or not. There is a book called *An Experiment with Time* by J. W. Dunne, which tells us that the author used to note down in the morning the dreams he had in the night, and that sometimes his dreams foretold what was going to happen in the future.

He suggests that when we are wide awake our sense of time is vertical, so that we are aware only of the present moment, but that when we are asleep, time becomes for us horizontal, so that we can travel into the past and the future. Other experts say that we dream of doing the things which for various reasons, we cannot do in our waking hours. So we try to realize in our sleep wishes that cannot be realized by day.

146

WHY do we have two eyes?   WHY do you get "pins and

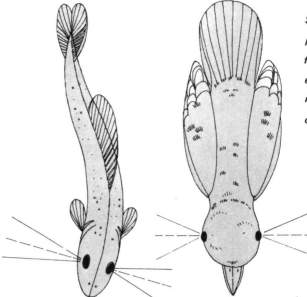

Stereoscopic vision is produced when the separate fields of vision of each eye overlap. This happens in man but not in the fish or bird.

TWO EYES

We have two eyes placed in the front of our heads because we need to be able to judge distances and to see in depth. The change in the position of the eyes from the side of the head in our remote ancestors probably came about because they needed to be able to judge distances accurately as they swung from branch to branch in the trees.

With both eyes in front, their separate fields of vision overlap. We see two images superimposed one upon the other but, because of the space between our eyes, the image from each goes a little way around its own side of the object. This is called stereoscopic vision, or vision in depth, which we share with apes and monkeys. Most other animals and fish do not have

this advantage. To them the world appears flat. One exception is the owl, who sees better than any of us, and has not only stereoscopic vision, but telescopic vision, too.

Our judgement of distance depends, with near objects, upon our stereoscopic vision. As the distance increases, there is less difference between the left-eyed and the right-eyed view. So we depend upon other factors as well.

Experience tells us that the farther away an object is, the smaller it looks. Its colour also changes, its details disappear, its outline softens. Nearer objects give us a measure against which to judge the distance of farther ones. Then there is perspective, the familiar illusion that parallel lines converge towards the horizon.

BRAIN

The brain directs and coordinates movements and reflexes, registers sensations and is the supreme nervous organ by which man acquires knowledge and the power to use and adapt it. It shapes our personalities, and without it we would be more helpless than the tiniest human baby.

There are three main parts of the brain: the forebrain (or cerebrum), the midbrain and the hindbrain. They have the consistency of soft jelly and are protected by three membranes (meninges), a tough outer envelope called the dura and a watery fluid (cerebrospinal fluid) which acts as a support and a cushion. The brain is connected to the spinal cord, and its surface is highly convoluted.

PINS AND NEEDLES

"Pins and needles" is the name given to a tingling sensation you feel in your hands, feet, arms or legs when the blood begins to circulate again in those areas after being impeded. When you sit with one leg doubled up underneath you, you probably find when you try to stand, that your leg has "fallen asleep" and is numb. As

the blood begins to flow again, the familiar tingling sensation will occur.

Blood has been called "the river of life" and its circulation both distributes supplies to the body's cells and removes their waste. The body's five quarts of blood make a complete circuit of the system once every minute.

Without this the cells would cease to function.

A tourniquet, a tie round a limb to halt the circulation, is sometimes used to stop bleeding from a wound into a vein or artery. But a tourniquet is generally loosened every 30 minutes and it should not be kept on for more than two hours at a time.

heedles''? WHY do we have a brain? WHY do we sleep? WHY does hair grow when a person dies?

SLEEP

Some scientists consider that sleep is an instinct, a basic need for the body and mind to relax and to escape from the responses needed while awake. We become tired in body and mind if we do not sleep, and scientists have proved that when we do sleep the electrical activity of the brain slows down, although it may be stimulated when we dream.

One chemical theory is that a substance needed to maintain the waking state becomes exhausted and may be replenished in sleep. A contrary suggestion is that some poisonous substances built up in wakefulness may be destroyed when we go to sleep.

Other theories connect the need for increased wakefulness with the development of the more sophisticated areas of the brain. This could explain why new-born babies whose powers of reasoning have not yet developed, spend most of their lives asleep. It has been demonstrated that a particular part of the brain, the reticular formation, if severed, causes continuous sleep.

Although we are not sure why we sleep, there is no doubt that we need to do so and so do most other animals. The pattern of sleep and wakefulness is closely associated with our habits and senses.

Animals which depend upon sight for food, shelter and defence, like man, are diurnal. That means they are for the most part active during the day and sleep at night.

The amount of sleep needed by a person to remain in full health varies considerably with age, with different individuals, and even, perhaps, with race. Pre-school children generally need ten to twelve hours sleep, schoolchildren nine to eleven hours and adults seven to nine hours. Adults seem to need progressively less sleep as they grow older, and exceptional cases are known of elderly people who have remained healthy on two to three hours a night. It has been said that the Japanese, both children and adults, sleep less than Europeans, but that may be due to habit rather than to race.

The cerebrum, which forms nearly nine-tenths of the brain, is divided into two halves (hemispheres). Generally the left half of the cerebrum controls the right half of the body, and the right half of the cerebrum controls the left half of the body. Some areas are connected with the special senses of man, but there are so-called "silent areas" which scientists believe are connected with memory and the association of ideas. The thalamus, a mass of grey matter which is buried in the cerebrum, is the source of instinctive feeling and emotion.

The midbrain is concerned with eye-movements, while the hindbrain contains the nerve cells responsible for breathing, heart action, digestive juices and so on. The cerebellum, a part of the hindbrain, plays an important role in the execution of the more highly skilled movements.

HAIR

Hair goes on growing after a person dies because the cells of the body go on working until they have exhausted their fuel supply.

Human cells have been described as power plants, chemical laboratories, furnaces and factories. They are marvellous structures, which carry out the functions for which they have been designed with great efficiency.

The hair follicle is composed of two layers—an outer layer of cells forming the outer root sheath and an inner horny layer of horny, fibrous oblong cells. The hair grows upwards from the bottom of the follicle by multiplication of the soft cells, which become elongated and pigmented to form the fibre-like substance of the hair shaft.

The soft cells at the base of the follicle need the nourishment brought to them and all the other cells of the body by the bloodstream.

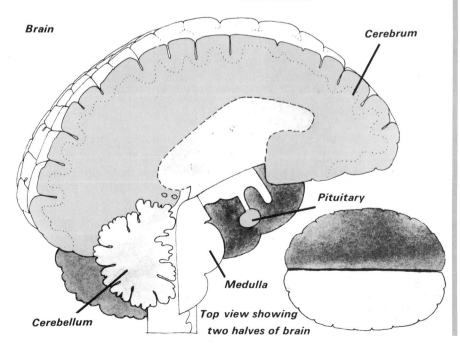

Brain

Cerebrum

Pituitary

Medulla

Cerebellum

Top view showing two halves of brain

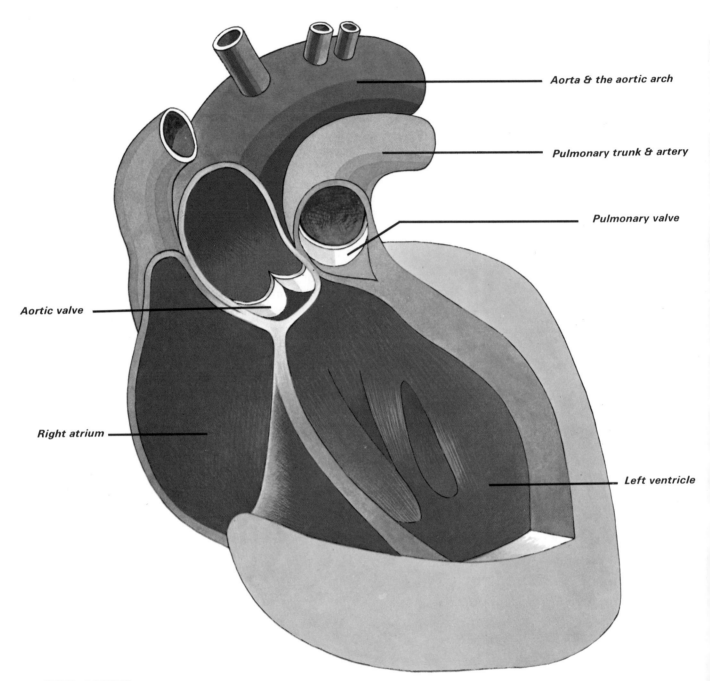

Aorta & the aortic arch

Pulmonary trunk & artery

Pulmonary valve

Aortic valve

Right atrium

Left ventricle

THE AORTA

The aorta is the great artery rising from the left side of the heart, through which the blood passes on its way to all parts of the body except the lungs, which are supplied by another system.

After rising from the heart, the aorta forms an arch, descending down the left side of the body. It passes through the diaphragm into the abdomen, where it divides into two lesser arteries. One of

these terminates under the end of the backbone, where man has the vestige of a tail. In animals it continues into the tail as the caudal artery.

The aorta is one of the elastic— or conducting—arteries, which take the blood to the muscular—or distributing—ones, which connect with the veins and smaller blood vessels.

Three valves at the exit of the

aorta protect the heart from any back pressure that might develop in the artery and force the blood in the wrong direction.

Inflammation caused by an illness such as rheumatic fever may sometimes cause these valves to leak. This is a serious condition requiring considerable medical care and attention. But in normal cases your aorta will continue to function reliably throughout your life.

WHERE is the cervix? WHERE are your nerves?

MALARIA

The most likely places to catch malaria would be in tropical and sub-tropical countries, especially in the forested parts of Central and South America, central Africa, Asia, and southern Europe. This is because the female anopheles mosquito, whose bite transmits the disease, breeds in the warm, stagnant, marshy pools found in those parts.

Malaria is said to derive its name from the Italian for "evil air". It causes chills, fever and anaemia, and is sometimes fatal. In India a million people are likely to die from it every year.

The first effective remedy for it, quinine, was used in the 16th Century. It is an infusion from the bark of the cinchona tree. Modern drugs, too, have greatly reduced the threat of malaria. In particular the use of sprays on the mosquitoes' breeding places has been highly effective.

In 1955 the World Health Organization started a mosquito-eradication programme of benefit to nearly 1,200 million people.

THE CERVIX

The cervix is the name doctors give to the neck of the womb. It is a small opening surrounded by folds of mucous membrane containing mucous-secreting glands. It is supported by two folds of tissue that attach to the backbone.

The first stage of a child's birth occurs when the cervix starts to expand under the influence of rhythmical muscular contractions, until the head can pass through.

The cervix is recognised as a possible cancer site. There is now a service that tests women at regular intervals—three years is usual—for signs of this disease, so that effective early treatment may be started. Scarring or infection following a difficult childbirth may make the cervix more vulnerable.

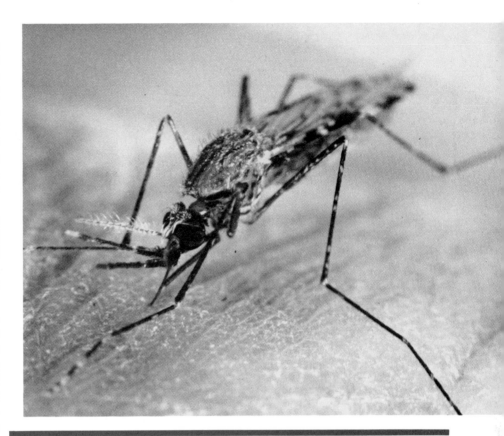

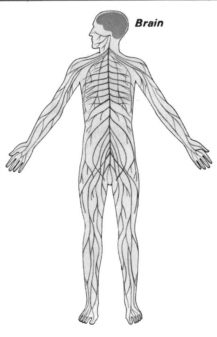

Brain

There are so many thousands of nerves spread throughout the body that a drawing cannot possibly show them all. This diagram gives a general idea of their distribution.

THE NERVES

Your nerves are spread all over your body. The organs of the body are composed of tissues. These in turn consist of microscopic units called cells, specialized to perform particular functions such as secretion (glands), contraction (muscles) or conduction (nerves). Likewise the tissues that pick up our nervous system are composed of billions of individual cells located all over the human body. No part of our body is completely insensitive to pain or some other sensation, because nerves are to be found in every part of the human anatomy.

The nervous system is usually considered to have two parts, the peripheral or outside system, which is in direct contact with the things that cause pain or pleasure, and the central system, consisting of the brain and the spinal cord. It is in our central nervous system that all our sensations and reactions are finally registered.

WHAT medical instruments did the Romans use?   WHAT are

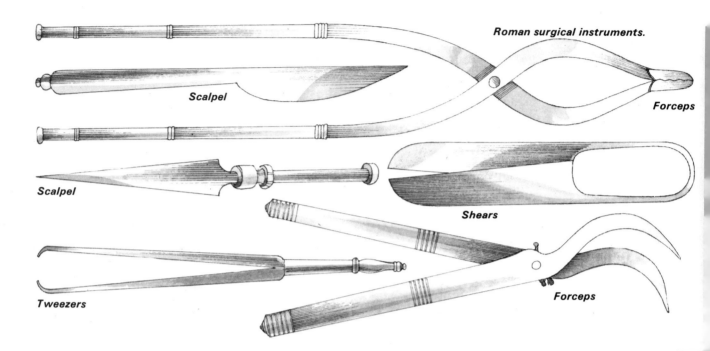

Roman surgical instruments.

Scalpel

Forceps

Scalpel

Shears

Tweezers

Forceps

ROMAN MEDICINE

Some 200 surgical instruments of various kinds have been discovered in the ruins of Pompeii but, in general, the contribution of Rome to medicine was not very great.

'The Romans', said Pliny, in the 1st Century A.D., 'got along without doctors for 600 years'. In fact, if it had not been for the Greeks they might well have never had any. In the early days the Romans relied on herbs and salts as well as some horrible potions like gladiators' blood and human fat. The first Greek doctor to win fame was Asclepiades in about 91 B.C. and he insisted upon regular diet and exercise, fresh air and cleanliness. Galen (c.A.D. 130–200), the most famous of all, emphasized the need to study anatomy.

Drills, scalpels, tweezers, forceps and even a four-jawed clamp were used as surgery, through trial and error, became more skilful. Fractures and dislocations were treated effectively and artificial legs were not unknown. However, there were no anaesthetics and antiseptics and many operations, such as appendicitis, were beyond the surgeon's skill.

CORNS

Corns and callouses are lumps or patches of hard skin, often painful, which can form anywhere on the feet. They are really extra thick layers of skin that grow specially to protect any part of the foot which is receiving more pressure than usual. When someone goes barefoot for a long time the whole of the sole of his foot will become calloused.

When people wear shoes which are too tight or too pointed for them, the shoes press hard on certain parts of their feet and corns develop at these points. This thick layer takes up more room inside the shoe. So the foot becomes even more pinched and sore. You may have noticed that women with tight shoes often take them off under the table—this could be a sign that their corns are hurting!

Why are corns so painful? The answer lies in the construction of our skin. The outer layer is quite thin in relation to the inner layer. Corns become painful when pressed because the toughened core has broken through the tissues of the dermis (or inner layer) of the skin.

WHITE HAIR

No one knows exactly what makes hair go white. Malnutrition or severe illness or shock have resulted in white hair, sometimes within a few days or weeks. But hair "turning white overnight" has never been authenticated.

Heredity plays an important part. You can see people in their 20s who have white hairs mixed with their normal hair. It is usually traceable to parents or grandparents who have had a similar pattern of hair colour change. The hair in these cases is usually coarse or medium coarse in texture.

Old age is the most frequent cause. As we grow older, many parts of the body economize and slow down. In the case of hair, the matrix or middle layer of the hair root "bulb" ceases to produce the colour granules which are normally distributed throughout the hair cells.

The colour of hair is produced by the amount and proportion of pigments within it. Dark brown hair contains a lot of black-brown and some red. Ash blond hair will have small amounts of black and some yellow.

corns?   WHAT makes hair grow white?
WHAT does an X-ray show?   WHAT gives you a stitch?

X-RAYS

X-rays are electromagnetic rays of very short wavelength which can penetrate matter through which light rays cannot pass. We call this opaque matter. An X-ray photograph shows a picture of the internal structure of the body allowing doctors to diagnose broken bones to examine the organs of the body. In order to show the position and shape of the stomach and intestine a harmless material such as barium is swallowed, and other opaque substances may be injected to show the outlines of other organs. Oxygen can also be injected into the brain to make its outline sharper.

The discovery of X-rays was recorded in January 1896 by Professor Röntgen, Professor of Physics at Würzburg. Chest X-rays led to the early diagnosis of pulmonary tuberculosis and from these beginnings the science of radiography and radiotherapy developed until now countless X-ray installations are in daily use throughout the world. X-rays are used both to diagnose and to treat deep-seated diseases like cancer. Scientific laboratories use them in experiments while industry uses them in work of investigation. By using high-tension apparatus giving up to 300,000 volts, steel can be examined for faults and hidden weaknesses can be discovered in aeroplane construction.

STITCH

A stitch is simply a sharp pain in one's side. What happens is that when we use muscles that are normally almost inactive, they contract and tighten, squeezing our nerves and causing pain.

This acute, internal pain is often experienced by runners, but it soon passes off, and is not serious.

There is a hedgerow plant called stitchwort which people once thought could cure stitch.

WHEN was acupuncture first used? WHEN do sounds hurt?

ACUPUNCTURE

Acupuncture originated in China as a form of medical treatment about 2,500 years ago. It has been practised by the Chinese ever since.

The treatment involves the insertion of small metal needles into one or many of 365 spots on the human body. Each of these spots, designated by ancient Chinese doctors, represents a particular function or organ of the human body. Accordingly a heart or liver line can be traced by linking the appropriate spots which relate to the particular organ. If a patient has eye trouble the needles will be inserted into his eye line, which may not necessarily come anywhere near the eye. The needles do not go deep, and are not painful. A single treatment may last only 10 minutes.

It is not clear why acupuncture works, but some scientists have suggested that the needles may relieve the nerves affecting a disease.

Since the beginning of this century the treatment has been introduced in the West. At first there was much scepticism, but recently acupuncture has been widely accepted and has been found to be not only a cure but also a valuable form of anaesthetic.

Acupuncture experts in China and Japan devised guide drawings for the positions of the punctures to cure certain complaints. These early drawings are typical of these guidelines which form a handbook for young students of the science. In acupuncture there are three main ways of pricking the needles into the skin and the material from which the needles are made is also an important point.
Altogether, classical acupuncture techniques recognize some 787 separate puncture points and all these points are carefully arranged to produce specific effects and cures.

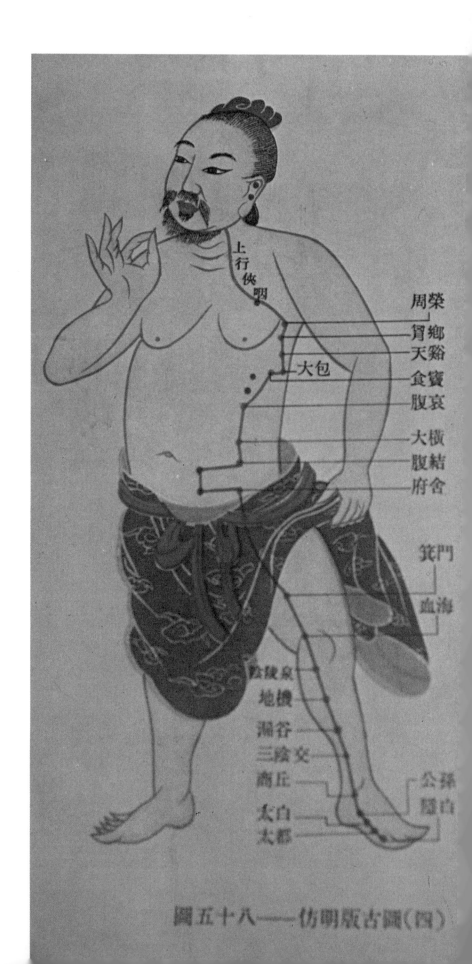

圖五十八──仿明版古圖（四）

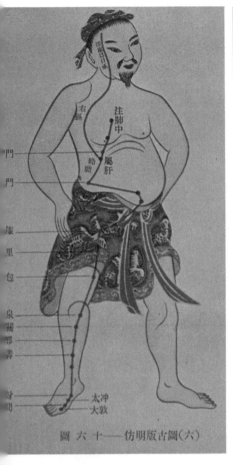

圖六十——仿明版古圖（六）

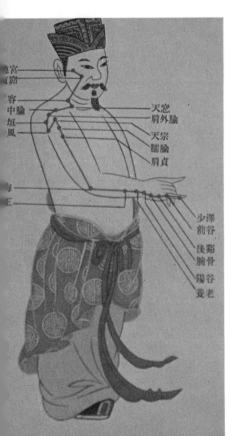

Here are some examples of sounds and their relative intensities in decibels

0 Almost complete silence

10 Leaves rustling in a slight breeze

20 A person whispering from a few feet away

30 A quiet office room

40 Subdued conversation

50 Ordinary conversation in an office area

60 Noise in a department store

70 Continuous traffic in a street

80 Noise of subway trains

90 Pneumatic drill close by

100 Metal drill

110 Hi-fi equipment at 10 watts

120 Aeroplane propeller at 16,000 r.p.m.

SOUNDS THAT HURT

Sounds hurt the ears when they register about 130 on the decibel scale. Decibels are units for measuring the loudness of sound. They show how strong the sound waves are.

The lightest sound—perhaps that of a butterfly landing—would register about zero on the decibel scale; the noise level of a house with the television turned on would be about 50; the din in a car factory would measure 95 or more; and some amplified pop music may be near the limit where the ears would be hurt.

Sound waves are formed by millions of molecules of air bumping and vibrating against one another. Weak sound waves move the eardrum only slightly, but strong ones cause it to respond violently and, in time, may damage hearing permanently. The waves get weaker the further they travel.

The word decibel was coined by scientists in honour of Alexander Graham Bell whose interest in sound waves led to the invention of the telephone.

WHY do some people go bald?   WHY do we usually get
WHY should you not watch television in a darkened room?

A gathering of the Bald-Headed Men's Society at the French town of Villechauve.

BALD PEOPLE

There are two reasons why people may go bald. The live hair germ centres have either been permanently destroyed or they have been temporarily damaged.

Permanent baldness or alopecia occurs in more than 40 per cent of men and may affect the whole head. In women it affects the crown of the head only and never leads to complete loss of hair. Three factors often lead to permanent baldness—heredity, age and hormone balance. There is no cure. Other causes of permanent baldness may be injuries or diseases which produce severe scarring, inborn lack of hair development and severe injuries to the hair germ centres by chemicals.

Temporary hair loss often occurs after a high fever, thyroid disease or tuberculosis, but it grows again in most cases after the disease is cured.

Drugs, X-rays, malnutrition and some skin diseases can also cause temporary hair loss, but usually it grows again within a year.

There is also a disease called alopecia areata, in which the hair falls out in patches all over the head. Usually the germ centres have been injured only temporarily, and in 99 per cent of cases the hair grows again without treatment.

Baldness may occur at almost any time of life after childhood.

MEASLES

We usually get measles or chickenpox only once because our bodies manufacture special chemical defences called antibodies. These antibodies are selective and are effective only against the particular microbe they have been formulated to fight. After the battle is won, the antibodies remain in the bloodstream, ready to repel another attack.

The antibodies are large complex protein molecules. One group, the antitoxins, act as antidotes, neutralizing the poisons that the microbes release into the body. The other group, the agglutinins, clump the microbes together so that they fall easy prey to the white

measles or chicken-pox only once?

WHY do we produce saliva?

TELEVISION

You should not watch television in a darkened room because you will not see the picture so clearly. The human eye functions best, and is able to see detail most acutely when viewing white light. So a lightish background makes for a better picture.

Of course, it is unwise to have the source of light shining directly on to the television set because some of the rays will be reflected and spoil the picture.

Viewing in a dark room can also cause an unpleasant glare. The intense light coming from a television screen against a black background causes a certain amount of stray light to be reflected internally from structures within the eye on to the retina. (The retina is the delicate tissue containing the photo receptors.) The effect is similar, if less intense, to that produced by a car with undipped headlights.

A third disadvantage of a darkened background is that "flicker" on the television screen becomes more apparent and can cause severe eye fatigue. In certain quite rare cases this "flicker" effect can produce epileptic fits.

blood cells, or leukocytes. These leukocytes develop in the bone marrow and are always present in the blood.

Some of them surround the infected area and quarantine it by making a wall with their own bodies. Within the barricade, the rest of them attack the microbes and eat them up. Like tiny amoebas, they crawl about and stretch out foot-like projections called pseudopods which they use to engulf bacteria and digest them. This explains their other name phagocyte, or eating cell. Each phagocyte can eat about a dozen bacteria this way—a process called phagocytosis.

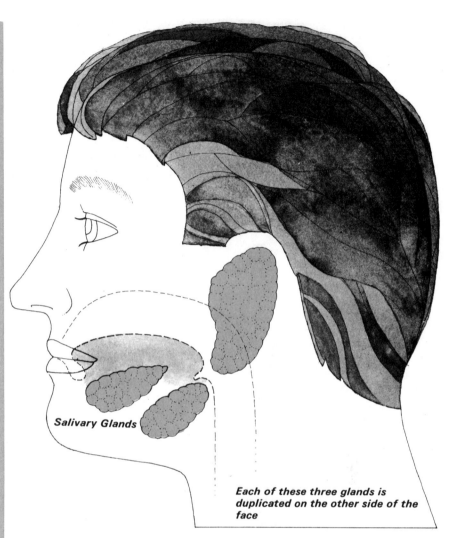

Salivary Glands

Each of these three glands is duplicated on the other side of the face

SALIVA

Saliva, the watery secretion produced in our mouths, has many functions. It moistens the mouth and tongue, making sure that the mucous membrane does not dry or crack. It also moistens our food so that it can be moulded into an egg-shaped mass (or bolus) for swallowing, and it lubricates the bolus so that it can be swallowed easily.

By means of the enzyme ptyalin, which it contains, saliva begins the digestion of carbohydrates inside the food. Saliva also acts as a solvent to make tasting food easier, for the taste buds are stimulated only by dissolved substances.

It is a cleansing agent, washing away particles inside the mouth. If salivation is stopped, for instance in the case of a high fever, the mouth becomes dirty and tastes and smells foul. If salivation slows down, our mouths feel dry, and we know we need water.

Saliva is secreted in the three pairs of salivary glands. The largest of these are the irregularly shaped parotid glands which are packed tightly into a space between the ear and the top of the jawbone. The glands are encased in an inelastic covering and that is why they are extremely painful if they swell. The next pair are the submandibular glands which are egg-shaped and lie under the front of the jawbone, and the third pair, the almond-shaped sublingual glands, lie on the floor of the mouth between the tongue and the jawbone.

MUSCLE

Muscle is the body tissue which, because it has the power of contraction, enables the higher animals to move their bodies. Muscles are divided into two great groups, voluntary and involuntary, the former being controlled by the will, while the latter act independently.

Most voluntary muscles are attached to the skeleton and range in size and shape to suit the particular jobs they perform. They can get into action within a few hundredths of a second, exert an enormous pull on the bone to which they are attached and, if necessary, support 1,000 times their own weight. Involuntary muscles include heart muscle and the muscles of the digestive system, and the fibres of which they are composed are very much smaller than those of voluntary muscle.

Because of its exceptionally rich blood supply, muscle is the most infection-free of the body's basic tissues. If it is over-taxed it tires and will stop contracting altogether, but if used normally will give little trouble.

DOUBLE JOINTS

A double joint is a joint which is capable of an unusual amount of movement, usually backward movement. Perhaps the most common demonstration of a double joint is to see someone bend his thumb downwards and backwards until it touches the inside of his forearm.

A joint is the meeting place between different bones of the skeleton. Joints are divided into fixed and movable ones.

Movable joints may be divided into gliding joints, such as the wrist and ankle; hinge-joints, like the elbow and knee; and the ball-and-socket type such as the shoulder and hip.

HYPNOTISM

Hypnotism is the art of putting a person's brain into a trance-like state which the hypnotist can then control. It is a way of exploring the deeper areas of the mind and, by so doing, releasing a patient from unconscious worries and strains.

For hypnotism to succeed, the patient must trust the hypnotist and cooperate with him. Once the patient is in a trance, his mind returns to a more simple, childlike state. He often remembers incidents that happened to him when he was young, incidents which may have affected him deeply and which have made him the sort of person he is. The hypnotist, who in these circumstances should also be a trained doctor, will help him to understand his fears.

The first doctor who used hypnotism as medical treatment was called Franz Mesmer. He was Viennese. His technique of hypnotism was known as Mesmerism.

joints? WHAT are eyes made of? WHAT makes teeth chatter? WHAT is a squint?

EYES

The outer shell of the eyeball is made up of three coats: the fibrous tunic, the uveal tunic and the retina. The fibrous tunic is tough and elastic. It is opaque at the back, where it is called the sclera, and transparent at the front where it is known as the cornea. The uveal tunic is so called because of its similarity to a grape (Latin: *uva*). It contains the choroid membrane which supplies blood to the eye. The retina, or innermost coat, is an extremely delicate tissue and is only a frac-

tion of a millimetre thick. Its inner layers carry blood from the central artery to the central vein.

At the centre of the eye is a circular opening, the pupil, and immediately behind it is the crystalline lens, which consists of a great many transparent fibres arranged in sheets like the layers of an onion and enclosed in a clear, elastic membrane, the capsule. The perfectly smooth surface of the lens is curved and it is suspended by a number of delicate threads.

TEETH CHATTER

Your teeth chatter when you are cold or afraid. This is because your muscles become tense and no longer control your teeth in the normal way.

Little children's teeth often chatter when they come out of the water. This is because the cold has cramped their muscles.

Similarly, your body may lose its normal controls. If you are frightened, for instance, you could be sick with fear if your diaphragm muscles contracted.

SQUINT

A squint, or *strabismus*, is the name given to a condition in which both eyes do not point in the same direction. The movements of the eyeballs depend upon the action of six muscles, four of which are straight and two slanting. Defects in these may produce a squint.

Long-sightedness in children often produces an inward squint, especially if the child is looking at something close at hand. Short-sightedness may produce an outward squint. Paralysis is the usual cause of a squint which appears after the years of childhood. This is caused by some disease affecting the brain or the nerves of the eye muscles.

If one eye has better vision than the other the good eye may be used much more than the other, which may begin to function less and less well. Treatment for squinting must begin as early as possible with the wearing of glasses, which may have one dark lens over the good eye to stop it being used. This prevents the bad eye from becoming worse. Special exercises, called orthoptic exercises, which help to strengthen the eye muscles, are given and, in some cases, an operation is necessary to strengthen a weak eye-muscle or to weaken an over-strong one.

Section of eye.

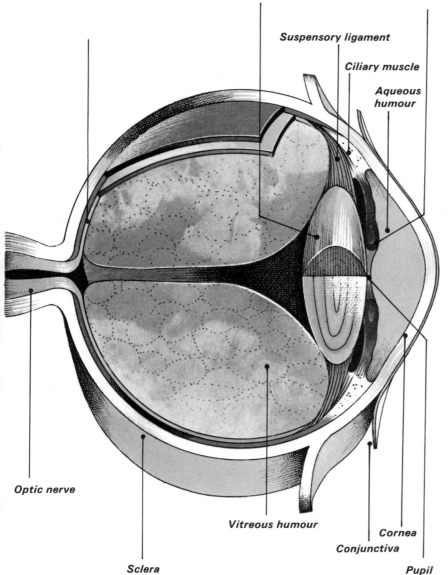

Crystalline lens

Iris

Suspensory ligament

Ciliary muscle

Aqueous humour

Optic nerve

Vitreous humour

Cornea

Conjunctiva

Sclera

Pupil

WHEN can a baby see clearly?　WHEN do bones break?

BABY'S SIGHT

Babies can generally see clearly by the time they are three to four months old. At birth they cannot focus on objects or control their eyes. Strong light upsets them.

After a month babies are able to focus on objects for a few moments at a time. After three months they can recognize things and follow their movements.

BROKEN BONES

Bones break under varying degrees of pressure according to age, health and other circumstances. They are made of hard, strong connective tissue and normally resist considerable force before breaking or fracturing. But when a bone has been softened by disease or grown fragile with age, fractures may follow very minor accidents or even occur spontaneously (pathological fractures).

The bones of children are not fully mature and are still relatively flexible. In childhood a severe blow or fall often results in a "greenstick" fracture, in which the bone appears to bend but does not completely break into two separate pieces.

An impacted fracture occurs when the broken ends of the bone appear to be jammed together by the force of the injury. A comminuted fracture is one in which the ends are shatted into many pieces. A fracture is called simple (closed) when the overlying skin is not broken, or compound (open) when the bone is exposed.

All fractures attempt to heal themselves by producing new tissue to join the broken pieces together. At first this tissue is like putty and easily injured. So, generally a fractured limb should be straightened, immobilized and protected by a plaster cast while the healing takes place. In time the new tissue, or fracture callus, changes into mature bone.

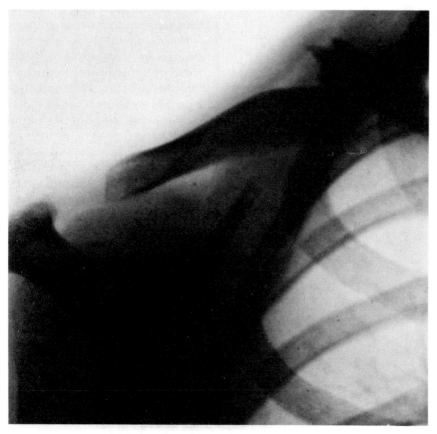

BLOOD TRANSFUSION

The first successful blood transfusion on record was performed in 1665 by Richard Lower. Using quills and silver tubes, he transferred the blood from the artery of one dog to the vein of another. Two years later, he transfused a man with the blood of a lamb. He gave a demonstration of this before

WHEN was the first blood transfusion?

WHEN was the thermometer invented?

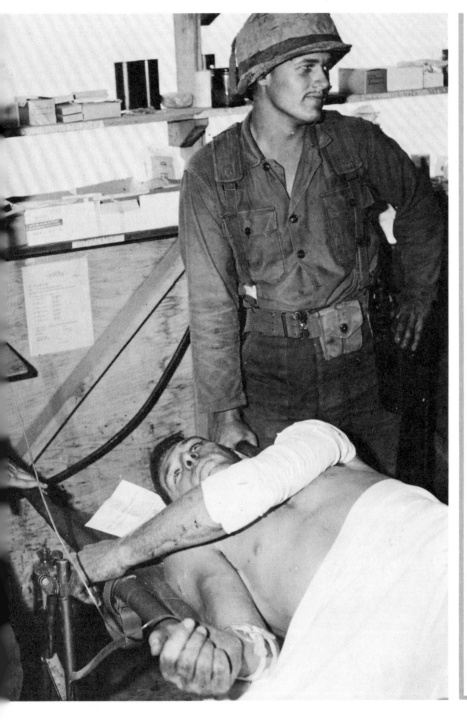

THERMOMETER

The first practical thermometer or instrument for measuring temperature was invented shortly before the end of the 16th Century by the famous Italian astronomer Galileo. It was an air thermometer giving only a rough indication of the degrees of heat and cold, and later he increased its efficiency by using alcohol instead of air.

The principle on which thermometers work is that the liquid or gas used for measuring expands or contracts with changes in temperature more rapidly than the glass containing it. Thus when a coloured liquid is confined in a thin glass tube the difference in expansion, as shown by the level of the liquid against a graduated scale, indicates the temperature.

About 1714 the German scientist Gabriel Daniel Fahrenheit designed a thermometer which, for the first time, used mercury as the measuring agent. He also introduced the scale named after him in which 32° is the freezing point of water and 212° the boiling point. Mercury is still used in most thermometers because it has a high boiling point (674°) and a low freezing point (−38°).

An alcohol thermometer, still in use in some countries, was made by René de Réaumur, a French naturalist, about 1731. About 11 years later Anders Celsius, a Swedish astronomer, used the centigrade scale for the first time, with freezing point at 0° and boiling point at 100°.

the Royal Society in London, and the incident is recorded in the diary of Samuel Pepys.

Richard Lower was able to perform these transfusions thanks to William Harvey who, in 1628, announced his theory of the circulation of the blood. Before Harvey, people had always realized that blood was vital to life, but they did not know how it circulated in the body.

A vital development in blood transfusion came in 1900, when Karl Landsteiner demonstrated the different blood groups in human beings. After that, people were transfused with blood of their own group whenever possible.

Nowadays blood transfusion saves many lives. People can be treated for shock by pumping plasma (the fluid part of the blood) into them. Large reserves of blood are necessary for open-heart operations, sometimes as much as 20 pints a patient.

WHY are some people colour blind? WHY do we sometimes

COLOUR BLINDNESS

Scientists think that some people are colour blind because they have an abnormality of the three pigments in the cones in the retina of the eye which, it is supposed, are necessary for colour vision.

The theory of colour vision depends on the fact that any colour in the spectrum can be matched by a mixture of three pure spectral colours of variable intensity but fixed wavelength. In colour blind persons, all three pigments are present, but are of an intensity different from normal.

They can see all the colours, but have difficulty in distinguishing between red, green and yellow, or between blue, green and yellow. Absence of one or more pigments is rare but does exist, while the complete absence of colour vision resulting from lack of cones in the retina sometimes occurs.

Most colour blind people are ignorant of their abnormality until it is demonstrated to them by means of a special test. Usually it is not a great handicap. But there are situations, and jobs, such as an air pilot, in which it may be important to distinguish colours quickly.

This chart is used for detecting red-green colour deficiency. People with normal colour vision will see a mug and a tea pot. Those affected will see only a mug. It should be noted this is only one of a series of tests for testing colour vision and is not sufficient by itself to prove defective colour vision.

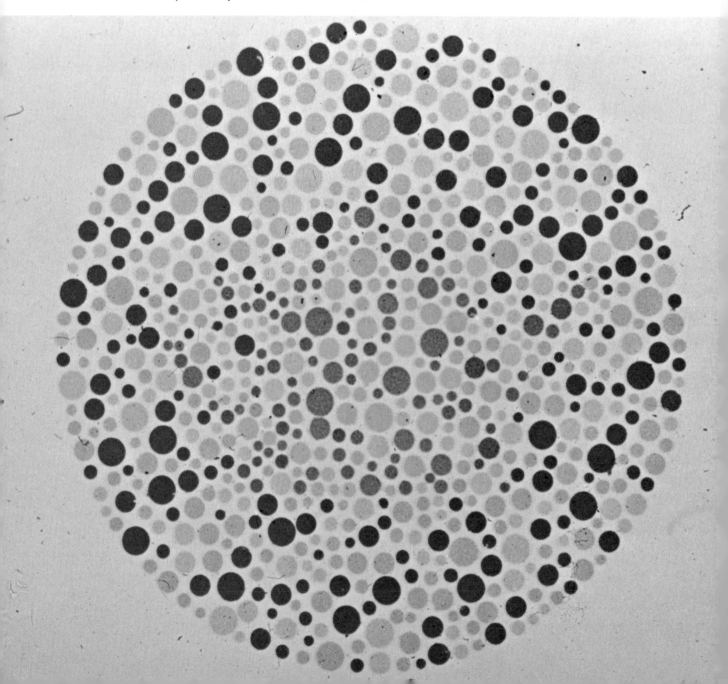

feel the need to scratch ourselves? WHY do we smile?

SCRATCHING

One of the commonest causes of an itchy skin is an allergy. The word was coined in 1906 by Professor Clemens von Puquet of Vienna to describe a special state of exceptional sensitivity of the body to certain substances brought into contact with it. Such substances are called allergens, and include furs, feathers, foods, dust, pollens and drugs.

Most people have experienced allergy in some degree at some time, and about 10 per cent of the population show more or less permanent symptoms of allergic illnesses.

An allergic reaction is always the same, no matter what has caused it. The reason is thought to be that a process similar to the antibody reaction is set off, not in the bloodstream but on the surface of the body cells.

This allergen-antibody damages the cell walls and sets free a substance called histamine which produces two responses. It allows fluid to escape from the blood vessels into the surrounding tissues and it brings about an involuntary contraction or spasm of certain muscles.

When contact with an allergen is external we develop an itch which may be caused by light, heat, cold, hair or fur. It can also be caused by eating foods such as shellfish, mushrooms and strawberries or by an allergy to some drugs and medicines. If the allergen is inhaled there may be, as in hay fever, an excessive secretion of mucous, or, as in asthma, a severe spasm of the lung's air passages.

A true allergen is always a protein, a complex substance which forms an essential part of animal and plant tissues, but the abnormal reaction is produced only by a particular substance or group of substances.

SMILING

We smile to show our pleasure or amusement in something or with someone. In fact, smiling seems to be an expression with which we are born, for most babies smile during the first weeks of life.

Charles Darwin (1809–1882), the great English naturalist who established the theory of organic evolution in his work, *Origin of Species*, also published, in 1872, a book, *Expression of the Emotions in Man and Animals*, in which he studied the facial expressions of men and animals. Most of the experiments connected with facial expression have been based on this book.

It has been suggested that a baby begins to realize within its first year of life that a smile is a "good" expression because it is greeted with pleasure by mother or nurse. The smile develops, some time after the twentieth week of life, into laughter but there are great differences between the frequency of laughter and smiles in individuals.

As the child grows up, the action of smiling becomes bound up with a growing awareness of what is socially acceptable in certain situations. In an adult it is often difficult to be certain whether the response is truly emotional or not. Recently different kinds of smiles have been more closely observed. It is notable that the pattern of the smile alters, according to the situation, from a wide spontaneous grin akin to laughter to a tight, nervous grimace which is nearer to a reaction of fear.

WHAT is St Vitus's dance? WHAT is a calorie? WHAT are

ST VITUS'S DANCE

St Vitus's Dance is a name given to the disease chorea. It is a convulsive disease of the nerves usually associated with rheumatic fever. When someone gets chorea, the muscles—particularly of their hands, feet and face—move irregularly and involuntarily.

The name St Vitus's Dance dates from the late Middle Ages, when hysterical dancing (similar to the dancing of dervishes and voodoo cultists) was very popular. People in the grip of this hysteria often went to the chapels of St Vitus, who was believed to have great healing powers.

Chorea is chiefly a disease of childhood, occurring most often between the ages of five and 15. It is more common in girls than in boys. Sometimes the disease is mild. Sometimes it completely incapacitates the sufferer. It is quite usual for someone with the disease to be unable to hold objects or to write properly, and to have difficulty in walking. Recovery is hastened by rest in bed in a sympathetic environment.

Facial grimaces and tics are frequency confused with chorea, but these repetitive movements are quite different from the uncoordinated, purposeless movements of the disease.

CALORIE

A calorie is a measure of heat. One calorie is enough heat to make a kilogram of water one degree Centigrade hotter. The energy which drives the human body is also measured in calories. When people talk about the calorific value of food, they are referring to the amount of energy it gives the person who eats it.

The amount of energy a person uses decides the amount of food needed. It depends on how big a person is and how much exercise is taken. A big, muscular lumberjack needs more than 2,500 calories a day, while a small secretary, who sits at a desk all the time, cannot take in more than 1,400 a day without getting fatter. Children need more calories for their size than adults because growing uses up energy fast.

When people put on weight it is because they are taking in more calories than they are using up in energy, and the extra is being stored as fat. The reverse is also true.

Calorific value is not the same as nutritional value. The body also needs special kinds of food to keep healthy. So people who are trying to lose weight must still eat a good deal of meat, or other form of protein, and vegetables. If they cut these out, their bodies will be undernourished and vulnerable to illness.

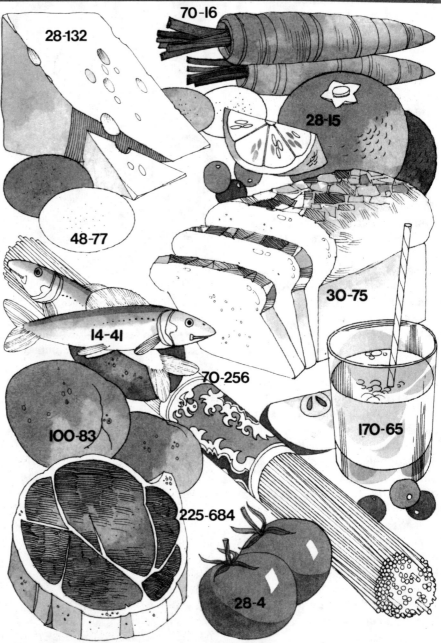

28-132
70-16
28-15
48-77
14-41
30-75
70-256
170-65
100-83
225-684
28-4

The first number gives the weight in grams (28 gms = 1 oz) and the second number gives the amount of calories in that weight.

Siamese twins? WHAT is serum?

SIAMESE TWINS

Siamese twins are babies who are born joined together. They are joined by a bridge of flesh through which the blood flows from one twin to the other. So the twins share the same blood circulation systems.

The name "Siamese" originated from a famous pair of such twins from Siam who were exhibited for many years in the 19th Century.

Nowadays, with the great advances in medicine and surgery, it is often possible to separate the twins, enabling them to live freely and independently from each other.

SERUM

Serum is the part of the blood in which the antibodies or antitoxins which the body uses to fight off infection are carried.

For every disease-carrying toxin there is another, called an antitoxin which cancels it out. The blood normally carries the antitoxins to combat the common infections which attack the body. But there are many diseases and infections for which we do not carry the right antibodies.

A cure or prevention is provided by injections of extra serum to which the correct antitoxin has been added. It takes many years of scientific experiments to work out which antitoxin will fight a particular disease. But once it is known, the antitoxin can be introduced into animals whose serum is then used to inject human beings.

Sometimes, as for snake bites, the serum injection is given only after the infection has set in. Often the antitoxin works only if given quickly. People going on long expeditions far away from hospitals take serum with them, so that they can inject themselves.

However, serums for some diseases can be given, as a precaution, before the infection appears. The tetanus injection which you are given if you cut yourself is one example. The diphtheria injection given to a baby is another.

These Dutch Siamese twins were successfully separated shortly after their birth and have since led perfectly normal lives.

COLOUR OF PEOPLE

People vary in the colour of their skin because of a network of pigment-forming cells called melanocytes. This network is interspersed between, and lies underneath, the cells of the deepest layer of the epidermis, or outer skin, which is called the stratum basale.

The melanocytes have slender, branchlike extensions which touch one another and also extend upwards between the cells of the deeper portions of the epidermis. There are about 1,000 to 3,000 melanocytes in each square millimetre of skin, and each one produces the dark pigment melanin formed as a result of oxidation.

This oxidation is catalysed by a copper-containing enzyme called tyrosinase, which gives the reddish spectrum of colour changes. Various stages of formation produce is pale yellow, tawny, orange, reddish, brown and, finally, intensely black.

Human skin contains greater or lesser amounts of melanin. In fair-skinned races the deep skin layer of melanocytes contains very little pigment. In the darker races, the deposits are heavy, and other melanocytes are to be found in the upper layers of the epidermis.

when frightened? WHY do we get indigestion?

Melanin is a natural protection from harmful sunrays and, on exposure to sunlight, man's skin normally undergoes gradual tanning. This increase of melanin pigment, helps to safeguard underlying tissues. In blondes and redheads the pigment cells respond only slightly and rather unevenly. The consequence of this may be a "freckling" effect rather than a sun-tanned look.

WHITE WITH FEAR

We turn white when we are frightened because the blood in our cheeks is diverted to do a more urgent job. At the same time our hearts begin to beat much faster, and we breathe more quickly.

When we sit still, our hearts beat at about 70 or 80 times a minute, pumping the blood through our bodies. The blood carries nourishment from food, and oxygen from the air we breathe, both of which are vitally necessary for the body to function.

If we take violent exercise, our muscles need to work much harder and faster than when we are sitting or walking. They therefore need extra nourishment and oxygen. The nerves carry the message to that part of the brain called the hypothalamus, the centre of an automatic nervous system in control of internal bodily functions such as the pumping of the heart, breathing and digestion.

Impulses from the hypothalamus travel down the spinal cord and excite other nerve cells— "sympathetic" neurons—which end in the centre or medulla of the adrenal glands just above the kidneys. These glands release the hormone adrenalin into the bloodstream which causes the heart to beat faster and more efficiently, dilates air passages in the lungs and the blood vessels that supply the muscles, and increases the concentration of energy-giving glucose in the blood.

In fact, when we are frightened, exactly the same physical changes take place and our bodies are immediately and efficiently prepared for the violent exercise of flight or fight without any voluntary effort on our part.

INDIGESTION

Indigestion is most often brought about by interference with a marvellous piece of engineering contained in 30 to 32 feet of continuous hollow tubing called the alimentary canal.

In this system the food is broken down, churned, diluted, dissolved and chemically split into simpler compounds which can be absorbed into the blood.

The alimentary canal is formed of membrane which has to resist a chemistry that dissolves bone, gristle, animal and vegetable matter far tougher than the membrane itself. The stomach's gastric juice, one of the chief agents in digestion, has a high concentration of hydrochloric acid. This can dissolve a hard-boiled egg in a few minutes.

Why does it not dissolve the stomach? One reason seems to be that the stomach secretes not only acid but also ammonia, an equally powerful alkali which acts as a neutralizing agent.

This powerful gastric juice can be hindered by many causes, with the result that we may get the pains we know as indigestion.

The alimentary canal makes its preparations for a meal well in advance. The sight and smell and even the thought of food set the salivary and gastric juices flowing, while the stomach blushes in anticipation as the glands begin working and the capillaries widen to bring in an extra blood supply for the activity of digestion.

But the prospect of an unappetizing meal or disagreeable company, and the emotions of worry, irritation, anger and fear may stop these preparations. They may even cause the stomach to turn pale. Indigestion is the result.

We may also get indigestion if we eat too quickly without chewing our food or eat too many foods which are difficult to digest, thus overloading and disrupting the system.

WHEN was the stethoscope invented? WHEN do we get

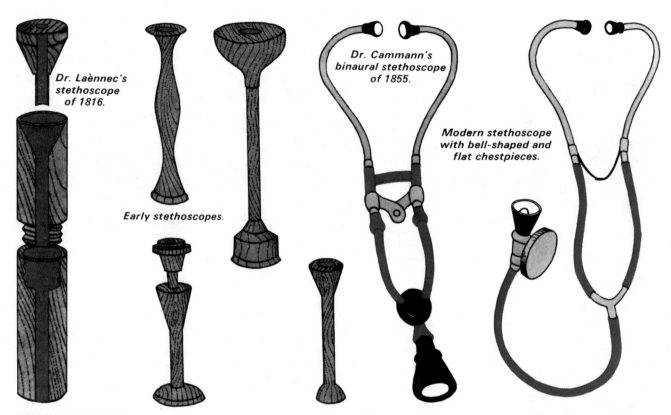

Dr. Laènnec's stethoscope of 1816.

Early stethoscopes.

Dr. Cammann's binaural stethoscope of 1855.

Modern stethoscope with bell-shaped and flat chestpieces.

STETHOSCOPE

The stethoscope was invented by a French doctor, René Théophile Hyacinthe Laënnec, in 1816. His stethoscope was a perforated wooden cylinder one foot long, and he got the idea for it from the sight of children scratching one end of a wooden beam with a pin and listening to the transmitted sound at the other end.

He put one end of the tube to his patient's chest and listened to noises made by the heart and lungs. He gathered evidence of what these sounds meant by comparing the various noises heard in living patients with the type of disease seen after they died. In 1819 he published his findings in one of the great books of medicine *De l'Auscultation Médiate*, and the stethoscope soon came into general use.

Auscultation (listening to sounds within the body) is most commonly used in diagnosing diseases of the heart and lungs. Nowadays a stethoscope is gener-ally binaural (for both ears) and has two flexible rubber tubes attaching the chestpiece to spring-connected metal tubes with ear-pieces. In listening it is often necessary to use both a bell-shaped, open-ended chestpiece for low-pitched sounds, and a flat chestpiece covered with a semi-rigid disc or diaphragm for high-pitched sounds. Many modern stethoscopes have both kinds of chestpieces, readily interchanged by turning a valve.

ULCERS

People get ulcers at various times, according to the kind of ulcers they are. Ulcers are wounds or breakages in the skin or tissues of the body.

The least serious are mouth ulcers. They usually arise from some minor infection, or through eating the wrong kinds of food. They are known as benign ulcers. People with varicose veins some-times get ulcers on their legs. This is because the blood in the skin is circulating too slowly.

If ulcers last for longer than a month, it may be because they are cancerous. These are known as malignant ulcers, and usually have hard edges. They can be dangerous if not discovered at once. The worst kind of ulcers are in the rectum. They cause pain constipation and bleeding, and are difficult to remove if left long.

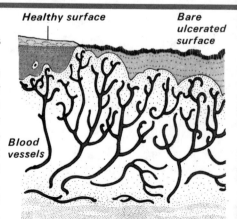

Healthy surface   Bare ulcerated surface

Blood vessels

ulcers?   **WHEN** was the iron lung invented?

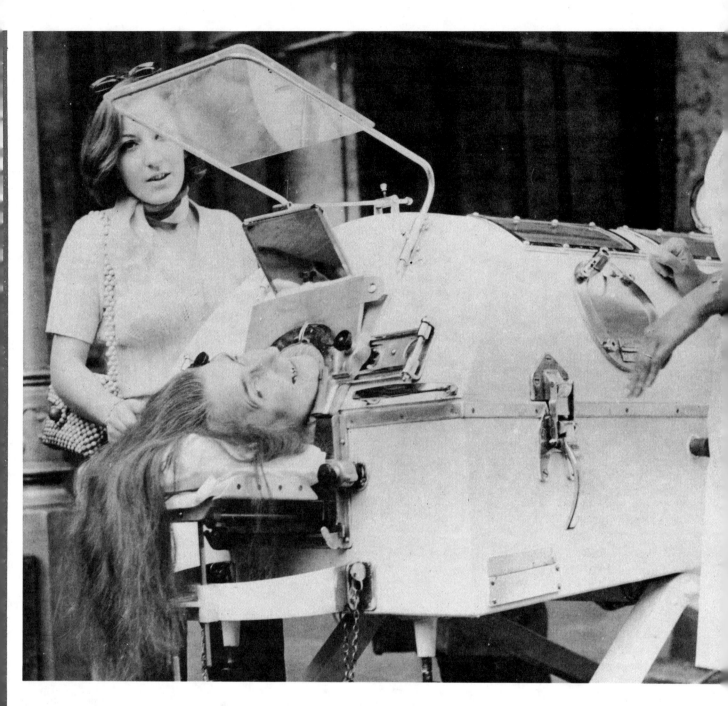

IRON LUNG

The iron lung was invented by Philip Drinker of Harvard, United States in 1929. This machine enables people whose lungs are paralysed by disease or accident to breathe. It does so by alternately reducing and increasing the air pressure round the patient's body. When the pressure is reduced, his chest expands and air streams into his lungs through the normal air passages in his head which is outside the machine. When the pressure is increased, the chest contracts and air is automatically expelled from the lungs.

This life-preserving apparatus is a tube on wheels in which the patient lies on a foam rubber bed with adjustable head and foot rests. It is operated by electricity, but has a safety device which gives a warning signal in the event of a power cut. The machine can then be operated by hand.

The cover on top of the iron lung can be opened to give access to the patient. When this is done, the patient's head is usually enclosed in a plastic dome in which the air pressure is alternately raised and lowered to enable breathing to continue.

168

WHY do we become sea-sick?   WHY do we have wax in

SEA-SICKNESS

We become sea-sick because our balancing organs, the labyrinthine portions of the inner ear, are disturbed by out-of-level movements, by sudden turning movements, and by sudden changes in movements in a straight line, either horizontal or vertical.

The three semicircular canals, filled with fluid are set on different planes in the ear. When sudden movements occur, each canal is affected differently. The nerve endings have no time to convey information to the brain so giddiness is likely to occur.

Nowadays, seasickness comes under the general heading of motion sickness, a name invented by Sir Frederick Banting in 1939, which includes the discomfort people feel while travelling in all kinds of vehicles.

Sea-sickness may vary with individuals from slight uneasiness to complete prostration. The symptoms are pallor, cold sweating, nausea and vomiting. People who have lost their ear labyrinths because of disease do not become seasick. Others become resistant to it. We say they develop their "sea-legs", but it would appear to be an adjustment of the central nervous system rather than the organs of balance. Some people find it helpful to keep their gaze firmly fixed on a steady object.

The red area in the diagram illustrates the semicircular canal, which is the major part of the inner ear. Its function is to help a person keep their balance through a delicate system of nerves. The sensation of sickness occurs when a conflict arises between the messages received by the brain through the nerves. The canals can just be seen on the right of the diagram below.

EAR WAX

Wax is deposited in our ear by special glands to prevent dust and similar foreign material from entering.

The part of the ear that we can see as a projecting flap on the side of the head is called the auricle. Leading from it is a short tunnel, the external auditory meatus or earhole, which is closed at its inner end by a thin membrane called the ear-drum, separating it from the inner ear.

This tunnel is lined with skin which, especially in men, carries hair and sebaceous glands, that is glands which produce an oily substance called sebum. The skin also contains specialized sweat glands (ceruminous glands), which secrete the brownish yellow wax.

Sometimes the glands secrete too much wax, and then it may collect in the external auditory meatus and deaden the hearing. As the ear is such a delicate instrument, the excess wax should be removed with a syringe by a doctor, although it can sometimes be softened by the application of warmed oil.

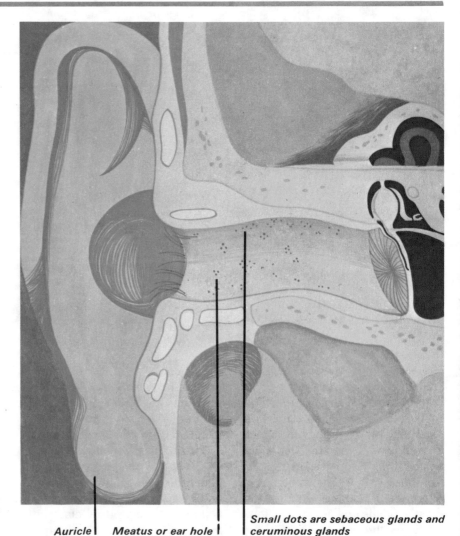

Auricle | Meatus or ear hole |

Small dots are sebaceous glands and ceruminous glands

our ears? **WHY** do babies cry so much?

BABY CRYING

Because a baby is unable to put its feelings and desires into words it communicates vocally with other people by crying. Crying in a baby is by no means only associated with unhappy experiences, such as being hungry or feeling unwell and tears do not normally appear unless the baby is really distressed.

Most mothers get to know the "vocabulary" of cries used by their baby and believe that they can tell with some accuracy what it wants from the nature of its cry. For instance, if a baby is hungry it will most likely continue to cry if picked up, but if it is crying from boredom it will stop crying when picked up or when moved to other, more interesting, surroundings.

Of course, it is not always possible to know why a baby cries. There are occasions when it is neither hungry, tired, uncomfortable, bored, frightened or wanting to be cuddled and a mother finds it impossible to quieten the baby's cries. Neither, it would seem, does the baby know what it wants and so it cries!

170

WHEN do people get hay fever?　　WHEN does the brain

HAY FEVER

People get hay fever when they are allergic to small particles existing in the air. The most common causes are the pollens of certain plants. Therefore the hay fever seasons vary greatly in different parts of the world according to the vegetation present.

In North America ragweed is the worst offender, causing a great deal of distress in late summer and early fall. In Britain, pollen from timothy grass causes hay fever in spring and early summer.

Other causes are dust, animal hairs, moults and, of course, hay itself. Particles of these substances inflame the membranes of the sufferers' eyes and nose.

Temporary relief is sometimes obtained from antihistamine tablets which prevent a certain amount of inflammation in the nose. The most effective treatment is immunization by a series of injections of pollen extract. Many sufferers get relief from this.

Timothy Grass.

Loading a haycart.

BRAIN DECLINE

The brain begins to show signs of decline after a certain proportion of the nerve cells or neurons of which it is formed have died. The age at which this happens varies.

A grown man has no more nerve cells than he did when he was born. These cells do not multiply as the body grows, as bone and skin cells do. Indeed, as a person grows older he has fewer and fewer nerve cells, because those destroyed are not replaced.

At the age of 70 or 80, as many as a quarter of the nerve cells may have died. That is the reason some old people cannot hear well or have poor memories. Yet others manage to retain their faculties and abilities until they are very old. Recent techniques have made it easier for scientists to study how our brains function, but there is still a great deal to discover.

BLOOD-LETTING

Blood-letting was a common form of medical treatment from before the time of Hippocrates (400 B.C.), the Greek "father of medicine" and was still much in fashion for various ailments a century ago. A bleeding-glass formed part of the symbol of the physician in ancient Egypt.

The old ideas about blood-letting, or phlebotomy, arose from a theory that certain body fluids, known as "humours", controlled a person's illnesses and decided his character. Today we call a person "sanguine" if he is optimistic or cheerful, but to a doctor in the Middle Ages a sanguine man was one in whom hot blood predominated over his other humours. A "phlegmatic" or stolid man was one who suffered from too much cold, wet phlegm.

For many illnesses it was considered that the best cure was to restore the balance of humours by relieving the body of diseased blood. Bleeding became almost a panacea, a cure-all. Monks were bled regularly to keep their minds from worldly thoughts. Madame de Maintenon (1635–1719) was said to have been bled to stop her from blushing.

Blood-letting was prescribed by doctors, but performed by barbers. The barbers took over as surgeons in 1163, when a papal decree forbade the clergy to shed blood, and they continued the profession for six centuries. On a barber's pole the red stripes represent the blood and the white ones the bandages, while the gilt knob at the end is the symbol of the basin in which the barber-surgeon caught the blood—or the lather.

In the 19th Century many people still had themselves bled regularly as a treatment for various illnesses, especially those due to over indulgence in food and drink. Frequently people did not from the disease but from the supposed cure. Blood-sucking worms called leeches were often used, being regarded as an essential part of a doctor's equipment.

Even today the withdrawal of blood is said to help certain conditions, and leeches are still used in some countries, particularly in the East.

PUBERTY

Puberty is a stage in human physical development when it begins to be possible to have or to father children. Puberty in girls is indicated by the development of breasts, and menstrual periods begin as the womb relines itself every month. Hair grows under the arms and on the pubis, as with boys. But girls change more rapidly than boys.

The glands of the body are very active. This sometimes results in acne and spots of various kinds which disappear naturally at the end of this stage.

In boys the most obvious sign of puberty is the breaking of the voice. The muscles develop, the penis grows and semen may be discharged.

The age at which puberty is begun is governed by climate and race. Doctors in some countries report that puberty there is being reached earlier in life. But they have not agreed on a conclusive reason for this.

Better living standards and a greatly improved and more nourishing diet are believed to be the main reasons for earlier development.

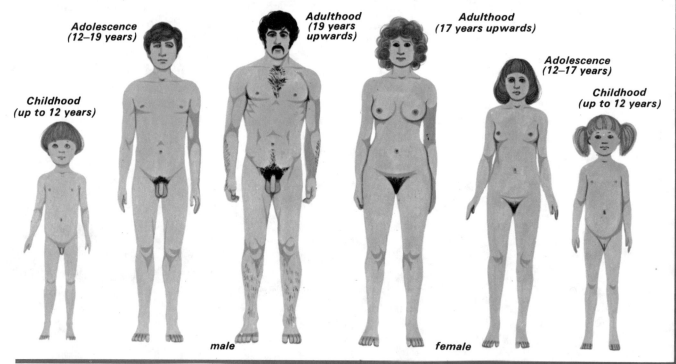

Childhood (up to 12 years)
Adolescence (12–19 years)
Adulthood (19 years upwards)
Adulthood (17 years upwards)
Adolescence (12–17 years)
Childhood (up to 12 years)
male   *female*

JAUNDICE

Jaundice is a condition in which the skin turns yellow because bile pigment is being deposited in its deeper layers.

Jaundice may arise from the breakdown of red cells in the bloodstream; because the bile passages from the liver are blocked so that the bile is re-absorbed into the bloodstream (as in gallstones) or because of disease of the liver cells, as in hepatitis or yellow fever.

Hepatitis and yellow fever cannot be cured by medicine alone. Careful nursing, plenty of rest, a protein-rich diet and time are needed for a complete cure.

HICCOUGH

Basically a hiccough is no more than a nervous reflex. Most hiccoughs are the result of shock or indigestion.

A hiccough is a catching of one's breath due to a sudden contraction of the diaphragm, the muscle separating the chest from the stomach. It appears to be a repeated but somehow ineffective and half-hearted attempt at vomiting.

Normally relief is brought about by deep, controlled breathing. This helps the sufferer to regain control of the diaphragm muscle. In very rare cases surgery is necessary to relieve the exhausted patient.

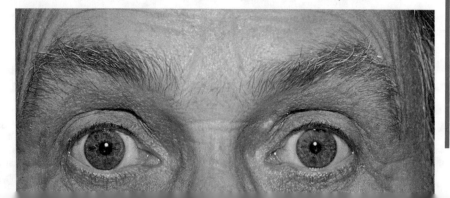

hiccough? WHAT is a hypochondriac?
you able to speak? WHAT makes eyes different colours?

HYPOCHONDRIAC

A hypochondriac is a person who has an exaggerated preoccupation with his own health. Hypochondriacs will find cause for alarm and evidence of disease or illness in the most insignificant symptoms.

To some extent we are all hypochondriacs. But too much concern can be a symptom of some mental disturbance.

There was a man called Samuel Jessup in Lincolnshire, England, who in 22 years swallowed nearly a quarter of a million pills. His record for one year was 50,000 pills. He is thought to have taken 40,000 bottles of medicine before his death at the age of 65.

SPEAK

Babies can babble almost as soon as they are born. Later, they learn the names of objects by copying their parents. Being able to speak sense, and producing sound from the mouth, are two different things. Over the centuries speech has become more complicated. We are able to say more, because man's intelligence has developed.

But our apparatus for producing the sound itself is still simple. The sound is made by means of vibrations of the vocal cords. These vocal cords are two bands of elastic tissue in the larynx, a valve guarding the entrance to the windpipe in the neck. When air is taken in and out, the vocal cords rub together and part again. Puffs of air escape rhythmically from the larynx into the cavity behind the mouth and the nasal passage, and then out by the mouth and nose, producing a tone. A man's vocal cords are longer than a woman's so his voice is lower. By moving our lips and tongue in different ways, we are able to pronounce the particular words we want to say.

The attempted speech sounds of babies of all nationalities sound very much the same. The actual sounds they ultimately fashion into words depends on the sounds they imitate from their parents.

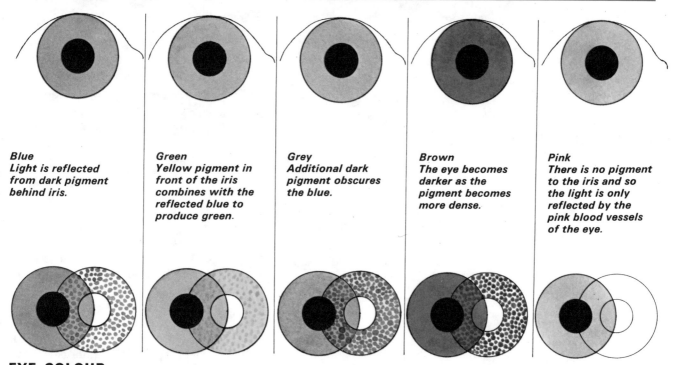

Blue
Light is reflected from dark pigment behind iris.

Green
Yellow pigment in front of the iris combines with the reflected blue to produce green.

Grey
Additional dark pigment obscures the blue.

Brown
The eye becomes darker as the pigment becomes more dense.

Pink
There is no pigment to the iris and so the light is only reflected by the pink blood vessels of the eye.

EYE COLOUR

What a baby is going to look like depends on the 46 genes in his body cells. Half of these genes he inherits from his mother, and half from his father. Some of these genes determine his eye colour.

All eyes contain blue cells, but some people have other coloured cells as well so that their eyes look green or grey or brown or hazel. Babies all have blue eyes because the other cells, if there are any, do not grow until the baby is about two. Sometimes people have eyes which are partly blue and partly brown or green. This is because half of their eye has only the usual blue colour, while the other half has some other colour as well.

When two blue-eyed people have a baby only blue cell-genes are being passed on, so all their babies will have blue eyes. But when one parent has brown eyes, a mixture of blue and brown eyes is being inherited, and the colour of the babies' eyes will depend on whether there are enough brown genes to dominate the blue ones. Even two brown-eyed parents may not have enough brown genes between them to have a brown-eyed baby.

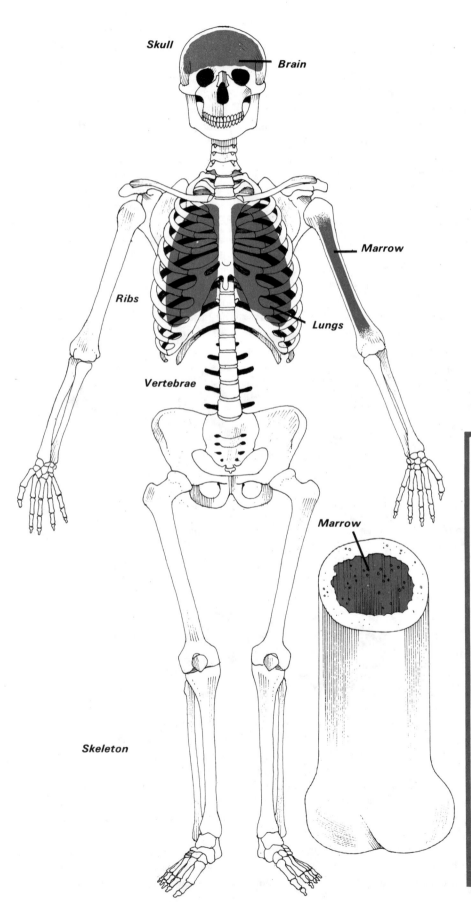

Skull

Brain

Marrow

Ribs

Lungs

Vertebrae

Marrow

Skeleton

BONES

We have bones to give us shape and support the body, to protect and contain the body's delicate vital organs, and to help us move about.

Bones are made from living tissue, composed of special cells which secrete around themselves hard material rich in calcium salts. In a child the bones are soft and cartilaginous (Cartilage is gristle, the elastic substance of the ear or nose). Bone-making, or ossification, is a gradual process. A baby has as many as 270 bones, but an adult only 206, for some bones grow together as they get older.

All bones have a middle cavity filled with a yellow or red fatty substance called bone marrow, the blood-making factory of the body, which also keeps bones light without reducing their strength.

WASHING HANDS

We should wash our hands before meals as a protection against infections. We live in a world full of germs (micro-organisms or microbes) and those which are dangerous to us prefer to live and multiply in organic material. So it is wise to remove as many as possible before coming into contact with food, which provides an ideal breeding ground.

Most of what are commonly called germs are harmless and some are even beneficial. Others, which are called pathogenic (disease producing), invade the body and live by feeding off body tissues.

Bacteria, which are tiny single-celled organisms, cause diseases such as diphtheria, cholera, leprosy, whooping-cough, typhoid fever, tetanus and scarlet fever, etc. Viruses are so small that scientists can see them only under immensely powerful electron microscopes. Yet they are responsible for an enormous range of human

before meals? **WHY** are wisdom teeth so called?
WHY do men have an "Adam's apple"?

The basic part of the skeleton is the spine, which has 33 bones or vertebrae. The spine carries the weight of the body, is extremely flexible and contains and protects the delicate spinal cord. The skull shelters the brain while the ribs protect the heart and lungs.

Bones fit together at the joints and are held firm by ligaments, which are made of tough tissue like cords or straps. Inside each joint is a thin membraneous bag which secretes a lubricant to make the joint move smoothly.

Some glide on one another, as the lower jaw slides on the upper. Some, such as the elbow and the knee, hinge on each other and others, like the hip, make a ball and socket joint. Bones are sometimes fused together and immovable, as in the five large, lower vertebrae called the sacrum.

diseases, from colds to rabies.

In hospitals, antisepsis and asepsis are used to maintain standards of hygiene. Antisepsis aims to destroy germs already present in a wound by applying chemicals. Asepsis keeps the germs away from wounds through the sterilization of the surgeon's hands, instruments, dressings and every other possible source of any infection.

The antiseptic system was introduced into surgery by Lord Lister (1827–1912), who worked on the discoveries of the French scientist Louis Pasteur (1822–95). At first he used pure carbolic acid, which was too strong and often damaged human tissue. Then better disinfectants were discovered.

The method of asepsis began with the sterilization of instruments by superheated steam. Penicillin and other new drugs have made the control of germs much less difficult.

WISDOM TEETH

Wisdom teeth are so called because they do not usually appear until the age of 18 to 20, by which time people were supposed to have become wiser. But surveys have shown that at least 19 per cent of the population of central Europe have failed to cut one or more wisdom teeth.

These teeth are the third molars and help in the process of grinding and chewing food. There should be four of them right at the back of the mouth next to eight other molars. Nearer the centre of the mouth are the eight bicuspids (or premolars) followed by the four cuspids (or canines) which are used for cutting and tearing food.

The eight front teeth, or incisors, are used mainly for biting and cutting, while the upper ones enable them to identify objects by nibbling.

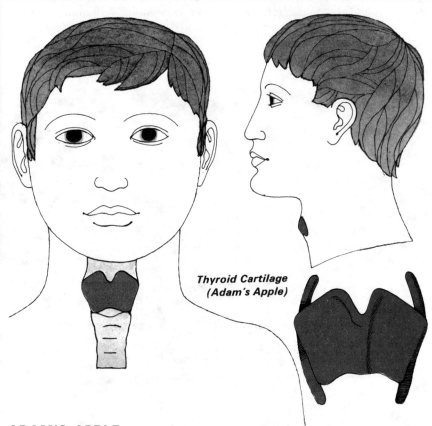

Thyroid Cartilage (Adam's Apple)

ADAM'S APPLE

An "Adam's apple" is to be found in both men and women and is part of the larynx, or "voice box", situated at the top of the windpipe in front of the neck. The larynx is a more or less rigid box created by a framework of cartilages connected by ligaments. The most important of these cartilages is the thyroid forming the prominence called "Adam's apple". The others are the cricoid cartilage and the epiglottis. The vocal cords are suspended in the larynx. These are two fibrous bands which are anchored fore and aft.

The chords are heavier and thicker in man than in woman, which makes the thyroid cartilage more pronounced. This led in olden times to the wrong belief that the "Adam's apple" was only to be found in man. The term itself arises from the ancient belief that it marks the place where the apple given by Eve to Adam got stuck!

CONGEALED BLOOD

Blood congeals when a part of the body is wounded. If it failed to congeal the injured person would die from loss of blood.

The congealing, or coagulation, of the blood, is the first step towards healing a wound. It closes the wound and builds a scaffold for new tissue by means of a chemical process in the plasma, the fluid part of the blood. In this process the platelets (small cellular bodies in the blood) produce thromboplastin. This changes fibronigin, a protein in the blood, into fibrin. Finally a spongy network of fibrin connects the edges of the wound and prevents the loss of any more blood cells. Often, a scab is formed over the wound as a protection.

ALBINOS

Albinos occur when there is an absence of yellow, red, brown or black pigments in an animal's eyes, skin, scales, feathers or hair. This peculiarity can be passed on from one generation to another. But albino animals do not often survive in the wild, because their normal colouring is designed to protect them against radiation or enemies.

In the case of human beings albinism is caused by the absence of the pigment melanin. It varies from complete albinism involving skin, hair and eyes, to localized albinism or spotting.

The complete human albino has milk-white skin and hair. The irises of his eyes appear pink, while his pupils take on a red hue from light reflected by blood in the unpigmented structures underneath. There is one complete albino for every 20,000 people.

do people stop growing?

WHEN does the body produce adrenalin?

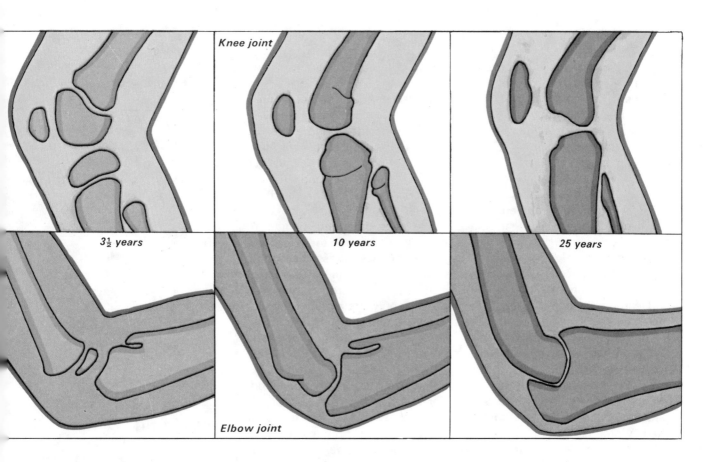

Knee joint

3½ years   *10 years*   *25 years*

Elbow joint

STOP GROWING

People stop growing when their bones do, and that is usually between 15 and 25 years of age.

Bones are made up of living tissue, composed of special cells which secrete round themselves material rich in calcium salts and as hard as marble. The formation of bone (ossification) is a complex process which usually begins in cartilage (gristle).

In a child the bone begins to form in the middle of the cartilage and spreads towards both ends, turning it all to bone with the exception of the tips. From these points the bone grows in length and so does the child. When the growing period is over the tips of the bones close by joining the main shaft of the bone.

Bones vary greatly in shape and size. Long ones act as levers. Flat ones are centres for muscle action. But each has a cavity containing bone marrow. Around this the bony substance is spongy in texture, becoming hard nearer the surface where the calcium is densest. On the surface of the bone is a special layer of fibrous tissue (the periosteum) which is rich in bone-building cells.

ADRENALIN

A person's body produces adrenalin when he is angry, frightened or challenged, or when he needs to be functioning at maximum efficiency to meet some sort of stress.

Adrenalin is a hormone, a substance which acts upon tissues and organs. It is secreted in the adrenal glands, which lie like a pair of pyramid-shaped caps, one on top of each kidney. Each gland has two parts, the outer shell, or cortex, and the inner core, or medulla. The adrenal hormones come from the medulla and are released into the bloodstream.

They stimulate the liver both to release its sugar and to speed up its manufacture for muscular action. They also contract blood vessels, diverting blood from the skin and raising the pressure at which it is pumped through the brain and lungs and muscles. The heart and pulse quicken, the breathing speeds up, the body heat rises and muscular fatigue is postponed. At the same time the ability of the blood to coagulate in the event of the person being wounded is increased.

This series of defence reactions occurs almost immediately. Adrenalin released by the glands is reinforced by more hormones produced at the sympathetic nerve ends. A hormone produced in the brain, called serotonin, stimulates the transmission of nerve impulses.

WHY do animals need oxygen? WHY is it harder to walk
WHY can you not breathe when you swallow?

OXYGEN

We must have oxygen to live. Every living animal cell needs oxygen for its vital metabolic activities (the process of converting fuel to energy), and every cell must also get rid of its carbon dioxide, the gaseous waste of its metabolism.

In the simple animal forms each cell gets oxygen for itself out of the surrounding environment and gives off carbon dioxide in the same way.

In the more highly developed organisms a special mechanism makes the exchange of oxygen and carbon dioxide on behalf of the entire body, and a carrier fetches the oxygen and carries away the waste for all the cells. The carrier is the blood in its circulatory system, and the special exchange mechanism is the respiratory system with the lungs as the key organs.

We have developed from water-dwelling creatures and still spend the first nine months from our conception lying in a bath of warm fluid, called the amnion,

receiving the oxygen necessary for the cells to do their work from our mothers.

In fact, we are still essentially water-dwellers, carrying our watery environment around within us, inside our skins. Because we have evolved lungs instead of gills we are able to live on land, but the air must be sufficiently rich in oxygen—about 20 per cent. Above 8,000 feet breathing begins to become difficult and the symptoms of mountain sickness, headache, nausea and vomiting may appear.

If we did nothing but rest, needing only a minimum supply of air, we would still need 300 quarts of oxygen every day. In a single minute of ordinary activity half a pint of oxygen has to be transferred from the air to the blood. For this half pint the lungs must process about five quarts of air every minute. An athlete running a race at sea level breathes as much as 120 quarts of air a minute to get the oxygen he needs to keep him going, which shows the importance of healthy lungs.

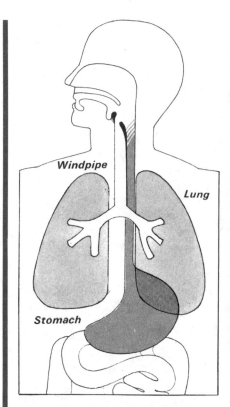

Windpipe

Lung

Stomach

BREATHING

You are not able to breathe when you swallow because your respiratory (breathing) system is closely linked to your alimentary (nourishing) system. In fact, both the air you breathe and the food you eat travel down the pharynx, a wide muscular tube situated behind the nose and mouth.

The air must reach the larynx or "voice box" on its way to the trachea (principal air passage) and the lungs, while the food has to go by way of the oesophagus (gullet) and stomach. Obviously, some kind of device must be used to prevent the two from becoming mixed up.

Swallowing temporarily interrupts breathing by closing the air passages while food is propelled from the mouth to the gullet and stomach. If a particle of food goes the wrong way the lungs respond immediately by trying to expel the food with a cough. Also some air does find its way to the stomach and can, if excessive, cause flatulence or "wind".

UP AND DOWNHILL

It is harder to walk uphill than downhill because you must lift the weight of your body and to do this requires greater energy than that needed for walking on the level. To create this greater energy your muscles require to give extra lift, your heart has more work to do to feed the blood cells and remove their waste matter and your lungs have more work to do to remove the carbon dioxide from your heart and replenish it with oxygen. That is why the steeper the climb and the more concentrated the effort, the more quickly you breathe. If you are out of condition you start to "pant" to gulp in extra oxygen. In comparison to the energy necessary for walking on a horizontal plane, the

total value of the extra energy needed for climbing is the weight of your body times the height you are to reach.

The steeper the incline of the hill, the quicker you use this extra energy. It is therefore harder for you to walk up a steep hill than a gentle one, although the energy used up in either case, where the height to be reached is the same, is identical.

When you walk downhill, very little energy is needed because the weight of your body carries you down the slope. Of course, this is the pull of gravity that is helping you down, in the same way that you have to overcome the force of gravity when you walk up a steep hill.

uphill than downhill? **WHY** do we have loops and whorls? **WHY** is it said "an apple a day keeps the doctor away"?

LOOPS AND WHORLS

The skin's surface is marked by a series of fine lines and ridges which deepen with age. The pattern on the tips of the fingers is peculiar to each individual and is used as a means of identification. In fact, the ridges of the skin on the lower finger joints and the toe prints are also unique, as are palm prints and foot prints. But fingerprints are by far the most simple and effective identification method.

Each ridge of the outer skin (epidermis) is dotted with sweat pores and anchored to the inner skin (dermis) by a double row of peglike objects called papillae. Injuries which affect the epidermis do not alter the ridge structure, and the original pattern returns in the new skin. If the papillae are destroyed, however, the ridges will disappear.

There are five general pattern shapes or types: the arch, the tented arch, the radial loop, the ulnar loop and the whorl. Whorls are usually circular or spiral, arches are shaped like a mound or hill and tented arches have a spike or "steeple" in the centre. Loops have concentric hairpin-shaped ridges and are divided into "radial" and "ulnar" to denote their slopes in relation to the radius and ulna bones of the forearm. Ulnar loops slope towards the little finger side of the hand and radial loops slope towards the thumb.

The pattern on our fingertips

Arches

Loops

Whorls

Composites

remains the same from birth until death, barring deliberate or accidental destruction of the papillae. Fingerprints therefore provide a positive identification, and the practice of fingerprinting (dactyloscopy) is an essential part of police procedure.

AN APPLE A DAY

The old rhyme, "An apple a day keeps the doctor away", was a polite way of saying that this would help to prevent constipation since it was believed that the juice of a raw apple aided the fermentation of undigested foods.

Although we might query such a sweeping statement these days, apples *are* good for you, but it is the dentist more than the doctor they keep away! Dentists will tell you that biting on a crisp crumbly apple is an effective method of removing food particles from between the teeth. Eating an apple after meals and cleaning your teeth night and morning is the best protection you can give them. To say this is not to deny the overall value of an apple and the presence of Vitamin C (ascorbic acid), as well as other minerals, lends some weight to the old adage. Some say you feel well in direct proportion to the amount of Vitamin C in your tissues.

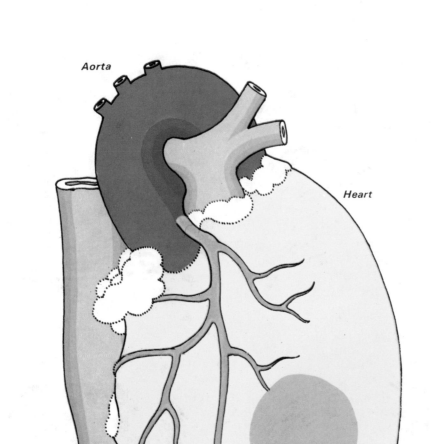

Aorta

Heart

Area of
dead tissue

Artery blocked by cholesterol deposit

GALL STONES

Gall stones occur most often in women who are overweight and have had children, for in the late stages of pregnancy cholesterol, which makes up a large proportion of gall stones, is deposited in the liver in such quantities that the organ may not be able to take it all in. The liver also stores sugar, but overweight people usually take more sugar than they need. So once again the liver may not be able to cope.

Lying on the underside of the liver, the gall bladder drains the bile, stores it and then conveys it to the intestines. However, if the stones block the tube called the bile duct, or the gall bladder itself, severe pain will result. This is felt under the ribs on the right radiating up to the right shoulder, and lasts until the stone causing it passes out of the bile duct. If the stone is wedged, cholangitis or infection of the gall bladder may occur.

The treatment of cholelithiasis, or gall stones, usually necessitates an operation, for there is no known drug that can dissolve the stones. Drugs can be given to ease the pain and to relax the smooth muscles of the ducts. Often small stones cause more trouble than large ones, which stay in the gall bladder without emerging to block the bile ducts.

HEART ATTACK

A heart attack, clinically known as coronary thrombosis, occurs when the arteries leading to the heart are blocked by contraction, a blood clot or cholestrol. In either case the heart will not receive enough blood for it to function properly.

As a general rule the possibility of a heart attack increases with age. But many victims of heart attacks recover completely and go on to lead normal, healthy lives.

Heavy smoking greatly increases the risk of a heart attack. Sudden bouts of exercise in older people can also be risky.

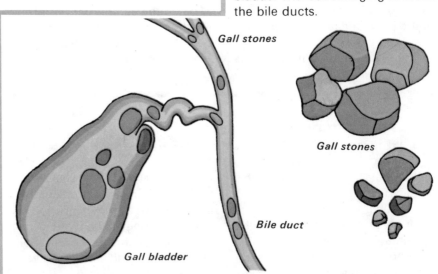

Gall stones

Gall stones

Bile duct

Gall bladder

expect gall stones to occur? WHEN was aspirin first used?

Meadowsweet, one of the many plants which contain the ingredients for aspirin.

ASPIRIN

Aspirin was first introduced into medicine in 1899 by H. Dreser of Germany. The word aspirin is actually the trade name for a preparation of acetylsalicylic acid.

During the last century many preparations of this acid were introduced for medical purposes, but Dreser was the first person to produce one which was considered satisfactory.

The main ingredients of aspirin occur naturally in the flowers, fruits, leaves and roots of many plants. South American Indians were familiar with the beneficial effects obtained from the bark of sweet birch and the leaves of the wintergreen shrub, which produce a medicine very similar to aspirin.

Aspirin is widely used for the treatment of headaches, sickness, colds and influenza. But too many aspirin tablets, instead of relieving the patient, may cause dizziness, headaches and sickness, and so they should be used carefully.

182

WHY do we grow old? WHY are young babies fed on milk?

This is a detail from Dürer's picture of his ageing mother.

BABIES AND MILK

Young babies are fed on milk because it is their natural food. The females of all backboned animals whose young are nourished with milk, store this fluid in their breasts, or mammae. The milk of each species of mammal is a complete food for its own young after birth.

Although the same ingredients are present in the milk of all mammals, the proportions differ a great deal. The ingredients are water, protein, fat and milk sugar. Milk protein contains all the essential amino-acids. The fat globules remain enclosed in a soft curd which milk forms in the stomachs of the young, so that digestion can proceed smoothly without the disturbance that fatty foods often cause.

Human babies, if not fed by their mothers, may be fed with pasteurized cow's milk, diluted and sweetened, or a liquid reconstituted from laboratory-prepared dried milk. In various countries babies have been fed on milk from the ass, goat, water-buffalo, reindeer, caribou, sheep, camel, llama, bitch and mare.

Other foods have been tried. In the 17th Century babies were fed on pap (bread cooked in water) or, as a French doctor advised, bread cooked in beer! After about four or five months human babies are gradually weaned from an exclusive diet of milk and given other forms of nourishment.

GROWING OLD

Scientists have evolved three main theories to explain why we grow old. The first concerns the loss of cells or of irreplaceable parts. Brain cells undoubtedly die off in their hundreds of thousands and cannot be manufactured again after a very infantile stage in human life.

However, this cannot be the complete explanation because people who suffer heavy damage to brain and body do not necessarily show the effects of ageing. Moreover, animals have totally different ageing rates, but suffer cell destruction at similar speeds.

A second theory concerns mutations or alterations. A dividing cell does not always divide correctly. All kinds of errors may creep in, aided by natural radiation. Sometimes the mutated cells may be harmful or put out of commission, with powerful effects on other cells, such as the endocrine glands or constituents of the blood. In the 1960s this theory was supported by the discovery that 10 per cent of the cells of very old women had lost an X chromosome.

A third explanation, which is not now so widely believed, is concerned with the accumulation of unwanted chemicals. It is suggested that some vital substances can only be replaced at cell division and that a general decline in the rate of cell division could lead either to a lack of needed substances or an excess of unwanted ones.

WHY do we vaccinate against smallpox?

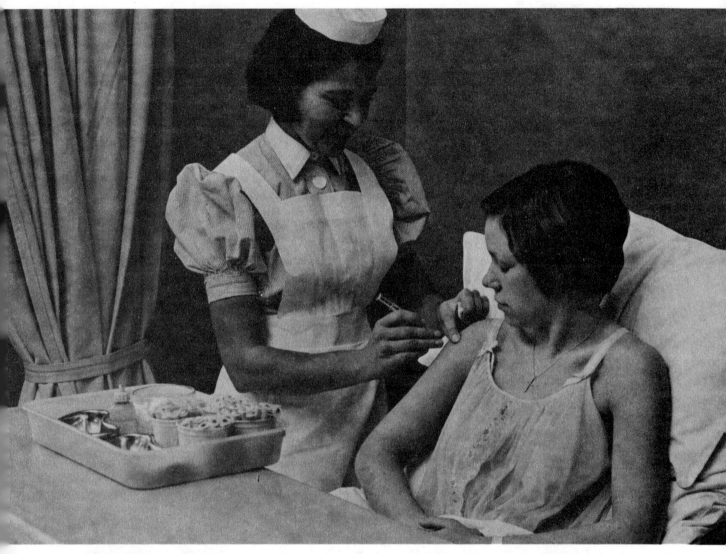

VACCINATION

We vaccinate against smallpox to allow the body to develop antibodies which will make it more or less immune to attack from the disease. In fact, by vaccination or inoculation we mean that a person is injected with the organism that causes the disease or its toxin (poison). This organism is modified physically or chemically, so that, without doing any damage, it triggers the body's immunizing defences. We call these modified cultures vaccines.

Vaccination against smallpox was first carried out in the East. Poisonous material taken from the blisters of a mild case of smallpox was inserted into the arm of the person to be protected. This produced a mild case of smallpox and enabled the body to manufacture the antibodies.

Vaccination was introduced into England in 1721 by Lady Mary Wortley Montagu, wife of the British ambassador to Turkey, who had her own children inoculated at Constantinople. However, this method could result in a severe or fatal attack of the disease.

Dr. Edward Jenner took the next step in 1796 when he inoculated a boy named James Phipps with poisonous matter from the arm of Sarah Nelmes, a dairymaid suffering from cowpox (a mild disease closely allied to smallpox).

Some weeks later he inoculated James Phipps with smallpox, but the boy did not contract the disease.

In 1798 Jenner published a book on his experiments, and the practice of vaccination spread throughout the world. The principle has been applied to many diseases. Babies and young children are particularly susceptible to complications from whooping cough and diphtheria, so they are immunized soon after birth. Poliomyelitis (infantile paralysis), cholera, yellow fever, and typhoid are all dangerous diseases which inoculation has been able to control.

WHAT is the umbilical cord? WHAT is hair for? WHAT makes

UMBILICAL CORD

Inside the womb of a pregnant woman or animal a placenta is formed, through which the unborn baby is nourished. The baby is connected to the placenta by the umbilical cord, which is joined to the unborn child at the navel.

The umbilical cord is the baby's lifeline. Everything the child needs to survive will pass through it— air, blood and nourishment. At most it is no more than an inch wide and, perhaps, only a foot long.

Once the baby is born the placenta and all other organs, which serve a purpose only during pregnancy, will be discarded.

The umbilical cord will be cut with scissors a few inches away from the newborn baby's stomach. This is quite painless because the umbilical cord has no nerves. The baby will now breathe on its own.

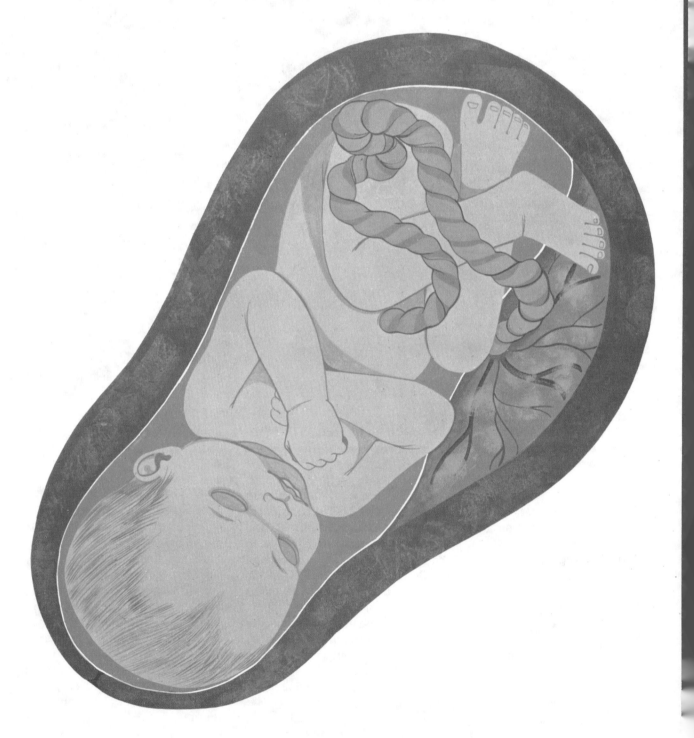

us sneeze? **WHAT** is the pituitary gland?

WHAT gives you flat feet?

HAIR

Hair has several functions. First, it keeps us warm. This is no longer as important as it was in the days of our Stone Age ancestors, who were worse off for clothes and heating, but a good deal hairier. There are, in fact, few areas of the body—the palms of the hands and the soles of the feet—which are not covered with fine hair.

A second function of hair is to protect delicate parts. Eyelashes, for instance, prevent dust entering the sensitive eye.

In the case of animals hair can act as camouflage. By matching the background, an animal's coat helps it to avoid enemies. The northern hare even grows a white coat in winter as camouflage in the snow.

The hair of both animals and human beings also serves to attract mates. People wear wigs and go to hairdressers to make themselves attractive to others.

But unlike many animals, we have no special sensory hairs helping us to feel our way around. A cat's whiskers are as sensitive as radio aerials. Being wider than the widest part of its body, they also help it tell whether it can get through a narrow space, even when it is dark.

A Skin surface
B Old hair
C New hair

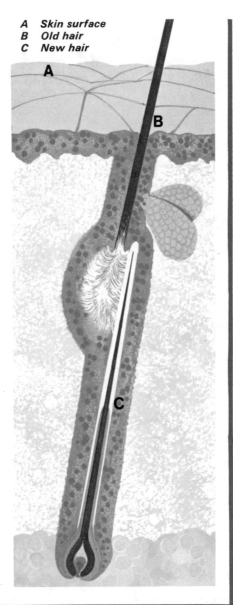

PITUITARY GLAND

The pituitary gland is a small structure about the size of a pea which is attached to the base of the brain. It consists of four parts and is the most important gland in the body for it controls the hormone output of all the other ductless glands, including the thyroid and sex glands.

The pituitary hangs by a little stalk just behind the nasal passage and was named after the Latin word for "nasal secretion" by the Belgian Andreas Vesalius (1514–1564), known as the "father of anatomy", who mistakenly believed that it discharged mucus into the nose.

If the pituitary is not functioning properly, gigantism or dwarfism may result. Premature old age, extreme thinness, extreme fatness and disturbances in sexual development are other disorders which may occur.

FLAT FEET

When you make wet footprints on the bathroom floor, you will see that there are blank patches in the middle between the toe marks and the heel marks. This is because the middle parts of the feet are raised off the ground by two sets of muscles, called the tibial and the peronal muscles which make the arches of the feet. If these muscles weaken, the feet spread out and the arches sink to the ground. The footprints are flat, with no gaps in the middle. This is called having flat feet, or fallen arches.

Sometimes people get flat feet because their jobs keep them standing around too much. Policemen, waitresses and nurses often suffer from flat feet.

The cure is exercise which tightens up the muscles again. Supports to be put inside shoes are worse than useless. They make the muscles slacken, weaker instead of stronger.

SNEEZE

A sneeze occurs when the white tissue or lining in our nose—called a membrane—gets inflamed or irritated. Our body reacts by letting out air as quickly as possible through the nose and mouth in an attempt to get rid of whatever is causing the irritation.

People used to make themselves sneeze by putting snuff, a kind of finely-ground tobacco, into their nostrils. This would tickle the membrane in the nose. Sneezing was thought to be healthy because it helped to get rid of germs.

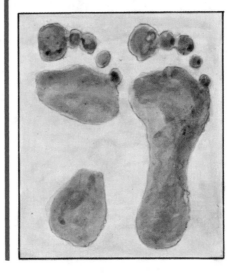

WHEN was penicillin discovered? WHEN was the first
WHEN can electric shocks help to cure people?

PENICILLIN

Penicillin was discovered in 1929 by Sir Alexander Fleming, then a professor and lecturer at the Royal College of Surgeons in London. He wanted to find a substance which would kill bacteria but would not also poison the tissues of the patient's body.

Fleming discovered penicillin by accident while he was researching into influenza. He was examining a staphylococcus, a kind of germ, when he noticed that it had created a bacteria-free circle of mould around itself. When he experimented further, he discovered that this liquid mould, which he named penicillin, prevented further growth of the staphylococcus germ even when diluted and made 80 times weaker. Also, penicillin had no poisonous effect on the human cells.

Sir Alexander Fleming published his results in the *Journal of Experimental Pathology* in 1929.

For some time it was thought that there was only one penicillin, but later it was discovered that the mould could produce four penicillins. They were distinguished by the letters F, G, X and K. The best known is penicillin G, which came into widespread use after the Second World War.

HEART TRANSPLANT

The first human heart transplant took place on December 3, 1967 at Groote Schuur Hospital, Cape Town, South Africa. A team of 20 surgeons, headed by Dr Christiaan Barnard, operated on Louis Washkansky, aged 55, using the heart of a 24-year-old donor, Denise Ann Darvall, who had been killed in a road accident.

Both the donor and the recipient were of the same blood group and the heart was kept in cooled oxygenated blood for more than three hours before transplantation. The operation took five hours and the new heart was only half the size of Washkansky's. The operation itself was a success, and within a few days Washkansky was sitting up, eating and talking happily. The doctors were anxious about transplant rejection by the body and also post-operative infection which, in fact, did kill Washkansky within a month of the transplant.

In January 1968 a second transplant was carried out on Philip Blaiberg, a 58-year-old dentist, who subsequently overcame a severe liver infection and lung condition, thought to be the result of his body trying to reject the new heart. By the end of 1968 more than 100 transplants had been carried out in the United States, Britain, France, India, South America, Canada, Czechoslovakia and Israel. More than 40 patients survived. Blaiberg remained alive until August 17, 1969 and other patients survived for up to two and a half years, but the number of operations declined. From December 1970 to May 1971 only six operations were performed. Caution took the place of optimism.

human heart transplant?
WHEN were antiseptics first used?

ELECTRIC SHOCKS

Electric shock treatment, or electro-convulsive therapy, is sometimes used with people suffering from mental illnesses in which severe depression is the main symptom.

It was first used in 1938 by U. Cerletti and L. Bini in Rome, and was recommended for the treatment of manic-depression and schizophrenia (literally, "splitting of the mind").

The technique of electrocon-vulsive therapy is to place two electrodes on the temples of the patient and pass alternating cur-rents through his head. This causes him to lose consciousness im-mediately and is followed by a convulsion of the body. It is claimed that the patient is much calmer and better-balanced when he regains consciousness. In general, treatment is given three times a week for periods from two to six weeks. Some acutely dis-turbed patients, however, have been given as many as two or three treatments in a day.

This treatment has become less common since the discovery of tranquillizing drugs which reduce feelings of anxiety and agitation without too many side-effects.

Weak electrical shocks are also used in physiotherapy to stimulate muscles wasted by disease.

ANTISEPTICS

Antiseptics were first used in 1865 by a surgeon called Joseph Lister, in London. He was helped by his knowledge of the work of Louis Pasteur, a French doctor, who had discovered that putrefaction (rot-ting), was caused by live bacteria and not by a chemical process.

Lister, shown above, thought that bacteria could be destroyed before they entered a wound and poisoned it. He first tried the treat-ment on a compound fracture. Carbolic acid was applied to the wound in the hope that this would provide a barrier against the germs in the atmosphere. The experi-ment was successful and led to a great advance in surgery. Various kinds of antiseptics came into general use to combat bacteria.

RESEMBLING PARENTS

We resemble our parents because of a complex of biological processes which we call heredity. Parents and children tend to be similar in many characteristics—structural, physiological and psychological. However, the young are not exact duplicates of their parents and usually differ in many traits. This difference we call variation.

The science of the study of heredity is called genetics, and the most famous name connected with it is that of Gregor Johann Mendel (1822–1884), an Austrian monk whose discoveries laid the foundation of the science.

Mendel studied plants, especially the garden pea, and showed that inherited characteristics were the result of paired elementary units of heredity, which we now call genes. These he symbolized by letters. A characteristic of one parent, such as tallness, which appeared in the progeny to the exclusion of another, was said to be dominant. A characteristic which tended not to reappear was called recessive.

Later studies have shown that the genes are carried by structures called chromosomes. The human body begins with the union of two sex cells, and the body of a new-born infant has some 200,000 million cells. These cells arise through the division of other cells. When they divide, their nuclei (or tiny central bodies) divide also by a remarkable process called mitosis.

During mitosis the nuclei resolve themselves into structures called chromosomes, which divide lengthwise. All body cells have true copies of all chromosomes that were present in the fertilized egg from which the body developed.

This detail from the famous painting by Goya shows the striking resemblance of the family to Charles IV of Spain.

TEMPERATURE

The body temperature of a human being is an indication of his physical condition, so that an abnormally high or low temperature is generally a sign that something is wrong.

The normal temperature is usually given as 36·9°C. (98·4°F.), but as the body temperature varies throughout the day, anything between 36·9°C. (or lower) and 37·5°C. (or 99·5°F.) may be taken, for all practical purposes, as normal.

For instance, the temperature rises after a large meal, during hot weather and after violent exercise. Your temperature is at its lowest at night when you are asleep.

Control of body temperature is exercised by a centre in the brain which ensures that a balance exists between heat production and heat loss. A raised temperature is often the sign of bacterial or virus infection. It may be due to heatstroke, to certain types of brain injury or disease or to shock.

A very high temperature, or fever, may begin with a "rigor" (an attack of shivering and cold), in which the whole body may tremble uncontrollably and the teeth chatter. Although at this stage the skin feels cold and clammy, the temperature within the body is raised. Soon the skin becomes hot and dry, pulse and breathing rate are speeded up and there is a feeling of exhaustion, aching muscles, headache, thirst and perhaps delirium and loss of the sense of time.

Finally this stage is succeeded by profuse sweating and a gradual relief of the symptoms.

your temperature if he thinks you are unwell?

190

WHAT is skin?   WHAT is a cold?   WHAT is the fontanelle?

SKIN

Apart from protecting our body, skin is a vital element in our physical make-up and well-being. It helps to regularize our body temperature and enables us to sweat. Thanks to the thousands of different nerve endings in our skin we can sense touch, pain, cold, heat and many other subtle sensations. In a minor way we can also get rid of certain waste substances through our skin.

In man the skin varies considerably in thickness according to the area of the body covered. For example, the skin of our eyelids is about one twenty-fifth of an inch or less than 1 mm, whereas on our palms and on the soles of our feet it reaches a thickness of about an eighth of an inch or 3 mm. Human skin has five layers —the basal cell layer, the stratum spinosum (which is several cells thick), the stratum granulosum, the stratum lucidum and, finally, the surface layer which is called the stratum corneum. This can consist of as many as 20 layers of cells but the cells nearest the surface tend to flake off.

Skin is practically waterproof and this quality allows the fluid "body" to live and function in dry air. There are many varieties of skin diseases and the skin also reflects in the form of rashes diseases that attack the body— chicken pox, measles and scarlet fever are examples.

One of the most obvious attributes of skin is its capacity to support hair growth but in man hair on the skin has little practical function or purpose. Hair is continually shed and replaced. The average life-span of the soft, downy hairs is only a few months while the long tougher hairs on the scalp can have a life of several years. Most of the human body's skin is actually covered by hair although for the most part the hair is so fine that we cannot see it without a magnifying glass. However, human beings do not grow hair on the soles of their feet or on the palms of their hands.

In one sense we can be said to register emotions through our skins, since any emotional stimulation can produce perspiration of the skin on the hands, feet and under the armpits.

One of the main functions of skin is to act as an early warning system to the rest of the body about outside conditions.

Skin remains taut and supple during most of our lives, but in old age, when the muscles begin to slacken, it loses this elasticity.

COLD

A cold is caused by a little organism called a virus. Colds most often occur in early autumn, midwinter, or early spring. The mucous membranes lining the nose and the breathing passages become inflamed.

No one really knows how to prevent colds. The virus (the poison that carries colds) is a difficult subject for medical scientists to study.

Colds are usually caught through being with people who already have them. The quickest way of catching a cold is through someone else's sneeze. One person with a cold in a crowded subway may well give it to many other people. So, when you do have a cold, it is kinder to stay away from other people as much as possible.

Getting wet or chilled does not directly give you a cold. But you are in a weaker state than usual, and more likely to catch a cold, if there is one going around.

FONTANELLE

The fontanelle is a gap filled with membrane in the skull of a baby. When it is born a baby's skull is not completely closed and there are some spaces between the bones. The largest is in the front of the head where, at the meeting-point of the frontal bone and the two parietal bones which form the side walls of the skull, there is at birth a gap about one square inch in size. It is called the anterior fontanelle and through it, if you put your hand very carefully there, you can feel the pulsation of the baby's brain.

By the time the baby is eighteen months old the fontanelle has normally closed and, if it has not, some delay in development may be the cause. It may bulge if the baby is ill or feverish or become depressed or sunken if the child is dehydrated. The name comes from an old French word meaning "little fountain".

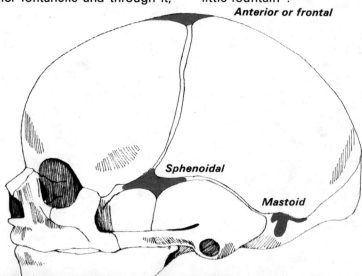

Anterior or frontal

Sphenoidal

Mastoid

WHAT is the uvula? WHAT makes you feel dizzy? WHAT is a virus?

UVULA

The uvula is a small mass of muscle covered by mucous membrane that hangs down from the middle of the soft palate at the back of the mouth. The soft palate is a movable fold of tissue and, with the hard palate, forms the roof of the mouth.

The word uvula comes from the Latin word "uva" or grape and the word describes its shape very well. Occasionally, if the throat is infected or relaxed, the uvula may become elongated, but it is never cut, since it recovers its proper size as the condition of the throat improves.

In certain animals, to whom the sense of smell is very important indeed, the uvula is joined to the epiglottis, a leaf-like piece of cartilage which stands upright between the tongue and the entrance to the larynx. This means that the animal is forced always to breathe through its nose. In man there is a gap between the two and consequently food may sometimes accidentally pass into the larynx and windpipe, causing great discomfort. Choking like this can even cause death.

DIZZY

Dizziness most commonly occurs when a person who has been moving around with speed stops suddenly. The sensitive liquid in the inner ear, which mainly controls balance, continues to move around for a time after the body has stopped. So the surroundings appear to be still in motion. However, it takes only a few seconds, for the fluid, and balance, to settle.

This sensation, which is also called vertigo, may also occur to someone looking down from a height or on board ship. Here the cause is probably not so much physical as a nervous reaction which affects the fluid in the inner ear.

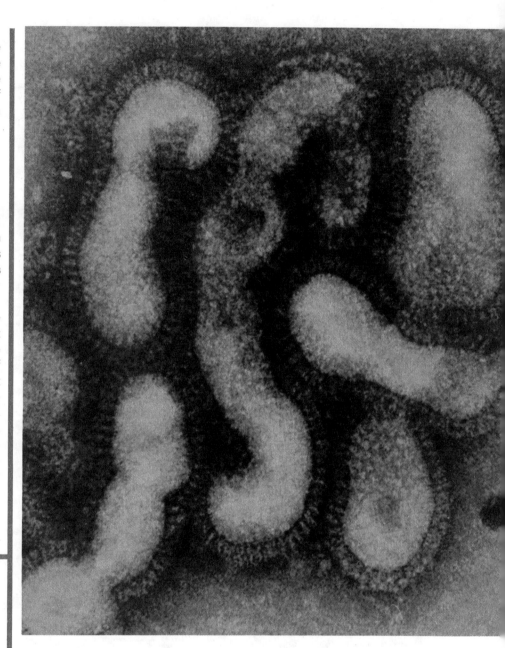

The photograph above shows an influenza virus greatly magnified.

VIRUS

A virus is smaller than the smallest bacteria visible through an ordinary microscope. Viruses can multiply only within the living cells of humans, animals or plants. They are responsible for a wide range of infectious diseases and illnesses.

Viruses can be investigated with the help of the electron microscope, and their measurements recorded. The virus responsible for foot and mouth disease in animals measures about one-millionth of an inch. The smallpox virus is about ten times as large.

Diseases caused by viruses vary greatly in danger and intensity from minor infections such as colds to extremely serious epidemic diseases. Either way, it is well worth taking careful precautions against catching a virus.

WHEN is a Caesarean operation necessary?
WHEN were contact lenses

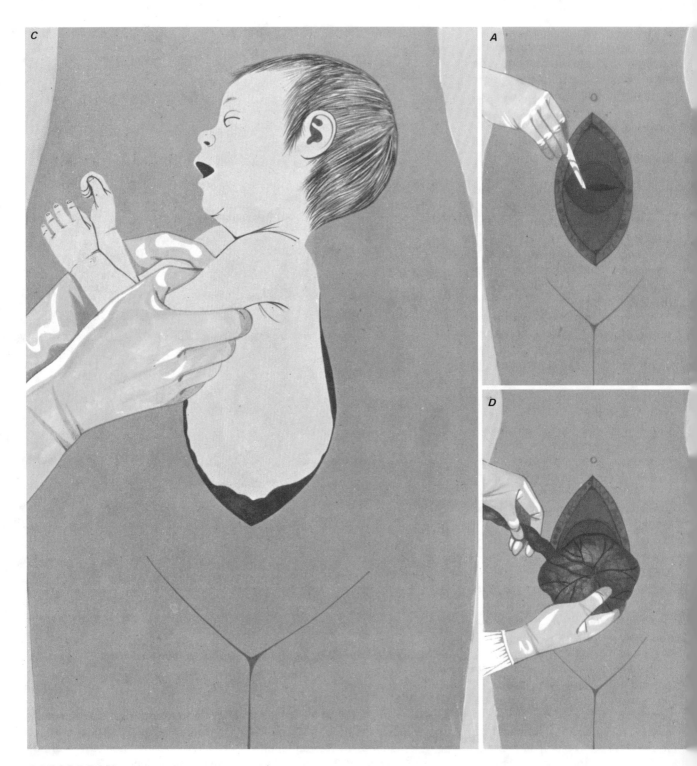

CAESAREAN

A Caesarean operation is necessary for the surgical delivery of a baby when a natural childbirth is difficult or impossible. The surgeon makes an incision into the mother's abdomen and delivers the baby through the wall of the womb.

The operation owes its name to the belief that Julius Caesar was born by this means. Deliveries of this kind were certainly known in ancient times. They are even mentioned in the Jewish law book, the Talmud, which dates back some two thousand years.

In the 19th Century, three-quarters of those who underwent such an operation died due to primitive techniques. Now they are nearly always completely successful.

invented? WHEN is it dangerous for a male to have mumps?

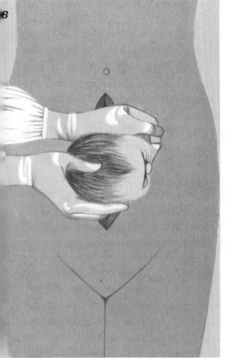

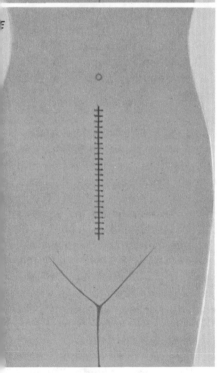

This is one kind of Caesarean operation A An incision is made in the abdomen B The baby's head is helped out first C Then the body is eased out D The placenta, or after-birth, is taken away E The abdomen is sewn up again

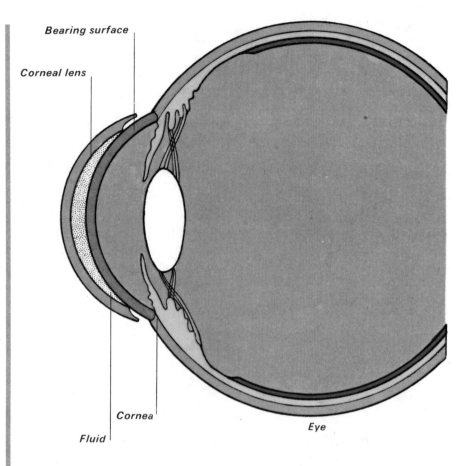

Bearing surface

Corneal lens

Cornea

Fluid

Eye

CONTACT LENSES

The first contact lenses were made by A. E. Fick in 1887, but were not successful. During the early part of this century opticians tried to produce extremely thin shell-like lenses to fit closely over the eye. An impression was taken of the eye and a glass shell made which, with a suitable fluid under it, covered most of the eye. After 1938, plastic was used instead of glass, and about 1950 smaller lenses were introduced which covered only the cornea and floated on a layer of tears. These lenses, only 7 to 11 millimetres in diameter and 0·1 to 1 mm thick can usually be worn all day without being removed.

Besides being invisible, contact lenses provide a much wider field of vision than spectacles. They are more practical for use in active sports because they are not easily lost or broken, and they can be tinted for use as sunglasses. But contact lenses are not effective in all cases of eye trouble. They are also expensive, and some people find difficulty in learning to wear them.

As research continues, even smaller and more flexible lenses are being developed.

MUMPS IN MALES

Mumps can be dangerous for a male after the age of puberty, because the illness can affect the testicles and, in severe cases, cause sterility.

Mumps is a virus infection and it is rare to have more than one attack. The parotid glands in the neck swell and opening or shutting the mouth can be painful. It is possible that only one side of the neck is affected.

WHERE is your funny bone? WHERE does the body store WHERE are the Islets of Langerhans?

FUNNY BONE

Your funny bone is in your arm. It is the long, almost straight bone which extends from your shoulder to your elbow. At the top end it is attached to your scapula, or shoulder blade. At the elbow it is attached to the two bones in your lower arm which are called the radius and the ulna, which in turn are attached to your wrist and hand.

The funny bone carries the very strong biceps muscles—the ones which bulge up on the top of your arm when you bend your elbow and bring your hand up to your shoulder. The bone is grooved to carry the nerves to your hand. These nerves convey messages to and from your brain so that you can control your hand and use it to feel things.

Some people think your funny bone is so called because, when you knock a particular part of your elbow, you get a funny, tingling sensation. The real reason is because the medical name for this bone is the humerus—and since it is pronounced "humorous", the description of "funny bone" has now passed into universal use.

THE BODY'S ENERGY

Certain cells of the body store surplus food in the form of fat or animal starch. This is released from storage when there is not enough food in the blood to supply the energy demands of the body.

Few of the things we eat can be used directly by the body cells. They must be changed chemically before they can supply the energy required. This is called digestion and is carried out in the stomach and in the small intestine, from where this digested food must be transported to the cells.

Now the food, in the form of digested sugars, proteins, and starches dissolved in water, passes into the blood system where, as blood, it can circulate through the body in less than one minute. Once the food is in the blood stream it is soon delivered to all the cells of the body by means of the red corpuscles in the blood.

It is when this supply falls low that the energy stores come into action.

ISLETS OF LANGERHANS

These islets are not to be found in an atlas but are located in the human pancreas, which manufactures juices to aid the digestion of fats and continues the work of the saliva and gastric juices.

Langerhans was a German anatomist (1847-88) who gave his name to two other parts of the body. He discovered cells in the epidermis called Langerhans Cells and also the Langerhans Layer which is a layer of the skin.

There are many groups of cells without ducts distributed through the pancreas. But the importance of the Islets of Langerhans is that their beta cells are a source of insulin. It is damage to or removal of the Islets of Langerhans that leads to pancreatic diabetes. Insulin, which is a protein, is synthesized by the beta cells.

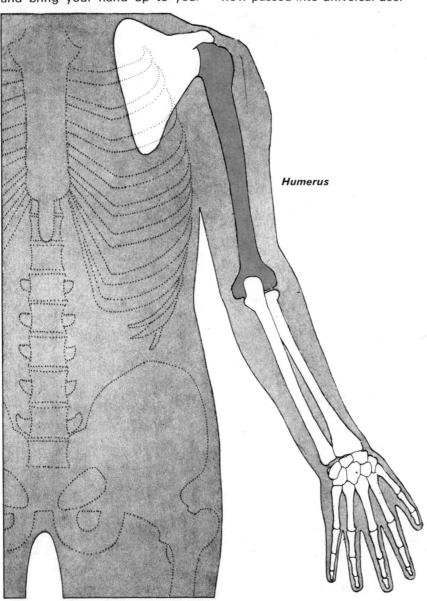

Humerus

its energy?   WHERE do teeth come from?
WHERE are your sweat glands?

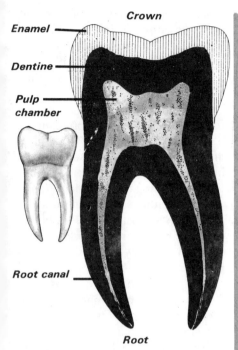

Crown

Enamel

Dentine

Pulp chamber

Root canal

Root

TEETH

Teeth are formed from specialized cells which produce the three parts of the tooth—root, neck, and crown. The outer coating of the crown is made of hard enamel. This covers the dentine which forms most of the bony framework of the teeth. Channels in the dentine contain blood vessels and nerves which make up the inner-most part of the tooth, the dental pulp.

Most of the higher animals, including man, are born without teeth. They develop two sets, called the milk teeth and the permanent teeth.

A human mouth contains 32 teeth. Their function is to cut, tear, and grind food, and they are specialized for this. So in each jaw there are four incisors (for biting), two canines (for holding or tearing), four bicuspids (chewing teeth with a cutting edge), and six molars (for grinding).

"Wisdom" teeth, the largest of all, are situated at the back of the jaw, and may not arrive until we are grown up.

SWEAT GLANDS

Sweat glands, of which everybody has approximately two million, are distributed all over the body on the skin surface. They are not, however, distributed evenly. The palms of our hands and the soles of our feet may have as many as 2,500 sweat glands per square inch, whereas on our backs there may be as few as 500 per square inch.

Each gland breaks the skin surface in the form of a sweat pore. These pores are too small to be visible to the naked eye, except on the palms and soles, where there are so many that they just become visible.

In some diseases nerve funtion is lost in certain areas of the body, and these areas also lose the power to sweat. Sweat is a solution of about 99 per cent water with a little sodium chloride (common salt). The body can produce from zero to 2,000 grammes of this substance every hour and even more in strenuous activities.

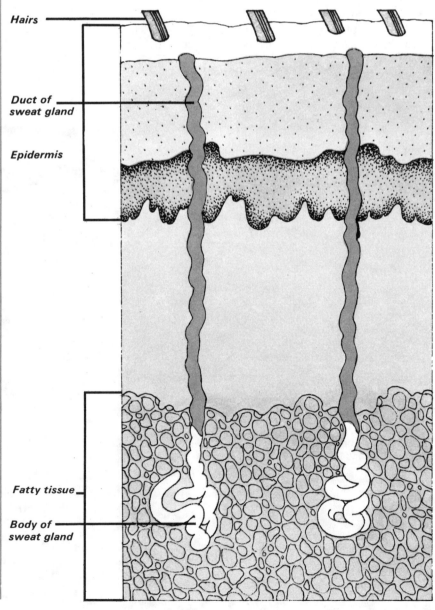

Hairs

Duct of sweat gland

Epidermis

Fatty tissue

Body of sweat gland

Geography and the Earth

anization. The first archeological surveys began in 1960 and U.N.E.S.C.O's response grew into what was to become the biggest archaeological rescue operation in history.

Abu Simbel consists of three temples of Rameses II built more than 3,000 years ago. The most important and impressive temple included four gigantic seated statues of the king, each 65 feet high. By 1968 these four enormous monuments to Rameses had been cut out of the rock and reconstructed, exactly as they were, high up on a cliff.

Six more great statues of Rameses and his queen (about 30 feet high) were also excavated and moved to a dry sanctuary above the old river bed, along with everything else that could be salvaged.

ABU SIMBEL

When construction began on the High Dam at Aswan, in southern Egypt, it was realized that the temples of Abu Simbel would be completely submerged as the waters of the Nile rose behind the dam to create a much needed reservoir.

In 1959 Egypt, and its southern neighbour Sudan appealed for help to the United Nations Educational, Scientific and Cultural Org-

Mercator's projection important to geographers?

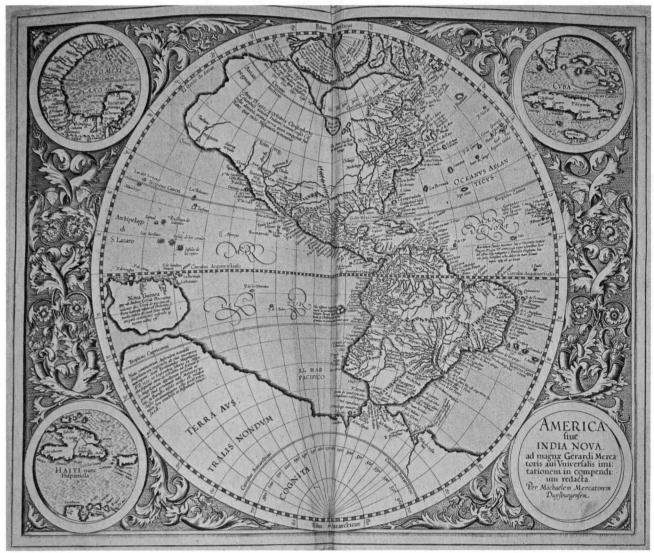

Mercator's original projection

MERCATOR

Gerardus Mercator's (1512–94) projection is important to geographers because, unlike other projections, a straight line drawn on it gives a true compass bearing.

A projection is simply a means of transferring a round section of the world on to a flat sheet of paper. This is more easily said than done, for, no matter how hard you try, you cannot do it without altering the shapes or sizes of countries or the distances between them.

You can try this for yourself. Draw a rough map of the world on an orange with a felt tip pen, then cut the orange into sections. When you have eaten the orange, try to arrange the curved pieces of peel into a flat map. You can see that if the lands by the Equator, or the widest parts of the orange peel, are touching, there are large gaps to the north and south. To make a map in which there are no gaps, it is necessary to stretch these lands in the north and south – and this is just what Mercator did.

The history of projections goes back to the Greeks who realized as long ago as 500 B.C. that the world was round. Eratosthenes, a Greek who lived at Alexandria in the Second Century B.C. even calculated the circumference of the world to be 25,000 miles. His estimate was only a little more than the correct distance which is 24,901·8 miles at the Equator.

Mercator's projection increases the distances between the lines of latitude (the lines parallel to the Equator) as one moves further north or south. While this makes the map useful for navigation, it also gives people many wrong ideas about the world. It makes some countries, such as Greenland, appear too large. The areas of land at the Equator on Mercator's projection are correct. But those at 45° North or South are doubled, and those at 75° are nearly 16 times too large.

WHERE is Fingal's Cave?   WHERE is the Hellespont?
WHERE is the will o' the wisp?

THE HELLESPONT

The Hellespont is the ancient name given to the strait of the Dardanelles which joins the Eastern Mediterranean to the Sea of Marmara. The Sea of Marmara is almost landlocked—except for the Hellespont and the Bosporus which flows into the Black Sea between the Soviet Union and Turkey.

The shores of the Hellespont are formed by the peninsula of Gallipoli in Europe on the north bank and by Asia Minor on the south. The Hellespont is only 38 miles long and between three-quarters of a mile and four miles wide.

Many famous castles overlook the strait including the Old Castle of Anatolia and the Old Castle of Rumelia. The strait has long been prominent in history. The army of the Persian king Xerxes crossed it by a bridge of boats. This expedition against the Greeks probably explains the origin of the name Hellespont: "Helles" comes from "Hellenic" or "of the Greeks" and "pont" means "bridge".

During the First World War, the Hellespont was the scene of much fierce fighting.

FINGAL'S CAVE

The great cave named after the legendary Celtic hero Finn Mac-Cool, or Fingal, is at the southern end of the isle of Staffa, seven miles west of Mull, one of the larger islands of the Inner Hebrides off Scotland's west coast. Fingal's Cave is 227 feet long, 42 feet wide and 66 feet high.

The entrance is an arch supported by basaltic pillars of awe-inspiring symmetry and, from there to the cave's end, there is a pavement of broken pillars. These pillars, either hexagonal (six-sided) or pentagonal (five-sided), form colonnaded walls elsewhere on the south and west of Staffa. The

71-acre island's name means Pillar Island in Norse.

Apart from its natural splendour, the cave is famous for its "music", heard from afar when heavy seas are running. Air, raised to a pressure of several tons to the square inch by the driving force of the sea surging into the cave, rushes out through cracks and fissures in the rock when the water recedes. This creates the musical sounds which have been described by some visitors as "like trumpets blowing". The composer Mendelssohn was inspired by this music as well as by the grandeur of Staffa in writing his *Hebrides* overture.

WILL O' THE WISP

The will o' the wisp is a pale flame, usually seen flickering over marshy ground. Another name for it is jack o' lantern. The phrase is often used in ghost or fairy stories to help create an atmosphere of mystery.

No one quite knows what causes will o' the wisp. Scientists think it is produced by gases catching alight in the air. These gases are probably formed by dead plant or animal matter, rotting in the ground. This would explain why the will o' the wisp tends to appear in such localities as stagnant marshes and damp moorlands.

WHERE are the antipodes?

ANTIPODES

The antipodes are places on the opposite side of the world to each other, such as New Zealand in the South Pacific, and Iceland near the Arctic Circle. Iceland might refer to New Zealand as "the antipodes".

"Antipodes" comes from a Greek word *antipous*, meaning "having the feet opposite". If you look at a globe, you will see why.

The illustrations below show two pairs of antipodes. Perth, at the top left, is the capital of Western Australia. It lies at the mouth of the Swan River. The beautiful island of Bermuda, shown at the top right, is almost exactly opposite Perth. Bermuda was once a British colony and is now self-governing. It lies off the west coast of the United States.

At the bottom of the page are Botswana, on the left, and Hawaii, on the right. These are also on almost exactly opposite sides of the globe. Botswana lies in the centre of South Africa, without any access to the sea. In contrast, the islands of Hawaii are spread out in the middle of the vast expanse of the Pacific Ocean. Hawaii, is also the 50th State of the United States.

WHAT is china clay?   WHAT is twilight?   WHAT are the
WHAT makes the wind?

CHINA CLAY

China clay is a type of clay first used by the Chinese for making chinaware and porcelain. From the hill, Kao-ling, close to the famous pottery-producing centre of China, comes the clay's other name of kaolin.

Kaolin is produced by the disintegration of muscovite-biotite-granite rock which is easily decomposed by atmospheric agents into its present form. It is composed of 46 per cent silica, 40 per cent alumina and 14 per cent water.

One of the most famous and largest of china clay deposits is to be found in the far west of England, in Cornwall and West Devon.

The uses of china clay are varied. By far the largest amount goes into the manufacture of paper. It is used also in the production of pottery, some chemicals and cosmetics, and in pharmacy.

WIND

Wind is the movement of air across the surface of the earth, caused by warm air rising and being replaced by cooler air.

Except for the monsoons, the chief global winds are constant in direction. The strength with which they blow is affected by seasonal changes in air pressure and temperature. The winds are named after the direction from which they come. For instance, a south wind travels towards the north and a wind from the sea is called a sea-breeze.

Instruments called the anemometer and the wind vane are used to measure the force and direction of the wind. To obtain accurate measurements, they must be in a position where there are no obstructions. The wind vane shows the direction of the wind, and the anomometer its force.

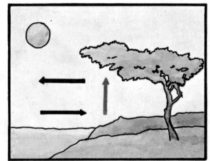

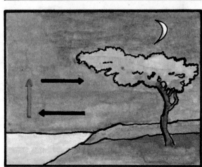

Land heats and cools quicker than sea. In daytime warm air rises over the land and draws in cool air from the sea (top). At night (bottom) the process is reversed.

TWILIGHT

Twilight is the faint light which appears a little before sunrise and again after sunset before it gets really dark.

On the moon there is no twilight. Darkness comes suddenly as soon as direct sunlight ceases to reach the moon's surface. This does not happen on earth because of the halo of air, called the atmosphere, which surrounds it. When the sun goes below the horizon, its light leaves the earth but is reflected downward from the upper atmosphere.

Poets and writers have written of the evening twilight—or "the gloaming", as it is called in Scotland—as an enchanted time. Perhaps one reason is that familiar objects become distorted in the half-light and we imagine we are seeing things that are not really there.

MOUNTAINS OF THE MOON

The Mountains of the Moon, or the Ruwenzori mountain range, forms an eighty-mile long backbone on the frontier of Zaïre and Uganda in East Africa, and extends northwards to within 70 miles of Lake Albert. Springing from the bottom of a rift valley, it reaches a height of 16,794 feet with Margaret Peak.

The name "Mountains of the Moon" is a very ancient one, for Herodotus, Aristotle and Ptolemy all had vague ideas that the source of the great River Nile lay in some far distant mountains, the fabled "Mountains of the Moon", the silver peaks whose glistening snows fed the lake sources of the Nile.

However, it was not until 1888 that the Ruwenzori Range was first discovered for the Western world by the great American explorer Henry Morton Stanley, and climbed for the first time in 1906 by the Duke of Abruzzi.

Several earlier explorers had camped within the area, but had been defeated by heavy rainfall.

SHALE

Shale is a fine-grained, earthy, sedimentary rock rather like clay, but, unlike clay, it is formed in thin layers. It is usually harder than clay and does not so easily dissolve in water. It is normally coloured grey, yellow, green or red.

Shales are made up of sediments that collected hundreds and thousands of years ago on the beds of lakes and oceans. Some of them contain other ingredients than clay minerals and may be called sandy shale, limy shale and so on. They are used a great deal in the making of bricks, tiles and portland cement.

The Rocky mountains are an example of shale rock which contains a great amount of oil. But the cost of extracting it is high.

Mountains of the Moon?   WHAT is the tundra?
WHAT is shale?

TUNDRA

The tundra is a desolate, flat region of land lying to the north of the coniferous forests along the shores of the Arctic Ocean, as in Russia. Winters are long and cold and summers short and cool. Snow covers the ground and ice covers the rivers and lakes for eight or nine months of the year.

Even in the summer only the surface of the soil thaws out and little grows but mosses, lichens and dwarf trees, shrubs and sparse brushwood. In some grassy spaces brilliant polar flowers flourish for a short time, in others, grey rocks and clay-like soil form a dismal landscape.

In the tundra there are many birds, rodents and carnivores, while reindeer roam the region in great herds. Until recently the inhabitants of the tundra led a precarious nomadic existence, based on hunting, fishing and reindeer breeding. Now coal, petroleum, mineral ores and some rare metals have been discovered and vigorous industries are growing in the tundra.

Tundra in the North-West Territory, Canada.

202

WHERE is the Dust Bowl? WHERE is the deepest part of the

THE DUST BOWL

The name Dust Bowl was given to the man-made desert in the central United States in the 1930s. There dust storms blew which were as severe as any on record. One storm in 1933 was traced for 1,300 miles to northern New York.

For the origin of the Dust Bowl we must go back to the late 1800s when homesteaders were advancing relentlessly towards the west and planting their crops in the short-grass country, land known previously as the American desert. The farmers brought with them strains of hard winter wheat that were resistant to drought, disease and insects. They ploughed into the thin grassland and sowed the seeds both of wheat and tragedy.

The states involved were western Texas, Oklahoma, Kansas, Nebraska and North and South Dakota to the Pacific coast. Wheat was the principal crop. Dry farming techniques were developed. These enabled farmers to conserve the meagre moisture in the soil by a process of dust mulching and by permitting the land to lie fallow to build up moisture for the following crop year. However, the farmers did not know how to conserve their soil and prevent the erosion of semi-arid earth which had been anchored only by the cover-crop of thin grass.

The great drought of 1932–7 led to the Dust Bowl and caused the abandonment of vast areas of land. Many people left their farms for California, where they joined other migratory workers in search of jobs as fruit and vegetable pickers.

Meanwhile the American government, with Franklin D Roosevelt as president, took action to aid the ravaged area. Starving cattle were moved to better ranges, or bought and slaughtered. Loans were extended to the distressed farmers. Mortgage foreclosures were stopped in 1933 by the extension of government credit. Soil erosion was attacked by encouraging farmers to use more effective methods of keeping their land in condition, and a great irrigation programme was begun.

OCEAN DEPTH

The deepest part of the ocean is the Marianas Trench off the Philippine Islands in the South Pacific. There the sea floor lies 36,198 feet below the waves. So the distance to the surface is more than a mile greater than the height of Mount Everest.

Jacques Piccard and Lt. Donald Walsh descended to the bottom of the Marianas Trench on January 23, 1960 in the United States Navy bathyscaphe Trieste. It took four and a half hours to make the trip to the bottom, where the water pressure was eight tons to the square inch. This is the nearest men have come to making a journey to the centre of the earth.

The average depth of water in the world's oceans is 12,000 feet. But, apart from the Marianas Trench, there are other trenches in the seabed more than six miles deep.

The floor of the ocean is, of course, as well defined with canyons and "mountain" peaks as the dry land of the earth, something we do not normally consider when we look at the ocean surface.

The imposing facade of St. Peter's in the Vatican.

SMALLEST COUNTRY

The smallest country in the world is the Vatican City. The Vatican is an independent and sovereign state within the boundaries of Rome in Italy.

Although the Vatican has always been the spiritual and administrative centre of the Roman Catholic Church, it did not become an independent state until 1929.

The city state has a daily newspaper, a railway station, and its own bank. It has an area of 0·17 square miles and a population of 1,000.

There are no frontier formalities for those entering Vatican City where millions yearly visit St Peter's and the exhibition galleries.

The chief treasures to be seen are the Michelangelo frescoes in the Sistine Chapel, paintings by Raphael, Fra Angelico and Caravaggio, the fescoes of Pinturicchio and the Codex Vaticanus of the Greek Bible.

ocean? **WHERE** is the smallest country in the world?

WHERE are the Everglades?

THE EVERGLADES

The Everglades are in Southern Florida in the United States. The peninsula of Florida, low lying and with a climate ranging from warm temperate to subtropical, stretches out from the American mainland towards Cuba. In the south of Florida lies the state's biggest stretch of inland water, Lake Okeechobee. Spreading south from this is the huge wet prairie called the Everglades which, after 100 miles, gives way to the mangrove forests fringing the peninsula's broad tip.

The Everglades have a slope to the south of only two inches to the mile and, along the eastern side of the great prairie, there is a river with an almost imperceptible flow. This river, which is only a few inches deep and 50 miles wide, moves slowly towards the south. Along the west side tall cypresses, hundreds of years old, stand in the Big Cypress Swamp. The whole area is waterlogged, for beneath the peat beds there is a porous rock which soaks up water like a sponge. All this freshwater-soaked land keeps back the salt water of the Atlantic Ocean, and the excess of water flows into the sea.

Grasses grow in the shallow, slow-moving river. Tall cypress trees flourish in the swamps. The area is rich in vegetation and wild life. A primitive world, thousands of years old, continues into the present and the Americans sought to preserve this by creating the Everglades National Park. But in spite of these efforts, civilization is destroying this primitive world. Agricultural land is being reclaimed by draining the swamps. Water is being taken from Lake Okeechobee and diverted from the river to quench the thirst of the Atlantic seaboard cities of Palm Beach and Miami. On the surface, the peaty soil dries out and becomes easily ignited tinder. Carelessly thrown cigarette ends create hundreds of fires.

As the swamps dry out and become barren, Nature's balance is destroyed and the wild life is threatened with extinction. The Everglades may well be doomed.

WHEN was the North-West Passage first sailed?
WHEN does peat form? WHEN was the Panama Canal built?

NORTH-WEST PASSAGE

The North-West Passage is a sea route along the north coast of North America between the Atlantic and Pacific oceans. It was first sailed by the Norwegian explorer Roald Amundsen in 1903–1906 in the 47-ton Gjöa.

The search for the Passage started in the 15th Century, when Bristol merchants commissioned the Genoese mariner John Cabot to find a direct sea route between Britain and the Indies by sailing west. He failed, but discovered the mainland of America on his voyage.

In 1845, Sir John Franklin made his ill-fated voyage. With 129 officers and men in two ships, the Frebus and Terror, Franklin's expedition became icebound in the Victoria Strait. Franklin died and the crew abandoned their vessels and eventually perished.

It was ironic that out of the Royal Navy's efforts to find Franklin came the first successful completion of the North-West Passage, although much of the journey was made overland. That was in the year 1854.

PANAMA CANAL

The Panama Canal was finally opened on August 15, 1914. It had taken ten years to build. At first much delay was caused by uncertainty over the type of canal that should be built. Some experts contemplated a high-level canal with locks at either end, while others suggested a canal at sea level. After two years the high-level plan was adopted. It was decided that the alternative system would threaten the land on either side of the canal with flooding and also put ships at risk in stormy weather.

The building of the Panama Canal, one of the great engineering feats in the world, was masterminded by John F. Stevens. The canal zone was formally acquired by the United States from Panama in 1904 for 10 million dollars plus an annual payment of 250,000 dollars. The United States was to be responsible for the construction of the canal and for its perpetual maintenance, sanitation, operation and defence. Since that date the treaty has been amended several times.

Since 1904 the canal, which is just over 40 miles long, has cost the United States well over 6,000 million dollars. But it has shortened the distance for ships travelling between that country's Atlantic and Pacific coasts by 8,000 miles. Ships going from Europe to Australia make a saving of nearly 2,000 miles.

Among the canal's many engineering marvels, its great locks attract particular attention. They are deep enough to take vessels drawing forty feet of water and have a length of 1,000 feet. Some of the "leaves" of the lock weigh as much as 730 tons and are more than 80 feet high.

PEAT

Peat bogs are formed in mild and humid climates when the land drainage is so bad that pools of water submerge masses of partially decomposed vegetable matter and prevent complete decay.

After being dug out of the bog, the peat is left to dry in the open air. When the water has evaporated it will burn readily. Vast quantities of peat exist in many parts of Europe, North America and northern Asia, but it is normally used as a fuel only in countries or regions where there is little coal. Large quantities are used for fires and ovens in Ireland, Scandinavia and the Soviet Union.

WHEN does an atoll take shape?

ATOLL

An atoll or coral reef begins to form when tiny marine animals called coral polyps attach themselves to rocks on the sea bed. The reef, which eventually takes the shape of a ring or horseshoe enclosing a lagoon, is made up of the lime-based skeletons of innumerable polyps.

After building skeletons round themselves, coral polyps produce new polyps, which in turn surround themselves with skeletons. The young polyps remain attached

to the parents so that succeeding generations combine to produce a great mass of coral.

Atolls occur only in shallow water where the temperature is over 65° Fahrenheit (18·3° Centigrade). They are found in the West Indies, the Indian Ocean, along the coast of Brazil and, notably, in the Pacific. North-east of Australia huge reefs have formed and some atolls may stretch 40 miles in diameter and more than a thousand feet in depth.

WHERE is nought longitude? WHERE is Tristan da Cunha?

LONGITUDE

Nought degrees longitude passes through Greenwich on the River Thames in London, England. 0° longitude is known as the "prime meridian". You can see at Greenwich the prime meridian mark from which all countries have reckoned longitude since 1884.

Longitude and latitude are fixed lines crossing the globe by which the location of any place on the earth's surface can be determined and described.

Lines of longitude go from north to south. All start at the North Pole and end at the South Pole. Longitude is measured both 180° east and 180° west of the meridian, the two together making the full 360° of the earth's circumference.

World time is also measured from Greenwich. Greenwich Mean Time is zero hour and, depending on whether you are west or east of the prime meridian, you are either so many hours behind or ahead of the time of Greenwich.

The Royal Observatory at Greenwich was founded in 1675 and was one of Sir Christopher Wren's great designs. In 1960 the building was opened as an astronomical museum.

Greenwich meridian

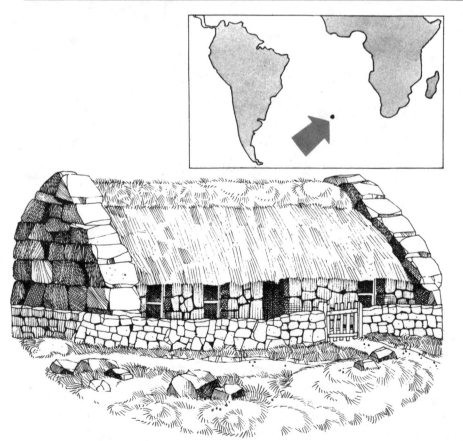

TRISTAN DA CUNHA

Tristan da Cunha is one of five small and remote islands in the South Atlantic midway between Buenos Aires in Argentina and the Cape of Good Hope, South Africa. Tristan is the only one of the five to be inhabited.

The island is 37 square miles in extent and was named after the Portuguese admiral who discovered it in 1506. Tristan da Cunha was created in prehistoric times when a volcanic eruption raised it 18,000 feet from the seabed. Cultivation is possible only on one part of the rocky outcrop, on a small plateau squeezed between the sea on one side and 2,000 foot cliffs on the other.

In 1816 Britain landed a small force of men on the island and took possession. The garrison stayed for a year. When it departed, one of its members, Corporal William Glass, was allowed to remain on Tristan with his family.

WHERE is Oberammergau?

With the arrival of shipwrecked sailors and of five women from St Helena, the population grew to 260 by 1961.

For 150 years the islanders' way of life changed little. But in 1961 the volcano erupted and forced their departure to England. This evacuation seemed to be the end of life on Tristan but, weary of contact with modern civilization and longing for their island ways, the people began to return two years later.

The Tristan da Cunha Development Company now provides the island's sole industry. By 1967 Tristan had a small harbour for the first time in its history. After that a road, a new hospital and a sewage system were built, and electricity was introduced. The island now has something approaching the best of both worlds, isolation and "away from it all" atmosphere but some modern amenities, too.

OBERAMMERGAU

Oberammergau is a small village in the Bavarian Alps near Germany's border with Austria.

In the winter of 1632 the village was struck by the Black Plague, which spread devastation through Europe. By the following summer one-eighth of Oberammergau's population of 1,000 people had died.

The village elders called all those who could walk to the church and everyone made a vow: "A solemn promise to devote one year in 10 to the preparation and presentation of the tragedy of our Lord's Passion to keep the Christian principle of the redemption of the world before men for all time."

There were no more deaths from the plague, and the villagers believed God had heard their vow.

Apart from an occasional lapse, due in the main to wars, the village people of Oberammergau have presented their Passion Play every 10 years. The first performance was held in the church in 1634. Nowadays a huge theatre, looking rather like a great aircraft hangar, is used. It seats 6,000 people and has room on the stage for crowd scenes with 500 actors. Only native-born villagers may be considered for the 600 parts in the play. Selection for the principal parts is made by ballot more than 12 months before the performance. Rehearsals begin in May for the first performance in May of the following year.

The Passion Play has given Oberammergau worldwide renown and visitors travel long distances to see the eight-hour play.

The play is divided into episodes. These episodes are introduced by the Passion chorus, which consists of fifty singers.

The whole community becomes involved in the production in a completely medieval way.

WHY does Ayer's Rock change colour?   WHY do clouds

AYER'S ROCK

The colour of Ayer's Rock alters continually according to the atmospheric conditions and the changing angle of the sun. The rock is an immense sandstone boulder rising 1,143 feet out of the flatness of the plain near the centre of Australia.

It is normally red, and measures over five miles round the base with relatively gentle slopes which can be easily scaled. The most dramatic effects occur at sunrise, when the sun's rays inflame the rock to a burning crimson, and at sunset, when marvellous purple shadows overlay the glowing blood-red monolith. The colours of the rock vary from a yellowish-ochre through all the various shades of oranges and reds to a deep purple and to black.

Ayer's rock is now one of Australia's most popular tourist attractions, though visitors of one kind or another have been travelling far for centuries to see the massive shape. There was a time when it was regarded with great awe as a religious shrine. People from the local tribes came to the caves around its base to worship and to decorate the walls with paintings. The rock was discovered by an Englishman, W. G. Gosse, in 1873 and named after Sir Henry Ayers, then Prime Minister of South Australia. The spot was so remote and inaccessible that for years few people ever visited the rock. Now they come by car and aeroplane and the rock forms part of the Ayer's Rock – Mount Olga National Park, 487 square miles in area, where the local plant and animal life is strictly protected.

Desert oak, mulga, mallee, bloodwood and spinifex are some of the exotic names of the plants that grow here. No less strange are the names and appearance of the animals—kangaroo, wallaby, bandicoot and euros.

This great highway through Brazil will greatly disturb the ecological balance of the jungle.

have different shapes? WHY do we study ecology?

209

SHAPES OF CLOUDS

Clouds vary in shape according to their height and temperature, and they contain minute drops of water or ice particles or a combination of both. And, of course, their formation is greatly affected by wind changes.

There are basically three groups of clouds: high clouds between 17,000 and 45,000 feet (cirrus, cirro-cumulus and cirro-stratus); middle clouds between 7,000 and 23,000 feet (alto-cumulus, alto-stratus and nimbo-stratus); and low clouds up to 7,000 feet (strato-cumulus, stratus, cumulus and comulo-nimbus. Their height and temperature decide how much pressure is exerted on them by the atmosphere.

Finally, the shapes of clouds differ according to the time of day. Towards evening clouds tend to thin out, rise a little and flatten out.

ECOLOGY

Ecology is concerned with the relationship between living things and their environment. This leads directly to the conservation of natural resources which is one of the most important problems facing the world today. Plants, animals and men are so closely associated and dependent upon each other that the ecologist's range of study is world-wide, although each special field has its own techniques.

The word ecology is derived from the Greek *oikos*, meaning house. Branches of ecology include types of environment, relationships between certain organisms and plants, game conservation, overcultivation, overpopulation and hundreds of others.

Most fields of study are inextricably bound up with the destiny of man. As it is such an enormous subject there is a danger that the information obtained will not be available soon enough to ensure proper conservation.

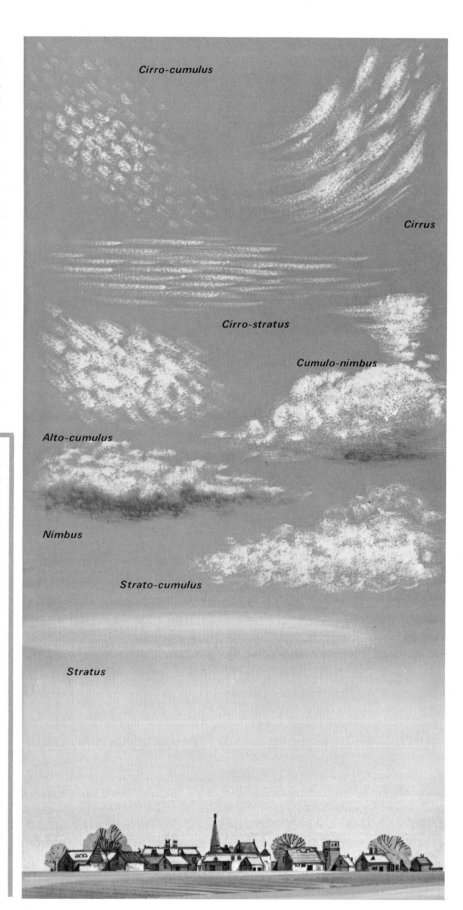

Cirro-cumulus

Cirrus

Cirro-stratus

Cumulo-nimbus

Alto-cumulus

Nimbus

Strato-cumulus

Stratus

volcanic eruption?

OLDEST REPUBLIC

The tiny country of San Marino, a few miles from Rimini on the Adriatic coast and surrounded by Italy, set up its own government in the 10th Century. This makes San Marino the oldest surviving republic in the world.

According to legend it was founded in the 4th Century by Marinus, a stone cutter from Dalmatia (now part of Yugoslavia). He fled to a mountain retreat, Monte Titano, to escape persecution by the Roman Emperor Diocletian.

Marinus bequeathed this retreat to his followers to remain evermore as an island of liberty in a tyrannical world. The republic's capital, San Marino, is built around the three craggy tops of Monte Titano, which rises to a height of 2,425 feet almost in the centre of the country's 24 square miles.

Over the centuries the republic has been invaded several times but has always regained its independence. In 1861, the people of San Marino, considerate of others, wrote to Abraham Lincoln expressing their concern over the troubles in America. An appreciative Lincoln wrote back: "Although your dominion is small, your state is nevertheless one of the most honoured in history."

Napoleon had offered this "model of a republic" additional territory in 1797, but San Marino declined to accept it.

The inhabitants are of Italian origin but they have one big problem. Over the centuries the families of the republic became so inter-related that the citizens found it impossible to provide a completely impartial system of law enforcement. Because of this they decided to "import" their judges and police forces from Italy. In this **way the San Marino families have avoided feuds and family charges of favouritism.**

VOLCANIC ERUPTION

The greatest volcanic eruption, in modern times, was on an island in the Sundra Strait between Sumatra and Java. On August 27, 1883, the volcano of Krakatoa suddenly erupted with a tremendous explosion that has been estimated to be the equivalent of 26 large atomic bombs. Rocks and ash were hurled up to 12 miles in the air and over half of the island was blown away. More than 160 villages were destroyed and 36,000 people were killed by 120-foot-high waves which were caused by the explosion.

The sound of the eruption was clearly heard four hours later nearly 3,000 miles away. Dust and ashes fell, days later, on Singapore and southern Java. Clouds of volcanic dust thrown high into the atmosphere travelled round the world and caused spectacular sunsets, even as far away as western Europe.

In the eruptions, which lasted two days, the highest part of the island became a huge crater which was filled by the sea. The remaining part was covered with layers of lava and ash which stayed hot for weeks.

No life was left on the island. But a small monkey was rescued from a floating piece of wood in the Sundra Strait. She was badly burned, but had survived one of the worst volcanic disasters ever recorded in history.

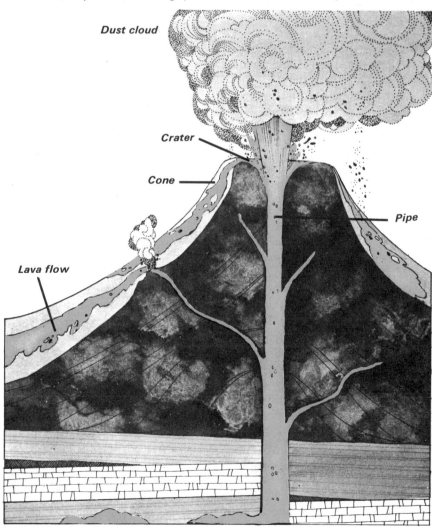

Dust cloud

Crater

Cone

Pipe

Lava flow

WHAT makes rain? WHAT is the Heligoland Bight? WHAT

RAIN

Rain comes from water which has evaporated from the surface of seas and lakes. If this water vapour hits a cold patch it condenses or turns into cloud. As long as the cloud meets only air of the same temperature it will go on holding its moisture without bursting. If the cloud meets warm air and is not too dense, it may evaporate again and disperse, leaving a clear sky.

But if the cloud meets cold air it will turn back into water and fall to the ground as rain. If the air on the way down is freezing, the rain may become snow before it reaches the ground.

Water vapour

Rain

HELIGOLAND BIGHT

The Heligoland Bight is an arm of the North Sea extending south and east of the red sandstone island of Heligoland. Heligoland is a small remote island of the German North Frisian group lying in the North Sea between the coast of Schleswig-Holstein and the estuaries of the Jade, Weser and Elbe. It is 5,249 feet long and 1,640 feet wide at its broadest point.

In 1807 Heligoland was a Danish possession but it was seized by the English in 1814 and given to Germany in 1890. Before 1914 Germany developed it as a great naval base with an extensive harbour in the south-east. There was a network of underground fortifications and coastal batteries and it was known as the "Gibraltar of the North Sea". The Heligoland Bight became famous as the scene of a naval battle between the British and the Germans on August 28th, 1914.

Heligoland became a stronghold again under the Nazis and the capital town of Heligoland was destroyed by Allied bombers. In 1947 the whole character of the island was changed by the destruction of the fortifications.

DATE LINE

The Date Line (usually called the International Date Line), is a north-south line through the Pacific Ocean where, according to international agreement, the date changes. East of the line it is one day earlier than it is to the west.

The line is necessary because the earth is divided, longitudinally, into 24 one-hour time zones (15 degrees longitude each) which make one full day on the earth. Since the earth rotates eastwards, the time on the clock progresses westward round the world. Thus, 12 o'clock noon arrives in London (0 degrees longitude) five hours before it does in Washington, D.C. (75 degrees west of London) and eight hours before it does at San Francisco (120 degrees west of London). When it is noon in London it is midnight 180 degrees to the west.

On either side of the 180th meridian the time is the same. But you would lose a day if you crossed it from the east and gain one if you travelled from the west.

The Date Line has some variations from the 180th meridian to allow for land areas or islands. The line bulges eastward through Bering Strait to take in eastern Siberia and then westward to include the Aleutian Islands with Alaska. South of the equator it bulges east again to allow various island groups to have the same day as New Zealand.

A   Siberia
B   Alaska
C   Bering Sea
D   Aleutian Islands
E   Fiji Islands
F   New Zealand
G   Australia

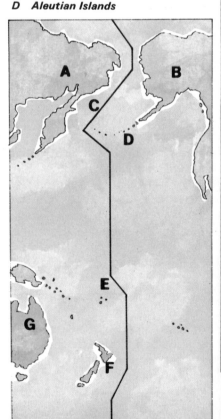

Top *Glacier National Park, U.S.A.* Bottom *Snowdonia, Wales.*

DEW

Dew is the result of condensation on the surface of the earth. At night the earth sometimes becomes colder than the air, and when water vapour in the air touches leaves and other objects on the earth's cold surface in the early hours of the morning, it condenses to form "dewfall". If the earth is very cold the vapour freezes and hoar frost, instead of dew, is formed.

If, on the other hand, water vapour rising from the earth meets a leaf colder than itself, it will condense to form a different kind of dewfall.

NATIONAL PARK

A National Park is an area where natural scenery and wildlife is protected by law to preserve them for future generations. It is only recently that man has realized that he must make a positive effort if many species of wildlife and areas of great beauty are not to disappear for ever.

There are many kinds of areas of conservation and their central priorities may differ slightly. In the U.S.A., a national park such as Yellowstone safeguards natural features and wildlife in a way that will contribute to public enjoyment. In Africa generally, as in the Amboseli Game Reserve, the chief purpose is the preservation of the remnants of the great herds of animals which once roamed the country.

National Parks depend on tourists for revenue but the animals must remain unmolested. To solve the problem many parks restrict visitors' movements by setting aside areas for hotels, restaurants and parking places and providing a limited number of roads through the park. National Parks may be small or large, privately or government owned.

WHERE are the Pillars of Hercules? WHERE does sulphur

The great promontory of Gibraltar, known to the ancient Greeks as one of the Pillars of Hercules.

PILLARS OF HERCULES

The Pillars of Hercules are on either side of the Strait of Gibraltar. The legendary Greek hero Hercules was said to have erected the Pillars on a journey to capture the Oxen of Geryon, a monster with three heads who lived on an Atlantic island. Passing out of the Mediterranean he threw up the rocks on either side of the Strait of Gibraltar. They were the Rock of Gibraltar and the headland on the Moroccan side.

Hercules' journey was one of the 12 labours that the son of Zeus had been set by Eurystheus, King of Tiryns, whose servant he had become. One of the most famous of these labours was the cleansing of the Augean stables. So innumerable were the herds of cattle that used these stables that, as they returned from pasture, they seemed to reach endlessly across the plain. Their stables were heaped high with manure and had not been cleaned for years. Hercules diverted the Rivers Alpheus and Pereus through them, and completed the task in one day.

For his last labour he braved the Underworld to capture Cerberus, its three-headed watchdog.

HIGHEST WATERFALL

The world's highest waterfall is in Venezuela, South America. It is known as the Angel Falls and lies on the River Carrao. This magnificent waterfall tumbles 3,212 feet down to the river.

The Venezuelans did not even know about Angel Falls or the surrounding country until the 1930s, because steep rocks made overland travel to the region impossible. It was not until aircraft started penetrating the region that the falls were discovered.

The falls get their name from the United States adventurer and explorer James Angel who crashed near them in an aeroplane in 1935.

ORIGIN OF SULPHUR

Sulphur is a volcanic product. It has many industrial uses. The volcanoes of Sicily and Japan were once the world's chief suppliers.

Today important sources are in Texas and Louisiana in the United States. In the coastal regions there are underground sulphur domes. Two pipes, one inside the other, are forced down to the domes.

Superheated steam is pumped down one of the pipes, melting the sulphur which is then forced up the other pipe. This method provides 92 per cent of the United States output.

The other source is from sulphides of various metals which are called "pyrites". It is the main source of sulphur in Sicily and Japan today.

come from? WHERE is the world's highest waterfall? WHERE do countries get their names from?

NAMING THE NATIONS

Countries do not all have universally accepted names. Holland is officially The Netherlands. Finland is called Suomi by its own people. The names of countries often spring from the discoverer and sometimes from a native tribe or even a conquering people. America is named after Amerigo Vespucci, the explorer, France after the Frankish invaders, and England after the Angles.

The Greeks and Romans called England "Albion"—which is probably derived from *albus* meaning white and is a reference to her white cliffs—the first things the Romans would have seen on their arrival. Spain in Spanish is Espana and in Latin, Hispania. An amusing story of the origin of Quebec in Canada is that it was so called because the French sailors who first saw the rocky promontory cried: "Quel bec!" or "What a beak!"

The white cliffs of Dover, England. "Albus" is the Latin word for white, hence the name of "Albion" for England.

Reindeer crossing a frozen lake in Finland known to the Fins as Suomi (derived from suomaa, the damp and frozen land).

Iceland's name derivation is self-explanatory—yet the island is also famous for its natural hot geysers!

WHEN does an underground river form?   WHEN will the

world's supply of oil run out? WHEN does a geyser erupt?

UNDERGROUND RIVER

An underground river is formed when the top soil of the land makes it extremely easy for water to pass through to a more solid soil structure. Another kind of underground river is created when a powerful spring in a mountain has to find a channel to the surface owing to the solidity and compactness of the rocks.

Finally, an underground river may form as an effluent to a larger river above ground, if there are faults in the surrounding land.

Some rivers travel underground only for a part of the journey, such as the Rhône in France.

An underground river at Wookey Hole, in Somerset, England.

WORLD'S OIL

Many experts believe that the world's oil supply may run out by the end of the century unless vast new oil fields are discovered.

At the end of 1969 the total known reserves of crude oil were calculated at more than 500,000 million barrels, or 21,000,000 million gallons. At the present consumption rate of 50 million barrels a day, this supply would run out in around 30 years from now. However, it has been estimated that consumption will be more than 80 million barrels a day by 1980 and more than 120 million barrels a day by the year 2000.

But by then more efficient methods may have been invented for getting the maximum amount of oil out of the ground. Also, extensive new deposits may have been found, possibly in Antarctica or under the sea, on a much bigger scale than the discoveries off the coasts of Britain and northern Europe.

The possibilities of producing oil from shale on a commercial scale are now being investigated in the United States.

GEYSER

A geyser occurs when a hot spring erupts, hurling a column of water and steam high into the air. These springs are situated in regions which were formerly volcanic and which have retained considerable heat near the surface.

They usually have craters with well-like shafts penetrating into the earth. The water which gathers deep down in these shafts becomes heated until the lower part is changed into steam. The pressure of the steam steadily mounts to a point when it suddenly hurls the water above it into the air, sometimes to a height of over 100 feet.

The chief geyser districts are in Iceland (home of the Great Geyser), in the Yellowstone National Park, Wyoming, United States, and in New Zealand. For four years Waimangu in New Zealand, the greatest of all geysers, was capable of spouting jets up to 1,500 feet.

WHERE is the "Moho"—or Mohorovicic discontinuity?

THE MOHO

The Mohorovicic discontinuity is to be found between the earth's crust and the earth's mantle. Mohorovicic was a famous Croatian scientist, a seismologist.

He specialized in the composition of the earth, and particularly in earthquakes and in faults in the structure of the earth, which are the cause of earthquakes.

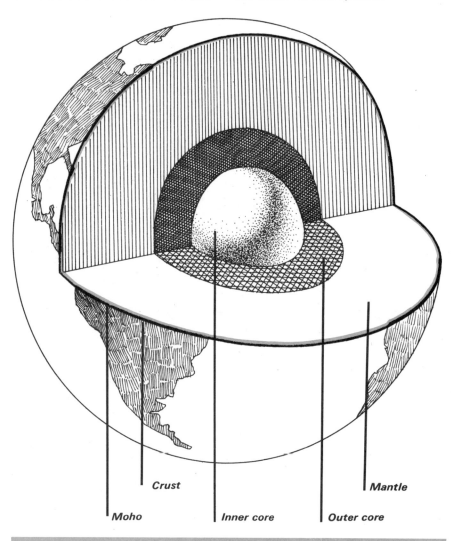

Crust

Mantle

Moho

Inner core

Outer core

Mohorovicic made a most important discovery. Scientists knew that the earth is made up of a series of layers, rather like an onion. There are many of these layers, all of different materials and all in a different state of development. The main layers are called the crust, the mantle, the liquid core and the solid core.

The great pressures inside the earth force the weaker areas of the rocky layers out of alignment and this pushing, twisting movement is experienced as an earthquake on the surface. These great forces set up a series of waves throughout the various layers of the earth, known as seismic waves.

Mohorovicic discovered a curious fact about the behaviour of these earth waves or tremors. He noticed that the shock waves travel comparatively slowly through the actual crust of the earth. But when they reach the lowest level of the crust—the layer called basaltic rock which rests on the next layer called the mantle—the waves increase dramatically in speed. Sometimes they also change direction.

This curious fact was proved by Mohorovicic's experiments. The importance of his discovery was that it proved the earth's crust is different from the mantle beneath.

So the "Mohorovicic discontinuity" is the scientific term used to describe this strange behaviour of the earth's shock waves.

Usually this level of the earth's composition is called the Moho, since even scientists found Mohorovicic's name difficult to pronounce! By plotting these earth waves on sensitive shock recording machines known as seismographs we have found that most of the outer crust of the earth is between 20 and 25 miles thick in continental areas, but only three miles thick under some oceans.

THE MISTRAL

This is the name given to a wind which blows in the Rhône Valley in France. The wind is caused by an exchange of air between the cold hinterland of France's Central Plateau and the warm Gulf of the Lion in the Mediterranean Sea.

High mountain ranges near flat country produce unpleasant winds, especially where the mountains descend to a warm sea. Atmospheric pressure is high above the cold mountains, but low above the sea. Air, therefore, flows towards the sea and is not warmed because it has not crossed enough land.

The north-westerly mistral, funnelling down the constriction of the Rhône Valley, blows at a speed of 30 to 60 m.p.h. on at least 50 days each year. It bursts out on to the Mediterranean coast, filling holidaymakers' caravans with sand and capsizing yachts caught unaware at sea.

WHERE is the mistral? WHERE is the Gulf Stream?

GULF STREAM

The Gulf Stream is in the Atlantic. It is a warm ocean current which flows steadily from the Gulf of Mexico north-eastwards. One branch reaches the Canary Islands, turns southwards and moves back across the South Atlantic. The other branch flows past the western coasts of northern Europe.

This current, which is like a river in the sea, is 50 miles wide at its narrowest and nearly 2,000 feet deep. It sweeps along with it many forms of warm water life from the tropics, but these die before they reach the European coasts where the warm water mixes with cold water moving down from the Arctic.

The Gulf Stream has a great effect on the weather of Britain and Norway. The prevailing south-westerly winds are warmed by it and collect moisture which turns into rain. In winter the warm water keeps open the cold northern ports, such as Hammerfest, in Norway, and Murmansk, in the Soviet Union, while harbours in the Baltic, many miles farther south, are blocked with ice. In summer it causes bright flowers to bloom on the west coast of Spitzbergen 500 miles north of Norway. In contrast, the east coast, cooled by Arctic water, is bleak and colourless.

In 1912 the United States Congress was asked for money to build a jetty which, it was thought, would divert the Gulf Stream and make it flow up the east coast of the United States. Although this scheme was unlikely to be successful, it was just as well for Britain and Norway that it was never tried. Without the Gulf Stream, Britain's winters would be very much longer and colder, and Norway's harbours, which are vital to the country, would be frozen over for many months.

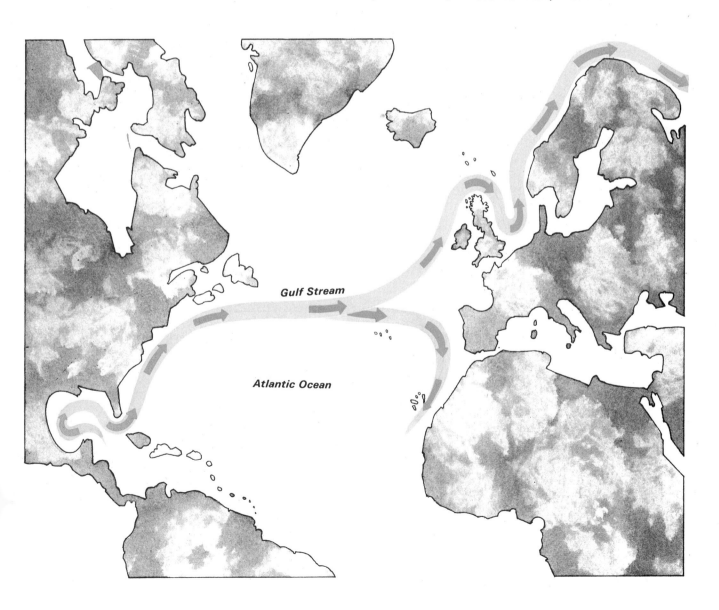

Gulf Stream

Atlantic Ocean

WHY does the Mediterranean Sea look blue and the Atlantic WHY are pebbles on a beach round? WHY

The blueness of the Mediterranean and the greenness of the Atlantic can be simply explained by the amount of sunlight reaching the water's surface. The more sunlight, the bluer the water.

However, in the case of the Atlantic, another factor helps to create the green effect and this is the colouring produced by plants decaying on the ocean bed. When these plants decay, yellow pigments are released, and this pigmentation added to the already duller blue waters of the Atlantic produces the characteristic greenish shade which distinguishes the Atlantic from the bright blue Mediterranean.

AGE OF FOSSILS

It is possible to estimate the relative age of fossils, that is whether they came before or after a particular period, because most fossils are found in sedimentary rocks. These are rocks made of sediment which has been compressed or cemented together in layers.

Older rock layers, or strata, are usually at the bottom. So each layer is younger than the layer below it and older than the one above. Fossils may be present in igneous rock (hardened volcanic lavas) and metamorphic rocks (formed by pressure and heat within the earth) but they are usually destroyed.

Telling the age of fossils in terms of years, or absolute time, is a much bigger problem. But scientists use several methods. The tree ring method, counting annual growth rings, can give a scientist a reasonably accurate date back to about 3,000 years ago.

The varve method, based on counting the annual layers of sand and clay deposited in a lake, bay

or river by melting glaciers, can be used for deposits less than about 15,000 years old. Similar calculations based on the rate of sedimentation, erosion, salt accumulation etc. have been successfully applied to very much older rocks.

The third method is concerned with radioactive decomposition and is based on actual changes in some of the rock elements or in the fossils themselves. Radioactive uranium gradually changes to uranium lead, radiocarbon to nitrogen and so on. From the proportion of uranium lead to uranium in the rock we can date the oldest rocks and fossils, nearly 3,000 million years old.

Ocean look green? WHY is it possible to estimate would you go to Death Valley? WHY the age of fossils?

PEBBLES

The pebbles that are to be found on a beach are invariably round and smooth owing to the constant battering they have received from the sea.

Originally pebbles were part of much larger rocks, but various natural phenomena, such as earthquakes and volcanoes, have gradually broken them down. Caught in the movement of the sea, and constantly rubbed against other hard materials, the pebbles finally lose their irregularities and present a smooth round surface.

Many of the rocks of today will be pebbles in thousands of years' time, and many of today's pebbles will eventually be turned into sand by the constant, wearing action of the sea.

DEATH VALLEY

You would go to Death Valley, as do half a million visitors each year, to look at its magnificently varied scenery and to recapture the flavour of those days of privation and hardship which gave the valley its name.

Death Valley National Monument is in the state of California in the U.S.A. In its 3,000 square miles can be found sheer-walled canyons, desert springs and sands, an extinct volcano, snow-topped mountain ranges, desolate wastes of salt crystals and gardens of fragile wild flowers.

There is a 200 square mile salt pan that contains the Western Hemisphere's lowest point—282 feet below sea level—and is the driest spot in the U.S.A.

Death Valley also contains long-abandoned mines, silent witnesses to the gold seekers of 1849 who lived and died in its inhospitable terrain. Coffin Canyon, Deadman Pass, Hells Gate, Starvation Canyon and Suicide Pass are names which perpetuate the despair and suffering of these pioneers.

SARGASSO SEA

The Sargasso Sea is in the Atlantic Ocean south of the Bermudas and several hundred miles east of the American mainland. It is famous for its seaweed and as a spawning ground for eels.

When these eels are eight or more years old and spawning time is due, they leave the pond or stream where they have been living and make their way, over land if necessary, to the sea.

When they reach the area known as the Sargasso, the females lay their millions of eggs at a depth of 1,500 feet and the males fertilize them. The baby eels hatch out after a few days and float to the surface. Vast masses of seaweed lie on the surface of the Sargasso.

Carried along by winds and ocean currents from the Gulf of Mexico and Caribbean Sea, this floating seaweed is concentrated into an area many thousands of square miles in extent. There it gives refuge to myriads of sea creatures, such as fish, sea-worms, molluscs, crabs and jellyfish. Sea birds find it useful as a resting place.

This floating "island" may have given rise to the famous legend in ancient times of the lost land of Atlantis. Christopher Columbus recorded taking two weeks to sail through it in 1492.

But what happens to the baby eels? Drifting at first, they eventually make their way to the ponds and streams of their parents. The American eels go to America and the European eels to Europe. The old eels do not return but die after spawning.

The Sargasso Sea is the subject of many legends. Ships are said to have vanished in it, but there is no truth in the legend that associates it with the lost land of Atlantis.

hanging gardens in history?
WHERE is the world's saltiest sea?

HANGING GARDENS

They were created by Nebuchadnezzar (605–562 B.C.) in Babylon and were regarded as one of the Seven Wonders of the Ancient World.

Babylon, situated about 50 miles to the south of Baghdad in what is now Iraq, had long been the capital in the time of the Chaldeans. Nebuchadnezzar, who ruled for 40 years and was the greatest of the Chaldean Emperors, enlarged the city and gave it enormous protective walls.

The hanging gardens, rising in terraces to a height of some 350 feet, were built, so the legend goes, for Nebuchadnezzar's wife, Amyhia, either to please her and thereby gain the support of her father's armies against her husband's foes, or simply because she did not like the flatness of the land after the hills of her homeland.

Each terrace had sufficient earth for trees such as oak, willow, pomegranate and palm to grow, as well as shrubs and flowers. Stairways led from terrace to terrace. Water cisterns were placed at the top to irrigate the lower terraces. Today, only a few ruins remain.

Believe it or not, she really is floating!

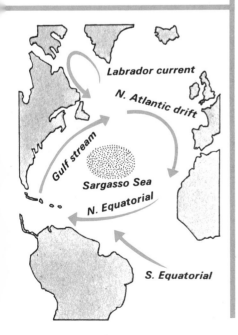

SALTIEST SEA

The Dead Sea is in south-west Asia and is really a big lake. Its northern half belongs to Jordan and its southern half is divided between Jordan and Israel.

It covers an area of 394 square miles and contains about 11,600,000,000 tons of salt. The River Jordan, which contains only 35 parts of salt to 100,000 parts of water, flows into the Dead Sea and each year adds 850,000 tons of salt to the total.

The lake's surface level lies 1,302 feet below the Mediterranean and is the lowest sheet of water on earth. In summer the absence of rain and the high rate of evaporation cause the water level to drop between 10 and 15 feet below that in winter. There is no outlet from the Dead Sea, but water balance is maintained by evaporation. Blue-white clouds, which form a mist over the surface of the water, carry off the evaporated moisture.

The Dead Sea is mentioned many times in the Bible. It gave its name to the Dead Sea Scrolls, groups of leather manuscripts and papyri first discovered in 1947 in caves on the lake shore. These scrolls date from the time immediately before and contemporary with the rise of Christianity. (No modern cities are to be found on its shore and no traces remain of the five cities said to have been near it in Abraham's time—Sodom, Gomorrah, Admah, Zeboiim and Zoar.)

Despite the lack of hotels, tourists come to the area because of the warm climate, the sense of history and the magnificent and awe-inspiring scenery. The climax of a trip is a swim in the lake, for the water is so full of salt that it is extremely difficult to sink in it.

The minerals and salts of the Dead Sea are being exploited for industry. But the lake itself is truly dead; no fish are able to live in it.

WHAT is brine? WHAT is an anticyclone? WHAT is a fiord?

BRINE

Brine is salt water. So the sea, which is the main source of salt water, is sometimes known as "the briny".

Salt water has various special properties and the fish that live in the sea and in salt lakes are usually not the same kinds that live in fresh water rivers.

Salt water cannot be drunk for refreshment, as it makes the drinker thirstier, or even sick. But it is possible by using expensive de-salinization plants to remove the salt and make the water drinkable.

The sea contains many valuable minerals and salts. In some parts of the world, such as coastal Brittany, in France, the sea is allowed to flood the marshes to a shallow depth when the tide comes in. The sun evaporates the water and leaves the salts to be collected.

ANTICYCLONE

The name anticyclone was first introduced by Sir Francis Galton, the English meteorologist, in 1861 to describe weather conditions opposite to those of a cyclone. Anticyclones are characterized by fine weather and weak winds.

In weather maps and climatic charts, anticyclones appear as a region in which the pressure is higher than in its surroundings. So when the weather forecaster starts to talk about anticyclones you can be prepared for the weather to remain stable for some time, usually sunny and with occasional light rain.

In a cyclone or low-pressure area the winds circulate anti-clockwise in the northern hemisphere and clockwise in the southern hemisphere. Cyclones are usually areas of strong, violent winds and indicate bad weather.

FIORD

A fiord is a long, narrow, deep inlet from the coastline where the water is often deeper than the sea-floor off-shore. Fiords are usually associated with Norway, but western Canada, southern Chile, the South Island of New Zealand and north-west Scotland all have fiord coasts.

The fiords may have originated where great cracks, or faults, were present in mountains. During the Great Ice Age that started a million years ago, the glaciers spread down from the mountains and deepened the fiords into the colossal troughs they are today.

LOAM SOIL

Loam soil is half way between clay and sandy soils. It is the best soil for horticultural and agricultural use, containing enough clay and humus for the retention of water and for the provision of food for plants. It also has sufficient sand to allow the passage of air and the drainage of water, which prevents waterlogging, and enough lime to prevent acidity.

River basins are often covered with a powdery, yellowish-grey loam called loess. This loam has been brought downstream by the river and is derived from glacial deposits of very fine silty, un-consolidated material. Some of the best farming land in the Rhine and Danube basins are composed of this soil. Other loess deposits have no connection with glacial action and are accumulations of fine material picked up by the wind in the world's arid regions. When water is introduced into these loess areas by means of irrigation they make unusually fertile soil.

There are loess deposits in the plains of south Russia, the Argentine pampas and China, and in Iowa and Illinois in the United States. These are among the richest agricultural regions in the world.

WHAT is loam soil?

WHERE is Arthur's Seat? WHERE is the highest tide in the

ARTHUR'S SEAT

Arthur's Seat (822 feet) is the name given to the highest of the seven hills on or around which Edinburgh, the capital of Scotland, is built. It stands in Holyrood Park, the Royal demesne which covers 648 acres. A broad road, the Queen's Drive, about three and a half miles long, encircles it.

The view from the top of Arthur's Seat is magnificent. To the south lie the Pentland and Moorfoot Hills; the Lammermuirs, North Berwick Law and the Bass Rock in the North Sea to the east; the Firth of Forth and Fife to the north; the Forth Bridges and Ben Lomond to the west; and just below, Edinburgh Castle.

Arthur's Seat is an extinct volcano. The cultivation terraces of the Iron-Age people who once inhabited the area can still be seen on its eastern slopes.

world? WHERE was the first canal built?

HIGHEST TIDE

The highest tide in the world is recorded in the Bay of Fundy which is between New Brunswick and Nova Scotia in eastern Canada. There the Petitcodiac River narrows, and forces the inrushing tide to the greatest height found anywhere on earth. The difference between high water and low water in the Bay of Fundy is no less than 50 feet.

Fishermen make use of these extreme tides as you see in the illustration. They set their nets at high tide and collect their catch of fish when the tide goes down.

Tides throughout the world are caused by the varying power of the pull of the sun and the moon on the oceans. They draw the water up in a great wave, and the rotation or spin of the earth every 24 hours sends this wave round the world washing the coasts of the continents and islands. The varying shapes of the coastlines and inlets also affect the tides, and, therefore, ports and navigation.

At certain times of the month, the sun and moon are said to be in conjunction—that is, they are pulling in the same direction, which causes tides to be higher. These are called spring tides. At other times in the month, the sun and moon are in opposition, which means they are pulling against one another. Then the tides are lower and are called neap tides.

FIRST CANAL

Archaeologists believe the oldest canals in the world are those whose remains were discovered near Mandali in Iraq in 1968. They believe these canals are nearly 7,000 years old (about 5,000 B.C.).

In 500 B.C. Darius the Great, the Persian emperor, ordered a canal to be built joining the River Nile to the Red Sea. This remarkable construction was the forerunner of the modern Suez Canal.

WHEN is a forest called a rain forest?

WHEN does sheet lightning occur?

RAIN FOREST

Rain forests are so-called because they grow in the wet lowlands of the tropics where the annual rainfall is more than 80 inches (2,000 mm) and the average temperature is between 20° and 30° Centigrade (65° and 85° Fahrenheit).

They consist of evergreen trees which never completely loose their luxurious leaves and grow over 100 feet high. Although it is possible to find as many as 100 different kinds of trees in a small area, most of them are similar.

Contrary to popular belief the rain forest is not a jungle. In most cases there is little vegetation apart from the trees and few flowers. This is because the tops of the trees are so dense that little sunlight reaches the ground.

Those plants that do grow beneath the tree line are mostly climbers winding their way up the barks of trees and such flowers as are found are usually the most exotic varieties on earth.

SHEET LIGHTNING

Sheet lightning usually occurs during a storm as the result of a discharge of excess electricity within a single thundercloud. The outline is obscured and the result is a diffused light spread over a large area of the sky in contrast to the vivid spiral or ribbon-like flashes of chain, forked or zig-zag lightning. The most favourable conditions for sheet lightning are provided when the electric field is equal throughout the area. Unlike other forms of lightning it does not reach the ground and the channel cannot be distinguished.

What is often referred to as sheet lightning is merely the lighting up of the sky by flashes occurring beyond the horizon.

All lightning is the natural discharge of large accumulations of electric charges in the atmosphere. It may take place between neigh-

Fork lightning taken with a five-minute exposure at night on Agfacolourfilm.

bouring clouds or between cloud and earth. Just before the discharge the cloud's electric poten-

tial is often built up by the action of falling raindrops or other natural processes.

WHEN does coal become a precious stone?

PRECIOUS COAL

Coal is basically a compound consisting largely of carbon. When a piece of carbon deep underground is subjected to great heat and pressure, it may gradually be transformed into a diamond. The heat turns the carbon into a liquid and the pressure causes it to crystallize.

Thus the carbon loses its black unattractive appearance and becomes the most precious of stones.

It has been calculated that this extraordinary process takes place at least 75 miles beneath the earth's surface, the diamonds being afterwards transported upwards by natural forces.

Some iron meteorites full of carbon have been found to contain diamonds deep inside. Here the heat and pressure conditions would be much the same as those formed underground.

Much the same conditions are created in the laboratory to make synthetic diamonds for industrial purposes, such as cutting hard materials. Only industrial diamonds are man-made. The diamonds that are considered the most precious stones in the world took thousands of years to form.

WHERE is the world's longest bridge?
WHERE are the Roaring Forties?

LONGEST BRIDGE

To measure the longest bridge in the world is not as easy as it may seem. After all, there are many different kinds of bridge. Another problem is: how do you start to measure a bridge? From its supports or simply the distance it covers over ground or over water?

There are many alternatives.

The bridge with the longest span is the Verrazano-Narrows Bridge, which stretches across the entrance to New York City from Staten Island to Brooklyn. Work on the project began on August 13, 1959. The bridge was opened to traffic on November 21, 1964. It measures 6,690 feet between supports and carries two decks, each of six lanes of traffic.

The centre span over water, is 4,260 feet, the world record. The bridge carries well over 20 million vehicles a year.

WHERE would you find whirlpools?

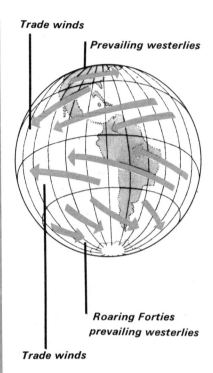

Trade winds

Prevailing westerlies

Roaring Forties prevailing westerlies

Trade winds

ROARING FORTIES

The Roaring Forties are westerly winds found between latitudes 40° and 60° South. They are prevailing winds resulting from the large, planetary circulation of the atmosphere.

The prevailing westerlies occur in both hemispheres in the middle latitudes (30°–60°), but in the Northern Hemisphere the great continental land masses of North America and Asia create a disturbance to the regular wind pattern and it is only in the Southern Hemisphere, with its small land masses, that these westerlies sweep unimpeded across the Southern oceans.

Intense, blustering, cold and often stormy, these winds were given their name by sailors who, in the days of sail, made the outward voyage to Australia by way of the Cape of Good Hope at Africa's southern tip and the return passage via Cape Horn, the southernmost tip of South America. In this way, sailing vessels would have the advantage of a following wind for both passages.

WHIRLPOOLS

Whirlpools occur quite frequently in the narrow sea passages between island groups and mainland shores. They are common in the fiords of Norway, the long, narrow inlets of sea between high cliffs.

What happens is that a rotary flow of sea currents is created by a head-on meeting of a rising tidal current with the returning ebb current of the preceding tide. Usually whirlpools are more likely to occur over a deep or depressed area of the sea bed.

In some cases, particularly between the Sea of Japan and the Philippine Sea, the whirlpool becomes so great that the rotary flow changes to a spiralling downward flow into a deep centre. This is capable of sucking under water objects as large as ships.

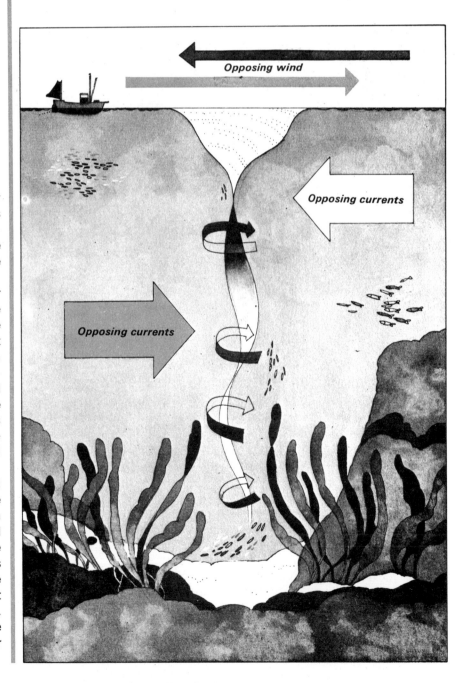

Opposing wind

Opposing currents

Opposing currents

WHY is there more sea than land on the earth's surface?

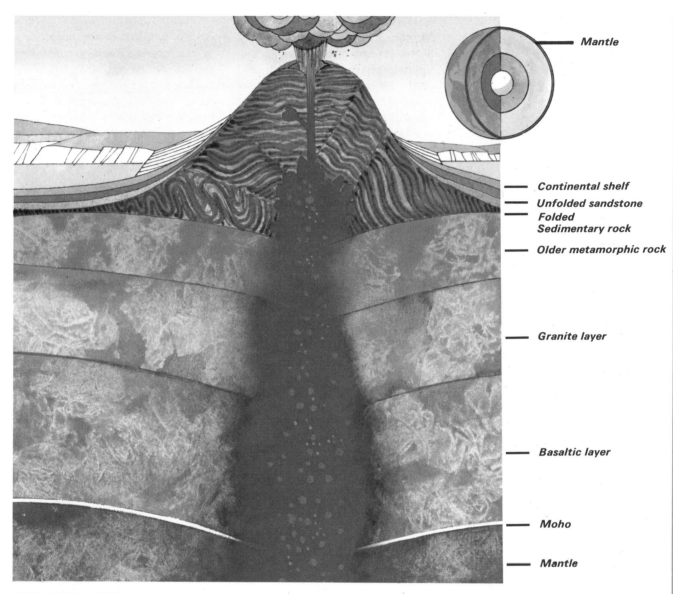

Mantle

Continental shelf

Unfolded sandstone

Folded
Sedimentary rock

Older metamorphic rock

Granite layer

Basaltic layer

Moho

Mantle

SEA AND LAND

The answer to this question lies in the composition of the rocks which make up the outer portion of the earth's crust. Over large areas of the earth's surface, these rocks are lightish in colour, relatively light in weight and are called granitic rocks, because granite is the most common type. Over still larger areas of the earth the rocks are darker, heavier and are called basaltic rocks, since among them basalt is the chief type.

We know that the earth at a depth of a few hundred miles below the surface is molten and that the surface or crustal rocks,

which are about 50 miles thick, are really floating on this liquid core.

The granitic rocks stand higher than the basaltic, just as a cork floats higher than wood, and therefore the granitic areas are the continents, and the basaltic, the ocean basins. If all crustal rocks were of the same composition, the earth's surface would be one vast ocean, more than a mile deep.

But why is there water in the sea? There are three reasons. First, molten rock holds much more water than when it hardens and cools. So, as the earth's crust

solidified, it gave off water vapour into the atmosphere. Secondly, the earth's gravity stops this vapour from escaping into space, just as it also retains the atmosphere we breathe. Thirdly, the pressure-temperature relationships on earth are such that the vapour is mainly in liquid form.

The water in the sea is salty because of the 2,000 million-years-old disintegration of the earth's crust. The soluble materials or salts remained in the ocean. The insoluble materials have formed sedimentary rocks and the ocean sediments.

WHY does Venice have so many canals?
WHY are there different kinds of soil?

CANALS OF VENICE

Unlike most canals, those in Venice are not man-made. If anything, man has made the land round the canals.

In the 7th Century this North Italian town was no more than a series of tiny islands and mud flats. After the fall of the Roman Empire, political exiles sought refuge in the Venetian lagoons. Gradually a town emerged with many of its buildings having been constructed directly over the water, supported by massive foundations on the sea bed.

The canals between the groups of houses were left, and consequently, the only form of transport in Venice today is by boat.

The vibrations of motor vehicles would soon shatter the foundations of this beautiful city, which in some cases are precariously poised on nothing firmer than sand. In the days of the gondola all seemed well, but the wash produced by motor boats has greatly weakened Venice's structure.

To add to this historic city's problems, much of the main island is slowly sinking into the sea, largely because of the dredging and water pumping activities of a nearby industrial area.

The Italian government has now embarked on the difficult project of trying to keep this marvel of medieval and renaissance architecture and engineering afloat.

DIFFERENT SOILS

The basic material of the surface of the earth is solid rock, and the surface of the landscape we see is nearly always the result of weathering, the action of sun, wind, frost, rain, ice or snow. Therefore, there are many kinds of soil depending upon the climate and the type of parent rock. There is also a third factor which influences the kind of soil formed. This is the vegetation.

The first step in weathering is the breaking down of the rock. Water plays an important part at this stage, either by freezing and shattering the rock as it expands or by washing away some of the minerals of which the rock is composed, thereby loosening its particles.

The climate is also important for most rocks contain much quartz as well as silicates. In a cold climate, the crystals of the silicates are dissolved more quickly than the quartz. In a hot moist climate however, the quartz is washed away and the silicates left behind. Every intermediate stage can be found between these two extreme types of soil.

Vegetation also plays its part by splitting rocks with its roots. Also dead branches and leaves fall on to the ground, decay and add a layer of humus to the soil, rich in nutrients which enable larger plants to grow. These larger plants support animals, some of which help to mix the soil still further.

There are other types of soil such as those formed from the silt deposited by rivers—alluvial soils— or where bogs and marshes occur. But one thing is common to all soils. They are very unstable if the vegetation which covers them and aids in their formation is removed. Then they are easily washed away and the result of centuries of slow development is lost.

WHAT is a tornado?   WHAT makes fog?

TORNADO

Unusually violent weather is called a storm, and is always accompanied by high winds. Some of these winds have spiralling internal movements, and the revolving storms they produce are variously called tornadoes, whirlwinds, willy-willies, waterspouts and hurricanes.

Near the centre of a tornado is an area of calm known as the "eye" of the storm. This is simply a hollow vortex formed by the spiralling of the air, rather like the centre of a vortex of water going down a drain. Because of the suction in this low-pressure "eye", houses collapse and roofs are carried off, corks are drawn from bottles, and window panes fall outward.

Around the edge of the funnel-shaped cloud of the tornado, which looks like an enormous spinning top and almost touches the ground, the wind may blow at 200 miles an hour. The storm belt, only a few thousand feet wide, travels at 25 to 40 miles an hour, to the accompaniment of a deafening roar.

A waterspout is a tornado at sea, sucking in water and carrying it in an upward spiral with the wind to the overhanging cloud. A ship entering a waterspout soon finds her bridge and rigging covered with insects and birds. They are exhausted by their struggle in the side of the waterspout they have just passed through and are seizing the chance to rest in the "eye" before being caught up in the fury of the other side.

Tornadoes occur in the middle latitudes of the earth.

FOG

Fog is a cloud which has come into contact with the ground. It is usually the result of condensation of water vapour in the air at the earth's surface. But on mountains a fog may merely be the result of clouds being formed in the free air and blown on to the slopes.

Fog is made up of water droplets, or sometimes ice crystals. It varies from a light haze or mist to the thick fog experienced in cities.

The densest kind—also called smog—may be caused as much by smoke as by water.

During the Second World War many attempts were made to dispose of fog artificially, so that runways for aircraft could be kept clear. A practical method developed in Britain was the burning of oil in jets arranged around an airfield. The water drops evaporated and an area up to 100 feet or more above the runway was cleared in a few minutes. But it was an expensive remedy and was not adopted for general use.

Chemical methods, such as "seeding" the fog with dry ice, silver iodide or calcium chloride spray to make the water droplets fall as rain, have been investigated since 1955. But no really satisfactory method has so far been discovered.

WHERE is the Emerald Isle? **WHERE** does gold come from?

EMERALD ISLE

This is a romantic name for Ireland, the second largest of the British Isles, which is farther into the Atlantic Ocean and the warm Gulf Stream current than its bigger neighbour to the east. The moist prevailing westerly winds bring between 30 and 50 inches of rainfall each year and maintain a temperature ranging between 0° and 21° Centigrade. All this gives the countryside a rare greenness— hence its popular description as the Emerald Isle.

Ireland

West coast of England

GOLD SOURCES

The main gold-producing regions of the world are in the Republic of South Africa, Ghana, Southern Rhodesia, the Congo, the Soviet Union, Canada, the United States, Australia, Columbia and the Philippines.

Many wars of ancient times were fought principally to secure gold as loot. Alexander the Great brought back vast quantities of gold from his Persian expeditions. During the Middle Ages alchemists sought the Philosopher's Stone, which would turn base metals into gold.

Exploration was stimulated by the search for the metal. The promise of it from the Indies helped Columbus to get support for his expedition. Spanish gold from Mexico and Peru greatly increased

the stock held in Europe. Rich deposits were discovered in Colombia and Brazil in the 18th and 19th Centuries, and these were the world's chief sources of supply for 200 years.

In 1848 a gold strike was made in California and hundreds of thousands of men poured into the Golden West. Many died, but some survivors became very rich, for California was soon yielding £10 million worth of gold every year. In 1851 new veins were found in Australia. The third great gold rush of the century occurred in 1896, when the Klondike goldfield was discovered in the far north-west of Canada.

The world's richest known source was discovered in 1884 in South Africa, near what is now

Johannesburg. This is the great gold-bearing reef of the Witwatersrand which has produced more than £4,000 million worth of gold. Its annual output is more than half the world's total supply.

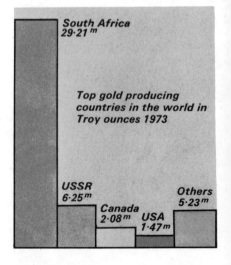

Top gold producing countries in the world in Troy ounces 1973

South Africa 29·21ᵐ

USSR 6·25ᵐ

Canada 2·08ᵐ

USA 1·47ᵐ

Others 5·23ᵐ

WHERE is Alice Springs?

ALICE SPRINGS

Alice Springs is a town situated in the heart of the continent of Australia, centred in the lower third of the Northern Territory.

The surrounding countryside, "the Centre" as Australians call it, is parched. The lakes and rivers are dry for most of the time and the cattlemen on the few homesteads depend on water pumped from bores hundreds of feet deep.

The town of Alice Springs was founded in the middle of the 19th Century after the discovery of a sheltered, watered plain among the MacDonnell Ranges, a series of hills which ripple for 250 miles across the land. By 1872 a telegraph station had been built at a water hole beneath a rocky hill. It was called Alice Springs after the wife of Charles Todd, superintendent of telegraphs in Adelaide, but it is always known as Alice to Australians.

Next came prospectors looking for gold. They left a ghost town at Arltunga not far from Alice. Once, back in 1880, they thought they had found rubies by the million, but the gems proved to be cheap garnets, not worth transporting. Cattlemen soon followed, for much of "the Centre" is marginal land that provides good feed when it rains. They knew the rains did not come often, but felt one good season could carry five bad seasons. Often it has had to carry seven or eight bad ones.

The growth of Alice Springs in recent years has astonished everybody. The railroad linked it to Adelaide in 1939 when its population was less than 100. By the Second World War 1,000 people lived there. It was used as a military base after the Japanese bombed Darwin. Stuart Highway— still called simply "the bitumen"—

was completed from Darwin to Alice, a distance of 954 miles.

Today, Alice Springs is a prosperous town of 6,000 people. It attracts crowds of tourists especially during the fine winter weather from June to September. They come for the spectacular scenery, the famous aboriginal artists, and to visit surrounding cattle stations.

Attractions include the tremendous monolith of Ayers Rock which towers 1,143 feet above the plain and is six miles around— the biggest "pebble" in the world, surrounded by a flat desert.

Since the 1950s the area has been suffering from the worst drought people can remember. It is feared that "the Centre" may turn into a huge dustbowl. So it looks as if the future of Alice Springs lies in its tourist trade and the mineral wealth which experts believe lies under the rugged landscape.

GLACIERS

A glacier moves when the pressure above it from rocks, loose ice and snow becomes greater than the strength of the ice. Under this enormous weight, the solid ice tends to flow like tar, although very slowly. The glacier must be quite old before enough material accumulates to exert the pressure needed to move it—usually when it is about 60 feet thick.

The movement of glaciers is too slow to be noticed by the eye, but measurements have shown they may travel as much as 150 feet a day. The bodies of mountaineers buried by avalanches have been carried several miles in a few years.

Glaciers cover 10 per cent of the earth's land surface.

The movement of the great glaciers is too slow to be measured by eye.

ICE AGES

The Ice Ages ended about 10,000 years ago after lasting about two million years. At its greatest extent the ice covered nearly 30 per cent of the land surface of the world, compared with about 10 per cent today. The great glaciers reached as far south in America as present-day Nebraska and Kansas and extended over the whole of northern Europe down to a line linking London and Berlin.

But there were a number of intervals when temperatures rose and the ice retreated temporarily to its present limits. During these warm periods, which totalled several hundred years, the liberated areas were repopulated. The climate is believed to have been warmer at times than it is today.

is Mohs' scale used?

geological period? **WHEN** was the Green Revolution?

MOHS' SCALE

Mohs' scale is used to measure the hardness of substances. The scale was introduced by the German mineralogist Friedrich Mohs in 1812. It is based on a classification of 10 minerals. These are arranged in a table so that each of them is hard enough to scratch those below it, but not hard enough to scratch any of those above it.

The scale in order of decreasing hardness is: 10, diamond; 9, carborundum and sapphire; 8, topaz; 7, quartz; 6, orthoclase; 5, apatite; 4, fluorite; 3, calcite; 2, gypsum; 1, talc. The divisions are, however, not equal. For instance, on an abolute scale, the difference in hardness between 10 (diamond) and 9 (carborundum) is four times greater than the difference between 9 (carborundum) and 1 (talc).

The 10 minerals thus provide a table of reference, against which the comparative hardness of other minerals can be measured.

EOCENE PERIOD

The eocene geological period began about 55 million years ago, and lasted between 15 million and 17 million years. During this period animals, fishes and plants made enormous evolutionary progress, in some cases coming very close to those familiar today.

During the eocene period the climate got warmer, and many plants became extinct. But new plants, especially flowering varieties, evolved, giving the world's vegetation a more modern appearance.

On land many familiar mammals appeared to replace more primitive animals now dying out. Horses were abundant, there were also tapirs and rhinoceroses. Pigs and camels began to appear but increased only slowly, because of constant attacks from the now extinct sabre-toothed tigers.

GREEN REVOLUTION

The increase in agricultural production throughout the world since 1945 has been so great it has come to be known as the Green Revolution.

World agricultural production in 1964 was one and a half times that of 1948. Much of this increase was due to the redistribution of land and to the grouping of small holdings into larger units.

Scientists have contributed new varieties of grass that provide better cover and strength, thus holding the soil in place. Advances have been made in the development of new kinds of plants capable of withstanding drought and maturing fast enough to avoid freezing. Research has led to the discovery of new production methods, fertilizers and pesticides.

Dawn horse or eochippus, Hyracotherium

Dinocerate Uintatherium

Phenacodus

Trees and vegetation appear gradually around the edge of the desert.

BIGGEST DESERT

The world's largest desert is the great desert of North Africa: the Sahara. "Sahara" in Arabic means wilderness, and this wilderness stretches right across Africa from the Atlantic Ocean to the Red Sea. From east to west it covers more than 3,000 miles. East of the Red Sea, desert conditions continue through Saudi Arabia into Persia.

To calculate the Sahara's breadth is not so easy. The desert does not simply "stop", and vege-tation begin from that point on. Indeed desert conditions disappear so gradually that nowhere to the south does it have precise boundaries. Nevertheless, the Sahara is seldom less than 1,000 miles wide, and consequently must have an area exceeding three million square miles. These enor-mous dimensions make the Sahara almost as big as the United States, including Alaska.

The Sahara is one of the hottest regions of the world and, on average, receives only 17 days of rain a year. When it does rain, delicate herbs and flowers grow rapidly and then disappear almost as quickly as they came.

Many people think of a desert as a flat expanse of sand. But in the Sahara there are many moun-tains, some rising to 10,000 feet. For part of the year some of these strangely shaped peaks will even be covered in snow.

Canyon? WHERE is the wettest place on earth?

GRAND CANYON

The Grand Canyon is in the northern part of Arizona in the United States. It is a tremendous gorge cut into the high plateau by the Colorado River. In some places it is 18 miles wide. At its deepest parts it goes down a mile below its rim.

The canyon is breathtaking to look at, partly because it is so huge, but also because of the colours of the rocks. The main colour is dull red, but other rocks are violet, pale pink, green and dark brown.

The canyon is an interesting place for geologists to study rocks, because it contains examples from many different periods of time. The rocks are marked by weather, earth movement, and water. Many animal fossils have been found there, including the remains of dinosaurs and elephants.

The most beautiful part of the canyon is the National Park, which was created in 1919.

WETTEST PLACE

The wettest place in the world is Kauai, one of the Hawaiian Islands.

Mont Wai, which is 5,000 feet high, is the wettest point of the island. Records over a period of 30 years showed that an average of only 14 days a year had no rain. During that time the average yearly rainfall was over 480 inches.

Kauai, west of Hawaii's capital Honolulu, is on the same latitude as the southern tip of the Sahara Desert.

WHY does Holland have so many windmills? WHY is a WHY could we sail

WINDMILLS

The large number of windmills in Holland, or The Netherlands, is due to the fact that they were needed to pump water into the canals off the rich, low-lying land reclaimed from the sea. Windmills are still used for this purpose today, but pumps worked by electricity are more usual.

There is an old Dutch saying, "God made the world, but the Dutch made Holland". They certainly did make a great part of their land by dragging it from the sea, and the battle to hold it never ceases. The name Netherlands (from the Dutch *nederland*) means low land, and more than one-third of Holland's land area of 12,530 square miles lies below sea level.

Along the coast are dunes of sand—nature's dykes—thrown up by normal tides. The Dutch plant them with marram grass, which holds the sand together with its long, strong, creeping roots. Behind the dunes the Dutch built three dykes of close-packed stone, clay and earth on wooden and concrete piles. The dyke nearest the sea is called a "waker". Behind it lies a "dreamer" and behind that again a "sleeper". Some of the dykes are 200–300 feet high and many have a road or, some, a railway running along the top.

In 1170 the North Sea swept into the country and formed the bay called the Zuyder Zee (South Sea). In 1421, another high tide flowed in to form the Hollandse Diep (Dutch Deep). The great spring tide of 1953 (two feet higher than any previously recorded) smashed the waker dykes, overflowed the dreamers and drowned about 1,900 people. About 50,000 were forced to flee from their homes.

A famous Dutch story tells of a brave boy who stood for hours with his hand thrust into a hole in a dyke and so prevented the sea from rushing in and widening the breach in the wall.

mineral different from an animal?
to the North Pole but not to the South Pole?

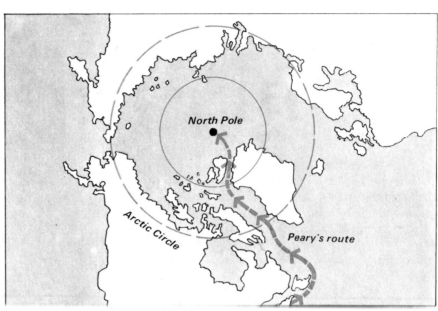

THE POLES

A journey by sea to the North Pole with an ice-breaking ship of sufficient strength and large amounts of explosives is possible in theory, although it has never been achieved.

But the South Pole is in the middle of a great land mass, the continent of Antarctica. This uninhabited land surface varies from basins more than 8,000 feet below sea level to mountains well over 13,000 feet high.

The South Pole was first reached, after a 53-day march, by a Norwegian party led by Raold Amundsen, in December 1911. Amundsen's expedition travelled on foot and on sledges drawn by dogs. It beat Captain Robert Scott's party by a month.

An American party first reached the North Pole, but there is no absolute proof which one it was. The honour is most often given to the team led by Robert E. Peary who reached the Pole on April 6, 1909. Claims that Dr. F. A. Cook reached the spot with two Eskimos, two sledges and 26 dogs in April, 1908 are now generally doubted.

ANIMAL AND MINERAL

A mineral is different from an animal in as much as it does not breathe and does not move. An animal is described as a living organism while a mineral is an inanimate organism.

Both minerals and animals can be classified exclusively in terms of their component chemicals. So in purely chemical terms a mineral cannot be described as dead because the atoms and molecules within are not dormant. They are capable of change and can even transform a mineral's shape.

But apart from chemical change the mineral, unlike the animal, cannot move.

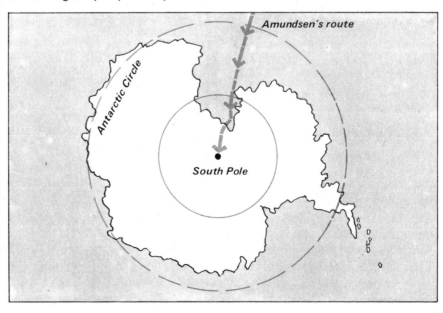

WHERE do icebergs go? WHERE is the biggest lake in the

VANISHING ICEBERGS

Icebergs are huge masses of ice which have broken away from glaciers in the Arctic and Antarctic regions. They gradually melt away as the upper part is warmed by the sun and the lower part by the warmer waters into which they drift.

An iceberg may be as much as 250 feet high, although only one-ninth is above the surface of the sea. It can be a hazard to shipping.

The worst disaster was to a British passenger liner, the Titanic. This fine ship was thought to be unsinkable, because she had a double skin and 15 watertight compartments. In April, 1912, the liner struck an iceberg in the North Atlantic. Despite her double skin and watertight compartments she was holed and quickly sank. Of the 2,207 people on board, more than 1,500 were drowned.

BIGGEST LAKE

The world's biggest lake is Lake Superior, between America and Canada. It covers an area of nearly 32,000 square miles. But Superior is not the lake with the most water. Lake Baikal in southern Siberia has far more water, because although little over 12,000 square miles in area, it is nearly 6,000 feet deep.

Lake Superior is nearly as big as Austria. It is nearly 400 miles long and receives the drainage of about 200 rivers.

There is virtually no tide. But during autumn and winter storms, waves can reach extremely dangerous heights. These waves are gradually eroding the shore, so the lake is slowly getting even bigger.

Owing to the lake's great industrial advantages and transport facilities the water has become seriously polluted. Since 1965, however, the United States Government has made efforts to purify the great lake.

world? **WHERE** is Surtsey?

SURTSEY

Surtsey is a volcanic island a few miles south-west of the Westman Islands which are situated off the south coast of Iceland. The island appeared as a result of a volcanic activity on November 15, 1963. The Icelanders took the infant island into their care because it appeared in their territorial waters.

They called the volcanic vent Surtur, and the island Surtsey (island of Surtur). In old Icelandic mythology Surtur was a giant who brought destructive fire from the south as a weapon in his fight with Frey, the god of fertility.

During its early life there was doubt about the island's chance of survival, and many thought it might disappear. A similar one did vanish in 1783 after erupting from the sea 65 miles south-west of Reykjavik, the Icelandic capital. Survival and long life were assured when repeated outpourings of thin flowing lava followed the first violent eruptions. The lava capped the volcano with a gently sloping regular dome which acted as a protective shield.

The arrival of Surtsey was no real surprise. For the 10,000-mile Mid-Atlantic Ridge, of which Iceland forms the largest above-sea land mass, had been active along its length for some years up to 1963, although since then things seem to have settled down, although further activity is always possible. The neighbouring Westman Islands were produced by volcanic activity 8,000 years ago.

WHAT is fire-damp? WHAT are the doldrums? WHAT is flint?

FIRE-DAMP

Fire-damp is a poisonous gas found at some time in most coal mines. It consists of a mixture of gases, the most important being methane or marsh gas, so called because it arises in marshy districts as a result of rotting vegetation beneath the water.

Fire-damp is dangerous because it is highly inflammable and explodes easily. Mines where the gas is known to be present are called "fiery" mines and are unpopular with miners. Because of the inflammability of the gas, lighting down mineshafts used to be a problem. A naked lantern flame was liable to explode if it met a leak of fire-damp.

However, in 1818 two British pioneers, George Stephenson, of railway fame, and Sir Humphry Davy, both invented mining lamps which solved this problem. They discovered that a cage of fine wire gauze surrounding the lantern completely would at the same time prevent explosion, and allow air and light to pass. This discovery made coal-mining a less dangerous operation.

Nowadays, only locked safety lamps of this kind are allowed down the mines. There are new electric versions, but the old type still has the advantage that it can be used as a fire-damp gauge. If fire-damp is present in a shaft, the flame in the lantern grows longer. If there is a considerable quantity of the gas about, the lantern fills with blue flame.

DOLDRUMS

The doldrums is a zone near the equator where the rising hot air creates calms and variable winds, together with thunderstorms, the zone of equatorial calms.

There are two areas of doldrum calms—one in the Atlantic Ocean between the west coast of Africa and the north-east coast of South America, and the other in the Pacific Ocean off the north-west coast of South America.

In the days of sail, ships were often delayed in these areas; the most famous being the Pinta, Nina and the Santa Maria, the ships of Christopher Columbus, which were becalmed in the doldrums during their famous voyage.

The expression "in the doldrums" means to be in low spirits.

Below left *a modern miner's lamp and* **right** *first Davy lamps.*

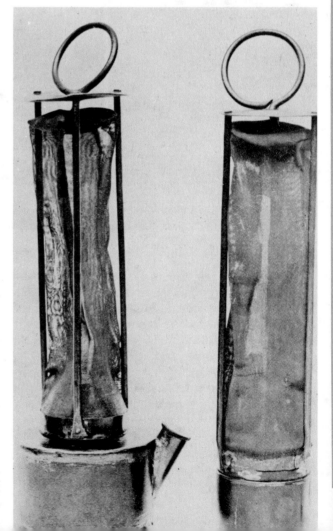

WHAT is a millibar?

FLINT

Flint is one of the various forms of silica, which is among the common materials making up the largest part of rocks. Some other forms of silica are quartz, opal, chalcedony, agate, jasper and onyx. Flint (essentially, silica with some water, a little lime, oxide of iron and, occasionally, carbon) can be grey, greyish-white, smoke-brown, brownish-black, red or yellow. It occurs as layers in other sedimentary rocks.

Because it flakes and can easily be chipped into a sharp cutting edge, flint was used by prehistoric man to make axe heads, arrow heads, knives and other such sharp-edged implements.

The study of implements from the Paleolithic, or Old Stone Age, and the Neolithic, or New Stone Age, has helped us understand how people lived then.

MILLIBAR

The millibar is the unit used to measure atmospheric pressure. The instrument which records the pressure is the barometer, first used in Italy, in 1643, by Evangelista Torricelli, an assistant to Galileo.

Pressure is measured in terms of force exerted on a unit of area. Thus the pressure of the atmosphere is given as about 14·7 pounds a square inch, or in metric terms a million dynes a square centimetre, of the earth's surface. Torricelli evolved the idea to balance this pressure against a column of liquid of which the height, density and value of gravity are known.

In 1953 the executive committee of the World Meteorological Society decided that "the millibar, defined as a unit of pressure equal to 1,000 dynes per square centimetre, shall be the unit in which pressures are reported for meteorological purposes."

HIGHEST MOUNTAIN

The world's highest mountain is Mount Everest, on the Nepal–Tibet frontier in the eastern Himalayas. Mount Everest was named after Sir George Everest who discovered it in 1856, when he was surveyor-general of India. At that time its height was estimated by trigonometry as 29,002 feet, but more recently it has been established as 29,028 feet.

Everest is not only the highest mountain in the world, but also the most magnificent and inaccessible. It is swept by icy winds and gripped in a coldness that often drops far below zero. There are great glaciers and crevasses, ice-

falls and sheer rock faces, and the rarified atmosphere at its greatest heights has defied generations of climbers.

It was not until 1920 that the Dalai Lama of Tibet was persuaded to permit a British climbing party into his territory. Until then both Nepal and Tibet had forbidden any such intrusion.

Several unsuccessful British expeditions were made to conquer the mountain and 16 men were lost in the attempts. In 1951 Eric Shipton made an approach from the south through Nepal. Before then all the expeditions had made their approach from the north.

Shipton had no intention of attempting an assault on the summit. His object was to gather information for future expeditions.

With the help of this information a British expedition, using light-weight oxygen-breathing apparatus and other weight-saving equipment, reached the summit in 1953. It was led by Colonel H. C. J. Hunt, later Lord Hunt.

Nine camps were made during the climb, and on the morning of May 29 a New Zealander, Edmund Hillary, and Sherpa Tensing Norkey made the final assault. At 11.30 a.m., after a hard climb, they reached the summit.

largest reef in the world ?

WHERE do thunderbolts come from?

LARGEST REEF

The largest reef in the world is the Great Barrier Reef off the north-east corner of Australia. From Anchor Cay (or island) above the northern tip of Queensland, the reef runs parallel to the mainland at a distance of about 60 miles, to Lady Elliot Island, 1,250 miles away to the south.

This reef, which is 80,000 square miles in area, was discovered in 1770 by Captain Cook. He called one of the many navigable passages Providential Channel after he had edged his ship through it to the coast. He named Endeavour Reef, where he ran aground, after the ship itself.

The fantastic coral forms give shelter to a collection of other living creatures, such as fish, crustaceans, worms, molluscs and starfish, of greater variety than can be found anywhere else. Ninety per cent of the reef is under water and the remainder is composed of some 200 islands dotted along its length. A few of these islands remain permanently dry and swarm with bird life. They are used also by turtles who come ashore to lay their eggs.

The Great Barrier Reef is a delicately balanced system suffering, from time to time, an upset in its regular routine. Such an upset began in the 1960s with the invasion of the large poison-spined starfish, which is still going on. Appropriately called "crown-of-thorns", this starfish has infested some parts of the reef and by feeding on the polyps has ravaged vast areas of living coral. Even so, the reef remains one of the most colourful regions of the world.

THUNDERBOLTS

Thunderbolts are actually lightning. A thundercloud forms when air carries moisture high into the sky. Raindrops form, and the movement of air currents causes them to be charged with electricity. When the charges become strong enough lightning flashes within the cloud. If the charge cannot be contained in the cloud the lightning flashes to earth with a loud clap, and a tree or other tall object on the ground may be struck and sometimes destroyed.

Occasionally the lightning fuses metal or sand, producing a hard, rough object which the ancients used to think was hurled down from the sky by an angry god. This was the so-called "thunderbolt". The word is now used to describe a sudden or overwhelming occurrence.

WHEN did a rift valley occur? WHEN does clay form?

RIFT VALLEY

The great rift valleys of the earth took shape during the pleistocene age, about two million years ago. They were caused mainly by volcanic eruptions powerful enough to split a mountain range, thus creating a rift between the two sides of the volcano.

Rift valleys are to be found in all parts of the world where volcanic action has been common. The most impressive example is the Great Rift Valley which extends from Jordan in south-west Asia to Mozambique in southern Africa. Many big lakes are situated within the valley's boundaries.

Extremely steep edges are characteristic of these valleys. In Africa their valleys rise to heights of 10,000 feet on either side.

CLAY

Clay is formed from earth and various minerals as a result of weather conditions such as heat and rain. Occasionally clay is produced by processes dependant on hot underground springs.

Wet clay has much the same constituency as a soft plastic and is capable of containing water.

When dry, clay becomes hard and takes on a permanent shape.

No other material on earth can be used in so many different ways. Clay provides the mechanical and chemical environment for almost all plant life and, therefore, can be said to support all the life on earth.

Once extracted from the soil, clays are used in a wide variety of industries, including engineering, paper making, brick making, cement and chemicals. The use of clay in pottery predates recorded history, and it has largely been due to pottery finds that archaeologists have been able to analyse and record past civilizations.

is marble formed?   WHEN was the sextant invented?

SEXTANT

The sextant was invented in England in 1731 by John Hadley. Hadley's instrument is used mainly at sea to determine a ship's latitude, or distance from the Equator. Its invention laid the foundation of modern navigation with the aid of the sun and stars.

The instrument is so called because it is equipped with an arc which is usually one-sixth of a circle, or 60 degrees. It measures the angle of the sun's or a star's altitude above the horizon. As this angle varies with the distance from the Equator, the information obtained helps the navigator to calculate his position. All he needs in addition is the time, the date and the longitude which can be found by comparing local time with the time at Greenwich.

To operate the sextant, the navigator looks through its small telescope straight at the horizon. At the same time, an image of the sun is reflected by mirrors into the user's field of vision. When the sun is made to appear exactly on the horizon, the arm which moves the mirrors gives the required measurements to calculate the ship's position.

The handling of a sextant is generally referred to as "shooting the sun"

A quarry of Carrara marble in North-West Tuscany, Italy.

MARBLE

Marble is formed when granular limestone or dolomite rocks crystallize twice under the influence of heat, pressure, liquids and chemical action. These rocks undergo what is known as metamorphism, a complete change from one state to another.

Most of the marble existing today was formed many millions of years ago and is usually quarried from deep under the earth. It is used for buildings and monuments, sculpture and table tops. The chief discoveries of marble have been made in Italy (Carrara marble), Mexico, the United States (onyx), Norway and Greece.

THE KREMLIN

The Kremlin was the palace of the Russian Tsars in Moscow until Peter the Great (1672–1725) moved the whole imperial court to the newly-founded city of St Petersburg (now Leningrad) early in the 18th Century.

In 1922 Moscow was chosen as the capital of the Union of Soviet Socialist Republics. Once again the Kremlin became the headquarters of government.

Encircled by great battlements erected in the 15th Century, the citadel covers an area of 65 acres and is almost a city itself. Around the walls are 19 towers and five gates, the finest of them being Spasskaya (Saviour's) Tower and Gate which houses the Kremlin chimes. Men used to doff their hats as they passed by this gate in Red Square.

Within the walls are churches, four cathedrals and many palaces. In 1955 the Kremlin was opened to the public and the palaces now exhibit the riches of Tsarist days.

Outside the walls is Red Square, 900 yards long by 175 yards wide, where the great military parades are held annually to commemorate the revolution of 1917. The embalmed body of Lenin (1870–1924), leader of the revolution, lies in its mausoleum in front of the Kremlin's wall.

The defensive fortresses at the centre of many medieval Russian cities were also called Kremlin, which is where the word comes from.

is Magyar spoken officially?

EASTER ISLAND

Easter Island, one of the most mysterious islands in the world, is in the South Pacific, 2,000 miles west of Caldera in Chile and 1,000 miles east of Pitcairn, its nearest inhabited neighbour. It was annexed by Chile in 1888. The island which is volcanic in origin, was discovered by the Dutch admiral Jacob Roggeveen on Easter Sunday, 1722. It is 11 miles long and 15 miles wide.

Easter Island is noted for its mysterious statues of remote and unknown origin. These statues, consisting of giant heads facing inland, fringe the island's coastline. They stand on huge ramparts or platforms which slope landwards, in some cases to a width of 250 feet. At the end of this sloping rampart there is a paved area.

There are some 260 of these platforms on the island and each one was designed to support between one and 15 of the strange giant heads, carved from compressed volcanic earth. The heads have upturned faces tilted towards the sky, and long ears. They vary in height from 12 to 20 feet. At one time they were topped by huge hats or crowns between six and eight feet in diameter. These hats are made from a red volcanic material different from the material used for the heads themselves.

The island is full of ancient curiosities including long, narrow boat-shaped houses flanked by stone chicken huts. The inhabitants are descendants of Polynesian people who migrated across the Pacific.

There is a legend of a war between the "long-eared" people and their "short-eared" attackers. The long-eared defenders of the island were said to have been burned in a vast earth oven, but the latest scientific evidence suggests that the "earth oven" was in fact a vast defensive ditch. Ashes in this ditch date from the 17th Century, only a short time before the island's discovery.

But the real truth about Easter Island and its mysterious statues will probably never be known until someone finds out how to read the curious sign language inscribed round the platforms. These signs, which are geometrical in form, are really symbols such as birds, plants and fishes. They may be like the "memory aids" of the ancient Aztecs, but experts believe they are an elementary form of writing.

MAGYAR LANGUAGE

The Magyar language is the official language of Hungary (or, in the Magyar language, the country of Magyarorszaq). In 1967 the population was 10,197,000 with another two million Magyar-speaking people living outside Hungary—mainly in Czechoslovakia, Rumania and Yugoslavia. Nearly half a million Magyars live in the United States of America.

Magyar belongs to the Arabic language family. Apart from Finland, where the language is closely related to Hungarian, the only part of the world where you are likely to hear anything similar is in western Siberia.

Because several suffixes, or smaller words, are often added, the Magyars can produce words of considerable length. For instance, "the very biggest" would be "legeslegnagyobb" in Magyar.

The first written example of Magyar dates from about 1200, when a short funeral oration was recorded.

WHY do deserts form? WHY are igneous rocks different from WHY are there locks on some canals and rivers?

DESERTS

Deserts in hot climates owe their origin to lack of water resulting from the capacity of warm air above the desert area to retain most of the available moisture. This, combined with the high evaporation rate, turn the land into desert.

Another factor in the formation of deserts is a high mountain range, such as the Andes. These enormous mountains lie across the path of the rain clouds and moist winds, thus forming a shield. So most of the rain clouds burst over the mountains before they ever reach the plains. Other deserts, such as the Gobi in Central China, are so deep within the continent that the moisture-laden winds hardly ever reach them.

IGNEOUS ROCKS

Sedimentary rocks are formed from the sediment, or broken pieces of the earth's rock structure worn down by weather and erosion. The fragmented pieces become compacted and in time much of it is cemented in to form rock.

Igneous rocks originate either from volcanic action as molten lava, which hardens, or from the slow cooling of molten masses beneath the earth's surface, which are exposed after a volcanic eruption or after much erosion.

Many important minerals, notably uranium, have been found enveloped in igneous rocks. The chief sedimentary rocks are sandstone, shale, dolomite and limestone.

RIVER DELTAS

A river winding its way down to the sea, from its mountain source, will inevitably choose the lowest land through which to flow. By the time the river approaches the sea the speed at which it is travelling will have decreased considerably, thus allowing the water to drop its load of sediment and other solids.

These solid particles (alluvium), therefore, form the land pockets which are characteristic of the various branches of a river delta. Owing to slow pace of a river at this stage, it will wind its way round any elevated land points rather than go over them.

Deltas are most likely to form where the sea, into which the river flows, is particularly calm for most of the year. Notable deltas in the world include the Mississippi (the largest) the Ganges, and the Nile. A delta is so called because it is the name of the fourth letter of the Greek alphabet whose shape it resembles.

sedimentary rocks? WHY do river deltas form? WHY does the Sahara constantly change shape?

SAHARA

The Sahara, the world's greatest dry hot desert, stretches right across the north of Africa where there is almost no rainfall and, consequently, little or no vegetation to anchor the soil. The sand is blown constantly by the wind, much of it into a landscape of great shifting dunes which constantly change shape, while the edges of the desert eternally encroach upon the land around.

The Sahara extends over three and a half million square miles of and, where the average rainfall is generally much less than 10 inches a year. The prevailing winds come from the heart of Asia and carry little moisture.

The temperature during the day exceeds 100°F. in the summer, and even in the winter averages 60°–70°F. The surface of the sand is sometimes as hot as 170°F. The sun beats down from a clear sky all day, but at night the same cloudless sky allows the land to cool quickly, and there is often frost at dawn in winter.

The wind acts as a great sand-blasting machine, constantly wearing down rocks and carrying sand and small pebbles along. The few desert plants survive because they have long roots or thick fleshy leaves, and stems that reduce water loss and may even store moisture.

A desert oasis is simply a place where there is water. The greatest oasis of all is Egypt, where for thousands of years life has depended on the careful use of the waters of the River Nile.

CANAL LOCKS

Locks are watertight chambers which enable boats to ascend or descend to different levels in a canal or river.

The lock is usually rectangular in shape with gates at either end. If a boat has to go to a higher level it enters through the bottom or downstream gates of the lock, which are then closed. The water level in the lock is raised to that of the higher part of the canal by filling from the upper level and the upstream gates are opened to let the boat out. The opposite procedure takes place when a boat needs to descend.

Locks used to be made of timber, brick or stone, but now concrete and steel piling are more usual. Originally the chamber was filled or emptied by sluices in the gates. Nowadays, as locks become big-

ger, these are often replaced by conduits or pipes running the whole length of the structure, with offshoot pipes running into the lock to give an even discharge of water. Old locks may be manually operated but new ones are worked by hydraulic power.

Locks vary tremendously in size from about 126 by 17 feet (38 by 5 metres) on small canals to the giant locks on the Mississippi River in America, which are 1,200 by 110 feet (366 by 33·5 metres).

WHERE is the world's largest island – apart from Australia?

WHERE is the driest place on earth?
WHERE is the hottest place on earth?

LARGEST ISLAND

The largest island in the world is Greenland—if we exclude mainland Australia, which ranks as a continent.

Most of Greenland, which has an area of 840,000 square miles, lies within the Arctic circle. More than 708,000 square miles are covered with ice. Greenland is about 1,650 miles long and nearly 800 miles wide. In the extreme north it is separated only by a 25-mile wide strait from the Canadian Arctic archipelago.

The island is divided into two natural regions. One is the coastal region, where the mountains rise out of the ice. The other is the ice sheet, which covers more than four-fifths of the country, burying all valleys and mountains far below its surface. The highest mountain in Greenland is Mount Gunnbjorn which rises up to 12,139 feet. As the whole country lies north of the tree line there are no forests, but in the south-west groups of trees do grow up to 10 feet in height.

The polar climate is uncertain and changes suddenly from bright sunshine to dense fog or heavy falls of snow. Temperatures can vary from 10° Centigrade (50° Fahrenheit) in July on the coast to about —47° Centigrade (—52·6° Fahrenheit) in the interior. The lowest recorded temperature in winter was —65° Centigrade (—85° Fahrenheit).

Greenland forms a part of the Danish kingdom. In 1960 its population was 33,140. The islanders speak both Danish and Eskimo.

DRIEST PLACE

The driest place on earth is to be found in Chile in the Atacama Desert at Calama. Weather reports for Chile date only from the Spanish conquest about 400 years ago. In those last 400 years not one drop of rain has fallen.

This part of the Deisorto de Atacama has suffered the longest drought in recorded history. Strangely, Chile also has one of the wettest places on earth. Not too far from the Atacama Desert is Bahia Felix. In 1916 it rained there on every day of the year.

HOTTEST PLACE

For sheer consistency the hottest place in the world is Lugh Ganane in Somalia, east Africa, where the temperature never falls below about 31° Centigrade (88° Fahrenheit.

However, the hottest temperature ever recorded was in 1933 at San Luis Potosi in Mexico where about 58° Centigrade (136° Fahrenheit) in the shade was recorded.

In California in 1917 temperatures about 49° Centigrade (120° Fahrenheit) were recorded on 43 consecutive days—in Death Valley, not surprisingly.

Western Australia also has more than its fair share of sunshine. At Marble Bar, for instance, the temperature remained around 100°F for 160 days and in 1946 at Wyndham, again in Western Australia, the temperature reached 90°F or more, for almost the whole year (333 days to be exact).

HEAVIEST METAL

The heaviest metal in the world is iridium. It was discovered in 1804 by Smithson Tennant of the United Kingdom. Iridium, which is a silvery-white metal of the platinum group, weighs 1,414 pounds a cubic foot or roughly two-thirds of a ton. Lithium, the lightest metal, weighs 33 pounds per cubic foot.

If you could stand an elephant weighing nearly six tons at one end of a seesaw, you would need only a two-foot cube of iridium at the other end to lift the animal. Such a cube would cost nearly £15,000,000.

BEAUFORT SCALE

The Beaufort Scale is a scale for measuring the strength or velocity of the wind; the various strengths are given in numbers. It was formulated in 1805 by the British Admiral Sir Francis Beaufort, and has been periodically revised since then. It ranges from Calm, when smoke rises vertically and the wind is less than 1 m.p.h. to Beaufort Number 12—a hurricane, when the air at sea is filled with foam and spray, and the wind exceeds 68 m.p.h.

DEPRESSION

A depression is an area of low pressure, usually bringing unsettled weather. A deepening depression has a lowering of pressure at its centre.

The profile of a depression would read as follows: "A warm front bringing a wide belt of layered clouds with steady rain. It will be followed by a cold front bringing first showers then brighter, more settled weather. In the warm sector between the two fronts we can expect quiet, dull weather broken by storms."

Official weather observers make their observations of the atmospheric conditions at the end of each six-hour period during the day. Daily reports from many different observers on land and at sea are collected together to make up a weather-map summary.

The weather-map consists of patterns of lines, very similar to the contours on a geographical map, along with various other signs and symbols.

Force 1 Direction of wind shown by smoke

Force 2 Wind felt on face

Force 3 Wind extends light flag

Force 4 Small branches move

Force 5 Small trees in leaf begin to sway

Force 6 Umbrellas turn inside out

Force 7 Whole trees sway; walking into wind is difficult

Force 8 Cars swerve on road

Force 9 Chimney pots and roof slates blown away

Force 10 Trees uprooted

Force 11 Widespread damage

Force 12 Houses collapse

COAL

Coal comes from the remains of trees, shrubs, and plants that grew millions of years ago, at a time when the weather was mild and moist.

The coal beds of today were once vast swamps. When the plants and trees died, they fell into boggy water. They did not rot away completely. They changed into a slimy material called peat. Then the sea washed over the peat, bringing up sand and stones, and changing the soil around it. Over millions of years, water, weather and the continual movement of the soil compressed and dried this original peat into good coal.

Coal is formed from the compressed remains of trees that grew in swampy land millions of years ago.

Open cast *mining is used when the coal is near the surface.*

Drift *mining uses horizontal shafts driven into the side of a hill.*

Shaft *mining is needed when the coal is deep beneath the surface.*

Galleries *have to be driven at angles to follow twisted seams of anthracite.*

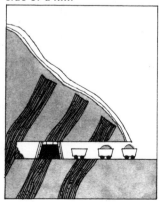
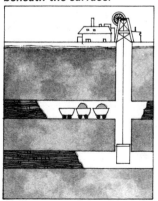
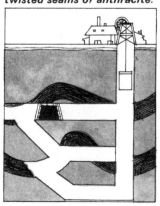

GOLDEN GATE

The Golden Gate is the name given to the break in the long chain of mountains running down the Pacific Ocean coastline of California. This gate, or gap, forms the sea entrance to San Francisco Bay.

The gap was mapped in 1846 by John C. Frémont, an American Army officer and explorer, who named it CHRYSOPYLAE—which is Greek for Golden Gate.

The bay itself had been discovered by accident in 1769, when a Spanish explorer, Gaspar de Portola, intending to establish a mission-cum-garrison at Monterey Bay, overshot his objective by several miles.

A small settlement was gradually established until, in 1848, San Francisco became the base for the gold strike in the famous Sacramento Valley. Within a year the population increased from 2,000 to 25,000. In the latter half of the 19th Century wharves and warehouses sprang up on the bay. Houses and offices, restaurants and bars spread rapidly over the steep slopes of its hills.

Rudyard Kipling, the English author, visited San Francisco in the 1880s and found it to be "a mad city inhabited for the most part by perfectly insane people whose women are of a remarkable beauty".

The great earthquake and fire of 1906 destroyed almost a third of the city. Apart from killing 450 people, it left over 100,000 homeless and did millions of dollars worth of damage.

Even so San Francisco continued to be an increasingly important maritime centre. Now about 12,000 ships use it annually. Whether liner, small cargo boat or yacht, every vessel must sail through the Golden Gate to reach the open sea.

Landlocked San Francisco Bay extends over an area of 422 square miles, but the Gate is only two miles across at its widest point. It has a tidal flow half as big again as the water flow of the River Amazon.

In 1937 work was completed on the Golden Gate Bridge to speed traffic along the coast from San Francisco. It is one of the world's man-made marvels with a central span 4,200 feet long.

of the Long White Cloud?

LONG WHITE CLOUD

The Land of the Long White Cloud is a translation of the Polynesian name for New Zealand. In the 12th Century, bands of Polynesian adventurers voyaged thousands of miles from their Pacific islands and made landfall in the country they named Ao-tea-roa.

The descendants of those adventurers are the friendly and highly intelligent people we know as the Maoris, the original settlers of New Zealand. The land and its people were discovered and named by the Dutch navigator Abel Janszoon Tasman in 1642, although he never landed.

It was not until 1769 that a European set foot in the country. Captain James Cook, the English explorer, landed in New Zealand and then sailed on to Australia. In the next eight years he came back three times.

The first settlers were sealers, whalers and traders. In 1814 a British missionary, the Rev. Samuel Marsden, began work among the Maoris. Within six years he had been joined by a number of British emigrants, and New Zealand was made a British colony. It became a dominion in 1907.

New Zealand consists of two main islands. From the top of North Island to the bottom of South Island the country is scarcely 1,000 miles long. Nowhere is it wider than 280 miles, and usually it is much narrower. But within this compass it is a land of strange and beautiful contrasts.

New Zealand's 3,000,000 inhabitants live a life where poverty is unknown and serious crime is rare. The climate is temperate and the scenery spectacular.

It is a curious fact New Zealand has no native land animals. The ancestors of the pigs, goats, rabbits, opossums, weasels and ferrets were imported. Some of the animals—rabbits for example—have since become pests. In compensation New Zealand has a huge variety of fish and birds.

In spite of its small population, the country has produced many outstanding writers, artists, musicians and scientists and has given support and encouragement to the revival and development of Maori arts and crafts.

262

WHEN is pumice stone formed? WHEN will man be able to

WHEN was coffee first grown? WHEN are contour

PUMICE STONE

Pumice stone is formed when molten volcanic glass, ejected from beneath the earth's crust, cools so rapidly that there is no time for it to crystalize.

After the pumice has solidified, the gases inside are suddenly released and the stone swells up into its characteristic light and airy form. If the substance had cooled under greater pressure it would have turned into solid glass.

The stones have long been used for cleaning and polishing. Since the Second World War it has been employed widely in railroad building, masonry and insulation. Good pumice is found in Iceland, the Canaries, New Zealand, Greece, the Pacific coast of the United States and many other areas with a volcanic background.

WEATHER CONTROL

Since the 1940s scientists have discovered techniques by which several weather conditions can be controlled. For example, it is possible to prevent lightning by using an electrical earth to diffuse the electrical content of a cloud. The American scientist V. J. Schaefer has shown that it is feasible to produce greater concentrations of ice in clouds than occur under normal conditions.

Weather experts already are taking advantage of these discoveries to increase snowfall on mountains for winter sports, to prevent damaging hailstones and to moderate, or even prevent, the development of dangerous storms. Scientists are now able, in some cases, to make a cloud burst to produce rainfall over parched areas.

These local efforts may lead the way to large-scale weather control. But before then scientists may have to learn to cope with the damaging effect of air pollution on weather conditions.

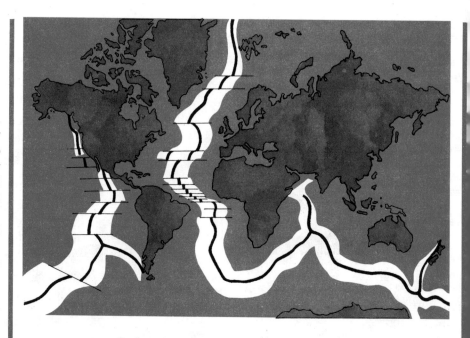

OCEAN MAPS

The shape of the ocean floor was not accurately determined until the 1920s. Until the end of the last century mapping had depended on the accounts by sailors of rock formations and deep troughs in the ocean bed.

Recent scientific developments, and new instruments and techniques have enabled maps to be drawn with greater accuracy and detail. By transmitting sound waves from ships to the sea bed, and back, it is possible to make a record of the changes in depth.

Mechanical, acoustical and electronic instruments have pictured the ocean floor not as a vast plain but as a series of mountain ranges, valleys, peaks and canyons. Some of the mountains are far higher than most of those on land and the deepest part of the ocean is much farther below sea level than the highest land mountain is above it.

COFFEE

A legend says the coffee plant first grew in Kaffa, a province in south Ethiopia, where it was discovered by a goatherd called Kaldi about the year 850. Kaldi's goats were reported to have skipped and pranced in a strange manner after feeding on an evergreen plant. The goatherd, so the story goes, tried some of the berries himself and excitedly dashed to the nearest town to tell of his find, which was called coffee after the name of the province.

Another theory is that the word coffee is probably derived from the Arabic *qahwah*. Certainly coffee was introduced into Europe from Arabia during the 16th and 17th Centuries. The first licence to sell coffee in the United States was issued to Dorothy Jones of Boston in 1670. The coffee houses of this time became famous meeting places for discussion.

As the drinking of coffee became more popular, its production spread to Java, Haiti, Dutch Guiana, Brazil, Cuba, Jamaica, Puerto Rica, Costa Rica, Venezuela, Mexico, Colombia, the Hawaiian Islands and, in this century, Africa.

Right: *coffee beans drying in the sun in a small Guinea village*.

control the weather? WHEN was the ocean floor first mapped? lines used on maps?

CONTOUR LINES

Contour lines are used when maps are designed to show the physical nature of the land. They do this by linking all points which are the same height above sea level. The width between the contour lines indicates the steepness of gra-dients or slopes in the area. The closer the lines are together, the steeper is the slope.

On physical maps giving the height of mountains, rivers, lakes and principal towns all areas between certain heights are gener-ally shown in the same colour. This is known as layer colouring.

Other methods for indicating heights include relief maps moulded in plastic to the physical feature raised as on a model. Spot heights may be shown, but these merely give the heights above sea level of certain points of the map and it does not follow that the ground rises evenly from one point to another.

Very old maps have mountains drawn on them. Later ones have lines called hachures radiating from a central point, with longer lines to show gentler slopes. Another system is to show the form of the land by hill shading. But none of these methods is so effective as the use of contour lines.

Thick line shows axial rift valley; white shows oceanic trenches.

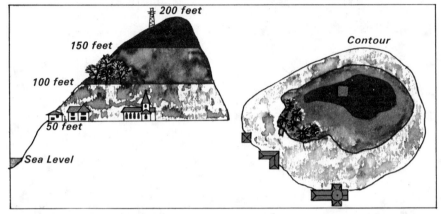

WHERE can you look for precious stones?   WHERE is the

PRECIOUS STONES

Precious stones, or gems, are minerals used for adornment, and they are found in rocks. Rocks are divided into three groups. The igneous (fire-formed) rocks may be fine-grained or coarse-grained; a very coarse-grained type, called pegmatite, is an important source of gem minerals such as diamonds. Gems are also found in the cavities of the igneous rocks granite and obsidian.

Sedimentary rocks are layered rocks and, except for turquoise and opal, are the source of very few gems. However, when the original rock contained heavy minerals— and gem minerals are heavy— pebbles of them tended to be deposited as pebbles in a river bed and such deposits form the gem gravels of Upper Burma, the "byon", and those of Ceylon, the "illam".

Metamorphic rocks — rocks which have been altered by pres-

sure—are a fruitful source of gem minerals, for instance the rubies found in Burma.

There are also precious materials of animal origin—pearls from oysters, ivory from elephants and coral from the tiny sea creatures which give their name to it. There are also amber and jet, whose origin is vegetable. Amber is the fossilized resin of a coniferous tree which grew in the Eocene period. Jet is a variety of fossil wood.

Gems are found throughout the world and are prized for their rarity and beauty. Their charm may depend on transparency and depth of colour as in the ruby and emerald, on colour only as in the turquoise, on purity and "fire" as in the diamond, and on "play of colour" as in the opal.

These beautiful emeralds came from uncut stones like the one shown.

MIDNIGHT SUN

The land of the Midnight Sun is the poetical name for Norway.

In that country from the end of April to the middle of August there is no real night darkness, but a long twilight. In the most northern part, the sun never sets com-

VICTORIA FALLS

These famous falls, among the most spectacular in the world, are on the boundary between Rhodesia and Zambia in southern Africa. The falls form the most remarkable feature of the Zambezi River. They are midway up the Zambezi near the town of Livingstone, which is named after David Livingstone, the Scottish missionary and explorer, who discovered the falls in 1855.

For some distance before the Victoria Falls the Zambezi flows over a level sheet of basalt—a hard, blue volcanic rock—in a valley between sandstone hills. Curiously, the Zambezi does not increase its speed of flow as it nears the mighty falls. The water pours over an almost vertical precipice, nearly a mile wide, at a rate of between four million and 75 million gallons a minute, depending on the season. The minimum flow is between November and December and the maximum between April and May.

The Victoria Falls are wider than Niagara Falls and more than twice their height. At the highest point the water plunges 355 feet.

The only outlet for this vast force of water is a narrow channel cut in the opposing barrier wall near its western end. The river is forced through this narrow, 100-foot gorge for nearly 400 feet. This part of the Falls is aptly known as the Boiling Pot.

From the Boiling Pot the water emerges into an enormous zig-zag which forms the beginning of the Batoka Gorge, about 60 miles long.

At one time it was thought that these fantastic falls were the result of a volcanic fault in the earth. Now it is believed they are caused by the check on the natural erosion of the river bed provided by the hard basaltic rock sheets.

pletely for about two months in the summer.

In winter, however, the most northern inhabitants are not so lucky. They have no sun for two months and have to eat their lunch in twilight.

266

WHY were early maps decorated?   WHY are some wells
WHY does a compass point north—south?

EARLY MAPS

Many early maps were decorated because the map-makers or cartographers had little real idea of geography and presented the world in symbolical terms. One map of Roman times showed the world as a T within an O. The O represented the ocean boundaries of the earth and the T the known world, with the Mediterranean as the upright and the horizontal bar as the meridian from the Nile to the River Don. Jerusalem was at the centre and elaborate decorations often included Paradise and the Last Judgment.

As the shapes of more coastlines were discovered, the unexplored land masses behind them were often filled in by map-makers with decorative portrayals of imagined animals and vegetation. The seas contained monsters and pictures of ships.

Even when maps became more accurate, decorations survived because cartographers saw their craft as a mixture of science and art.

Some maps were specially commissioned to be given as gifts to noble patrons or sovereigns. Unlike ordinary maps for use at sea, these special productions were magnificently decorated, with the seas and lands full of fabulous animals and the winds portrayed as human. The houses and ships shown were usually accurate pictures of those in use at the time the maps were made.

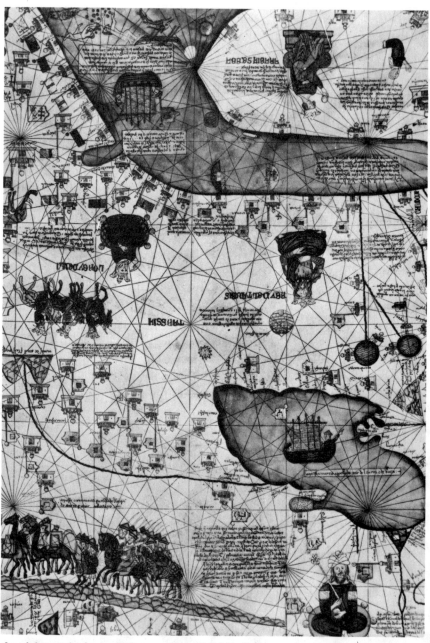

An elaborately decorated map of the Middle East

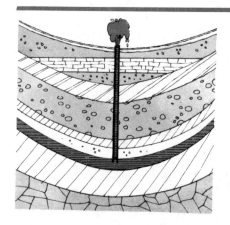

ARTESIAN WELLS

Artesian wells are those from which water flows freely. These wells are man-made and are created by boring into the rock to a channel that is lower than the water source.

The resulting artesian well has the advantage over vertical wells of not requiring a pump. The water will pour out naturally without the aid of any mechanism until the well runs dry. For this reason artesian wells, although often several hundred feet deep, may be only a few inches wide. This prevents undue loss of water.

The term "artesian well" is derived from Artesium, the ancient name for Artois in Northern France, where a famous free-flowing well was excavated early in the 12th Century.

called artesian wells?

WHY does India have monsoons?

COMPASS

When the magnetic needle of a compass is allowed to move freely it will automatically place itself in line with the earth's magnetic field, one end pointing to the magnetic North Pole while the other indicates the South.

Natural magnets, such as loadstone or pieces of iron which have been touched by a loadstone, are to be found the world over. It was the discovery that loadstone would always place itself so as to lie in a magnetic north-to-south position that led to the invention of the magnet.

During the 15th Century it was realized that the magnetic North Pole and the Geographic North Pole were not exactly in the same place. The small angle between the two is known by seamen as "the variation". Some experts have claimed, however, that the Chinese were already aware of the existence of variation as early as the 11th Century. Again, in the 15th Century, it became apparent that the earth itself was a great magnet.

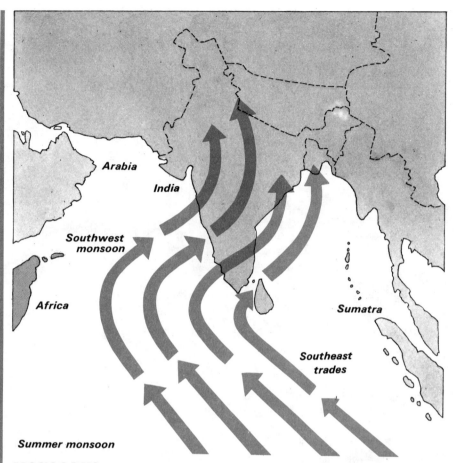

Summer monsoon

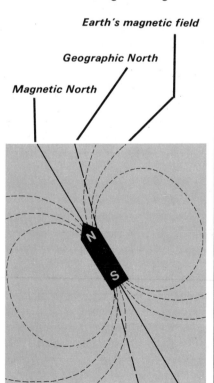

Earth's magnetic field

Geographic North

Magnetic North

MONSOONS

The seasonal winds of south-west Asia known as monsoons are associated particularly with India because of the tremendous effects they have on the lives of the inhabitants. The winds are drawn to India by changes in the temperature of the great land mass. A good monsoon season with plenty of rain means a comparatively good supply of food. A bad monsoon with little rain means a bad rice crop and, perhaps, starvation for many millions.

Monsoon comes from the Arabic *mausim*, meaning season. The summer season monsoon is a great inrush of moisture-laden air from the ocean. The winter monsoon blows from the land to the sea.

In India there are three seasons: the hot dry season from March to June; the hot wet season from June to November; and the cool dry season from December to March. During the hot dry season the great plains of northern India become like a furnace and a region of low pressure develops.

By mid-June, the pressure is low all the way to the Equator and draws the south-east trade winds to India, filled with water-vapour as they cross the Indian Ocean. When they meet the hot dry air over India, violent thunderstorms result, followed by steady rain in July. By November India has received three-quarters of its annual rainfall.

Then the land mass cools and the high pressure attracts the north east trade winds. These bring no rain to India except to the Coromandel Coast and Ceylon, where the rainfall in late September is heavy, because the winds have picked up water vapour as they move across the wide expanse of the Bay of Bengal.

WHAT makes a river wind? WHAT are the Northern Lights?

RIVER

A river always takes the easiest course through channels and soft ground to the sea, flowing swiftly down mountain sides but much more slowly on the level plains.

On the plain the river takes advantage of every difference in gradient. This winding course is accentuated by the process of silting and erosion. As a river flows round a curve, the water on the outer bend moves more swiftly to cover the greater distance in the same time as the water flowing past the inner bend.

The more rapidly moving water will tend to wear away the banks of the channel, while the slower movement of the water on the inside wall will allow silting to take place. When the curve becomes more pronounced it is known as a "meander". Notable examples of meanders are to be found in the Wye in England, and the Meuse in France.

Sometimes the river erodes the bank so fiercely that a new channel is formed, leaving an island of earth in the middle of the stream.

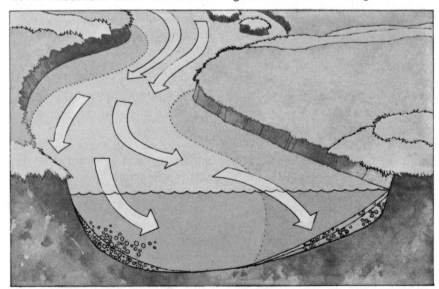

WHAT causes mountains?

NORTHERN LIGHTS

The Northern Lights are long, waving streamers of light, often seen in the night sky in the Northern Hemisphere during both warm and cold weather. These marvellous, wavering illuminations are also called the Aurora Borealis, from the Latin words meaning a "northern dawn". They are most frequently seen between 65 degrees and 80 degrees northern latitude, but the area of visibility extends further south in North America than in Europe. The aurora of the southern hemisphere is called the Aurora Australis, from the Latin for "southern dawn".

The bands of light in the aurora seem to radiate from an arc and send their rays far across the heavens. They are most often white, but are sometimes green, red or yellowish. The luminous streamers may be almost straight, or they may wind backwards and forwards like glimmering snakes in the sky. Sometimes the rays look like a fan, or form a crown round a dark centre. At other times the long beams of light may seem to fall downwards like the folds of a gigantic, shimmering curtain. Their apparent movement is often so rapid that they have been called the "Merry Dancers".

Scientific studies of auroras began in 1716 with a spectacular display that was visible over the whole of Europe. The English astronomer Edmund Halley (1656–1742) proved a connection between them and the earth's magnetism. But the exact cause of the auroras is still not completely understood. The most likely theory is that they have their origin in streams of electrically charged particles from the sun, which are turned aside to the north and south magnetic poles on reaching the upper layers of the earth's atmosphere.

Auroras are most pronounced during magnetic storms, that is during the time that the earth's magnetic field is most disturbed. They also tend to occur when there have been signs of unusual activity in the sun.

MOUNTAINS

The first mountains and valleys were the crust formed as a result of the cooling of the molten mass of the earth. As the planet contracted the crust twisted and cracked, forming new mountains.

Mountains are still being formed by volcanic eruption. A crack in the earth's crust allows molten rock and ash to be forced out, forming a cone-shaped mountain growing as it continues to erupt.

Fault-mountains are formed when the earth's crust cracks, or faults, under pressure from inside, and one side of the break is pushed up against the other to form a cliff.

The highest mountains are in the Himalayas where some are over 25,000 feet. Only in the Rocky Mountains and in the Andes are there any others over 20,000 feet.

270

WHY did the continents drift apart? WHY is a seismograph

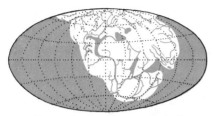

Upper Carboniferous period

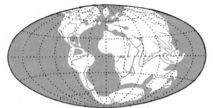

Eocene period

Lower Quaternary period

CONTINENTAL DRIFT

One of the most convincing explanations of why the continents drifted apart is that the earth expanded considerably after its creation. This theory can be illustrated by imagining the earth as a balloon and the continents as pieces of paper stuck on the outside. As the balloon is blown up the pieces of paper will grow farther apart.

Other theories suggest that the continents only appeared to drift apart because masses of land were drowned under volcanic waters. But it has been demonstrated that land masses are, in fact, made to drift, by the heat generated from the earth's interior and from earthquakes.

Probably a combination of various theories may be necessary to provide a complete explanation.

SEISMOGRAPH

A seismograph is used to measure the vibrations of the earth and to locate the source of earth vibrations. Phenomena capable of being detected by a seismograph include earthquakes, volcanic eruptions, explosions such as bombs, powerful winds, violent storms at sea and even, in urban areas, traffic.

Thanks to the seismograph whole populations can be warned and prepared for a variety of natural disasters. Seismic observatories around the world, have provided information increasing our knowledge of the earth's structure.

The seismograph operates on one of two basically simple mechanisms which are devices responsive to strain and pendulums. The earliest form of seismograph known was developed in China in the 2nd Century.

There are many examples of the usefulness of seismographs in a wide variety of fields. They have been used to measure the thickness of the ice sheets covering the polar regions of the earth and, when used in conjunction with artificial explosions created under special test conditions, seismographs can help geologists trace oil fields.

AVALANCHES

An avalanche occurs when a mass of snow which has built up on a mountain side begins to slip and finally to fall. There can also be avalanches of earth, stones, rock and ice, but usually the word is used to describe a rapid fall of snow.

Snow builds up to great thickness on steep slopes, especially if the surface is not smooth. Even a very small disturbance may set it in motion. The vibration of a passing vehicle, the movement of a man or animal, the fall of a tree branch or even a sound can cause thousands of tons of snow to crash down a mountainside.

The speed of an avalanche varies enormously, but some have been estimated to move at about 200 miles an hour. A big avalanche hurtles down the side of the mountain with a thunderous roar, crushing or sweeping away anything in its path.

The swiftly moving mass of snow pushes the air in front of it with such violence that it fans out sideways as well as driving directly ahead. This wind sometimes reaches a force almost equal to that of a tornado. This great wind is often a more powerful force of destruction than the avalanche itself.

EARTHQUAKES

Earthquakes occur mainly in the regions of the earth where mountains are being formed, and where the earth's crust is under strain.

Some mountains are formed of great thicknesses of folded sedimentary rock laid down beneath the sea. Heat currents deep within the earth are thought to suck down sections of the undersea crust and so produce great trenches thousands of feet deep. When the heat currents die away the material forming the bottom of the trench begins to rise because it is lighter in weight. Eventually it is thrust up as a mountain range.

This is never a smooth process but is accompanied by great friction and heat, as well as by rending and shearing and tearing. The tearing and shearing of deep underground rocks connected with mountain formation cause earthquakes. Even small underground movements may produce violent surface shocks. The great Tokyo earthquake of 1923 which is believed to have killed 200 thousand people was caused by the twisting of a section of the earth's crust in Sagami Bay.

As might be expected, ocean trenches are the seat of a great many earthquakes, for there the earth's crust is in an unstable state. Indeed all the deep earthquakes — those taking place more than 160 miles below the surface — originate around the Pacific trenches. About 90 per cent of the intermediate earthquakes (30 to 160 miles deep) also originate there, as do 40 per cent of the shallow earthquakes (less than 30 miles deep).

Some shallow and intermediate earthquakes are caused by volcanoes or by a slight shifting of layers of rock at a weak place or "fault" on the earth's surface. One of the most famous and widely publicized of these is the San Andreas fault on which San Francisco is built.

272

WHEN does litmus paper turn red? WHEN will man land on

Science and Technology

LITMUS PAPER

Litmus paper turns red when placed in an acid solution, but blue if the solution is alkaline. This absorbent paper is the oldest and most commonly used indicator of the presence or absence of acid. Its special qualities are due to the fact that it has been soaked and impregnated with a mixture of dyes called litmus.

The litmus mixture was originally produced by the action of air, ammonia and an alkali carbonate on certain lichens found in the Netherlands. It is now made from azolitmin and erythrolitmin.

A litmus solution is sometimes used. But the message is the same. A few drops added to a liquid turns it red if acid and blue if alkaline.

NEON SIGN

The first neon sign was made by Georges Claude in France in 1910. Neon, an inert gas, was discovered in 1898 by the British scientists Sir William Ramsay and M. W. Travers. It is colourless, odourless and tasteless and is widely distributed in nature. Neon is called an inert gas because it is not affected by the usual chemical reactions.

In 1850 a German physicist, Heinrich Gessler, demonstrated that a brilliant light is produced when electricity is discharged through such a gas. Neon proved to be ideal for advertising because of its unusually high electrical conductivity, its adaptibility, its high luminosity and the brilliant colours obtainable by the addition of other inert gases and mercury vapour.

But neon light tubes do not give enough light for general illumination, and the colours that can be produced from it are not suitable for indoor lighting.

MAN ON A PLANET

No definite date can be given for man's first landing on another planet, but it is not expected until after the next decade. The first planet to be visited is likely to be Mars. Venus, the nearest to earth, is too inhospitable, for it is enveloped in gases and has a surface temperature of about 900° Centigrade (1,650° Fahrenheit).

Already much effort has been devoted to finding out the conditions which would have to be overcome on a planetary journey. The Russians have organized "sampler" expeditions with unmanned, radio-controlled space vehicles. At the same time Americans aboard the "sky laboratory" in orbit round the earth have concentrated on the problems of enduring long periods of space travel.

another planet? **WHEN** was the first neon sign made?

274

WHAT is an alchemist? WHAT makes silver tarnish? WHAT

ALCHEMIST

An alchemist was an early student of the science of chemistry. According to one theory the word "alchemy" is derived from "Khem", the ancient name for Egypt. That country was the source of a great deal of the pioneer work in the various sciences.

Much of the early work of the alchemists is frowned on by to-day's scientists because it was bound up with experiments to find "the elixir of life" and "the philosopher's stone" which would turn all base metals into gold. The alchemists also studied magic and astrology.

However, we have to thank the alchemists for such words as "hermetically sealed", alcohol and alkali, and for the discoveries of sulphuric, nitric and hydrochloric acids, and of metals such as antimony, bismuth and arsenic.

The "hermetic art" is another name for alchemy. Hermes Trismegistus was the name given by the Greeks to the Egyptian god of alchemy. Thus hermetic sealing is derived from the method of air-tight sealing used by alchemists in their experiments.

The alchemists also associated the planets with certain metals and used the astrological symbol as a shorthand sign for the metal. The sun stood for gold, the moon for silver, Venus for copper, Mars for iron, Jupiter for tin and Saturn for lead.

SILVER TARNISH

It is the sulphur in the air, which often comes from coal-gas used for cooking and heating, that causes silver to tarnish or blacken. Silver combines with sulphur to form the black silver sulphide sometimes found on forks and spoons which have been in contact with egg yolk.

Silver is a precious metal which the Greeks called shining. In spite of its tendency to tarnish silver has long been used for the manufacture of coins, jewellery and other articles of value, on account of its comparative rarity, brilliant white colour and resistance to corrosion.

Sterling or "solid" silver is an alloy containing 92·5 per cent silver with 7·5 per cent copper to harden it. This alloy can be drawn into wire finer than a human hair, or beaten into sheets thin enough to be stacked 100,000 high in a one-inch pile. It is used for standard hall-marked silverware in the United States, Britain and the Commonwealth. But cupronickel, an alloy of copper and nickel, has largely replaced silver in the world's coinage.

Silver plate is a thin layer of silver put on to another metal. Various alloys and compounds containing silver serve many commercial purposes, especially in the photographic and electrical industries. Silver is also very useful as an excellent conductor of electricity.

STRONGEST MATERIAL

The strength of any material is its ability to resist stretching, pressing together, and tearing—what the scientists call tension, compression and shear. No one material is the strongest for all purposes. For example, cast iron is immensely strong in resisting steady compression, but is easily broken by a sharp hammer-blow.

Some materials are made stronger by the addition of other substances. A little carbon added to iron makes it stronger and produces steel. The addition of silicon or magnesium to low-strength aluminium forms a lightweight, high-strength alloy used for aircraft engines and other highly-stressed mechanisms.

Nylon and similar plastics have introduced new standards of strength in non-metallic materials. They are made from basic substances such as coal, salt, petroleum, air and water, and are very tough and resistant to wear.

is the strongest material known to man?

WHAT is a prime number?

PRIME NUMBER

A prime number is one that cannot be split up by division. Think of 11. Twice six is 12, three fours are 12. But the only number you can divide 11 by is one, and when you have done that you still have 11 left.

Prime numbers lie at the very roots of arithmetic, and have always fascinated those concerned with figures. Choose at random 17, 23, 29, 41, take the sequence as far as you like, and you will never find a prime number divisible by another. Over the centuries the world's finest mathematicians have tried to do so and failed—although they have also been unable to prove that no such number exists.

That is because there is an infinity of prime numbers, and, in theory, anything may happen in infinity. But so far the theorists have not even been able to find a rule governing the gaps between prime numbers, which is a great mathematical mystery.

276

WHY is Newton famous?   **WHY** are fertilizers used
WHY do oil and water not mix?

NEWTON

Sir Isaac Newton (1642–1727), the great English physicist and mathematician, is best known for his work on gravity and light.

In his twenties, Newton sent a paper on light and colours to the Royal Society of London, and devised a telescope in which the principle component was a concave or magnifying mirror. He enquired into how light was produced and developed what was known as the "emission or corpuscular theory of light", according to which light is the product of a luminous body of tiny particles.

The theory was also used to explain the colours seen when light is reflected from a thin film (e.g. a film of soap) and a series of dark and light rings circling round a central black spot is seen.

Newton said that some of the particles of light were reflected and others were refracted.

Rings of colour from the reflected and refracted light were known as "Newton's Rings".

OIL AND WATER

Oil and water do not mix because the molecules (tiny particles) of which they are composed are so different. The molecules in oil are much bigger and contain many more atoms than those of water.

When different liquids mix, it is because they have similar types of molecules which readily link up with each other, like milk and water. In the case of oil and water the groups of molecules prefer to stay apart.

The patches of oil floating on top of the water are usually circular because of another characteristic of molecules, which produces what scientists term surface tension. This is a cohesive force caused by the attraction of the molecules to each other. They cling so tightly that they produce a surface layer which acts like an elastic skin or the rubber envelope of a balloon. The molecules are trying to pull the liquid into as small a space as possible. As well as producing a circular shape, this tension makes the surface area of each oil patch as small as possible.

FERTILIZERS

Fertilizers are used on farms to increase crop yields by ensuring that soils contain the chemical elements required by growing plants. These chemical elements include oxygen, carbon, hydrogen, nitrogen, phosphorous, potassium, sulphur, calcium, magnesium, and iron. If soils are lacking in any of these, the deficiency can be made good by the right fertilizer.

Until the 19th Century, farmers relied mainly on the application of natural fertilizers to put "goodness" back into the land. They used manure from the stock-yards and, in the case of coastal areas, seaweed from the shore. Lime was also applied to prevent acidity. This method of soil rejuvenation went a long way to maintain the presence of chemical elements. But it often did little to improve soils already lacking in certain chemicals.

Nowadays soils are analysed to find out deficiencies which can be made up by the application of the appropriate chemical fertilizers. Of course, the chemicals alone do not guarantee a successful crop. The continued application of the natural fertilizers, such as manure and humus (decayed vegetable matter) is also essential.

CARBURETTOR

An automobile is driven by an internal combustion engine which will work properly only if the right amounts of petrol and air are mixed together. The carburettor is the part of the engine where the mixing takes place.

The burning of fuel in the engine is a chemical reaction in which petrol combines with the oxygen of the air to produce water, heat energy and oxides of carbon. A chemically correct mixture should have 15 parts of air to one part of petrol, both by weight. The amount of air then present is just sufficient to burn the petrol com-

on a farm? WHY does an automobile have a carburettor? WHY are ice-skates made of steel?

ICE-SKATES

Ice-skate blades are made of steel for three reasons. First, because steel is immensely strong, hard and resistant to wear. Second, because it is a relatively low conductor of heat. And third, because it can be sharpened to a keen edge.

A skate blade has to resist tremendous pressure because it is hollow-ground, so that only the edges rest on the ice.

The smooth gliding movement associated with skating is made possible by a thin film of water on the ice produced by heat friction as the blade strikes the surface. As it is a relatively poor conductor of heat, the steel allows the heat to remain for a longer time at the edge of the blade, thus ensuring the necessary film of water.

There are specially designed blades for different kinds of ice-skating. The figure skater's blade is hollow ground and curved with saw-like teeth at the toe to enable the skater to get a better grip on the ice when carrying out certain movements. The speed skater uses a thinner blade, about 16–17 inches long, sharpened, with a flat surface. This type of blade gives the racer a longer stroke.

pletely. If the engine uses a mixture with an excess of petrol—a rich mixture—a small amount of unburnt petrol will be present in the exhaust fumes.

A carburettor has to produce the required mixture in varying strengths to suit different engine conditions, such as starting, idling, acceleration, cruising and application of full power. It must be able to pass the correct mixture at all engine speeds and under varying loads, and has to atomize the petrol into tiny droplets and vaporize the resulting spray into a combustible mixture.

Inside the carburettor is a throttle valve which can increase or decrease the amount of mixture passing into the cylinders, which in turn controls the power of the engine. This valve is mounted on a spindle which is operated by the accelerator pedal.

A special device called a "strangler" is also incorporated to help in starting the engine in cold weather by allowing an extra-rich mixture. This is commonly referred to as the choke.

The diagram shows the principle of the carburettor.

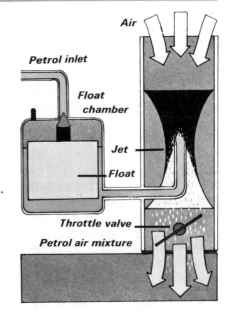

WHAT is a star? WHAT is the Milky Way? WHAT is a watt?

STAR

A star is a body of luminous gas, like the sun. But as stars are much farther away from the earth than the sun, they appear to be only small points of twinkling light. With the naked eye it is possible to see about 2,000 stars at any one time or place but with the most powerful telescope over 1,000 million stars are visible. Although light travels at 186,000 miles a second, the light from the stars takes many years to reach the earth.

Stars are not fixed in space, but are travelling in different directions at different speeds. Seen from the earth, these movements appear to be so small that groups of stars, or constellations, seem to have a permanent relationship. The star patterns we see in the sky are almost the same as those seen by our ancestors hundreds, or even thousands of years ago.

The sizes of stars vary tremendously, from about a tenth of the diameter of the sun to 20 times its diameter. Most stars appear to be white when looked at with the naked eye, but some are bluish-white, yellow, orange and red. The varied colours are due to differences in surface temperature. The brilliant, white stars are the hottest with temperatures of several hundred thousand degrees. The less brilliant, orange and red stars have a temperature of about 2,000 degrees.

There are exceptions, however. The red giant, Betelgeux, in the constellation (or group) of Orion, appears to be brilliant because of its size. Its diameter is 250 million miles, which is greater than the diameter of the earth's orbit round the sun.

Shooting stars which are sometimes seen moving across the night sky for a few seconds are really meteors. These small particles flare up as they strike the earth's atmosphere but soon burn out.

MILKY WAY

The Milky Way, or Galaxy, is the whole concourse of stars and other bodies which can be seen stretched across the heavens. It includes our own sun and its planets, as well as all stars visible to the naked eye. But the name is commonly restricted to the luminous band or belt where most classes of stars are concentrated.

The spiral arms of the Milky Way are rich in hot, bright stars, interstellar clouds of gas (mainly hydrogen) and dust. The first evidence of spiral arms was obtained in 1951 by the American astronomer W. W. Morgan, who identified three.

Our own system of sun and planets appears to be situated towards the inner edge of one of the arms, which is about 1,300 light-years away. The Andromeda nebula, a vast mixture of gaseous and solid matter, is visible as a small luminous patch in our sky. But it is comparable in size to the Milky Way and seems remarkably similar to our own galaxy.

The Palomar telescope, 200 inches in diameter, situated on Mount Palomar in California, has perhaps 1,000 million galaxies within the scope of its vision.

WHAT makes a mirror reflect?   WHAT is soap?

WATT

A watt is the term used to describe a unit of power. It is named after James Watt (1736–1819), the inventor of the first practical steam engine. The definition of the watt is based on the definition of power —the rate at which work is done. Although power was used in mechanical engineering long before electricity was heard of, the use of the watt as an electrical term is now universally accepted.

. Electric power may be a thousand kilowatts for an electric locomotive, a hundred watts for a light bulb, or only the very minute fraction of one watt which a radio receiver picks out of the air.

MIRROR

It is the brightness of the mirror surface that makes it reflect light.

When light falls on a surface some of the light may be reflected or thrown back, some absorbed and some allowed to pass through. In a mirror the surface is made so bright that as much light as possible is reflected and as little as possible absorbed.

The earliest mirrors consisted of thin discs of metal, generally bronze, slightly convex and polished on one side.

The method of making mirrors by backing glass with thin sheets of metal was known in the Middle Ages, and a guild of glass-mirror makers existed in Nürnberg, Germany, in 1373. The commercial manufacture of mirrors was developed in 16th Century Venice. Coated mirrors were made from blown cylinders of glass which were slit, flattened on a stone, polished, and their backs silvered by an amalgam of tin and mercury.

These mirrors had a high reflecting power, but a considerable improvement came in France in 1691 when the art of making plate glass was introduced. The chemical process of coating a glass surface with metallic silver was discovered by Baron Justus von Liebig of Germany in 1835.

Mirror surfaces are used inside lighthouses, lightships and search-lights, where it is necessary to produce a high degree of reflection in order to throw the beam of the light over a distance of several miles. Even a hand flashlight has a slightly mirrored surface behind the bulb.

SOAP

Soap is made largely from fats or oil, with a variety of other ingredients.

Before the introduction of soap in the 1st Century A.D. people "washed" themselves and their clothes with fuller's earth, a fine clay-like substance that loosens oil and dirt.

People first made their own soap by saving scraps of fat and boiling them in an iron pot. They added an alkaline solution, made from wood ash, called lye. This formed a yellow "soft soap", the yellow coming from the potash in the lye. Hard soap was made by boiling for longer, and by adding salt, usually from sea-water.

Soap is still made in much the same way, but on a far larger scale in modern factories. The chief things that go into its manufacture are still fat or oil (but oil from coconuts or cotton seeds), lye containing potash, or sodium, and salt. Coloured dyes, perfumes and super-fats, such as almond oil and glycerine, are added to make the expensive toilet and shaving soaps.

WHERE was the world before it was made?

This is a nuclear explosion. Explosions far greater than this formed the Universe.

THE WORLD

In the beginning our universe was a mass of white-hot vapours and molten materials whirling about in space. Our world was formed from this. Astronomers believe it took millions of years for the cloud to cool, contract and begin to turn into molten rock.

Modern astronomers think that many millions of years ago there was a huge explosion in space. They do not know exactly what happened. But it is possible that our sun exploded or that a much bigger companion star of the sun became a supernova—that is, it broke up violently. The debris and blazing gases from this explosion were, it is thought, flung far into space.

For more millions of years our universe boiled and bubbled. But slowly, very slowly, the fiery redness began to cool and condense into the nine planets and many more smaller bodies. All these planets now revolve around the sun.

After further vast periods of time the lava of the earth began to solidify, developing over many millions of years, into the world as we know it today.

WHERE do shadows go?

SHADOWS

Shadows need light before they can appear. If the light goes out, the shadow goes out too.

A shadow is that part of an an illuminated surface which is shielded from oncoming light rays by an object through which the light cannot pass. If the source of light is small, the outline of the shadow will be sharp and pronounced and its shape will be that of the object producing it. If the source of light is large, the shadow is very dark in the middle (the umbra) and much lighter on the outside with indistinct outlines (the penumbra).

Shadows cast by the sun always have a penumbra and the shape of the shadows cast varies with the position of the sun in the sky and the angle of its rays. An upright pole will cast a long shadow in the morning when the sun is rising but grows shorter as noon approaches. As the sun declines in the sky, the shadow grows longer again.

Human shadows have often had a mystical or magical significance. In the picture above you can see a masterly use of shadow to give form by the English painter Wright, of Derby.

ACIDS

Some acids burn because they have a strong tendency to absorb water, giving out a great deal of heat in the process. Since most living cells contain water the strong acids, such as sulphuric acid, hydrochloric acid and nitric acid, react with them and kill the cells, causing very serious burns.

These three acids, as well as others such as perchloric acid and benzine sulphuric acid are called mineral acids because they are manufactured from minerals. They are all strong and dangerous acids. They have tremendous industrial value, but great care must be used in handling them.

Most organic acids—that is to say, those made from living things—are weak acids. Vinegar or lemon juice are examples. All acids taste sour and most attack metals, turning them into salts and releasing hydrogen.

Special clothing is worn by men handling acids to protect them from serious burns. Acid must always be poured *slowly* into water, never water into acid. If you are burned by acid you should wash your skin with large quantities of water and then with a weak ammonia solution. If your eyes are affected, flush them immediately with lots of water and then with bicarbonate of soda solution, which neutralizes any acid left.

ASTRONAUT

A space suit enables an astronaut to survive by providing him artificially with conditions like those he is used to on earth.

These conditions can be reproduced in a large space craft or space station in orbit, but an astronaut still needs a space suit for operations outside the craft or for an emergency.

In space men lack the air needed for breathing, the pressure required to stop their blood from boiling and the natural protection of the atmosphere against radiation. All these must be supplied by the space suit which also must withstand the cold of space.

When an astronaut ventures into space, he leaves behind the safety of the atmospheric blanket which we, on earth, take for granted. His space suit becomes his own personal little world.

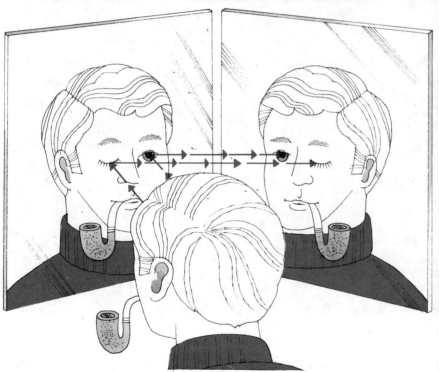

MIRROR

Objects will appear reversed in a mirror because what you are seeing is a reflection and not a reproduction of the image. If you stand in front of a mirror with your right eye closed the image in the mirror will appear to show your left eye closed, because the image is facing the opposite direction. In all reflections images and directions are reversed.

By using a combination of two mirrors at right angles to each other, the reversal will be eliminated. This is because the reversed image will be reversed yet again in the second mirror, thus giving a true likeness of the original object.

in a mirror?　**WHY** does an astronaut need a space suit? **WHY** are there different types of saw?

DIFFERENT SAWS

Saws are of many shapes and sizes, according to the special purposes for which they are to be used and the materials they are meant to cut. Most are designed to cut through wood but others have the particular qualities needed for cutting metals and stones.

There are two types of large hand-saw. Both have steel blades with wooden handles, but the teeth are shaped differently to fit the job they have to do. One is a cross-cut saw for cutting *across* the grain of the wood. The leading edges of the teeth slope backward and are also bevelled, or angled, transversely. In other words, they are cut away at the edges to give an oblique angle like the edge of a chisel, thus producing a sharp-pointed profile or shape designed to avoid splintering the wood.

The second type is the rip or tenon saw, which is used for cutting *along* the grain of the wood. This has a smaller blade, strengthened by a steel strip along the top edge, and smaller teeth. It is used, as the name suggests, in cutting tenon or slotted joints.

Smaller hand saws, like the fretsaw, are used for cutting intricate shapes. These have a narrow blade stretched across an open frame. The hacksaw, which is used for cutting metal by hand, also has an open frame, but its blade is deeper and more closely-toothed.

Machine saws are of three types: first, a larger and stronger hacksaw operated by an electric motor through a crank and connecting rod; second, a circular saw, which has a rotating, disc-shaped blade with teeth on the circumference; and third, a bandsaw which has a blade formed like an endless flexible band and tightly stretched over pulleys.

The bandsaw, which has fine teeth along one edge, operates at a higher speed than the circular saw. It can cut round curves of quite small radius because the blade is so narrow.

For stone-cutting in quarrying there are swinging gang-saws with teeth like chisels and flat-bladed circular saws, which are either fed with a mixture of hard sand and water or fitted with rims of a hard abrasive substance called carborundum.

The hand-held power saw driven by an electric or petrol driven engine is used for felling trees and cutting logs. This is also known as a chain-saw because it is much like a bicycle chain equipped with saw teeth.

1. Combination: large teeth for general cutting.

2. Planer: hollow ground gives smooth finish.

3. Crosscut: to cut across the grain of the wood.

4. Friction: for corrugated materials and thin metals.

DIAMONDS

Industrial diamonds are used for such a wide variety of purposes that a sudden shortage would cause havoc in many branches of manufacture and mining. This is because diamonds, as well as being the most brilliant and precious of stones, are also one of the hardest materials known to man.

Their earliest use in industry was as an abrasive powder for sawing and polishing operations and for grinding metal-cutting tools.

Many kinds of drills use diamonds as cutters. The introduction of the carbonado or black diamonds of Brazil—less brittle than other forms—greatly improved rock drilling for geological and mine prospecting. But they have become so scarce that other suitable varieties have had to be substituted.

Diamonds are also employed for cutting glass and porcelain, for fine engraving, for dental surgery, and for bearings in watches.

PLANET

The word planet comes from the Greek *planetes*, meaning "the wanderer". Originally the term was applied to the seven heavenly bodies, which changed their places by revolving, so men believed, round the earth. The seven were Mercury, Venus, Mars, Jupiter, Saturn, the moon and the sun.

While we now realize that the planets (including the earth) revolve round the sun, the distinction between planet and star is still valid. Planets are too cool to give off any light of their own. We

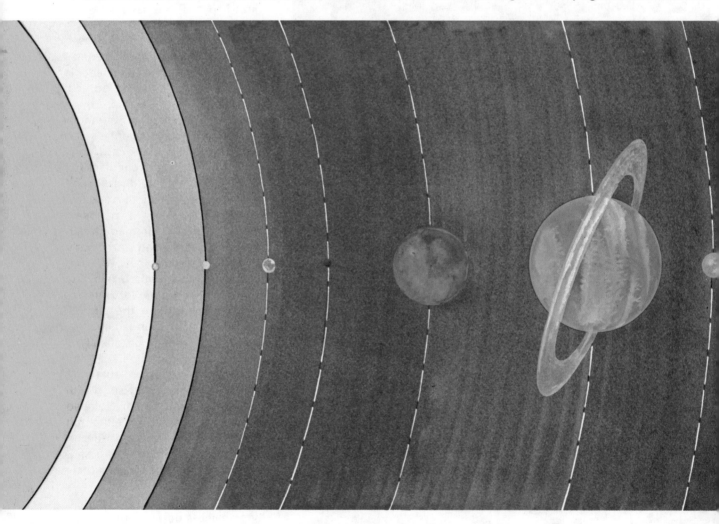

can see the other planets only because they reflect the light of the sun, which is now known to be not a planet but a star.

The planets are only a few million miles away, but distances to the stars are so vast that they have to be calculated according to the time taken for their light to reach the earth.

Three more planets joined the list in comparatively recent times. In 1781 William Herschel discovered Uranus. Neptune was added in 1846 and Pluto in 1930.

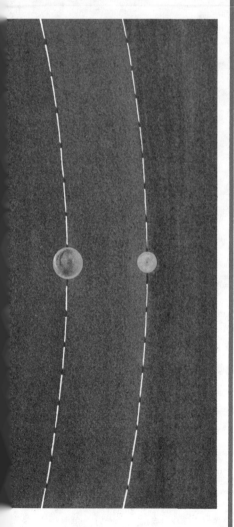

MAGNET

A magnet is a piece of iron which will attract or repel pins, tacks, nails or anything else made of that metal.

The word comes from a district in Thessaly, Greece, called Magnesia. It was here that men first noticed that certain black stones attracted iron. These stones were composed of an iron ore called magnetite and were natural magnets.

Later it was discovered that if a piece of magnetite or lodestone (leading-stone) was hung by a thread or floated on a piece of wood, it would always turn to point north and south. This proved very useful to the early sailors.

Next it was found that a magnet could be made by winding an insulated wire round a piece of iron, and passing an electric current through the wire. This is called an electromagnet and is used in an electric motor.

Magnets can be made by stroking a piece of iron with lodestone or with another magnet, thereby passing on the power of magnetism.

In the middle of the 13th Century a Frenchman, Petrus Perigrinus de Maricourt, carried out experiments in magnetism, especially about its connection with the use of the compass as an instrument of navigation. In 1600 William Gilbert of Norwich, who was Court Physician to Elizabeth I, published a book on magnetism called *De Magneti*.

TELEPHONE

Alexander Graham Bell (1847–1922) invented and patented in 1876 the first telephone that was of any real practical use. In 1874 he said: "If I could make a current of electricity vary in intensity precisely as the air varies in density during the production of sound, I should be able to transmit speech telegraphically." This is the principle of the telephone.

On March 10, 1876, the first historic message was telephoned to Thomas A. Watson, Bell's assistant, who was in another room: "Mr Watson, come here; I want you."

Bell's first machine gave electrical currents too feeble to be of much use for the general public. In 1877 the American scientist Thomas A. Edison (1847–1931) invented the variable-contact carbon transmitter, which greatly increased the power of the signals.

The telephone was immediately popular in the United States, but Bell found little interest in Britain when he visited the country in 1878. Then Queen Victoria asked for a pair of telephones and the royal interest resulted in a London telephone exchange being formed in 1879 with eight subscribers.

Bell inaugurating the New York–Chicago telephone line, October 1892.

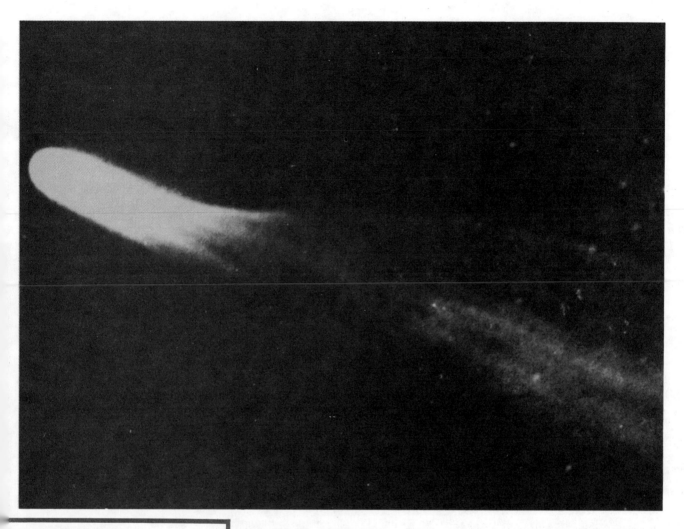

WRISTWATCH

The exact time the first wristwatch appeared is not known. But soon after the beginning of the 20th Century women's small pocket watches began to be fitted into specially made leather or gold adaptors to be worn on the wrist. They were immediately successful, and their popularity rapidly increased in the First World War because they could be consulted without undoing a coat or uniform jacket.

The first self-winding wristwatch was invented by John Harwood, an Englishman who patented it in 1924. Today the largest watchmaking industry in the world is concentrated in the Jura mountains and the valley of the Aar in Switzerland.

HALLEY'S COMET

Halley's Comet was last seen in 1986. It is the most famous of all periodical comets — those which move round the sun and reappear in out skies at known intervals.

The comet is named after the British astronomer, Edmund Halley (1656–1742) who observed it in 1682. He predicted accurately that it would return in 1758, but died too soon to see it. Halley's Comet has a period of 76 years and was last seen in 1910, when this photograph was taken.

Comets have been called the stray members of the solar system, but the description is misleading as a comet's orbit can be calculated like that of a planet, though they may appear unexpectedly.

A comet is formed of relatively small particles contained in an envelope of thin gas. A large comet has a concentrated head or nucleus, from which streams a long, brilliant tail, but a small one may have no tail. Although a comet may be larger than the earth or even Jupiter, it contains only a small quantity of matter. This lack of substance makes it invisible until relatively close to the earth.

A comet's tail always points away from the sun, probably because of the intense radiation which repels the tail's tiny particles. Its orbit is much more elliptical than that of a planet, and, because they are so insubstantial, they can be seen only when relatively near the Earth.

pencil "bend" when it's put in water?

METEORITE

Meteorites begin as bodies of matter travelling at great speed through space. In the solar system there are numberless such bodies, usually chunks of rock or metal. When they enter the earth's atmosphere friction makes them hot and bright. The small chunks burn away, but the larger ones fall to the earth as meteorites.

Their crater hollows are found all over the world. A meteorite which probably weighed hundreds of tons is believed to have fallen near Winslow, Arizona, in the United States several thousand years ago. The Barringer crater, as it is known, is about one mile across and over 500 feet deep. Another large meteorite is known to have fallen at Grootfontein in South-west Africa. This weighed about 60 tons. An iron meteorite in New York City, which was brought from Greenland, weighs 36 tons.

HARD WATER

Hard water is water that contains certain dissolved chemicals that act on soap to form a scum. If water comes from limestone areas, some rock is dissolved in the water, and this makes it hard.

There are several disadvantages in hard water. More soap or soap powder must be used to obtain a suitable lather. Also, the scum clings to the object being washed. Hard water leaves a scaly deposit in kettles and boilers, which reduces the efficiency of both.

But hard water can be treated to remove the unwanted chemicals. In the home small amounts of washing soda or borax can be added. At large water softening plants which serve a community, the water is filtered through a mineral called zeolite which removes the chemicals. After a time zeolite ceases to be effective, but it can be restored by washing it with salt water.

PENCIL

The pencil appears to bend owing to the refraction of light, or the change in direction of light when it passes through transparent materials. The light rays coming from the submerged part of the pencil are bent as they leave the water.

Light rays are reflected and absorbed by opaque materials such as iron, lead and rubber. Transparent materials, such as glass, air, water, oil and certain plastics, allow the light rays to pass through them. But in doing so they bend them to a greater or lesser degree.

Refraction occurs in nature. The stars not directly overhead are in different positions from those they appear to be in, because the light rays from them are refracted by the earth's atmosphere. Desert travellers sometimes see mirages which are caused by refraction through the atmosphere.

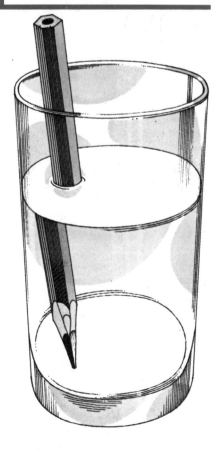

290

WHERE was Morse Code first used?   **WHERE** does the lead
WHERE is plasma found?   **WHERE** was the first aeroplane

PLASMA

Plasma is the liquid part of the blood, in which the red and white blood cells float. It is the red oxygen carrying cells that give the blood its red colour. The plasma itself is straw-coloured. You may have seen some oozing out round a burn. Plasma is 90 per cent water, with various proteins and salts.

Along with the red cells, the plasma helps to carry oxygen from the lungs to the body tissues which need it to break down their food. When the tissues have finished with the oxygen, the blood carries the carbon dioxide waste back to the lungs in order for it to be breathed out.

It also carries food, at various stages of absorption, round the body to the tissues, and takes the waste away to the kidneys from where it is passed out of the body as water.

Plasma is also a vehicle for toxins and antitoxins, special substances designed to fight infection in our bodies.

MORSE CODE

The first message in Morse code was tapped out in the United States over a telegraph line from Baltimore to Washington by Samuel Morse in 1844.

Morse is often credited with the invention of the telegraph on his return to the United States from a trip to Europe in 1832. During this trip he became acquainted with the works of Michael Faraday on electro-magnetism, which forms the basis of the telegraph. This gave Morse the necessary impetus to go ahead with his work.

In 1837 Morse exhibited his first truly successful telegraph instrument. By 1838 he had developed the Morse code, an alphabet which consists of dots and dashes representing letters and numbers. In the same year he attempted unsuccessfully to persuade Congress to build a telegraph line.

It was not until 1843 that Congress voted to pay Morse to build the first telegraph line in the United States from Baltimore to Washington. In the following year Morse sent his famous message— "What hath God wrought!"—on this line.

Later, Morse was caught in a mass of legal claims among his telegraph partners and rival in-

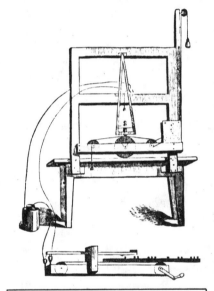

A ·—	B —···	C —·—·	D —··	E ·
F ··—·	G ——·	H ····	I ··	J ·———
K —·—	L ·—··	M ——	N —·	
O ———	P ·——·	Q ——·—	R ·—·	
S ···	T —	U ··—	V ···—	W ·——
X —··—	Y —·——	Z ——··		
1 ·————	2 ··———	3 ···——		
4 ····—	5 ·····	6 —····	7 ——···	
8 ———··	9 ————·	0 —————		

The Morse Code and original instrument.

ventors. He was probably the most successful propagator of the telegraph although there were many pioneers in the same field long before him.

EXHAUST FUMES

The lead in exhaust fumes comes from the petrol used to drive internal-combustion engines. Crude oil straight from the wells is thick, black and sticky. It has to go through a complicated refining process before it can be used as fuel for the engines of cars, lorries, buses and aircraft.

During refining, various substances are added to improve the petrol and for other reasons. For instance, small quantities of dye are put in to standardize the colour. Other substances prevent the formation of gum which would clog up parts of the engine.

Lead, in a liquid form called tetra-ethyl lead, is added to petrol to reduce "engine knock". This means that it prevents the petrol from igniting in the engine at the wong moment. When an internal-combustion engine is running, the petrol is lit by sparks from the sparking plugs. The petrol burns in what is really a series of small explosions and produces gases which come out through the exhaust pipe as dirty, smelly fumes. And the lead comes with them.

Ill-health can be caused if quite small quantities of lead in the air are inhaled over a long time. For this reason, the governments of such countries as the United States, Britain, Sweden and Japan are passing laws to reduce the amount of lead in petrol.

They are also encouraging car manufacturers to design internal-combustion engines which will work efficiently on lead-free petrol and have cleaner exhaust fumes. These engines will be more expensive at first, but they will help to make the air cleaner and pleasanter where there is a lot of traffic.

Work is in progress to invent a satisfactory car engine that runs on alternatives to petrol, such as a battery.

in exhaust fumes come from?
flown? WHERE does candlewax go when a candle burns?

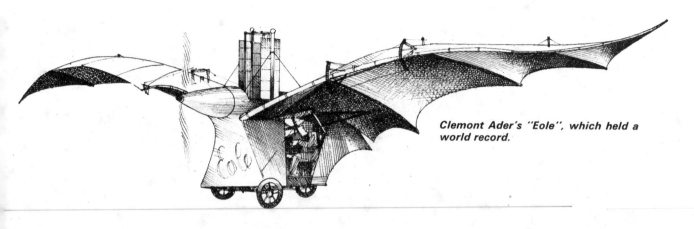

Clemont Ader's "Eole", which held a world record.

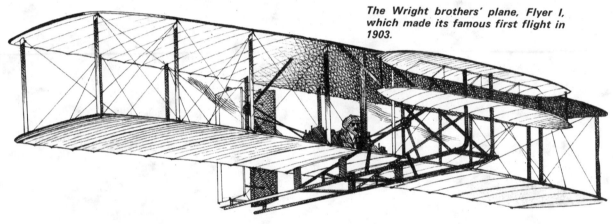

The Wright brothers' plane, Flyer I, which made its famous first flight in 1903.

FIRST AEROPLANE

The first aeroplane ever to fly was built by a French naval officer, Félix du Temple de la Croix. In 1874 his monoplane, powered with a hot-air engine, took off from the top of a hill near Brest in France. It did not get far, just a short hop, but it was a beginning. A few years later, in 1890, Clément Ader of France flew his own plane, Eole, entirely under its own power for about 50 metres. It was a world record.

The first truly successful aeroplane flight was in 1903. In December of that year Orville Wright flew his chain-driven plane Flyer I at a speed of 8 m.p.h. and at an altitude of 12 feet for 12 seconds in North Carolina, United States. It was several years before the Wrights' achievement was fully appreciated in America.

VANISHING CANDLE

Nowhere—it simply changes into other substances. That is what burning does to everything.

The moment you put a match to the wick, you start a change in the candle by turning the solid wax into a liquid. The liquid wax rises to the wick by an irresistible process called capillarity, the simplest example of which is the way blotting paper soaks up ink or water. Then the liquid wax changes into a gas which burns—a chemical reaction which releases energy in the form of light and heat.

The presence of the gas can be demonstrated by blowing out the candle and immediately holding a lighted match an inch or so above the wick. The inflammable vapour instantly catches fire, and the candle lights up again without the match having actually touched the wick.

Other changes are taking place while the candle burns. The wax is a complex chemical compound of carbon and hydrogen. The process of burning is simply the combination of the wax with the oxygen in the air. If you put a jar over the candle, it will quickly use up the oxygen and go out.

During the time the candle burns, the carbon joins with the oxygen in the air and makes carbon monoxide and carbon dioxide, and the hydrogen combines with the oxygen to produce water.

While all these changes in the substance of the candle are taking place, the candle, of course, is becoming shorter. But it is not "going" anywhere. Its materials are simply changing into other substances.

WHAT are sunspots?   WHAT makes a helicopter work?

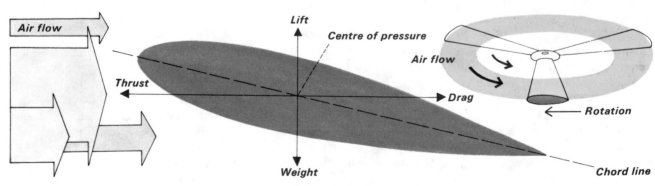

Air flow

Thrust

Drag

Lift

Centre of pressure

Weight

Air flow

Rotation

Chord line

WHAT is an aerosol?

SUNSPOTS

Sunspots are dark patches on the surface of the sun, which can usually be observed only through special telescopic lenses. They are caused by the magnetic activity of the sun, which cools certain regions of the sun's surface so that the gases there no longer shine as brightly as the rest. Sunspots often have diameters of over 20,000 miles when they first appear.

During regular 11-year cycles, the number of sunspots may increase to as many as 100. The sunspot cycles coincide with a build-up of solar violence, but scientists are not yet certain what causes these disturbances.

Observers should remember that it is dangerous to gaze directly at the sun without protecting the eyes with a densely-smoked special glass.

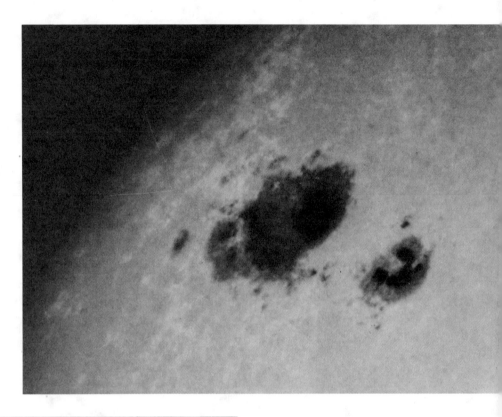

HELICOPTER

The aerodynamic theory behind the flight of a helicopter is that thrust is produced by giving a downward velocity or speed to the mass of air flowing through a large horizontal rotor. This rotor acts as a rotary wing and gives the heavier-than-air machine sufficient lift for take-off and hovering.

As the helicopter flies forward, the flow of air through the rotor is increased when the rotor is inclined forward to propel the helicopter. The amount of power required drops off as the speed increases. At about 50 m.p.h. it reaches a minimum value of about half that required for hovering. Then it rises with increasing forward speed as the drag of the fuselage grows.

This minimum power characteristic is of importance in considering the ability of multi-engine helicopters to maintain altitude after failure of an engine during take-off.

AEROSOL

An aerosol consists of fine particles of liquid or solid substances suspended in the air, or in any other gas. It is not, as many people think, merely a spray for use in applying paint easily, or getting rid of unpleasant smells.

The germs of diseases, for example, are to be found suspended in the air, and these dangerous aerosols can be dealt with by spraying chemicals to form another aerosol which destroys the germs. Leaves of plants attacked by pests can be treated in the same way.

Chemicals in the container part of an artificial aerosol spray are stored there under very high pressure. When the release trigger is pressed a valve opens, and the chemicals are forced out through a tiny hole in a fine spray. This invention is useful not only in the home, and to gardeners and doctors, but also to a wide variety of specialist users.

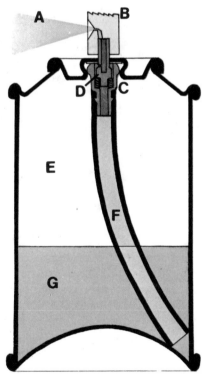

A   Jet
B   Operating button
C   Valve
D   Spring
E   Air gas pressure
F   Plastic tube
G   Liquid

294

WHY is uranium important?   WHY do motor vehicles have

WHY do some liquids burn?   WHY are some

URANIUM

The importance of uranium today lies in its value as a producer of nuclear power. Uranium was first discovered by the German chemist, Martin Klaproth in 1789. But for a century and a half afterwards few uses could be found for the new metallic element.

Some suggested making filaments for lamps out of it. Uranium has actually been used success-fully in large lamps for photo-graphy. Also, it was of some value as a dye for wood and leather.

In 1938, two scientists, Hahn and Strassmann, discovered that uranium could yield nuclear energy. One pound of uranium would give as much energy as three million pounds of coal. The first nuclear chain reaction was conducted by Enrico Fermi in 1942. This made possible the exploding of the first atomic bomb in 1945.

Apart from its destructive ap-plications, the use of uranium in nuclear power stations has proved a valuable substitute for the world's dwindling supply of oil and coal. Also, isotopes extracted from uranium have proved immensely useful in medicine by helping to diagnose and treat illnesses.

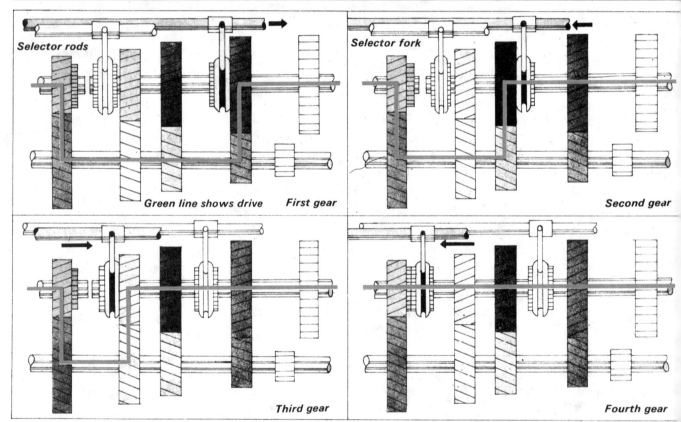

Selector rods

Green line shows drive   First gear

Selector fork

Second gear

Third gear

Fourth gear

GEARS

A transmission gear system is used in motor vehicles because petrol engines have little power at low speeds. So to make the vehicle move off or climb a hill the engine has to turn fast while the wheels are revolving slowly. The gears provide the means of altering the ratio between the speed of the engine and the speed of the wheels.

The gear box is so arranged that the driver can link the engine shaft to the transmission through large to small gears for the vehicle to move faster, or through small to large gears for it to move more slowly. Some of the gears are fixed to the shafts while others can be slid along the shafts but they will still turn when the shafts revolve.

With the gear lever, various combinations of these gear wheels can be brought into action. These combinations give first—or bottom —gear for slow speeds up to, say, 20 miles per hour, and two, three or four more up to top gear for speeds of 65 m.p.h. and over. On some vehicles an extra high gear is incorporated by means of a device called an overdrive. This is a great advantage for long runs since it reduces engine speed by 22 per cent for any given road speed, thereby reducing petrol consumption and engine wear.

Many motor vehicles are fitted with automatic gear boxes which adjust engine speed in correct relation to road speed without the driver having to change gear.

gears? **WHY** do people study cybernetics?
metals chromium-plated? **WHY** are tuning-forks used?

CYBERNETICS

People study cybernetics to gain knowledge with which to improve mechanical things. Cybernetics is the scientific study of automatic control and communication in the functions of animals and in mechanical and electrical systems. It is chiefly concerned with physiological and psychological mechanics of animal behaviour.

These methods have been used in deciphering garbled messages, in anti-aircraft gunnery, in constructing artificial limbs, in building computers and in making models of the human brain.

Cybernetics comes from the Greek *kubernetes* meaning steersman. It is a word much in vogue among engineers.

LIQUIDS THAT BURN

Some liquids will burn because when their molecules mix with the oxygen in the air the mixture becomes combustible.

The application of heat promotes the necessary chemical reaction to put the molecules into more violent motion, so that they collide at high speed. The jolt loosens the bonds and makes it easier for the molecules to rearrange themselves and escape from the liquid to form a vapour, mixing with oxygen in the air.

The most important liquid which will burn is crude mineral oil from which petrol and paraffin are produced. Others include tar and creosote, and the very explosive nitro-glycerine.

TUNING-FORKS

A tuning-fork vibrates to give a musical note of definite pitch or frequency and is marked on the fork by a letter or symbol referring to its position in the musical scale.

The instrument has two hard steel prongs and a handle or stem. It is sounded by giving one of the prongs a light tap on a wooden surface, and then holding the handle on a wooden board or table.

Tuning-forks are used by piano-tuners and musicians. Most forks give the same musical note as Middle C on a piano and are usually marked 256. The number gives the frequency and means that it vibrates at a rate of 256 times a second. In 1939 a frequency of 440 for A was agreed.

CHROMIUM PLATE

Some metals are chromium-plated to make them look more attractive and to prevent them from corroding or rusting. Chromium is a silver-white, hard, brittle metal which was discovered in 1798 by N. L. Vauquelin. Its non-corrosive, high-strength, heat-resistant characteristics are utilized in alloys and as an electroplated coating.

In electroplating, the article to be plated is connected to the negative terminal of a battery and placed in a solution known as electrolyte. Direct electric current is introduced through the anode or positive terminal, which usually consists of the metal with which the article is to be coated. Metal dissolves from the anode and forms a deposit on the article. The electrolyte for chromium contains chromic acid and sulphuric acid. It deposits a bright top layer but this is not the most important part of the electroplating. The chromium is only about 0·00002 inches thick. Under it lies a thick layer of nickel and beneath that again may be a layer of copper.

Many household appliances are chromium-plated and so are the bright parts of an automobile. Tools, chemical equipment, electric appliances, gears, packing machinery, and hundreds of other articles are similarly treated to give them brightness, beauty or resistance to wear and rust. Electroplated and polished chromium is bright bluish-white with a reflecting power which is 77 per cent that of silver.

WHAT is glass made from?   WHAT is the stratosphere?

GLASS

Glass is made naturally from a fusion of silica (sand), soda and lime. This fusion can be achieved merely by lightning striking in a place where the right ingredients happen to be adjacent to each other. When glass is made by man, other ingredients are added, such as potash, lead oxide and boric oxide. Some of these ingredients are used to make glass clear, some to colour it, and others to give it a frosted effect.

Glass was made by potters in Egypt for glazing stone beads as early as 12,000 B.C. As Egyptian culture progressed, craftsmen used glass for the manufacture of personal ornaments and bottles.

A tremendous step forward in the use of glass was made by the Phoenicians in about 300 to 200 B.C. by the invention of the blow-pipe. The blowpipe is a hollow iron tube with a mouthpiece at one end and a knob shape at the other. The knob-shaped end is dipped into hot, viscous glass. A "gather" of molten glass remains on the end when the pipe is withdrawn. This hot glass can be blown by the worker into a hollow ball. The harder he blows, the larger the ball.

During the Roman civilization the art of glass-making reached near-perfection. In the 3rd Century, the Romans cast glass on flat stones and produced the first window panes. The break-up of the Roman Empire and the ensuing Dark Ages brought an end to such cultural developments. The glazing of windows did not become widespread over the whole of Europe until the 15th and 16th Centuries.

WHAT is liquid air?

STRATOSPHERE

The earth's atmosphere has several layers of air extending upwards into the sky. The first is about seven miles high and is called the troposphere. The second, 50 to 60 miles high, is the stratosphere.

In the stratosphere, the density of the air is so thin that it is only about a third of normal atmospheric pressure at the bottom of the layer and about a hundred-thousandth at the top. In spite of this, the lower half of the stratosphere is a region of turbulent jet "trade winds" of 50 to 100 miles an hour, which vary in strength and direction with the seasons.

Higher in the stratosphere the temperature is raised by the action of the sun's ultra-violet rays on the ozone (a condensed form of oxygen) that accumulates there.

The stratosphere is bounded on its outer side by the ionosphere, a region of electrical activity, which reflects radio waves. We exploit this characteristic to enable us to make long distance transmissions around the world far beyond the range of ordinary radio.

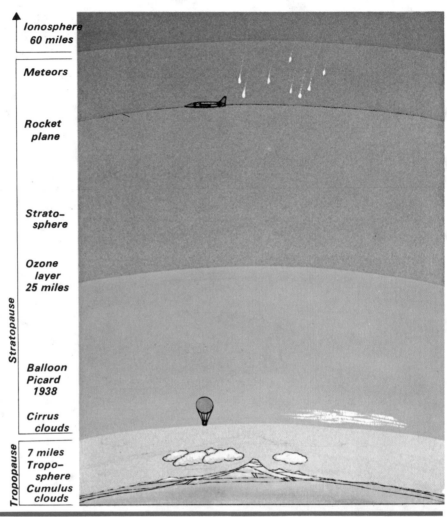

Ionosphere
60 miles

Meteors

Rocket plane

Strato-sphere

Ozone layer
25 miles

Stratopause

Balloon Picard 1938

Cirrus clouds

Tropopause

7 miles
Tropo-sphere
Cumulus clouds

LIQUID AIR

Liquid air is a mixture of oxygen and nitrogen which have been compressed until they form a liquid. When the pressure on the liquid is released, it turns back into these two gases. The liquid is kept under great pressure in strong steel cylinders.

Liquid air has a great many uses, because it enables large amounts of these two gases to be stored in small spaces. The aqualung used by skin divers consists of small cylinders joined to a mouthpiece. Liquid air is also used by pilots, firemen and astronauts.

Once liquid air has been made, the liquid oxygen can be separated from it for use in hospitals. People with lung trouble are helped by being given an increased amount of oxygen to breathe. Other gases, liquefied in the same way, are used as anaesthetics to put people to sleep during operations.

Liquid oxygen is widely used in industry because a flame fed with additional oxygen is much hotter than an ordinary flame. The oxy-acetylene torch consists of two cylinders, one of liquid oxygen and the other of acetylene. The two gases are mixed together and fed through tubes to a special blowpipe. When they are lit, they can produce a flame with a temperature of about 3,000° Centigrade (5,432° Fahrenheit) or twice the melting point of iron. This torch is used to cut and to weld metals.

WHEN was the first supersonic flight? WHEN did talking

This is the Bell X-1A, which succeeded the Bell X-1. In 1953, Yeager flew at 1,600 m.p.h. in the Bell X-1A.

SUPERSONIC FLIGHT

The first time a manned aircraft exceeded the speed of sound (Mach I) on a level flight was on October 14, 1947. Captain Charles E. Yeager of the United States Air Force flew America's Bell X-I rocket-propelled research aircraft 42,000 feet over Edwards Air Force Base, Muroc, California, at a speed of Mach 1·015 (670 miles an hour).

Known as Glamorous Glennis, this aircraft was the first rocket-propelled aircraft in the world designed for research into high speed aerodynamics. It was a single-seater monoplane with an enclosed pressurized cabin lying flush to the surface.

In 1946 the X-I underwent a series of tests during which it was released from a Boeing B-29

Superfortress in flight and allowed to glide to earth. The aircraft first flew under its own power after one such drop on December 9, 1946. But its first take-off under power did not take place until January 5, 1949.

Glamorous Glennis is now in the National Air and Space Museum of the Smithsonian Institution, Washington, D.C.

movies start?   **WHEN** does a car use overdrive?

WHEN does an atom split?

TALKING MOVIES

The first talking movies were produced in France before 1900 by Léon Gaumont. They were short films, starring great performers such as Sarah Bernhardt, in which the moving pictures were synchronized with a gramophone record. By 1912 Eugene Lauste had discovered the basic method for recording sound on film, while Thomas Edison produced several one-reel talking pictures in the United States. An American, Lee de Forest, improved the system.

In all this the public showed little interest until the presentation on October 6, 1927, of *The Jazz Singer*. This was a silent picture, starring Al Jolson, with four talking and singing interludes. Jolson's electric personality and the very much improved sound began a movie revolution. Within the year every important picture was being produced as a "talkie". By 1930 silent films were a thing of the past, and many film stars found themselves has-beens because their voices recorded badly.

OVERDRIVE

A car uses overdrive when it is travelling at high speed over long distances. Overdrive, or cruising gear, is a device which enables the engine to run at a relatively low speed even when the vehicle is travelling fast.

All internal combustion engines fitted in vehicles need some kind of gearbox because their efficiency at low speeds is poor. The use of different gears enables the speed of the engine to be harmonised with that of the car. The gears may be engaged or shifted by hand or operated by an automatic gearbox.

Most cars have a four-speed gearbox. The driver uses first gear for starting and changes to second and third gears as the car gains speed. Finally in top or fourth gear the engine speed is transmitted unreduced through the gearbox. In overdrive a large gear wheel drives a smaller gear wheel on the propeller shaft. This shaft then rotates faster than the engine, thus reducing wear and tear and saving petrol.

SPLITTING THE ATOM

An atom splits when it is struck by a neutron. The nucleus of the atom then breaks into two roughly equal parts and, at the same time, shoots out several high-speed neutrons.

Atoms are so small that they cannot be seen under the most powerful microscope. They are the building bricks of which each element is composed. The Greek word "atom" means "cannot be cut". But we know now that atoms can be cut, or split. Each one contains minute particles carrying two sorts of electricity: first, the electrons which are negatively charged; and secondly, the central core or nucleus which is made up of protons (positively charged) and neutrons (no charge).

In the 19th Century it was discovered that all elements with atomic weights greater than 83 are radioactive and that the nucleus could be divided into several parts. Albert Einstein (1879–1955) calculated in 1905 that heat ought to have weight and that, if we could destroy a piece of matter and turn all its weight into heat, we should obtain vast amounts of heat by using up only a small amount of matter.

Between 1934 and 1938 the Italian Enrico Fermi and the German Otto Hahn discovered that atoms of uranium (atomic weight 92) split when struck by a neutron. In 1939 Frédéric Joliot-Curie found that this splitting, or fission, released two or three more neutrons which in turn produced fission in more uranium nuclei, and so on. It is this chain reaction that makes possible not only the benefits of nuclear power but also the horrors of nuclear warfare.

Al Jolson appearing in "The Jazz Singer—the film which delivered the first-ever spoken dialogue from the cinema screen—"You ain't heard nothin' yet folks, listen to this."

300

WHY is pollution a problem?   WHY does a satellite remain

POLLUTION

Pollution is a problem because man, in an ever-increasingly populated and industrialized world, is upsetting the environment in which he lives. Many scientists maintain that one of man's greatest errors has been to equate growth with advancement. Now "growth" industries are being looked on with suspicion in case their side effects damage the environment and disrupt the relationship of different forms of life.

The growing population makes increasing demands on the world's fixed supply of air, water and land. This rise in population is accompanied by the desire of more and more people for a better standard of living. Thus still greater demands for electricity, water and goods result in an ever increasing amount of waste material to be disposed of.

The problem has been causing increasing concern to living things and their environment. Many believe that man is not solving these problems quickly enough and that his selfish pursuit of possessions take him past the point of no return before he fully appreciates the damage. It would then be too late to reverse the process.

Ecologists say we are so determined to possess a new car or washing machine, or to obtain a greater yield from our crops by the use of fertilizers, that we ignore the fact that life depends on a lot of micro-organisms working efficiently.

For example, if new chemicals were released into the environment, a combination of them might well poison one or more of the different types of bacteria in soil and water, which are essential to keep nitrogen being circulated from the air into organic material, and being cycled back into the air again. If this should happen on a world-wide scale, the air would become unbreathable.

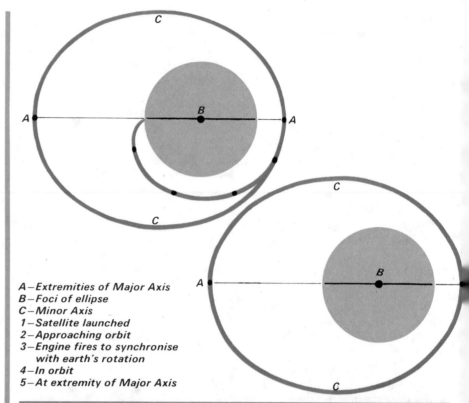

A—Extremities of Major Axis
B—Foci of ellipse
C—Minor Axis
1—Satellite launched
2—Approaching orbit
3—Engine fires to synchronise with earth's rotation
4—In orbit
5—At extremity of Major Axis

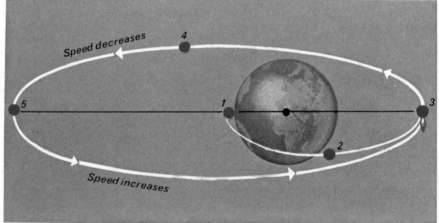

SATELLITE

An artificial satellite remains in its regular course around the earth even after its motors have been turned off. This is not because the satellite has been lifted beyond the reach of gravity but because its centrifugal force just balances the gravitational pull of the earth.

Launching a satellite calls for a propellant, such as a rocket which can move it high enough and fast enough to make it orbit the earth at a constant height indefinitely. There is no air in space to slow it down.

Since the pull of gravity grows less as the distance from the earth's surface increases, the speed required—its orbital velocity—also grows less.

At a height of 200 miles the orbital speed required is 17,200 m.p.h. At about 22,000 miles, the required speed would cause the satellite to take 24 hours to complete an orbit. It would thus rotate with the earth and maintain a fixed position above it.

in orbit? WHY were the Galapagos Islands important to Charles Darwin?

Above: A Galapagos iguana.

GALAPAGOS ISLANDS

In 1831 Charles Darwin sailed in H.M.S. Beagle on an expedition which would take him to the Galapagos Islands. On arrival he was so impressed by the animal life that the islands inspired many of his ideas on evolution, in particular his monumental work *The Origin of Species.*

Here he had proof for his views on natural selection. In front of his eyes were albatross and cormorant that could not fly, and giant land tortoises weighing over 500 pounds and considered among the oldest living creatures on earth.

There were also such extraordinary curiosities as a four-eyed fish and tame finches which would use sticks as tools to obtain food. Also, Darwin discovered a species of penguin unlike any others and large spiny iguanas, the only lizards that take to water.

The Galapagos Islands are in the Pacific Ocean, off the coasts of Ecuador and Peru, in South America.

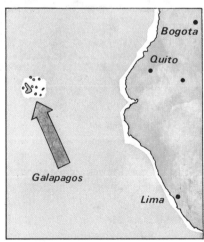

WHAT is glass fibre? WHAT is a light year? WHAT is the man

An experimental lifeboat with a glass reinforced plastic hull and deck used to test glass fibre in severe weather conditions.

GLASS FIBRE

Glass fibre is a mass of very fine strands of glass. When ordinary glass is spun into thin threads it is strong and bendable, unlike normal glass objects, which are brittle and break easily.

These silky strands of glass can be woven into a material or massed together like cotton-wool. Glass fibre does not decay or corrode. It is a good insulator and a poor conductor of electricity. Curtains made of this material do not rot in damp conditions or in sunlight. Now that technical dyeing problems have been overcome, glass fibre can be patterned.

Many plastics tend to crack or bend under stress or impact, but combining them with strands of glass fibre results in very light, strong and useful materials. Glass fibre increases their strength in much the same way as concrete is

in the moon?

LIGHT YEAR

A light-year is a unit of measurement used by astronomers and represents the distance light travels in one year. This distance is approximately 6,000,000,000,000 miles, the speed of light being just over 186,000 miles a second.

Astronomers adopted this unit because they found ordinary measurements impractical for coping with the vast distances of space. Using this means, scientists calculate that the Milky Way must be about 100,000 light-years in diameter.

The light from some stars takes millions of years to reach us. Andromeda is about 1,800,000 light-years distant from earth, although it can be seen with the naked eye. Our nearest star, Proxima Centauri, is about four light years away, while the most brilliant star, Sirius (the Dog Star), is eight and a half light-years from us.

MAN IN THE MOON

The moon, like the earth, is covered with ranges of mountains. People imagine in the shapes of these mountains the pattern of a face, which they call the "man in the moon".

His facial expressions vary according to whether the moon is full—completely free of the shadow of the earth—or partly in shadow. When the moon is only a crescent no face can be seen.

No one mentions the "woman in the moon", although most poets through the ages have regarded the moon as feminine. St Francis of Assisi referred to the moon, his sister.

reinforced with steel rods. These mixtures are moulded to make such things as aircraft parts, car bodies, boats and fishing rods. Coarse mats of glass fibre are used for filters and washers, and blankets of the material provide good insulation for houses.

WHEN is the best time to launch a rocket to the moon?

ROCKET LAUNCH

There is virtually no "best time" to launch a rocket to the moon, because, in terms of space travel, the journey is so short. The average distance is 238,000 miles, with a maximum variation of only 25,000 miles.

A space shot, whether to the moon or some other object, is made by a rocket already in orbit. To take a rocket out of orbit and put it on course for the moon calls for a boost in speed to 25,000 miles (40,000 kilometres) an hour. This is necessary to overcome the pull of the earth's gravity. The moment when the engines are refired to start the rocket on its journey does not depend on the position of the launching base in relation to the rocket or the moon.

In contrast, the great variations in the distances between the earth and Mars or Venus make the launching of a rocket to the planets impractical for periods of nine to eighteen months.

WHEN were dish telescopes first used?

DISH TELESCOPES

The first dish (or radio) telescope was made in 1942 by an American, Grote Reber, of Wheaton, Illinois. He constructed his apparatus after studying the experiments of K. G. Jansky, another American. Jansky discovered in 1935 that the intensity of radiowaves increases as a highly sensitive aerial is directed progressively nearer to the Milky Way. The maximum intensity is reached when the antenna is pointing towards Sagittarius— that is to say, towards the galactic centre.

Radio telescopes are called dish telescopes because of the steerable dish-shaped or parabolic reflector which gathers the radiation and focuses it on to a centrally mounted aerial. The surface of the dish is made of a good electrical conductor and the radio waves are reflected from it. The parabaloid shape ensures that all the reflected rays arrive at the central point, where they are "swallowed" by an electromagnetic horn and fed into a receiver.

Since the Second World War the development of radio telescopes has gone ahead rapidly. A 250-foot diameter instrument was installed at the Nuffield Radio Astronomy Laboratories at Jodrell Bank, Cheshire, England. It is under the direction of Professor Sir Bernard Lovell and has already contributed a great deal of new information to astronomy.

WHAT is a mirage?   **WHAT** keeps you afloat in the water?

WHAT is a

MIRAGE

Mirages are optical illusions produced by extraordinary atmospheric conditions. They can be non-existent sheets of water or similar visions, inverted or oversized images of distant objects or various other distortions. All are caused by the refraction, or bending, of light rays as they pass through two layers of air with different densities. The differences in density are usually due to unequal distributions of temperature in the atmosphere.

A common type of mirage is seen in deserts where the heat of the sand raises the temperature of the lower air to make it substantially less dense than the rest of the atmosphere. This bends the light to such an extent that images of the sky are projected on to the ground as patches of water. The phenomenon is known as an *inferior* image.

If the layers of hot and cold air are reversed, the result may be a *superior* mirage, where distorted images of distant objects on the ground are projected into the sky.

In this kind of mirage there are sometimes two images, the lower one being upside down.

A famous mirage known as the Fata Morgana can be seen in the Strait of Messina, between Italy and Sicily. Here the distorted images of houses on the opposite cliffs are transformed into imaginary castles in sea and sky. The Italians named this mirage after the Fata (or Fairy) Morgana, a legendary enchantress with the magical power of raising phantom castles from the waters.

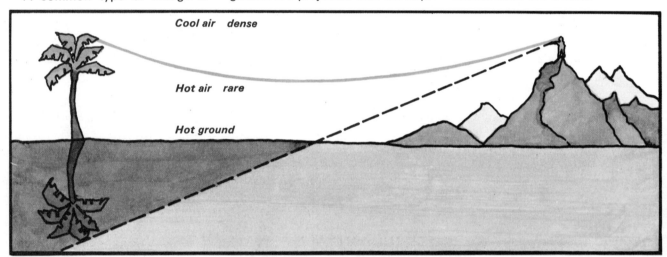

Cool air   dense

Hot air   rare

Hot ground

The illustration shows an inferior image. The reflection of the sky and tree appear on the ground.

AFLOAT

The main reason we are able to float is that the density of our bodies is relatively less than the density of water. A large part of the human body is made up of air and water.

Buoyancy—the ability to float —depends on the individual. But with experience it is possible to improve your body balance, in other words to distribute your weight evenly throughout your body. This makes floating easier.

In learning to float the beginner often experiences difficulty in keeping the legs horizontal. This can be remedied by extending the arms beyond the head to act as a counterbalance.

WHAT is a Bunsen burner?   WHAT is a vacuum?
Daguerrotype?   WHAT makes the ring around the moon?

BUNSEN BURNER

A Bunsen burner is a gas burner consisting of a tube with a small gas jet at the lower end and adjustable air inlet by means of which the heat of the flame can be controlled. It is used in laboratories and produces a hot non-luminous flame if the air and gas mixture is about three parts air to one of gas.

The inventor of the burner was Robert Wilhelm Bunsen (1811-1899), a German chemist, although Michael Faraday (1791–1867), the English physicist and chemist had previously designed a burner that worked on very much the same general principle.

Over the years several varieties of Bunsen burners have been made with improvements in the control and mixing of the air and gas, giving greater heat and enabling different sizes of flames to be obtained. There are devices for spreading the flame and numerous fittings are made to go on the top of the tube for holding retorts, test tubes, etc.

Burners may be constructed to burn coal gas, oil gas, acetylene or natural gas.

DAGUERREOTYPE

A Daguerreotype is a photograph taken by a process in which the impression is taken on a silver plate sensitized by iodine and then developed by vapour of mercury.

Louis Jacques Mandé Daguerre (1789–1851), a French painter and physicist, opened exhibitions of pictorial views, or dioramas, in Paris and London. His London exhibition was destroyed by fire in 1839, but Daguerre was by that time totally engrossed in discovering the photographic process to which he has given his name. He worked on his "heliograph pictures" until he perfected the process and was appointed an officer of the Legion of Honour in France, as reward for his work.

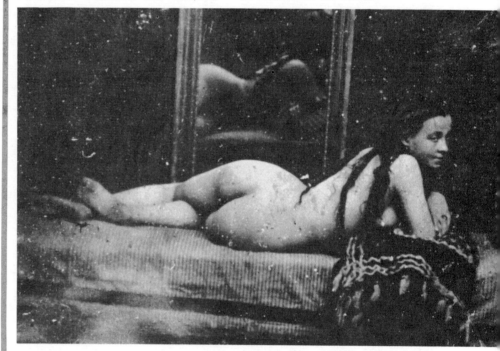

VACUUM

A vacuum, in theory, is a space entirely devoid of matter. But no method has been devised for producing one. In practice, therefore, a vacuum is an enclosed space from which air or other gases have been expelled to such an extent that the pressure inside is below that of the atmosphere. There are partial vacuums and high vacuums, according to the proportion of air pumped out of the container.

Vacuums can be put to a wide variety of uses, thanks largely to the truth of the old saying, "Nature abhors a vacuum". The tendency of air to rush into empty spaces under pressure from the atmosphere provides vacuums with suction power. This can be used to operate vacuum cleaners, pumps, milking machines and powerful brakes for heavy vehicles. Vacuums speed up evaporation and are, therefore, used in refrigeration and the dehydration of drugs and food.

High-vacuum processes are used to produce extra-hard steel, blend new materials and make components for radio and television sets. Perhaps the best-known vacuum is the electric light lamp in which the glowing wires are deprived of the oxygen which would cause them to burn up almost immediately.

MOON RING

The ring around the moon is the glow, or halo, which surrounds any light visible in intense darkness. Technically the ring is known as the moon's albedo.

It is faint because of the roughness of the moon's surface. This reduces the light reflected by the moon to slightly less than 0·1 per cent of the amount it receives from the sun and other stars.

The result is that the moon's reflected light, as seen on earth, amounts to only half a millionth of direct sunlight. Its faint, mysterious and gauzy halo was considered by ancient peoples to be like the illumination round the heads of their gods.

SPACE FLIGHT

On October 4, 1957, the Soviet Union launched the world's first satellite, Sputnik I, into space from a secret launching pad north of the Caspian Sea. The satellite continued to orbit the world for 92 days, ending its journey on January 4, 1958. The Russians spent 12 years developing their Sputnik.

The first manned space flight was made when Yuri Gagarin of the Soviet Union orbited the earth once in his spacecraft Vostok I in April, 1961. His journey lasted 108 minutes. He took off from Baikonur in western Siberia and landed near Engels in the Saratov region— probably close to the Sputnik's launching pad.

Man first set foot on another celestial body on July 21, 1969 when Neil Armstrong stepped on to the moon's surface. His first words were: "That's one small step for a man, one giant leap for mankind".

Below is Vostok 1 on exhibition

invented? **WHERE** will water not boil?
WHERE is the longest ocean cable in the world?

EARLY CLOCKS

It is believed that the Babylonians first used a pole fixed in the ground to measure the passing of time. They noticed that the position of the shadow changed during the hours of sunlight. They found that the shadow was long at sunrise and that it slowly grew shorter until it reached a point when it started to lengthen again. They noticed that at sunset the shadow was as long as it was at sunrise.

The simple shadow and pole arrangement was the basis of the various shadow clocks or sundials used by the ancient Egyptians. Eventually sundials were provided with the hour figures engraved on a metal plate.

The Egyptians also used a clepsydra or water clock. This was a basin-shaped, alabaster vessel filled with water that ran out through a hole in the bottom. The time was indicated by the level of water remaining inside.

Monks were the first to operate clocks by wheels and weights. Clocks of this type, found in monasteries, date back to the 14th Century. The first spring clock is dated about 1500.

BOILING WATER

Water will boil anywhere, but it boils at different temperatures in different places. For example, it will boil at a lower temperature up a mountain than at sea level.

The boiling point of water is the temperature at which its vapour pressure becomes equal to the outside atmospheric pressure.

As the atmospheric pressure is always changing so the boiling point of water will vary from day to day. Water boils at 100° Centigrade only when the atmospheric pressure outside is at the "standard" value.

At Quito in Ecuador, which is about 2,700 metres (or 8,800 feet) above sea level, water boils at 90° Centigrade.

People who explore in mountainous regions find a pressure-cooker very useful. The time required to cook food can be greatly reduced if the boiling point of the water is raised. The pressure-cooker does this, since it is an aluminium container fitted with a sealing ring but with a loaded pin-valve which allows steam to escape. The valve can be set at varying pressures, enabling the food to be cooked at a temperature of about 120° Centigrade.

OCEAN CABLES

The laying of the first successful transoceanic cable was completed on July 27, 1866, from Newfoundland, Canada, to Valencia Island off the south-west coast of Ireland. The cable was laid by the famous steamship Great Eastern. Since that time submarine telegraph and telephone cables have been laid all over the world.

Today the longest submarine telephone cable is the Commonwealth Pacific Cable (COMPAC).

It runs for over 9,000 miles from Australia, via Auckland, New Zealand and the Hawaiian Islands to Port Berni in western Canada. This cable was officially inaugurated on December 2, 1963. Its total cost was about £35 million.

Now that communications by satellite are being extensively used, it seems unlikely that another cable will ever be built to match COMPAC's record.

See the marine cables below

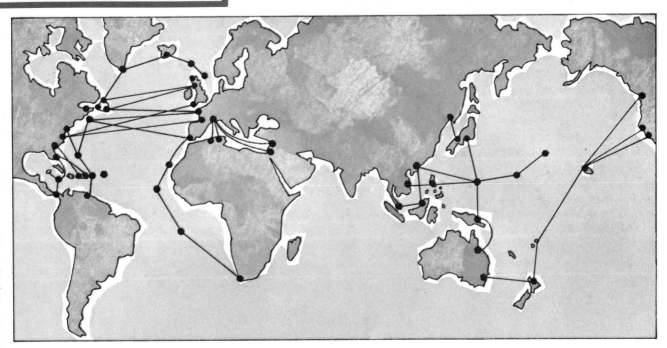

WHAT is safety glass? WHAT is the Doppler effect? WHAT

SAFETY GLASS

Safety glass is glass that has been strengthened. There are two kinds of this protective glass—laminated and toughened—and both were discovered by accident.

In the early 1900s Edouard Benedictus, a French chemist, knocked a glass flask on to the floor. Although the glass starred and cracked, it did not break. After examining the flask he realized that a coating of dried celluloid on the inside had held the fragments together.

Some years later, when injuries from broken car windscreens increased, Benedictus recalled this incident. Using glass sheets and celluloid bonded together in an old letter press, he produced the world's first sheet of laminated, or layered, glass. Since then the clarity of the glass has been improved to equal that of ordinary glass. But it will withstand the impact of a half-pound steel ball dropped from a height of 16 feet. Toughened glass was developed later, although in the 17th Century, Prince Rupert, nephew of King Charles I of England, discovered that molten glass was turned into immensely strong pear-shaped drops when tipped into cold water. Prince Rupert's Drops, as they are called, can be hammered on an anvil without breaking, but if the tail of the drop is broken they crumble into dust.

In 1874 a French scientist, de la Bastie, heated small sheets of glass and then quenched them in oil, increasing their strength dramatically. However these sheets of toughened glass were very small, and it was not until the 1930s that sheets large enough for use in cars could be toughened.

Laminated or toughened safety glass is now used all over the world in cars, buses, trains, aircraft, ships and shops and has proved its safety value.

Fracture patterns on toughened glass.

is a catalyst? WHAT is a teleprinter?

DOPPLER

Christian Johan Doppler (1803–1853) was an Austrian scientist born in Salzburg who made an important discovery about the effects of sound and light when the sources are moving in relation to the observer. You may find the Doppler effect easier to understand if you consider what happens to the noise of a train as it approaches you and then fades away.

The Doppler principle states that the pitch of a sound is changed, if the object emitting it is moving relative to the observer.

The light emitted, being a moving source, is changed in colour, as seen by a relatively stationary observer.

In each case the actual sound and light frequency remains constant. That is to say, a diesel locomotive travelling at a constant speed will be producing exactly the same engine noise or "note" whether it is half a mile or a 100 yards from you. But, as it gets closer, a change of tone appears.

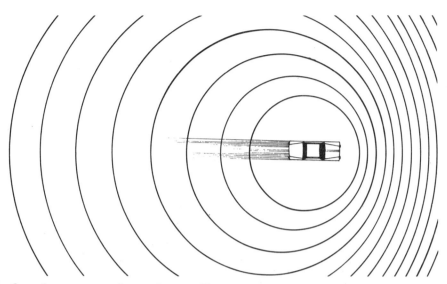

Sound waves around a moving car. The waves are bunched up in front of the car and spread out behind. The high-pitched sound that you hear as the car passes is the result of the bunched-up waves and the deeper roar comes from the more widely spaced waves behind the car.

The second part of the principle can be applied to the change in colour of a moving star.

A more complex example is the Doppler navigational system for aircraft, which requires no ground installation. In a typical system four separate beams of microwave energy are radiated from an antenna on the aircraft to the surface of the earth, and some of the energy is reflected back. The frequency of the reflected signal from each beam is shifted by an amount proportional to the plane's speed. This information is processed by a computer and enables the pilot to fix his position.

CATALYST

A catalyst is any substance which causes a chemical reaction without itself undergoing any chemical change. Many industrial processes depend on this property.

A simple example is when oxygen and hydrogen combine together quickly in the presence of platinum. Platinum is, therefore, the catalyst. It is believed that this is due to the gases being absorbed on the surface of the metal.

Magnesium is used as a catalyst for removing unwanted oxides and sulphur during the making of alloys, such as bronze, nickel, or brass.

Some of the most remarkable examples of catalysts are to be found in the human body. These are organic catalysts, or enzymes. At body temperature they bring about chemical reactions, like the burning of sugar. In a laboratory this could be done only at very high temperatures which would kill any form of life.

Each of the body's catalysts has its own function. Ptyalin, found in saliva, is concerned in the digestion with converting starch into sugar. Pepsin, produced in the stomach, plays a major part in breaking down the proteins in our food.

TELEPRINTER

A teleprinter is a telegraph transmitter which has a typewriter keyboard and type-printing telegraph receiver. It is widely used in commercial offices and for public and news services.

The machines were developed so that telegraphing could be carried out by competent typists rather than highly-skilled telegraph operators. During the 1920's and 1930's they were developed by E. E. Kleinschmidt and the Morkrum Company in the U.S.A., Creed and Company in England and Siemens-Haske in Germany. The teleprinter has become the commonest telegraph instrument and is capable of speeds of 60–100 words per minute.

WHEN was concrete invented? WHEN is the earth nearest

CONCRETE

Concrete can be said to have been used for thousands of years, if the word is taken generally to mean a hard building material produced from a mixture of cement, sand, gravel and stone. The Assyrians and Babylonians used clay to bind sand and stones, and the ancient Egyptians discovered lime and gypsum. The Romans mixed slaked lime with volcanic ash and constructed aqueducts, bridges and buildings, some of which survive.

Lime remained a popular cementing material until the discovery of the process of making Portland cement shortly after 1800. The name was given to it by Joseph Aspdin, an Englishman, because he thought its products resembled the limestone quarried at Portland in Dorset, England. It is a man-made cement which, since 1900, has been almost the only cement used in the building industry.

Concrete mixtures for small jobs and repairs at home are easily made, but the design and erection of important concrete structures calls for a combination of artistic and scientific skills. Scientists have developed reinforced concrete strengthened with steel, pre-stressed concrete and concrete shells which may be simple and functional or more complex to give a building added beauty.

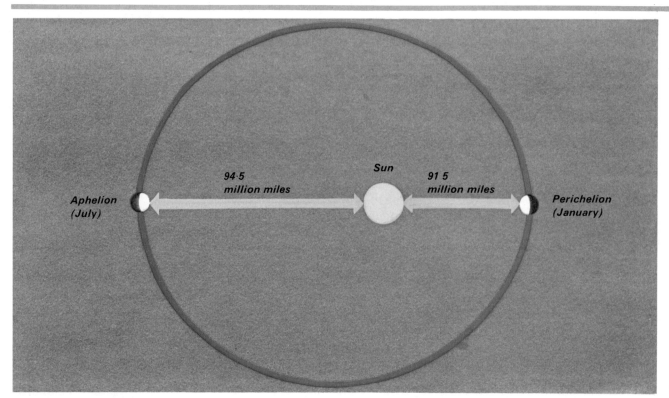

Aphelion (July) 94·5 million miles Sun 91 5 million miles Perichelion (January)

EARTH AND SUN

The earth is nearest to the sun on about the second or third day in January. The distance varies because the earth spins round the sun in an elliptical orbit or path. The time when the earth is closest to the sun is called the perihelion. The time when it is farthest away—the aphelion—comes six months later on the first or second day in July. During the perihelion the earth is 147 million kilometres from the sun (about $91\frac{1}{2}$ million miles), but during the aphelion it is 152 million kilometres away ($94\frac{1}{2}$ million miles).

When planetary distances in the solar system are compared, the average distance between these two extremes is used. This is called the astronomical unit and in the case of the earth and sun, measures 149 million kilometres (about 93 million miles). If it were possible for an aircraft to fly from the earth to the sun at a constant speed of 1,000 miles an hour it would have to travel non-stop for 10 years to reach its destination.

The earth takes $365\frac{1}{4}$ days to travel round the sun and moves at a speed of nearly 19 miles a second. As can be seen from the dates of the perihelion and aphelion, the nearness of the sun does not determine the seasons. Our seasons are decided by the amount of daylight and directness of the sun's rays on the earth's surface.

These conditions vary as the axis on which the earth spins is tilted.

to the sun? WHEN was plastic invented?

WHEN does colour fade?

PLASTIC

A plastic, in the modern sense of the word, is a synthetic or man-made material which can be formed into various shapes. The first plastic material was Celluloid, made in 1868 by an American, John W. Hyatt, by dissolving nitrocellulose under pressure.

The use of plastics began slowly, but shortages of natural materials caused by two world wars forced scientists to develop substitutes. Since the Second World War the making of plastics has become a gigantic industry, which has grown so fast that many people still have only a hazy idea what plastics are. In fact, the term "plastics" is as general as the word "metals". The high-temperature cone of a rocket and the highly inflammable table-tennis ball are both plastics, just as lead and steel are both metals.

However, all plastics have some things in common: first, they are entirely man-made and not found in nature; secondly, they consist of large molecules of an organic nature; thirdly, at some stage in their manufacture they are liquid and can be shaped; and fourthly, in their final state they are solid.

Most of the raw materials for plastics are produced by the petroleum and coal industries. Scientists are able to produce different properties in plastics so that they can be used in a tremendous variety of articles.

This giant plastic air-bed makes an ideal playground.

COLOUR FADE

An article's colour fades when subjected to a chemical reaction in which oxygen is released. This oxygen combines with the natural colouring matter or with the dye to produce a colourless compound. Thus the colour of the article becomes paler and is finally taken out altogether, or bleached.

The most famous bleaching agent is the sun, and the process by which it makes colour fade is called photo-chemistry. The old-fashioned method of bleaching textiles by laying them out flat in the sunlight is still used in places.

Chemical bleaching is much quicker, but needs to be controlled with great care. In about 1790 it was discovered that chlorine gas and its compounds were good bleaching agents and chloride of lime (calcium hypochlorite), made by the action of chlorine on slaked lime came into use. This "bleaching powder", as it was called, was dissolved in water. It was removed when the bleaching was complete by washing the article or immersing it in neutralizing solutions. More modern bleaching agents are sodium hypochlorite, hydrogen peroxide and sulphur dioxide.

WHAT is the greatest distance you can see?
WHAT is pasteurized milk?   WHAT are the rings of Saturn?

DISTANCE

If you stood on the shore looking across the sea to the horizon (the line appearing to separate earth from sky), you might be able to see about two and a half miles. But the higher you stood the further you would be able to see. As the earth is curved, the horizon would appear farther away with every increase in height above sea level.

At a height of 20 feet you might see for six miles. From the top of a 300-foot cliff your view could extend for 23 miles, while on the summit of a 3,500-foot mountain, it could lengthen to 80 miles. From an aircraft flying at 16,000 feet you might have an uninterrupted panorama for 165 miles.

If you look straight up into the sky, the distance you can see is immense. The moon is about 239,000 miles away and the stars are millions of miles distant.

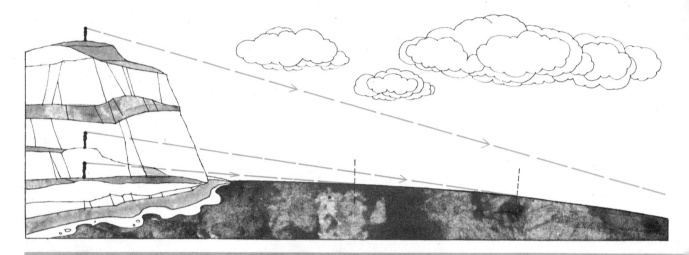

PASTEURIZED MILK

Milk is pasteurized by heating it to a temperature of about 62° Centigrade (about 143° Fahrenheit) and maintaining that temperature for half an hour. The treatment kills most of the bacteria which cause milk to go sour quickly or may produce disease in human beings.

This temperature is chosen because it is the lowest temperature that will kill the microbacterium tuberculosis, the carrier of tuberculosis which used to kill people of all ages in their millions. At the same time the temperature is low enough not to alter the taste and quality of the milk too much.

Pasteurized milk is therefore much safer than untreated milk, especially for babies, and in many countries is the only milk allowed to be sold. The process is named after the French scientist Louis Pasteur (1822–1895) whose discoveries revolutionized knowledge about the effects of bacteria.

WHAT is dry ice? WHAT makes stainless steel stainless?

RINGS OF SATURN

The magnificent bright rings surrounding the planet Saturn are made up of large numbers of small particles of matter revolving round the planet like thousands of tiny moons. It has been suggested that they are the fragments of a former satellite which went too close to Saturn and was broken up but this has not been proved.

There are three main rings round the planet. The two outer rings are bright, but the one closest to Saturn is dusky.

The two brighter rings were discovered in 1610 by the great Italian astronomer Galileo, although he admitted he did not know what they were. But it was not until 1850 that the third ring was discovered through independent observations both at Harvard College University in the United States and in England.

DRY ICE

Dry ice is frozen carbon dioxide. When this gas is cooled to a temperature of $-78 \cdot 5°$ Centigrade ($-109 \cdot 3°$ Fahrenheit) it becomes a solid without first becoming a liquid. That is why it is called dry ice. When frozen carbon dioxide is exposed to the air, it evaporates slowly as a gas without going through the melting stage in the way that ice made from water does.

The fact that dry ice has a freezing point much lower than that of water makes it useful as a refrigerant, particularly for the storage of things that need to be kept very cold. When powdered dry ice is added to such liquids as acetone (used in the manufacture of chloroform) or ether, it is possible to produce a mixture which has a constant temperature of as little as $-110°$ Centigrade ($-166°$ Fahrenheit).

STAINLESS STEEL

Stainless steel resists rust because it contains a high proportion of chromium to carbon. Before the arrival of this alloy just before the First World War, knives and other household articles made of steel easily rusted unless very carefully dried.

It was an English researcher named Harry Brearley who discovered that rust was encouraged by the carbon in steel and other metals. The less carbon and the more chromium in steel, the better it would resist rust.

But a careful balance had to be struck. Completely carbon-free steel was impossible to make, and only a limited amount of chromium could be included, because it tended to make steel brittle. Brearley discovered a satisfactory formula only after many experiments.

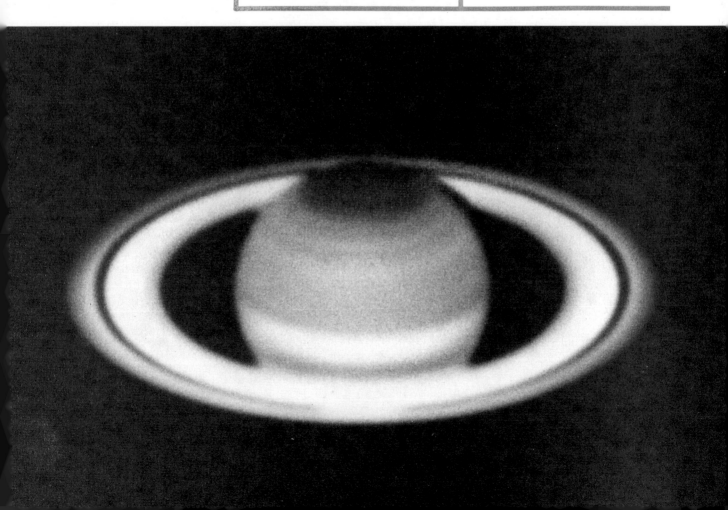

WHY does iron go red when heated? WHY does a magnifying

WHY is a diesel engine more efficient than the petrol engine?

IRON

Iron goes red when heated because its atoms radiate vibratory waves of an electrodynamic nature which are visible as light at a sufficiently high temperature. At 800° Centigrade the iron is at low-red heat. But as the heat increases the iron will turn bright red, and finally white-hot and molten.

Heat is passed through the iron by conduction—the contact of one iron particle with another with no visible movement of the particles. The heat which is given off as light when iron glows red-hot can be reconverted into heat by the substance on to which it falls. When iron is heated to a temperature below 300° Centigrade it gives off invisible rays of infra-red radiation which are similar in nature to light. But they do not contain quite enough energy per unit (photon) to stimulate the optic nerve and so be seen by the human eye.

MAGNIFYING GLASS

A magnifying glass consists of a double-convex lens which bends the rays of light that pass through it and so makes objects appear larger. This bending of the light rays deceives our eyes. We do not see the actual object we are looking at, but rays of light from the direction from which they would come if we were looking at a much bigger object.

A convex lens is a circular piece of glass which has been ground, or shaped, so that its centre is thicker than its outside edge. A concave lens is thinner at its centre than at its outside edge, and this makes objects look smaller.

Magnifying glasses, or convex lenses, are used in telescopes and microscopes. A telescope makes distant objects appear nearer by means of two convex lenses. This can be shown by using two old spectacle lenses. The one held nearer the eyes should be thicker than the one nearer the object.

LIGHT BULB

A light bulb gives off light because an electric current is passed through its filament, a thread of tungsten metal thinner than a human hair, which then becomes white hot.

Sir Joseph Swan (1828–1914) in England and Thomas Alva Edison (1847–1931) in the United States constructed the first incandescent electric lamps in 1879. They succeeded in preventing the rapid burning up of the filament by oxidization, but their problem lay in the choice of a suitable material for the filament.

Edison sat in his laboratory watching a filament of charred cotton thread glow in a glass bulb, which had been exhausted of air, for 40 hours. But the thread was too fragile to sustain the heat provided by the electric current. A material was needed that would stand great heat, for the hotter the filament, the brighter is the light

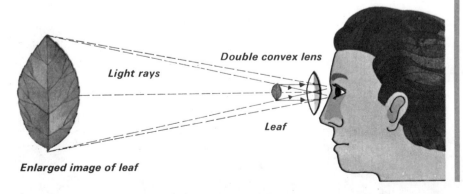

Double convex lens

Light rays

Leaf

Enlarged image of leaf

317

glass magnify? WHY does an electric light bulb give off light? WHY don't cranes topple over?

DIESEL ENGINE

The diesel engine is more efficient than the petrol engine because of its greater thermal efficiency. This means that the ratio of the work done by the engine to the amount of heat supplied is higher. Since the heat in this case comes from fuel-oil, it is not possible to convert all the heat energy in the fuel into useful work. There are losses due to friction, exhaust and radiation.

The compression-ignition, or diesel engine was invented by the German engineer Rudolf Diesel in 1897. It is much simpler in construction than the petrol, or spark-ignition engine. Pre-ignition troubles are avoided because only the air in the engine cylinder is compressed and the fuel is introduced only at the instant of combustion. The engine requires no spark-plugs and burns fuel-oil which is less expensive than petrol.

The basic construction of the diesel engine is similar to the petrol engine. The main difference is the way in which the fuel is introduced and ignited. With an average compression ratio of 16:1 the air in the cylinder during the compression stroke reaches a pressure of about 500 pounds a square inch.

At the right instant a precise amount of fuel passes from the injector pump to the injector at high pressure and enters the cylinder as a fine spray. Owing to the high temperature of the air, the fuel starts to burn without the need for a spark.

But the high pressure means that diesel engines have to be stronger than petrol engines. They are, therefore, heavier and more expensive.

CRANES

Cranes do not topple over because their jibs or booms are counter-balanced at the opposite end from the lifted load, thus keeping the centre of gravity over the base.

The first cranes were simply long poles fixed in the ground at an angle, with a pulley at the top through which passed a rope. They were called "cranes" because they looked rather like the neck of the bird with the same name.

The derrick crane, which looks like a gallows, is named after Dick Derrick, a 17th Century hangman. In the middle of the 18th Century, steam engines began to be used on cranes, while today the lifting may be done by varieties of power.

Jib cranes may be portable, being mounted on a wheeled carriage, or they may be self-propelled. Gantry cranes with long booms are used for unloading ships while overhead cranes are used in factories. Goliath cranes, with steel towers at either side, capable of lifting 200 tons are used at some atomic power stations.

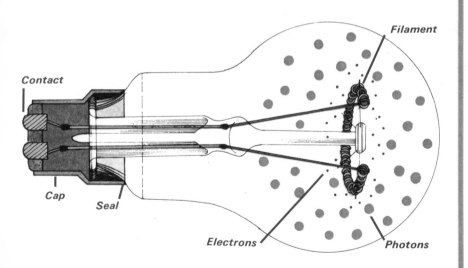

Contact · Cap · Seal · Electrons · Filament · Photons

given by the lamp.

But even with the present day use of tungsten, the problem still remains in that the more a filament is heated, the sooner it will burn away. To solve this problem, gas discharge lamps were invented. These consist of glass tubes filled with sodium or mercury vapour, or neon gas. At each end of the tubes are electrodes, or contacts. When an electric current is applied to one of the contacts it passes through the gas to the other contact, causing the gas to glow and give out light.

WHEN does a car engine stall? WHEN does a firestorm

Ruins in Dresden after an incendiary attack.

ENGINE STALL

A car engine will stall—that is to say, it will suddenly stop when you do not want it to—if it is unable to provide sufficient power to overcome the load on the back wheels.

This power is provided by the explosion of the petrol and air mixture pushing down on the pistons. If the load on the pistons from the crankshaft is exerting a greater force than that created by the explosion, the pistons will not move down the cylinder and the engine will stop. This can happen if the clutch is engaged too rapidly or if the hand brake is left on.

FIRESTORM

A firestorm occurs when flames from a large number of individual fires merge into a single convective, or circulatory, column. This produces so much heat that all the buildings below are set on fire. Firestorms cover a whole area, trapping the population within them.

During the Second World War enormous destruction was caused by fire in British, German and Japanese cities. In Britain and Germany the thousands of fires started by incendiary bombs burned individually, with relatively little spread from building to building. This was because of the materials from which the buildings were constructed, their size and the lay-out of the cities.

However, in Japanese cities mostly made up of low wooden-framed houses the American bombing attacks brought about a number of annihilating firestorms. The most terrible of all was that caused by the atomic bomb dropped on Hiroshima, on August 6, 1945. This storm contributed in great measure to the death toll of 70,000 to 80,000 people. In the second atomic bomb attack on Nagasaki on August 9, 1945, fire damage was again severe.

occur? **WHEN** was the first lighthouse built?

LIGHTHOUSE

The first known lighthouse was the Pharos of Alexandria in Egypt, a 400-foot tower built about 280 B.C. A wood fire was kept burning on the top of the tower, which became one of the Seven Wonders of the World. Before this the light from volcanoes had acted as a guide for sailors. The first lighthouse in Britain was built by the Romans at Dover in about A.D. 43.

Lighthouses continued to be built to the plan of the Pharos until about the 12th Century. Then oil lamps and candles inside lan-terns began to be substituted for fires. Shortly afterwards light-houses suffered a decline which lasted until the great expansion of overseas trade and shipping began in the 16th Century. This led to a revival and many light-houses were built around the coasts of Europe. The first American lighthouse was constructed on Little Brewster Island off Boston, Massachusetts in 1716.

Electricity was introduced for this purpose by Britain in 1862, when electric carbon arc lamps were installed at Dungeness light-house on the coast of Kent. But this source of light did not come into general use until the 1920s, when high-powered filament lamps were employed. A small but powerful high-pressure electric arc lamp containing a gas called xenon was installed at Dungeness in 1961, and mercury arc lamps provide the power for one of the most modern lighthouses in the United States, that on Oak Island, North Carolina.

Scientists are now investigating the possibility of harnessing solar energy to operate lighthouses.

PHAROS

320

WHAT enables an aircraft to stay in the air?   WHAT doe

AIRCRAFT

The flight of an aircraft is the outcome of a conflict between four forces—drag and thrust, and weight and lift. Drag and thrust are opposites, and so are weight and lift.

When the aircraft is in level flight, lift is pulling upwards, weight is bearing downwards, drag is pulling backwards and thrust is pulling forwards. Briefly, that is the theory of flight, which was first expounded by the British scientist Sir George Cayley (1773–1857) almost 100 years before men first flew in a heavier-than-air machine. Cayley made many simple experiments, some with pieces of paper. He also used leaves and kites, and finally designed a wing for a model glider. His design was the forerunner of the wings on today's aircraft.

Wings are designed to give as much lift as possible with the least drag. This is achieved by giving the wing cambered surfaces, causing the air to create a region of negative pressure or push beneath the lower surface. About 70 per cent of lift is created from this negative pressure. The air flow must reach the required minimum speed for a particular aircraft before the amount of lift necessary for flight is obtained.

WATERLOGGED

Wood becomes waterlogged when all its cells are filled with water. It can absorb water only up to about 30 per cent its own weight. As it does so, the wood swells until it reaches "fibre saturation point" or its maximum volume.

If further water is added, it will penetrate to the cavities of the cells, but no further swelling will take place. Waterlogged wood no longer floats because the air spaces within are filled with fluid making it too heavy.

The word "waterlogged" is used to describe ships that have been flooded and sunk, or meadows and fields that are so wet that they must be drained before they are any use for growing food.

A meadow becomes waterlogged in the same way as wood. The land can no longer absorb more water or drain it away. Many areas of land remain permanently in this condition unless they are reclaimed for farming.

waterlogged mean?   WHAT is radar used for?

RADAR

Radar, or radiolocation, as it was called in the early days, is the use of radio waves to find the whereabouts of aircraft or ships.

Electro-magnetic waves, which include radio and light waves, all travel at the same speed. When small bursts of radio waves, fired into space from a transmitter, strike an object such as an aircraft some of them bounce back and are collected by an aerial. Special equipment calculates the distance of the object from the time taken for the waves to go there and back.

Direction is obtained by rotating the aerial, and the course being taken by the object is shown as spots of light on the face of a cathode ray tube. So direction, position and movement can be judged accurately.

Radar was first used to detect enemy aircraft in wartime, and to guide fighter aircraft and bomber pilots. Since then it has proved invaluable in civil aviation by helping the pilot to guide his aircraft in the air and to land it safely in fog or at night.

At sea it can give the position of land and other ships. Some buoys are fitted with radar, so that they can be located in the dark or in fog. Radar is used also to give warning of turbulent weather.

Display of Decca Super 101 yacht radar.

EINSTEIN

Albert Einstein is famous for his Theories of Relativity which say that nothing in the universe is absolutely still and that all motion is connected or comparable. Einstein worked out a method of measuring the speed of moving objects, using the three dimensions of space—length, height and thickness—and adding the fourth dimension of time. The three space dimensions tell us where the object is, while the fourth tells us when.

In the relativity theories the movement of any object is represented by lines, called "world-lines", with the dimensions of time and space—as a four-dimensional graph. If an object moves with uniform speed and in a straight line, its world-line will be straight. If it moves under the force of gravity, such as a falling stone, it will drop not at a uniform pace, but at an increasing speed. So its world-line will be a curve.

Einstein was born in 1879 at Ulm in Germany of German-Jewish parents. He published his first paper on the Special Theory of Relativity in 1905, his second paper on the General Theory of Relativity ten years later. In 1921 he was awarded the Nobel Prize for Physics. In 1950 he published another paper, an extension to the General Theory designed to include magnetism and electricity and called the Unified Field Theory.

His remarkable ability as a scientist did not stop him from taking a keen interest in other affairs, and he held passionate views on peace and world unity. He was also an accomplished violinist.

In 1952, three years before his death, he rejected a suggestion that he should be nominated to be President of Israel.

RADIOACTIVITY

Radioactivity is dangerous because it can expose people to a harmful dose of radiation even without being aware of it. A number of small doses received over a very long time could lead to leukaemia or cancer in later life.

Radiation can lead to the retention of a potentially harmful amount of radium in one's bones. Radioactivity resulting from nuclear bomb tests can cause ingenuous quantities of radio-strontium and radiocaesium to get into food.

A radium compound was once used in the manufacture of luminous paint for the numbers on clocks, watches and instrument dials. The girls who painted these had a habit of putting the brush in their mouths to get a fine pointed tip. In those days the danger was not realized, and, over a long period, many workers absorbed enough radium to cause death in later years.

CONVECTOR HEATER

Heating appliances specially designed to create a circulating movement of warmed air are called convection heaters because they use convection currents of air.

When air is heated it becomes less dense and, since warm air is lighter than cold air it duly rises and is replaced by cold air.

Convector heaters consist, basically, of metal cabinets with openings at the top and bottom to produce and direct this flow of rising warm air. At the base of this cabinet there is a heating element and this warms the air within the cabinet.

This warm air rises and, as it rises, cold air is drawn into the convector from the bottom of the appliance. The cabinet of the convector acts as a flue or chimney and creates a continuous current of warm air.

MOTOR OIL

Every moving part of a motor vehicle engine needs lubrication. Oil provides this lubrication, without which much of the power generated by the engine would be wasted through friction.

Lubrication creates a protective film between all those parts of the engine that rub together. This minimizes wear, and prevents breakages and possible fire. Oil also reduces noise and stops the engine from overheating too easily, by cooling the working parts.

An engine that is regularly oiled will automatically be clean. The oil acts as a detergent and prevents rust.

oil? **WHY** do aircraft break the sound barrier with a bang?
so called? **WHY** can transistor radio valves be so small?

Path of double sonic boom

SOUND BARRIER

The loud double bangs produced when aircraft break the sound barrier are caused by shock waves from the plane's wings.

An aircraft travelling at a speed less than that of sound produces waves which travel ahead of it. At this speed the waves seem to prepare the way for the machine, so that the air slides over and under the wing surfaces easily.

As the plane approaches the speed of sound, the waves travel at the same speed as the machine and the air tends to swirl and break unevenly over the wing surfaces.

At the speed of sound shock waves are projected outwards and backwards from the leading and trailing edges of the aircraft. These waves are heard as two quick loud claps like thunder and are usually followed by a somewhat diminished roar as the aircraft breaks through the sound barrier.

TRANSISTOR

Transistor radio valves can be small because they are made with a class of material called semi-conductors.

In the early days of radio it was essential to have a rectifier, a component which allowed an electric current to flow with a low resistance in one direction and a high resistance in the opposite direction. This involved the use of a piece of carborundum crystal and a steel point.

Then a diode-valve was used as a rectifier. This consisted of two separated metals in a vacuum. They were contained in a thin glass tube, two inches long and one inch in diameter. More progress was made by the discovery of materials with an electrical resistance between high-value insulators and low-value substances such as plastic and copper. Two such materials, now widely used in industry and called semi-conductors, are silicon, a non-metallic

element and germanium, a metallic element.

Only a small amount of the elements is required and only a few volts are needed to carry the current. By a special industrial melting process, these semi-conductors can be joined together in layers like a sandwich. A transistor is basically a sandwich of three layers of semi-conductors, and it is possible to obtain several combinations.

Since the resistance of all semi-conductors is sensitive to light, the sandwich is housed in a sealed capsule and coated with black lacquer.

Transistors can be any size from a grain of rice to $\frac{1}{4}$ inch long. They can perform many of the functions of multi-electrode valves, need only a small voltage battery, are less liable to breakage, are considerably cheaper to produce and can be very much smaller.

ENERGY

Energy is the power to act. There are several different forms of energy, and one kind can be changed into another kind. But although it can be changed from one form into another it can never be lost. The total amount of energy in the universe remains constant.

If you strike a match on the side of a match-box, mechanical and chemical energy is changed into heat energy. If you use a saw, the blade gets hot because the energy of movement or mechanical energy becomes heat energy. The end of a bicycle pump becomes warm after several minutes of pumping, because heat is generated when air is compressed.

In a simple electric circuit there are several changes. The battery has chemical energy, which passes along the wire as electrical energy, which lights the bulb as light and heat energy.

We depend for a large part of our power on steam, diesel and petrol engines in which the chemical energy stored in a fuel is converted first into heat energy, which is then turned into work.

AEROFOILS

Racing cars capable of moving at speeds well in excess of 100 m.p.h. need aerofoils to counter the effect of lift created by their highly streamlined shapes.

Drag is caused by the turbulence of the air as it flows in to fill the vacuum left behind a forward-moving object. The less stream-lined the object, the greater the space to be filled in and the greater the turbulence. Therefore, the greater the "drag".

As designers improve the streamlining effect of racing cars to reduce drag, the cars' shapes become more and more flattened and a new problem arises. The car has taken on similar properties to an aircraft wing and the movement of air over and under it at high speed begins to provide lift. The aerofoil placed at the rear of the car is so designed as to create a downward force when it passes through air at speed, and thus counteracts the lift. If this did not occur the cars' wheels would make too little contact with the road surface and the driver would quickly lose control.

EARTH SPIN

The earth originated from a swirling cloud of blazing gases, and its rotation has been gradually slowing down over millions of years. Its spin is now kept practically constant by the movement of the oceans causing a tidal bulge. This movement is just enough to keep the earth revolving at a speed which diminishes with almost imperceptible slowness, detectable only by refined scientific instruments.

The earth's axis is the imaginary spindle on which it revolves, stretching from Pole to Pole. It is not vertical, but is inclined at an angle of $23\frac{1}{2}$ degrees and remains tilted in the same position as it makes its journey round the sun.

Moon

Earth

Tidal bulge

WHAT makes the earth spin?
WHAT makes the holes in a piece of bread?

HOLES IN BREAD

The holes in a piece of bread are made by bubbles of gas. In bread-making flour and water are mixed to form a dough. Then a small amount of yeast is added to the mixture. Yeast is a type of fungus which grows very quickly when it is warm and damp. While growing, it gives off a gas which bubbles up through the dough, making it expand. It is yeast which gives bread its particular flavour and appetizing smell.

No one knows when yeast was first used to make bread, but it must have been many thousands of years ago. According to one story, the idea was the result of an accident. Some yeast is said to have got into the dough by

chance and made it rise. Because this loaf was twice as big as normal, people thought it must be magic. But as the bread tasted better than the usual flat, heavy loaves, they soon used yeast to make all their bread.

Cakes also have holes in them made by bubbles of gas. But these are made by a different substance which leaves practically no flavour. This substance is baking-powder, which is a mixture of tartaric acid and bicarbonate of soda. When these two chemicals are mixed together, wetted and heated, they react to produce carbon dioxide. This gas bubbles through the cake mixture to make it rise while being baked.

VIDEO TAPES

Video tapes were introduced in the years following the Second World War. The idea of storing information on magnetic wire was first put into practise by a Dane, Valdemar Poulsen, in 1900, but little was heard about it until the 1920s when magnetic tapes were made in the United States and Germany.

The recording of most television programmes is done on magnetic tape or video tape. This technique produces good pictures which can be played back immediately without processing. The magnetic tape, two inches wide, is moved at a speed of 15 inches a second past a magnetic recording head which imprints, by means of electrical signals, a magnetized

pattern of the sound and picture.

The tape is a band of plastic which has a film of magnetic iron oxide coating—one ten-thousandth of an inch thick—spread over one side of it. When the tape is played back, the changing magnetic fields of the pattern of iron oxide particles create weak currents which exactly correspond to the sound and picture which has been recorded.

Recording enables programmes to be re-broadcast or edited. In sports television it is often used for the "instant replay" or reproduction of a particularly interesting event during a live broadcast. Videotape is also employed in slow-motion and stop-action techniques.

SLIP CURRENT

A slip current occurs when a steady stream of air tries to resume its even flow after being diverted by an object at right angles to it. The less streamlined the object, the greater the disturbance, or turbulence, of the stream of air.

A good example is provided by a bus moving along a road. The

IMPLOSION

An implosion is the opposite of an explosion. It occurs when something violently shatters a container in which the internal pressure is less than the external pressure. A good example of such a container is an electric light bulb in which the pressure has been lowered by the withdrawal

current occur? WHEN does an implosion occur?

WHEN was the first gas balloon?

GAS BALLOON

The first gas balloon, filled with hydrogen, was released in Paris in August, 1783 by a French professor of physics, J. A. C. Charles. Two months earlier, the first hot air balloon was sent aloft by the Montgolfier brothers, Jacques, Etienne and Joseph, of France, and it was with balloons of this type that the first manned flights were made.

A rubberized silk balloon filled with hydrogen carried Professor Charles and M. N. Robert on a flight of 27 miles and rose to 2,000 feet. Ballooning became a popular sport in spite of the fact that hydrogen-filled balloons were always liable to catch fire. Some amazingly long trips were undertaken, including an unsuccessful attempt in 1958 to cross the Atlantic.

Balloons play an important part in meteorology, the science concerned with the weather. The first aerial photographs were taken from balloons, and in the 1930s pressurized cabins or gondolas were designed enabling observers to rise over 60,000 feet into the stratosphere.

Military observation balloons fastened to the ground by cables came into use at the end of the 18th Century and were employed by both North and South in the American Civil War (1861–1865). The Austrians used pilotless hot-air balloons to bomb Venice in 1849. During the Franco-German War of 1870–1871 balloons transported mail and carrier pigeons. Barrage balloons tethered to the ground were used in the Second World War to provide barriers against low-flying enemy aircraft.

The Robert brothers help J. A. C. Charles to inflate the first hydrogen balloon.

air pushed aside by the bus is turned back to fill the empty space when the vehicle has passed. Thus air currents are set flowing in the same direction as that being taken by the bus. A sensation of being pulled forward may be felt if you ride a bicycle too close to the rear of a large moving object.

of air. When a bulb is suddenly broken, the atmospheric pressure against all sides causes the glass to collapse inwards with tremendous force and noise.

In contrast, an explosion is caused by a sudden increase of pressure within a confined space, which directs the force outwards.

328

WHAT is fire?   WHAT is a volt?   WHAT makes a boomerang

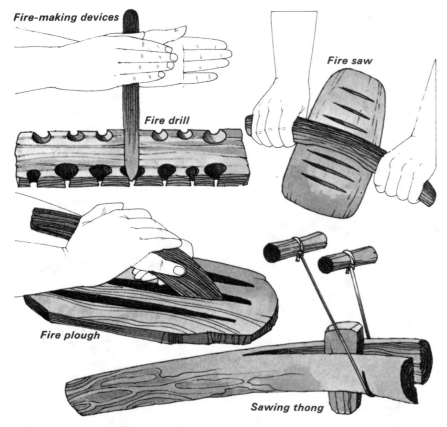

Fire-making devices

Fire saw

Fire drill

Fire plough

Sawing thong

FIRE

Fire is the outward sign that oxygen is combining with other substances in a spectacular chemical reaction. As the air is rich in oxygen, many materials will burn freely in a process scientifically called combustion, if their temperature is raised high enough. This explanation of what had been considered a mysterious phenomenon was discovered by the French chemist Antoine Lavoisier in 1783.

The discovery of fire may have changed early man's wandering mode of life to a more settled one because of an urge to keep the fire burning. It provided him with a new weapon for survival, warmed his cave and huts, enabled him to cook, and helped to scare off dangerous animals.

In ancient times people in Persia, Egypt and India believed fire to be sacred and worshipped it as representative of the sun.

VOLT

A volt is the practical unit of electromotive force, or electrical pressure, as distinct from an electric current. In terms of measurement it is that electrical motive force which applied to a conductor of 1 ohm resistance produces a current of 1 ampere.

Imagine water stored in a tank on a tower, with an outlet near the ground. The head of water will give varying pressures at ground level, depending on the height of the tower. In electricity the head corresponds to the voltage.

The volt is named after the Italian physicist Alexandro Volta (1745–1827), who invented the voltaic cell.

In a dry battery the chemical composition determines the voltage or pressure of each cell. This cannot be increased by making the cell larger. A larger cell will merely last longer.

BOOMERANG

It is the built-in skew or twist in a bommerang combined with its spinning motion that makes it return to the thrower. At first people believed that air, pressing on the lower flat surface and passing over the upper rounded face, was responsible for the return flight. But T. L. Mitchell, a Scottish explorer of Australia, gave the true explanation early in the 19th Century.

The curved throwing stick is used chiefly by the aborigines of Australia for hunting and warfare. (They also use a non-returning kind of boomerang.)

The boomerang is held at one end, above and behind the thrower's shoulder, with the concave edge to the front, and swung forward rapidly with the flat side underneath. Just before it is released, it is given extra power with a strong wrist movement.

If thrown downward or parallel to the ground it sweeps upward to a height of 50 feet or more. When thrown so that one end strikes the ground, it ricochets into the air at terrific speed, spinning endwise. It completes a circle 50 yards or more wide and then several smaller ones, up to five, before it drops to the ground near the thrower.

come back? WHAT is a flying buttress?

The cathedral in Palma, Majorca.

The flight path of the boomerang.

FLYING BUTTRESS

The name "buttress" in architecture is given to a mass of masonry which stands out from the face of a wall, either to strengthen that wall or to resist the thrust from an arch or a roof. The flying buttress was a Gothic innovation and is a kind of half-arch or half-bridge of masonry spanning the space from the buttress proper to the neighbouring wall.

Buttressing began in the great buildings of the later Roman Empire but it was not until the Romanesque period that really large outside buttresses began to appear. As the naves of churches became roofed with ribbed vaults, a tremendous number of thrusts were concentrated into each bay and the flying buttress was evolved to counter them. Where the nave wall was of great height, as at Beauvais Cathedral, in France, two, or even three half-arches— one over the other—formed the flying buttress. By the 15th Century, few large buildings were without flying buttresses, which were often pierced and richly traceried. Many cathedrals in England, such as Exeter, Salisbury, Winchester and Sherborne Abbey in Dorset, show magnificent examples of flying buttresses as well as the richly decorated buttress pinnacles which often accompany them.

Poultry Cross, Salisbury, England.

WHERE was the wheel invented?   WHERE is Ursa Minor?

FIRST WHEEL

The earliest wheels so far discovered were found in graves at Kish and Susa, two ancient Mesopotamian cities. These wheels are believed to date from 3,500 B.C. They were made from three planks, clamped together with copper clasps. This kind of wheel also existed in ancient times in Europe and the Near East. No one is sure where the wheel was invented, but this archaeological evidence suggests it was probably in ancient Mesopotamia.

A wheel with proper spokes was not invented until after 2,000 B.C. There are records of this wheel in northern Mesopotamia, central Turkey, and north-east Persia. By the 15th Century B.C., spoked wheels were being used on chariots in Syria, Egypt, and the western Mediterranean.

The solid wheel was used mostly in farming. Tripartite wheels—wheels with three spokes—were being used in the Bronze Age in Denmark, Germany, and northern Italy for carts.

The invention of the wheel made it possible for people to transport heavy objects much more easily. It also enabled them to travel farther and trade with each other more easily, and so find out about other countries and customs.

URSA MINOR

Ursa Minor is the name of a group of stars in the Northern Hemisphere. The word used in astronomy for a group of stars is "constellation".

The stars and constellations have Latin names. Ursa Minor means The Little Bear. Its brightest star is called Polaris, and is centred over the North Pole. It is of great importance in helping sailors to find their bearings when navigating at night.

Star maps of the sky will help you locate the constellations.

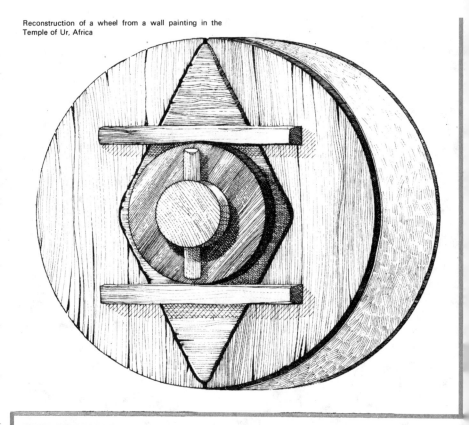

Reconstruction of a wheel from a wall painting in the Temple of Ur, Africa

THE BICYCLE

The first rideable bicycle was made by Kirkpatrick MacMillan of Dumfriesshire, Scotland, in 1839, although an attempt to construct one had been made by Jean Théson at Fontainebleau, France, in 1645.

Before this, crude machines had been made, which had no form of steering and had to be propelled by pushing the feet against the ground. Machines of this type appear on bas-reliefs in Babylon and Egypt and on frescoes in Pompeii. In England, a stained glass window, dated 1580, in the church of Stoke Poges, Buckinghamshire, shows a cherub astride such a machine.

But all these machines seem to have been four-wheeled. The true bicycle belongs to the 19th Century.

MacMillan's bicycle was driven by rods attached from pedals to a sprocket on the rear wheel. The first chain-driven bicycle was produced by Tribout and Meyer in 1869. In this year the first bicycle show—in Paris—and the first cycle road race—from Paris to Rouen—took place.

An Englishman, James Starley, of Coventry in Warwickshire, is known as "the father of the cycle industry". In 1871 he introduced a bicycle with a large driving wheel and a smaller trailing wheel. This was the "ordinary" bicycle, known to everyone as the penny-farthing. In 1874 a chain-driven bicycle with two wheels of equal diameter was designed by H. J. Lawson. This was known as the Safety bicycle and became enormously popular from about 1885 when the Rover Safety bicycle was built by John K. Starley, James's nephew.

The pneumatic tyre—in other words, a tyre filled with air—was invented in 1888 by John Boyd Dunlop, a veterinary surgeon of Belfast, Northern Ireland. By 1893 the design of the bicycle had been developed into the modern diamond frame with roller-chain drive and pneumatic-tyred wheels.

WHERE was the first bicycle made?
WHERE was the first radio signal sent from?

RADIO SIGNALS

Guglielmo Marconi is usually credited with sending the first radio message. Marconi was born in Bologna, Italy. He came to England in 1896 and obtained a British patent for his wireless telegraphy system. In 1897 he established a radio transmitter on the roof of the Post Office at St Martins-le-Grand in London, and sent a message a distance of a few hundred yards.

He continued to improve his apparatus, and in 1898 radio was installed aboard a ship at sea, the East Goodwin lightship off the south-east coast of England. In the following year wireless messages were sent across the English Channel.

The first radio transmission across the Atlantic was on December 12, 1901 from a station on the cliffs at Poldhu, in Cornwall, and the message, three dots representing the letter S in the Morse code, was picked up at St John's in Newfoundland.

The existence of radio waves was first demonstrated by Heinrich Hertz, a German professor, in 1887. Marconi based his experiments on Hertz's research.

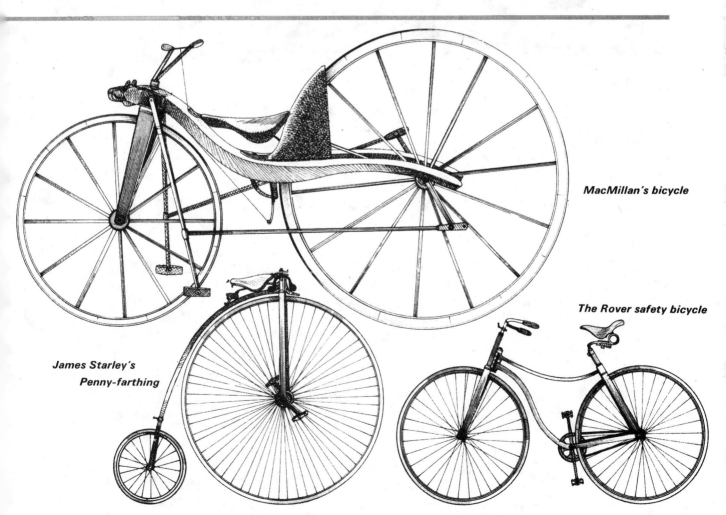

MacMillan's bicycle

The Rover safety bicycle

James Starley's Penny-farthing

FIREWORKS

The use of fireworks, or pyrotechnics, probably began when some prehistoric man mixed saltpetre (potassium nitrate) from his cooking with charcoal from his fire. Saltpetre is a pyrotechnic composition—a substance which does not need oxygen from the air in order to burn, but instead supplies it. Two more such compositions are potassium chlorate and potassium perchlorate. These are combined with finely ground gunpowder, sulphur, aluminium dust and many other chemicals to produce force and sparks, or white or coloured flame. Other substances produce noise, smoke and whistling sounds.

It is believed that fireworks were used in the East, especially China and India, for centuries before they spread to Europe. The Chinese fired pyrotechnic war missiles and produced dazzling displays of fireworks for ceremonial occasions. Arabia, in the 7th Century, also used pyrotechnics in war. In the 14th Century came the invention of gunpowder, a pyrotechnic mixture of saltpetre, charcoal (carbon) and sulphur.

Spectacular firework displays in celebration of victory or peace became popular during the 17th Century. Colour was introduced into the entertainment in the 19th Century through the use of potassium chlorate, which was first prepared by Claude Louis Berthollet (1748–1822). Later magnesium and aluminium was employed to make fireworks still more brilliant. Every year displays are given to mark such widely different occasions as the discovery of the Gunpowder Plot to blow up the British Parliament, and Independence Day celebrations in the United States.

RETRO ROCKET

A spaceship uses a retro rocket when those aboard wish to slow the craft down. The rocket acts as a brake by giving thrust in the opposite direction to the motion of travel. Such a brake is needed to reduce a spaceship's speed sufficiently for it to fall out of orbit and re-enter the earth's atmosphere safely.

A spaceship in orbit travels round the earth at about 17,000 miles an hour. At this speed it has a centrifugal force which counter-balances the inward pull of the earth's gravity, causing it to continue orbiting indefinitely. The problem is overcome by using retro rockets which fire forwards so as to push backwards. This reduces the spaceship's speed and centrifugal force, and allows it to spiral towards the earth. The craft is further slowed down by atmospheric friction and finally by parachutes.

When landing on the moon, where there is no atmosphere, a lunar module is turned round so that its retro rocket is facing the direction of travel. The descent is then controlled by bursts from the retro rocket until just before the module settles on the surface.

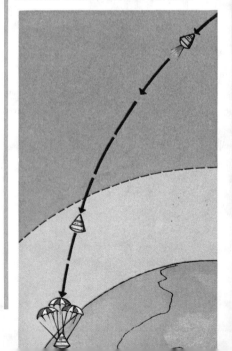

use a retro rocket? WHEN was the hydrofoil invented?

HYDROFOIL

The hydrofoil, a boat supported clear of the water by underwater wings called hydrofoils, was invented by an Italian, Forlanini, in 1898. In 1918 a hydrofoil, powered by an aircraft engine, gained the world's water speed record. The commercial hydrofoils now used in Europe are based on the work of German engineers who carried out research into the design of high-power, lightweight engines.

In the early 1950s hydrofoils were developed in the United States, Canada and Russia using high-powered gas turbines. They are used for both military and commercial purposes.

Since water is 775 times heavier than air, very small hydrofoil wings will support relatively heavy boats. But, since operating in water puts great loads on boats, the hulls are usually built of high-strength steel.

The object in raising the hull of the hydrofoil from the water is to avoid the resistance caused by friction and drag. This means the power needed to drive the boat at high speeds is cut by half. Another result is that the hydrofoil travels smoothly in quite rough water, and is not slowed down.

WHAT makes a stone fall when it is thrown in the air? WHAT
WHAT is a theodolite used for?

FALLING STONE

This is due to the pull of the earth's gravity. If there were no gravity the stone would remain in the air.

When the stone is thrown into the air, a force is applied to it which is greater than the pull of gravity. But as it rises higher the force becomes weaker until the stone reaches a point where force and gravity are equal. Then the pull of gravity becomes greater, and the stone begins to fall back to the ground.

Everything on earth, including the atmosphere, is held to it by gravity, and all the members of the solar system—the sun, planets and other bodies—are attracted towards one another by this force. They would all fall into the common centre, the sun, if it were not for the balancing force of their circular motions.

Sir Isaac Newton discovered that the gravitational pull of one body upon another increases with the amount of matter in the two bodies. It was one of the greatest discoveries in science.

ELECTRON

Electrons are negatively charged particles of electricity, which circle a positively charged nucleus—like planets round a sun—to make up an atom.

An atom is the smallest particle of an element—and electrons are even smaller. Yet since their discovery and naming by the English physicist Sir Joseph Thomson in 1897 our knowledge of them has come to play an important part in our lives.

The key to their importance is that electrons can be detached from their atoms and formed into a controllable stream of negative electricity far more sensitive and flexible than a current in a wire.

Television, transistors, computors, all depend on an electron stream for their working.

PHOTOMICROGRAPHY

Photomicrography is the art of photography through the microscope. It is important in chemistry, biology, geology and medicine.

Most photomicrography is done by using the compound microscope with a camera arranged opposite the eyepiece so that the image can be focused on a film or plate. For detailed photographs, an electron microscope is used.

The advantage of photography in sciences is that we are able to record visible images in black and white or in colour. These images make quite permanent records which can be examined and studied at leisure when the original subjects may no longer be available. Photomicrography extends the range of our vision, allowing photographs to be made of things the eye cannot see because they are too faint or too small.

Carbon arc lamps and incandescent tungsten filament lamps are normally used for illumination but, for special purposes, flashbulbs, electronic discharge lamps and sodium lamps are used.

Contrast is obtained by staining with dyes and using filters that transmit light which complements the staining dye.

Ultraviolet light is used for maximum detail but infra-red, which has a longer wavelength, may be used for materials which are opaque to ultra-violet.

Colour photography is important in some branches of science (e.g. metallography) but great care has to be taken with length of exposure and filters.

Electron microscope photograph of virus particles in the lymph gland of a leukemic mouse.

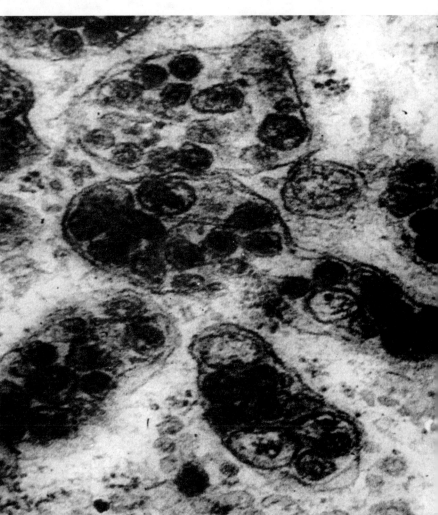

is an electron? WHAT is photomicrography?
WHAT is a detergent?

THEODOLITE

A theodolite is a surveying instrument used for measuring horizontal and vertical angles. To measure long distances we use a system known as triangulation – we can use it, for instance, if we want to know the distance to the moon.

Astronomers measure the angle of the moon above the horizon at two places on the earth's surface —as far apart as possible and at the same moment. This gives them a triangle and a base line (the distance between the two observations). Since they have measured two angles of the triangle, they know the third, because the three angles of a triangle always add up to 180°. They therefore have enough information to find the distance between the apex (moon) and base line (earth).

The same system is used in surveying and map-making, but the surveyor's base line is, of course, much shorter; in fact, both ends of the base line must be within sight of one another and of the next point to be observed. The theodolite is the basic instrument used in surveying, especially in precise triangulation.

DETERGENT

A detergent is a substance which has the power to cleanse. This description applies to soap, as well as to soapless shampoos and washing powders. A detergent must have surface activating properties, which means it must be able to break down the surface tension of water.

In the process of cleaning the detergent acts as a bridge between the solid matter and the water. Soap molecules are shaped like tadpoles. The head is soluble, but the rod-like body is composed of an insoluble fatty substance. When mixed with water part of the soap tries to get away and the rest stays,

A theodolite in use on the right of the picture during a British Antarctic survey.

thus breaking down the water's surface tension. There is not sufficient room for all the soap molecules on the surface of the water. So they form bundles with the water-resisting rods on the inside.

The dirt attracts the fatty part of the soap molecules which lift and surround it, while the soluble part of the molecule lifts and rinses the dirt away. There are some stains which respond better to soap.

WHY do fire extinguishers stop flames? WHY do lunar
WHY does iron rust? WHY is it

FIRE EXTINGUISHERS

Fire extinguishers stop flames either by dousing them in water or by excluding the oxygen which a fire needs in order to burn.

There are three main kinds of fires. First are those occurring in ordinary materials like paper and wood for which the quenching and cooling effects of water or water solutions are the most effective. Second come those involving inflammable liquids or greases for which a blanketing or smothering effect is essential. Finally there are the fires occurring in "live" electrical equipment where a special extinguishing agent must be used.

The most common extinguisher for the first type of fire is a bucket of water, or a manufactured extinguisher with water containing a chemical. The chemical reaction expels the water which puts out the fire.

For the second kind of fire the most common method is to use a chemical extinguisher to spray the burning material with foam which puts out the fire by excluding oxygen. This foam usually consists of bubbles of carbon dioxide. As the foam is not a conductor of electricity, it may also be used safely on the third type of fire.

Foam-type extinguishers can generally be employed safely in nearly all cases, but water or water solutions should never be used on oil, grease or electrical fires.

LUNAR MODULES

A lunar module needs a blast-off platform because it is propelled by a rocket engine.

This engine carries its own fuel and oxidizer and can, therefore, operate at great heights where little or no air is present. It can thus be used on the moon's surface where there is no air.

Very hot gases are expelled from the rear of a rocket. The engine depends for its operation on the upward thrust (on the rocket and the load carried) being equal and opposite to the downward thrust (of the burnt gases). That is why a blast-off platform is needed.

modules need a blast-off platform?
dangerous to take electrical appliances into a bathroom?

IRON RUST

Iron rusts, or corrodes, in air because it dissolves in the acid solution provided by the moisture and the carbon dioxide of the air to form hydrous oxide. In an atmosphere which is rich in sulphur compounds—for instance, very smoky air—the process will be accelerated.

Our industrial system is largely based on the use of iron and its alloys. It is the world's most important metal, but rarely found in a pure state. Iron ore has to be smelted to separate the metal from other elements. The molten iron which flows from the blast furnace after smelting is called pig iron. This contains many impurities, but is a raw material for cast iron and wrought iron.

Cast iron is made from pig iron by resmelting it with coke in a blast furnace. The coke raises the temperature and helps remove the impurities. The molten cast iron is tapped from the base of the furnace and poured into moulds. Although it is brittle, cast iron melts and moulds easily. Because it does not distort when red hot and corrodes only slightly in water, cast iron is used for stoves, fireplaces, manhole covers, water pipes and rain gutters.

If cast iron is resmelted, the result is wrought iron—an almost pure form of iron, which is not much made today. It can be easily shaped (or wrought) and, until the 1870s, was used for bridge building and engineering. Nowadays it is used mostly for decorative purposes. It gave way to the master-metal steel, which was first mass produced in the 1870s and which combines the easy-to-handle qualities of wrought iron with the toughness of cast iron.

BATHROOM ELECTRICS

It is dangerous to take electrical appliances into a bathroom or indeed anywhere that there is a lot of moisture, because water is such an excellent conductor of electricity. A person could receive an extremely severe, if not fatal, electric shock if the appliance fell into the bathwater.

There are two kinds of electricity. One is static electricity which remains stationary in an object. The other is current electricity which flows, as in a wire. An electric current is formed by the movements of electrons. It is possible to transfer electrons from one thing to another by rubbing them together. One object is given a positive charge, and the other a negative charge of electricity. Objects with like charges repel each other while those with unlike charges attract each other.

Some things lose their charge at once. Others retain it for a long time. Substances which do not retain an electrical charge are called conductors, while those which keep the charge are called non-conductors or insulators. All metals and water are conductors. The human body is also a conductor, but not a good one. Insulators include glass, paper, plastic and silk. In fact, materials which are good conductors of heat are also conductors of electricity.

Water is at least a million times better at conducting electricity at room temperature than any other non-metallic liquid. So never take the risk of a terrible accident by handling any electrical gadget in the bath. You should also remember to turn off the current before touching anyone who has had an electric shock and is still in contact with the appliance. If you don't do this you will probably get a shock too!

338

WHEN was the gyroscope invented? WHEN were the first

GYROSCOPE

The first gyroscope was made in about 1810 by a German, G. C. Bohnenberger. But the name was the idea of a French physicist, Leon Foucault, in 1852 when he used the device to demonstrate the rotation of the earth. It comes from two Greek words *gyros*, meaning "turn" or "revolution", and *skopein*, meaning "to view". Therefore gyroscope means "to view the turning".

This instrument is based on the principle of a spinning top which remains upright in resistance to the force of gravitation as long as it keeps revolving. In a gyroscope a wheel is mounted in such a manner that it is free to revolve round any axis. When rotating the wheel gives this framework the same tendency to remain at the angle at which it is placed as a top has when it is spinning alone.

Any spinning object resists attempts to change the direction of its axis, the imaginary straight line round which it revolves. Thus you can move a gyroscope up, down, forwards, sideways or backwards and feel no resistance, but you will meet opposition if you try to turn it through an angle.

The gyroscope's other important characteristic is called "precession". This means that when you do overcome the resistance and push the axis out of the straight, the gyroscope does not tilt the way you push it but at right angles to the push and axis.

The peculiar qualities of gyroscopes have been exploited in complex instruments used for stabilizing purposes at sea, on land and in the air. They are used in compasses, gun sights, and instruments for ships and aircraft.

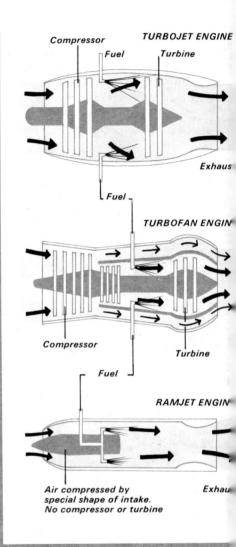

TURBOJET ENGINE

Compressor

Fuel

Turbine

Exhaust

Fuel

TURBOFAN ENGINE

Compressor

Turbine

Fuel

RAMJET ENGINE

Air compressed by special shape of intake. No compressor or turbine

Exhaust

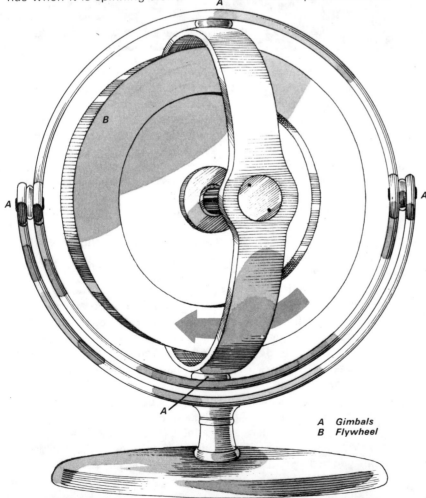

A Gimbals
B Flywheel

SCIENCE

Science began with the wish of some prehistoric man to find out about the workings of the world about him. But the first recorded scientific discoveries are those of the ancient Babylonians who observed the positions of the sun, moon and planets. The ancient Egyptians invented simple arithmetic and geometry around 4,000 B.C. and acquired a considerable knowledge of engineering, medicine and anatomy.

From about 600 B.C. the Greeks made great progress in philosophy and geometry, where intellectual effort only was required. But they achieved little advance in practical science, except for the discoveries of Aristotle (384–322 B.C.), who

scientific discoveries? WHEN was the jet engine invented?

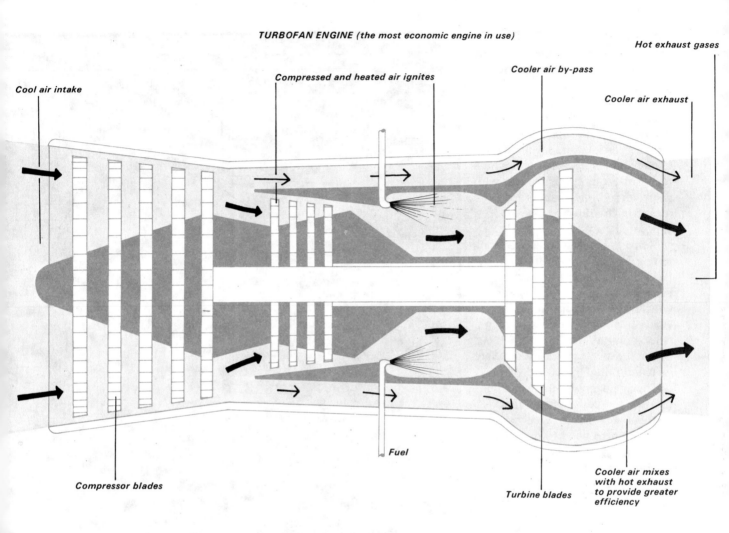

TURBOFAN ENGINE (the most economic engine in use)

Cool air intake

Compressed and heated air ignites

Cooler air by-pass

Hot exhaust gases

Cooler air exhaust

Compressor blades

Fuel

Turbine blades

Cooler air mixes with hot exhaust to provide greater efficiency

JET ENGINE

founded the study of biology. Archimedes (287–212 B.C.) discovered many simple principles of physics and Ptolemy (about A.D. 140) made advances in astronomy.

Under Rome progress slowed down. Then the barbarians overran Europe and for almost 1,000 years—from 300–1100—science was kept alive first in Byzantium and then, from about 700, by the Arabs. From the 15th Century, practical experiments in science began in earnest. Galileo (1564–1642) carried out physical measurements and laboratory experiments. Francis Bacon (1561–1626) and René Descartes (1596–1650) pioneered the new scientific philosophy.

The first flight by a jet-propelled aircraft was made in Germany on August 27, 1939. Its engine was designed by Hans-Joachim von Ohain, who had conceived the idea while a student at Göttingen University in Lower Saxony. Unknown to von Ohain, the British inventor and aviator Frank Whittle had thought of the idea some years earlier. But his engine did not have its first flight until May 14, 1941.

Briefly, a jet engine takes in air from the atmosphere, compresses it, and expands it by burning fuel. The mixture of hot gases is then expelled through a nozzle in a powerful backward jet which propels the aircraft forwards.

This forward thrust is the effect of a scientific principle first ex-

plained by the English scientist Sir Isaac Newton (1642–1727). He pointed out that with every action there is a reaction which is equal but opposite to it. Thus when a gun is fired, the forward movement of the shell is matched by the backward recoil of the barrel. In a similar way the reaction to the jet exhaust drives the engine forward. The thrust is obtained by the pressure of the jet against the inside of the nozzle and not, as many people suppose, by the exhaust gases "pushing" against the atmosphere.

The jet engine, whether turbojet, turboprop, ramjet or turbofan, weighs less than a piston engine of comparative power and can be much more streamlined.

ROCKETS

The rocket, as far as can be established, was invented by the Chinese during the 12th or 13th Century. The Chinese used their rockets as fireworks to mark special celebrations. A rocket has no moving parts. It is a fuel-filled container with a hole at one end where the exhaust or gases escape with such force that they propel the rocket in the direction in which it is pointed.

Rockets were used as weapons in the East until the 18th Century. Sir William Congreve added improvements in his artillery rocket, which was used in the American War of Independence and in the Napoleonic Wars. Rockets fell out of use in the 19th Century but were revived in the First World War.

Their peaceful use as line-carriers in sea rescues and as distress signals is well known. They are also used to deliver mail and to aid aeroplane take-off.

There are two categories of rocket fuel: liquid and solid. Also, rockets which are used outside the earth's atmosphere must carry their own oxygen or they would be unable to get a "burn". The space rockets carry both liquid and solid fuel. Some burn at least 1,000 pounds of fuel a second. Control of the rocket is carried out by radar and intricate design is required in directing the exhaust gases to maintain the correct flight path.

The Germans developed the rocket in the 1930s and used it in the V1 and V2 weapons which were directed at London in the Second World War.

Since then enormous advances have been made by technicians and scientists working all over the world, culminating in rockets as tall as small skyscrapers and weighing thousands of tons, which are used in the exploration of space.

weigh nothing?　**WHERE** does sound go?
　　　　　　　WHERE were kites first flown?

WEIGHTLESS MAN

This happens whenever the pull of gravity or the "G" factor is overcome. It can occur when an aircraft is put into a steep dive.

Astronauts experience this "weightlessness" in space. So that they can get used to its effects before leaving the earth's atmosphere, special machines have been built in an attempt to create the same conditions. Astronauts also train for space weightlessness in large water tanks.

It is essential that an astronaut should get used to the feeling of weightlessness which occurs when earth's gravity is no longer effective. For instance, he cannot pour liquid into a cup or drink from it. With enough practice, however, he can learn to move about, eat, drink and sleep without difficulty.

When an astronaut goes outside his vehicle in space, there is some gravitational pull between him and his cabin. But owing to the small mass of both, the attraction between them is negligible. It is far too small to bring him back if he jumped off. So he has to use a special life-line to prevent himself from drifting into space.

SOUND

The simple answer, of course, is that the sounds you hear go into your brain by way of your ears. But what is sound?

When you are listening to pop music, you are at the receiving end of sounds. But what is going on at the sending end? The players are making vibrations on their instruments and sending sound waves through the air to you. The point to remember is that sound waves must have something to carry them. Usually this is air, but it can also be water or the earth under your feet, both of which are better sound wave conductors than air.

The Indians of North America used to put their ears to the ground to hear the sound of their enemies' horses, when the air gave them no warning. But in a vacuum no sound can be heard. The loudest pop music, if it could be played in a vacuum, would make no noise.

The question "Where does sound go?" can be put another way—"When does sound stop?". The answer to this one is that sound stops when the vibrations sending out the sound waves come to a standstill.

FIRST KITES

Kites have been used in Asia since time immemorial. Some evidence dates their invention at around 1,000 B.C. Kite flying has been a national pastime for many centuries among the Chinese, Japanese, Koreans and Malayans. Kites held great religious significance in Asia, as they were believed to keep evil spirits away when flown at night.

But there is also a tradition that they were invented nearly four centuries before Christ by Archytas of Tarentum, in southern Italy. He was a Greek philosopher and scientist, and a friend of Plato, the great philosopher.

Kite flying strictly for pleasure has many supporters in China, where the ninth day of the ninth month is designated Kite Day.

Kites have often been used in simple bridge building by attaching a cable to the kite and flying it across the river or gap. In meteorology kites have been used to carry weather recording instruments aloft.

The current kite flying record of four and a half miles was achieved with a string of 10 kites. The total surface of the 10 kites was 683 square feet. The line used for this record-breaking flight was more than nine miles long.

342

WHY is DDT dangerous? WHY do pipes sometimes burst
WHY is a screw so strong? WHY do road vehicles have

DDT

After extensive use as a pesticide, DDT was found to have many harmful after-effects on human beings and animals. The control of insects was revolutionized by the introduction of DDT after the Second World War. It was employed to combat a wide range of insects which attacked food crops and was also instrumental in bringing the world malaria problem under control.

But by the 1960s it was found that DDT affected the metabolism of many birds so much that their eggs became too fragile to survive. As a result many species have nearly become extinct. Several kinds of fish have also been seriously affected. Large numbers of insects which served as food for both fish and birds have been destroyed.

The effects of DDT on food for human consumption have been extremely serious. Food becomes poisonous if the amount of DDT in it exceeds a certain limit. However, such pesticides are now heavily restricted by most governments.

BURST PIPES

Cold water pipes may burst in winter when the outside temperature falls below 0° Centigrade (32° Fahrenheit) and the water turns to ice. The pipe's walls crack to relieve the pressure caused by the fact that ice requires nearly one-tenth more space than the water. One cubic foot of water makes 1·09 cubic feet of ice. To prevent a freeze-up, a heat insulator is wrapped round the pipes.

Water has very unusual properties. Apart from expanding when frozen, it requires more heat to warm it than any other common substance. In other words it has a high specific heat. In nature there are some obvious advantages in these peculiarities. The expansion of ice causes the breaking up of clods of water-filled soil on cold winter nights to leave a fine tilth admirably suited to spring sowing. Water's high specific heat means that the sea takes longer to warm up than the land and longer to cool down. Thus the sea acts to prevent extreme changes in temperature between the seasons.

STRENGTH OF SCREW

The screw provides a means of converting a small force into a large one. Once in use, it allows pressure to be applied from different directions. These factors give the screw its relative strength as compared with a nail of the same size.

In the first case, the force applied to a screw is like the smaller force necessary to lift an object up an inclined plane rather than straight up. In a screw a form of inclined plane is provided by the spiral groove, called a thread, which is cut round the shaft. By contrast the force applied to a nail can be compared with lifting an object straight up. If it were possible to unwind an inch-long screw, you would find that it was longer than an inch-long nail.

In the second case, the holding power of a screw or nail in a piece of wood depends on the pressure exerted on its shank by the wood fibres. A screw creates a far stronger grip because it presents a much greater surface area to the pressure of the wood.

GLASS

We can see through glass because it allows the light rays to pass through. Glass is a hard, brittle material made by fusing silica with the oxides or silicates of such metals as sodium, magnesium, calcium and potassium. The product is cooled rapidly to prevent the formation of any crystalline material which would interfere with the passage of light. The melting point of glass is about 800–950° Centigrade (1,472–1,742° Fahrenheit).

In fact, light does not travel straight through glass but is bent or refracted. The light is bent twice, first when it enters the glass and then back to its original direction. when it comes out at the other side. Every transparent material bends light, but the amount (described by a number called the index of refraction) varies with the density of the material. The denser the material, the greater is the amount of bending and the higher the index. The speed of light also varies as it enters another material becoming slower as the density of the material increases.

The ability of glass to refract light rays has made possible the designing of lenses which are essential for the important science of optics. A convex lens—a lens with one or both of its surfaces bulging outward—bends light rays inward. A concave lens—with one or both of its surfaces curving inward—spreads light rays outward.

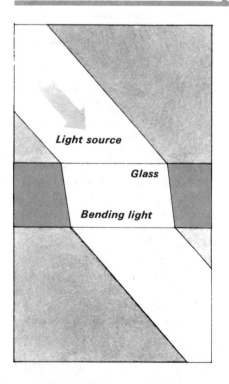

Light source

Glass

Bending light

in winter? WHY can we see through glass?
pneumatic tyres? WHY does frozen food keep for a long time?

PNEUMATIC TYRES

Pneumatic tyres help to cushion the vehicle against bumps, ruts and other inequalities in the road surface. This levelling effect of the tyre is achieved because of the compressed air which is inside the rubber casing.

Until about 1900 all road vehicles were fitted with solid tyres. These were very unsatisfactory. When a tyre struck an obstacle on the road surface the shock often damaged the vehicle's mechanism permanently. In any case the effect was most uncomfortable for the passengers, and the roads then had holes and potmarks, which made driving over them dangerous.

The adaptability of pneumatic tyres gives them a firmer grip on the road and enables the driver to steer, change speed and go round corners more safely.

FROZEN FOOD

Frozen food keeps for a long time because the freezing of the water inside the food forces the bacteria, which cause it to decompose, into inactivity. Like all living things, bacteria need water in order to thrive.

Bacteria are microscopic organisms, or forms of life which occur in air, water and soil all over the world. But they flourish and multiply particularly wherever organic matter is present. Some may cause disease, others are harmless, or even beneficial, but their activity causes organic matter, including food, to decompose.

Modern discoveries have en-abled sub-zero temperatures to be obtained by cooling air to about −300° Centigrade (−508° Fahrenheit) by compressing it and passing it into low pressure chambers through fine nozzles. The result is a sudden and violent expansion, causing the air to be drastically cooled. In home refrigerators Freon-12 gas is used instead of air, and the temperatures are much less drastic. The temperature in the freezing compartment of a domestic refrigerator is about −4°C or 25°F, and that of a deep-freezer about −15°C or 5°F.

Preserving food has an ancient history. The salting and smoking of fish and meat have been carried out for centuries. Another long-used method of preserving food is to change its form, for example turning milk into butter and cheese, and grapes into wine. More recently preservation has been effected by canning, heat being used to kill bacteria, or dehydration.

Most fresh food contains 75 to 90 per cent of water. When this liquid is removed, great savings in packaging, storage and transport are made. Potatoes, milk, eggs, tea and coffee are among the well-known products now sold as dry powders that need only the addition of water to reconstitute them.

344

WHAT is a solarium? WHAT makes a wheel sometimes look

SOLARIUM

A solarium may be a sundial. It may also be a terrace, a balcony or a room exposed to the rays of the sun, especially one used for the treatment of illness by sunbathing.

A sundial tells the time by means of the shadow cast by the sun's rays. The earliest known sundial still preserved is an Egyptian shadow clock dating from at least the 8th Century B.C.

The Greeks and Romans constructed very complex sundials, and the Renaissance produced many beautiful designs. By the 19th Century, clocks and watches were so accurate that the sundial was used only as an ornament in gardens. But some specially designed for scientific purposes were made as late as the beginning of the 20th Century.

The fact that the sun's rays may be beneficial to man was not scientifically proved until fairly recently. Vitamin D is now known to be activated by the ultra-violet rays in sunlight. Nevertheless, in the late 19th Century, it was observed that many people found "sunshine baths" of great help when recovering from an illness. Many hospitals and large private houses had solariums or sun rooms.

The rays of the sun not only induced a feeling of well-being, but helped to clear up some skin diseases and imparted a glowing colour to the body. Before this time, a light, delicate complexion had been a mark of wealth, an indication that one had no need to toil in all weathers to earn a living.

WHEEL

Sometimes when we are watching a film of a wheeled vehicle, especially of one with a spoked wheel, it seems to be going backwards instead of forwards as the vehicle slows down. This is be-cause the film is made up of a series of individual pictures taken in quick succession. Our eyes blend the individual images together and we see a smooth movement rather than a series of still pictures. If the eye does not blend the images correctly, the wheel seems to turn backwards.

This effect can also sometimes be obtained by looking at a spoked vehicle through railings.

Submarine P.C.8. This kind of submersible has developed from the original Bathyscopes and Bathyspheres.

BATHYSPHERE

"Bathos" is Greek for "deep". A bathysphere means a "sphere of the deep". The first bathysphere was built by an American, William Beebe, and made its first descent into the unknown ocean darkness in 1930. It reached a depth of about 1,300 feet.

Beebe's bathysphere was held by a cable. Free descents were first made by Auguste Picard in a bathyscaphe. "Scaphos" means "ship" in Greek.

Now special submarines, able to cruise at great depth, are used for specific oceanographic tasks in many parts of the world.

TAR MACADAM

Tarmac is a hard black material used for roads, parade grounds or anywhere that a hard, even and durable surface is needed. It is a mixture of tar (which accounts for the colour) and macadam, which consists of hundreds of tiny even-sized chips of granite pressed together.

Macadam is named after a Scotsman, John Loudon Mac-Adam, who first used it in the late 18th Century. Until MacAdam's time roads were tracks, sometimes covered with stones, which easily got muddy and waterlogged and whose unevenness made travel-

ling by stage coach so uncomfortable that most people stayed at home. MacAdam, who was on the roads committee in his home county of Ayrshire in Scotland and wrote several books about road-building, persuaded the government to let him make experiments which resulted in vastly improved highways.

The original macadam is still used on roads and looks much better than tarmac. But tarmac and other more recently invented surfaces fare better where there is heavy traffic and when loose stones would be quickly dispersed.

WHERE does the sun go in a total eclipse? WHERE does
WHERE would you look for a needle beam?

TOTAL ECLIPSE

An eclipse of the sun occurs when the moon passes between the sun and the earth, thus blocking from view either the whole of the sun or part of it.

A total eclipse begins when the moon starts to move across the western side of the sun travelling towards the east. When the sun is completely covered, the beautiful halo of light surrounding it, called the corona, can be seen. This is the ring of burning gases which envelopes the main body of the sun. It is dangerous to look directly at an eclipse, since the sun's rays can burn the eyes badly.

Since the moon is far smaller than the earth it cannot block all of the earth from the sun at the same time. The moon as it sweeps across the surface of the earth blots out the sun rays only for those parts of the world in the moon's shadow.

The longest a total eclipse can last in one place on earth is seven and a half minutes. The last total eclipse of the sun occurred on June 30, 1973 and the next one will take place on July 11, 1991.

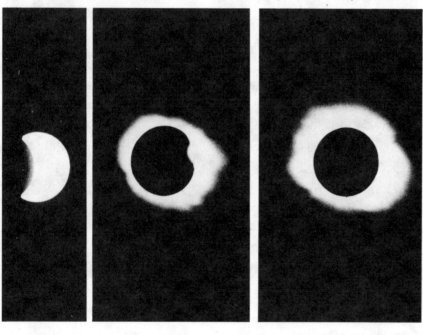

PAPER

A sheet of paper consists of vegetable fibres of different sizes, twisted and intertwined with each other and finally squeezed together to make a sheet with a surface smooth enough to write or print on.

Originally it was discovered that if a mixture of wood pulp and water was spread on a sieve, the water would drain away and leave a deposit which, when dry, could be peeled off as a sheet of paper.

Although the Chinese had been using paper since A.D. 105 it was not introduced into Europe until the 15th Century. The raw materials used for modern hand-made paper are cotton and linen rags. Such paper is very expensive to produce.

Machine-made paper is processed in paper mills from esparto grass, wood and straw, and is much cheaper. The materials for both types of paper-making have to be put through the same basic procedure of repeated washing and bleaching to get rid of impurities.

ELECTRICITY

The real answer to this question is that electricity is not stored at all. It is generated—that is, made—as it is used. Gas can be stored in huge cylinders. Electricity is produced and used immediately.

Electricity can be produced in several ways—by hydro-electric stations, which use the power of waterfalls and rivers to drive the generators; by thermal power stations, where fuel like coal and oil is used; and by nuclear power stations.

The basic method of production is the same, but the most usual source of electricity is the thermal power station. The fuel is used to heat water in the boilers to produce steam at very high pressure—up to 5,000 pounds a square inch. This steam is directed at the blades of a high-speed turbine which is connected to the generator. The generators are of two-pole construction, turning at 3,000 revolutions a minute.

These generators work on the principle of the rotation of a wire coil through a magnetic field, the application of the earliest principles discovered by pioneer scientists.

To supply this tremendous electrical energy where it is wanted, three component parts are required. First, the generating stations themselves. Second, the transmission system for transmitting large amounts of electricity to whole areas where it is needed. Third, the distribution system for distributing the power at low voltages to homes, shops and individual consumers.

So electricity is not stored. It is made, and at once used. Great skill has to be employed to keep the balance between the supply and the demand.

The current world oil shortage has made the problems of electricity production more difficult, especially in Europe and Japan.

paper come from? **WHERE** is electricity stored?

WHERE is cobalt used?

NEEDLE BEAMS

This has nothing to do with needles and nothing to do with light. A needle beam is a term used by builders and architects to describe the supports used when the foundations of a wall or a column need attention.

If a wall needs underpinning to enable the foundations to be strengthened, steel needle beams are inserted through slots cut into the wall a foot or so from the bottom. The ends of the beams are supported by screw jacks which can be moved along the beams according to the extent of the foundation area needing attention. Once the work has been done and the foundations have been restored, the needle beams are removed and the holes in the wall filled.

When a needle beam is used to shore up a column it is usually bolted on.

The needle beam is so called because it is "threaded" through the wall it has to support (see illustration).

USES OF COBALT

Can you think of any connection between a delicate Ming vase and a nuclear explosion? Difficult, isn't it? And yet there is a connection in the sense that different types of one particular substance—cobalt—have been used in the production of both.

In ancient China the beautiful blues used in the finest porcelains came from a cobalt ore. Until the early years of this century most of the world's production of cobalt went to provide colour for the porcelain and glass industries.

Today cobalt, which in its natural state is a hard silvery-white metallic substance, serves many purposes. A "cobalt bomb" can be a terrible weapon capable of distributing lethal radioactive cobalt-60 through a nuclear explosion. It can also be the means of treating certain illnesses by deep X-rays.

About a quarter of the output of cobalt goes into the making of magnets, since the metal has a high magnetic quality. It has many engineering uses. It can be employed to take away the slightly yellow tint of the iron in plate-glass windows. There is a call for it in dentistry and bone surgery.

In Australia and New Zealand ranchers were puzzled by the poor condition of sheep and cattle grazing on apparently good pasture land. Eventually it was discovered that the land did not have enough cobalt. Today small quantities of a cobalt-based compound are added either to the water supplies serving the cattle or to the land itself in the form of fertilizers.

Cobalt is also an essential food ingredient for human beings. Liver, cabbage, spinach, lettuce and watercress all contain comparatively high levels of it. About 20,000 tons of cobalt are produced every year.

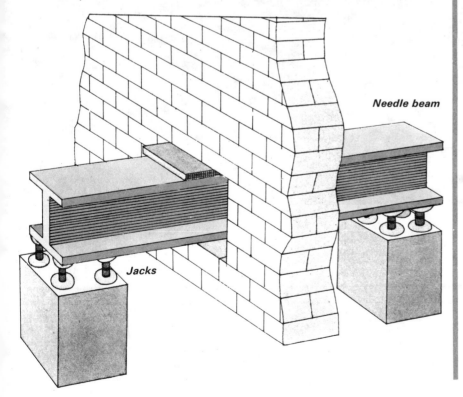

Needle beam

Jacks

WHEN does copper turn green? WHEN was the first televisior

GREEN COPPER

Although copper is highly resistant to the chemical action of the atmosphere and of sea water, it turns green if exposed to them for a long time. The colour is caused by the formation of a thin coating of green basic copper carbonate known as patina or verdigris. The latter name comes from the old French *vert de Grece*, (green of Greece), but the reason for it is unknown. This beautiful green is often seen on copper roofs or statues, especially if they are near the sea.

Copper was the first metal man learned to use. Five thousand years ago, when men discovered deposits of pure copper in what are now Iraq and Cyprus, they found that this fairly soft metal could be easily melted, cast in moulds and hammered into tools, weapons and ornaments.

About half the copper produced today is used by the electrical industry. Pure copper is the best cheap conductor of electricity and can be drawn into threads one-thousandth of an inch thick.

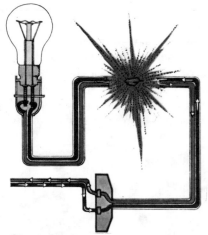

Short circuit
Electricity flows back through wires

ELECTRIC "SHORT"

An electric "short" or short circuit can occur when two wires which are supposed to be separate come into contact, perhaps through loose connections in a socket or worn out insulation. A screwdriver inserted into a socket can also cause a short circuit and severe injury to the person holding it.

Ordinarily the circuit followed by an electric current forces it to overcome certain resistances by generating energy which heats an electric toaster or lights an electric lamp. But when the two sides of an electric circuit are accidentally connected by a path which cuts out this resistance, a short circuit occurs, because electric current always flows through the path of least resistance.

When this happens the current flow becomes so high that it melts the piece of wire or fuse inserted in the circuit as a safety measure and so cuts off the voltage. Damage to an appliance is thereby avoided, for, if the excess current continued to flow, it would cause the appliance to become very hot.

TELEVISION

The first public television demonstration or broadcast was given by the British inventor John Logie Baird (1888–1946) in 1926 at the Royal Institution in London. Twenty years earlier Baird had set up a small laboratory at Hastings to study the problem of "seeing by wireless".

Experimental television broadcasts were made by the British Broadcasting Corporation between 1929 and 1935. The pictures were formed of only 30 to 100 lines and flickered badly. It was obvious that a method of high-definition, with more scanning lines, was badly needed.

Research in the United States made possible an increase to 343 lines, and other improvements quickly followed. In November, 1935, the first high-definition television service in the world began with the opening of a B.B.C. station at Alexandra Palace, London, using 405 scanning lines. British television continued with 405 lines until 1964, but now uses the international 625-line standard.

The United States began regular television broadcasting in 1941, but the Second World War held back other countries, and television services did not become

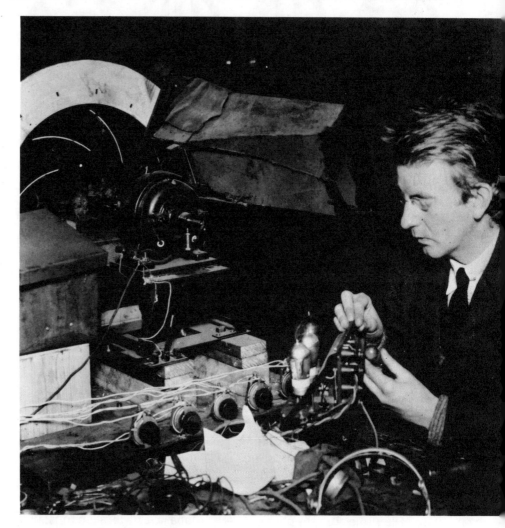

widespread until the 1950s.

Although the first colour television transmission was given by Baird in 1928, its use did not become general until 1954 in the United States, 1960 in Japan and 1967 in Britain, Germany, France, Russia and other countries.

ELEMENT

The English chemist Robert Boyle (1627–1691) defined an element as a substance which cannot be broken down into other simpler substances.

It is known that there are about 100 such basic substances. They include iron, gold, carbon, oxygen, nitrogen, mercury and radium. Some have been made artificially.

Thus sugar is not an element because it can be broken down into oxygen, hydrogen and carbon. Salt is a mixture of sodium and chlorine. Air includes nitrogen, oxygen and other gases, and water can be broken down into hydrogen and oxygen.

Elements are each given a recognition symbol for use in chemical formulae and equations. Iron has Fe, gold Au, carbon C, Oxygen O, mercury Hg, radium Ra, and plutonium Pu.

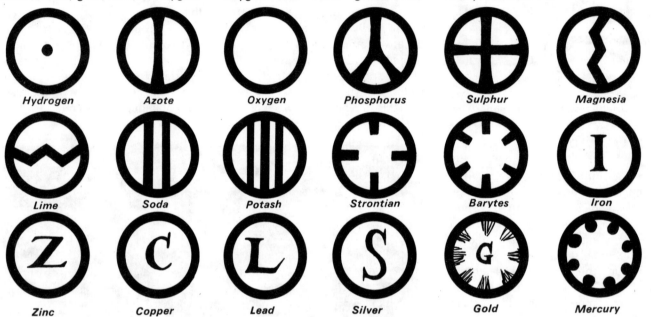

Early symbols of the elements as conceived by the Quaker John Dalton in 1806.

WATERGLASS

Waterglass, as the name implies, is soluble glass—a solution of silicate of soda. It is a thick, treacly, translucent substance prepared by fusing silica (sand or flint) with sodium carbonate. It can also be prepared under pressure using silica and caustic soda.

A familiar domestic use of waterglass is in the preserving of eggs. They are left in a container of waterglass solution which coats the shell, thus preventing the entry of bacteria. It is also employed as a protective coating on artificial stone for buildings to prevent weathering. Other uses are in soap manufacture and the making of fireproof cement.

You can also use it in the preparation of a chemical garden. To do this, make a mixture of one-quarter waterglass to three-quarters warm water. When this is cool, drop in one alum, one copper sulphate and one iron sulphate crystal. Within a few days they will grow coloured strands. These strands are composed of very small crystals.

GAMMA RAYS

Gamma rays are streams of electromagnetic waves. They are given off from elements such as radium, as the elements disintegrate and become radioactive.

In 1899 the British physicist Ernest Rutherford began a study of radioactivity. He found three types of radiation which he called alpha, beta and gamma rays. Alpha rays were stopped by a thin sheet of paper, beta rays could get through several millimetres of aluminium, and gamma rays could pierce quite thick pieces of lead.

Alpha rays travel at up to 12,000 miles a second, beta rays from 80,000 to 180,000 miles a second, and gamma rays at 186,000 miles a second, the speed of light.

Gamma rays have proved very helpful in medicine and industry. These rays are also given off by radioactive isotopes obtained as by-products in production processes. They can produce radiographs of forgings and the seams of boilers and other pressure vessels, where freedom from flaws is vital.

gamma rays? **WHAT** is Orion's belt?

WHAT is an Instrument Landing System?

ORION'S BELT

Orion's Belt is a row of three bright stars across the middle of a constellation or group of stars. One of the three is easily distinguishable by its yellowish-red colour, which contrasts strongly with the whiteness of the others.

The whole constellation was named after Orion, the great hunter of ancient Greek mythology. When Orion was killed by the goddess Artemis, he was changed, according to the myth, into a group of stars. These took the form of a warrior wearing a girdle of three stars (Orion's Belt) and a lion's skin, and carrying a club, a sword and a shield. Below the belt a hazy line of stars representing the jewels on Orion's sword can be seen.

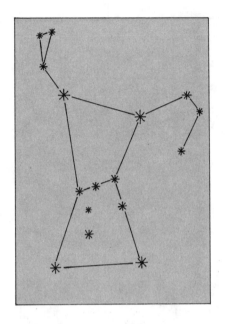

AIRCRAFT LANDING

An Instrument Landing System is used by a pilot in bad weather to bring down an aircraft in perfect line with an airport's runway. Two radio beams are sent out by a ground transmitter. The "localizer" is a narrow, upright beam which positions the aircraft in line with the runway. The "glide path" is a thin, flat beam which gives the aircraft a perfectly angled approach path to the end of the runway.

In the case of large, busy airports such as London's Heathrow, a pilot is in close contact with Air Traffic Control on his approach to the airport for, at peak periods, aircraft can be landing at 45 second intervals.

The Ground Control operator tells him to "lock on", a phrase used to tell the pilot to switch on his Instrument Landing System. The pilot informs Control that he is "established", which means that he has locked on to the two radio beams and is keeping them crossed. The point at which the beams intersect is the spot on the runway where the aircraft must land.

352

WHEN was the Scout movement formed? WHEN did yoga

General Knowledge

YOGA

Yoga started about the 2nd Century B.C. when its main principles were set forth in the *Yogasutras* by the sage Patanjali. This system of Hindu philosophy is based on the idea that man's bondage results from the identification of the soul with the body and that his freedom comes when he realizes the two can be separated. In yoga the mind is controlled by the constant practise of meditation and non-attachment to material objects.

There are different types of yoga designed for different temperaments. Karma Yoga is suited to active minds, and deals with the performance of duties in which the doer renounces attachment, motive and the result of what he does. Jnana Yoga is for philosophical minds, and teaches how to discriminate between the real and the unreal, and how to renounce the unreal. Bhakti Yoga shows the way to cultivate the love of God for His own sake, deals with self-control and concentration.

The final aim of all these systems is the liberation of the soul from the bondage of matter. Hatha Yoga deals mainly with physical exercises and is chiefly concerned with health and long life. Yoga is a Sanskrit word signifying the union of a person's soul with the supreme spirit. A person who practises yoga is called a yogi.

Two yoga positions. Top: *locust.*
Right: *variation on the fish.*

SCOUT MOVEMENT

The Scout movement was formed in 1908 after the appearance of a book, *Scouting for Boys*, written by the then Inspector General of Cavalry in the British Army, Lt. Col. Sir Robert Baden Powell. The author had intended his ideas to be used by existing youth organizations, but it soon became evident that a new movement had begun.

Baden Powell had held an experimental camp on Brownsea Island in Poole harbour, Dorset and put into practice his ideas on the training of boys. He thought they should organize themselves into small, natural groups of six or seven under a boy leader. Their training should add another dimension to their education by including mapping, signalling, rope-knotting, first aid and all the skills needed in camping and similar outdoor activities in which self-reliance is important.

Before being accepted as a scout, a boy had to promise to do his duty to God and his country or sovereign, to help other people at all times and to obey the Scout Law. This was a simple code of chivalrous behaviour easily appreciated by boys. It was not long before the movement spread from Britain to other countries.

ALPHABET

The oldest known alphabet was found in Greek inscriptions of about 2000 B.C. The word comes from the first two words of the Greek alphabet, alpha and beta. The alphabet invented in Greece was based on north Semitic writing and was made up entirely of consonants. This was suitable for a Semitic language, but not for a Sudo-European one, such as Greek.

There are two forms of the Greek alphabet called Chalcidic and Ionic and generally known as Western and Eastern. The Western symbols were brought to Italy by Etruscans and Greek colonists, and adapted to form the Latin alphabet used today in most English-speaking, European and American countries.

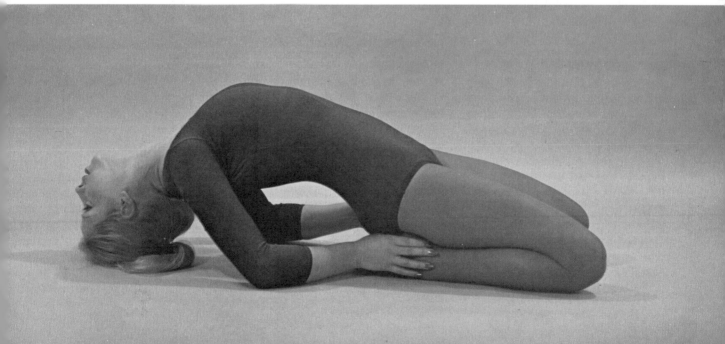

354

WHAT is a madrigal? **WHAT** happens to worn bank notes?

MADRIGAL

A madrigal is a song for several voices, unaccompanied by any musical instrument. The madrigal originated in Italy in the 14th Century as a short poem about love or the countryside, set to vocal music.

It became very popular in the 16th Century when some Italian composers took the light-hearted, but often bawdy, songs sung in the streets and turned them into suitable entertainment for their rich patrons. They wrote songs which could be sung by ladies and gentlemen at home. These part songs were usually for five voices.

At the beginning of the 17th Century several books of madrigals by the composer Claudio Monteverdi were reprinted. This indicated their great success, for music printing had been invented only 20 years earlier.

The fashion for madrigals spread to England where they were sung at the court of King Henry VIII. The Puritan Revolution of the 1640s put an end to this type of singing, but madrigals again became popular in the early 18th Century. It became customary for people to entertain themselves at home by gathering round a table and singing madrigals. A Madrigal Society, formed at that time, still exists.

BANK NOTES

Bank notes that are worn out, soiled or torn are collected by the banks and sent to a central office where they are usually destroyed in a furnace.

Of course, these notes are still money, not just waste paper. So the utmost care is taken with their destruction. The bank that sent them in to be destroyed has to be credited with the amount of money which the old notes represent. Careful account has to be taken of every note burnt.

WARLOCK

A warlock is a male witch, wizard, or sorcerer with supposed supernatural powers, usually considered to be evil. Belief in witchcraft survives in modern civilized societies and remains a strong force in most primitive ones.

Throughout the Western world most alleged witches have been women, and the number of warlocks has been comparatively few. The last execution of one in Germany was that of Johannes Junius who was burned alive in 1628. On the other hand, one of the most famous figures in the history of magic and witchcraft is Merlin, the benevolent wizard of Arthurian legend.

The earliest evidence of belief in witchcraft survives from the prehistoric past. A horned creature, thought to be connected with witchcraft, is to be found carved or painted at archaeological sites dating back to 30,000 B.C. and in areas spanning the territory from the Soviet Union to Spain.

WHAT is a warlock?   WHAT is a Gordian Knot?
WHAT are invisible exports?   WHAT is a swan-song?

GORDIAN KNOT

"Cutting the Gordian Knot" is an expression describing the solution of a problem by quick, decisive action.

In ancient Greek mythology, the Gordian Knot was devised by Gordius, King of Phrygia, the ruins of whose capital lie near Ankara in Turkey. He had bound his chariot yoke so tightly and with such intricacy that it was impossible to loosen. An oracle foretold that he who could untie the Knot would go on to conquer Asia.

When the Greek king Alexander the Great (356–323 B.C.), one of the supreme soldiers and statesmen of history, invaded Asia Minor in 334 B.C., with the object of defeating the Persians, he came to the ancient capital of Gordium. According to story, King Gordius's chariot still stood with the Knot unbroken.

Alexander is said to have resolved the problem in characteristic fashion by drawing his sword and cutting through the Knot at a stroke! The conqueror went on to bring the empire of the Persians, 50 times larger than Greece, under his dominion.

INVISIBLE EXPORTS

Invisible exports earn a country money without any goods being sold abroad. They relate to income from services a country can perform abroad such as banking, insurance, shipping and other forms of transport and communications. All these services earn the country foreign currency. Yet nothing has physically left the country.

Another way of earning foreign currency is by encouraging tourism. The money tourists spend on holiday forms part of the host country's invisible exports.

SWAN SONG

A swan song is a phrase used to describe a person's final appearance or performance, a last gesture or piece of work before retirement. The phrase arises from the legend that the mute swan (the most common British swan) sings for the first and last time just before it dies.

WHERE is the Mona Lisa? WHERE is the Alhambra?

MONA LISA

The world's most famous portrait, painted by Leonardo da Vinci (1452–1519) between 1503 and 1506, hangs today in the Louvre in Paris. The Louvre, formerly a palace of the French kings, is now a museum of art and antiquities which is beyond all valuation.

The Mona Lisa is also called La Gioconda because the sitter's married name was Giocondo. It has been in France from the day in 1516 when Leonardo left Italy to settle there—except for two occasions. Once, in 1911, the picture was stolen from the Louvre and found two years later in Italy. The second time it left France for 26 days, on a fantastically well-guarded and highly insured visit to the United States as a guest of President John F. Kennedy.

Leonardo da Vinci began painting Lisa when she was 24 and he was 51. She used to come to the great master's studio in the late afternoon when the light was soft. Over the three years, Leonardo became fascinated by his model, and perhaps that was the reason why her husband, Francesco del Giocondo, never received the finished portrait. The artist always made the excuse that he had not quite finished it. He carried it with him wherever he went—to Milan, to Rome and, finally, to France where King Francis I offered the artist a palace in the beautiful Loire valley, the Chateau de Cloux.

It is believed that Francis I paid 4,000 gold crowns for the Mona Lisa, but it was not until after Leonardo's death that the king was able, at last, to possess the painting of the Florentine lady with the enigmatic smile. Thereafter, it remained in the possession of the kings and emperors of France. The picture hung at Fontainebleau, at Versailles and at the Tuileries. There in 1800 it hung on the wall of Napoleon Bonaparte's bedroom!

THE ALHAMBRA

The Alhambra is a palace and fortress at Granada, in Spain, overlooking the River Darro. It was built by the Moors who occupied Spain in the Middle Ages. The Moors were the inhabitants of Mauretania, an African province of the Roman Empire, which we know today as Morocco. The Alhambra was begun in 1248 and completed in 1354. Its name comes from the Arabic *qal'at al hamra* (the red castle) and was given to the building because of the red brick of the outer walls.

Today only some splendid remnants of its former glory are to be seen, for in the 16th Century Charles V had much of it rebuilt or replaced. Over the outer arch of the Gate of Judgment is carved an open hand, and legend said that the fortress would never be captured until the hand grasped the key sculptured on the inner arch.

The largest room is the Hall of the Ambassadors and the most romantic the Hall of the Abencerrages, which is called after a famous Moorish family who settled in Spain in the 8th Century. According to legend, 36 knights of the Abencerrages family were massacred in the hall of Boabdil, the last Moorish King of Granada, who died about 1495.

CREMATION

Cremation is the burning of human remains to ashes. Reasons given for adopting this practice include considerations of hygiene, a shortage of land for cemeteries and the rapid growth in population.

Many peoples of the ancient world, including the Greeks and Romans, practised cremation. But in Europe it ceased to be popular with the growth of Christianity and belief in the resurrection of the body.

The modern development of cremation dates from 1874 with the formation of the Cremation Society of England. The society's aim was to replace burial with a method of disposal which would "rapidly resolve the body into its component elements by a process which would not offend the living and would render the remains perfectly innocuous".

The society met with much opposition, and it was not until after the Second World War that local authorities decided to encourage cremation because of the shortage of land. Today cremation is permitted either by law or by custom in about three-quarters of the countries of the world.

WEDDING RINGS

The modern custom of wearing gold wedding rings originated in Roman times, but the idea took many centuries to become established as a universally accepted tradition. At first rings made of iron were introduced as tokens of betrothal. In those days the privilege of wearing gold rings was reserved for Roman senators and magistrates.

As the Empire became more affluent and permissive, this right was allowed to spread through the various levels of society, and engaged couples took advantage of the freedom to use the coveted gold for their betrothal rings.

A great writer of the early Christian church, Tertullian (about 155–222) said that gold "being the nobler and purer metal and remaining longer uncorrupted was thought to intimate the generous, sincere and durable affection which ought to be between the married parties". Gold marriage rings, as distinct from betrothal rings, came into use from the 5th Century, but do not appear to have been generally adopted by the Church for use in the wedding ceremony until much later. At first they probably simply received the Church's blessing.

In English-speaking countries the wedding ring is usually worn on the third finger of the left hand, perhaps because of an old belief that a nerve ran from that finger directly to the heart. But in Germany and France and other European countries both husband and wife wear the ring on the third finger of the right hand, the hand traditionally used for making vows.

This large wedding ring is unusually decorated. The smaller engagement ring is worn on the same finger.

SIKHS AND TURBANS

Sikhs wear their symbolic turbans because they have long hair. The turban keeps the hair free of dust and dirt and keeps it out of the way so that they can live and work comfortably. The Sikhs' religion, which forbids them to cut their hair, is a mixture of two faiths—the Muslim and Hindu. Drinking and smoking and, indeed, all practises that are bad for the health of the body are banned. The Sikh religion allows both men and women to perform religious ceremonies. The Sikhs believe that all men and women are equal.

At the Hindu New Year in 1699, the Guru (or teacher) Gobind Rai, assembled his followers in the foothills of the Himalayas and initiated five of them as members of a fraternity which he named Khalsa, which means pure. They drank amrit (nectar) out of the same bowl, although they all came from different castes. Also, they received new names with the suffix Singh (lion) and swore to keep the five K's which were: to wear long hair (kesh), a comb (kangha) in the hair, soldiers' shorts (kachha), a steel bangle (kara) on the right wrist, and a sabre (kirpan).

In the days that followed, 80,000 people were initiated into the Khalsa fraternity.

Sikh boys and girls now undergo the initiation ceremony of the five K's at the age of puberty. Boys take the additional name of Singh, but not all persons named Singh are Sikhs. The corresponding name for Sikh women is Kaur.

The Sikhs are excellent farmers, soldiers and mechanics. The proportion of literacy among them is higher than among any of the other major communities of India.

traditionally made of gold?
Leonardo da Vinci so famous? WHY do we need passports?

LEONARDO DA VINCI

Leonardo da Vinci is the perfect example of the all-round educated man of the Renaissance. Born in Florence in 1452, he soon became famous for his remarkable paintings. His painting the "Mona Lisa", now in the Louvre, Paris, is possibly the best known painting in the world.

His enormous talents encompassed a wide variety of subjects ranging from sculpture to military engineering. He devoted much time to the concept of flying machines and carried out experiments, without success, in this field. From his work as an artist he developed a knowledge both of anatomy and of the science of light. His anatomical drawings are of a rare beauty and of great precision.

Leonardo was also knowledgeable on such varied subjects as astronomy, geology, botany, and geography. In architecture his studies produced both beautiful designs and practical scientific information. The great man's interests were so diverse that he even gave specific and most serious instructions on how to make and launch stink bombs.

PASSPORTS

Passports have been used for centuries as a means of identifying and protecting people travelling in foreign countries in times of both peace and war. But the adoption of the passport as an essential travel document is fairly recent.

The development of compulsory passports was accompanied by the introduction of visas. These are endorsements by officials of foreign states that entry is permitted.

Originally a passport, as the word indicates, meant permission to leave a port or to sail into it. Later this was extended to include a general permission of exit and entry.

360

WHAT is a Sherpa?   **WHAT** is the origin of Santa Claus?

SHERPA

Sherpas are a hardy people living in a rugged, mountainous region of north-east Nepal, of which Mount Everest (29,000 feet) forms the northern boundary. Originally they came from Tibet.

Today they number about 6,000 and live at heights of about 13,000 feet. Potatoes form their main crop.

Accustomed to living in a thin atmosphere, Sherpas became world famous for their part in helping Everest expeditions since General G. C. Bruce's attempt on the mountain in 1922. They are excellent high-altitude guides and porters, cheerfully carrying loads of supplies and equipment seemingly out of all proportion to their small size. They also act as cooks and assistants.

The most famous Sherpa is Tensing Norkey, who on May 29, 1953, stood with Edmund Hillary of New Zealand on the top of the world—the first men to reach the summit of Everest.

SANTA CLAUS

The jolly old man with white whiskers who brings children toys in his sack at Christmas time had his origins in the popular St Nicholas (4th–5th Century A.D.), the patron saint of school-children and sailors.

Little is known about the life of St Nicholas, but it is probable that he was bishop of Myra in Lycia (Asia Minor). The earliest miracle attributed to him was the rescue of three army officers who were unjustly condemned to death but saved by St Nicholas's appearance in a dream to Constantine I.

In the 17th Century the Dutch Protestant settlers in New Amsterdam (now New York) replaced St Nicholas (known as Sinter Claes in Dutch) by a generous magician called Santa Claus. Gradually, this transformation spread to many countries in Europe, especially those where the Reformed churches were dominant. The kind old man was also given the names of Father Christmas and Father January, and his special day became either December 25 or New Year's Day.

INFLATION

Inflation is what happens when prices in a particular country rise so high and so quickly that they upset the nation's economy.

Prices may start rising rapidly because people want to buy more goods than there are goods to go round. Fears of still higher prices may cause people to rush out and buy things while they can still afford them. Thus the demand for goods increases and the cost of them goes up even faster.

One cure would be for people to stop buying, but, of course, it is difficult to persuade people to stop buying things they want. Workers whose wages buy them less, old people whose pensions are no longer enough to live on, students whose grants no longer support them, all press for increased money to keep up with prices. Higher wages often mean dearer goods.

WHAT is inflation?   WHAT is a witch doctor?

WITCH DOCTOR

Among many tribes the most important member, after the chief, is the witch doctor or medicine man. He combines the roles of priest and healer and is regarded with fear and respect. Often he may claim to have power over the spirit world, or to be able to read the secrets of the past and foretell the future.

The witch doctor is responsible for the magical rites for ensuring rain, fruitful crops or good hunting. He also enforces obedience to taboos and rituals, and may cast a spell upon any man who disobeys them. Such a spell may prove fatal to a victim who believes in it.

In his capacity as healer, the witch doctor acquires a specialized knowledge of herbs, many of which form the basis of modern medicines. Even so, the cure will not be tried without the use of magical charms, spells and ritual.

CHESS

Chess was invented in the East, probably by the Hindus in India. In the 6th Century it was introduced to Persia.

But the game of the Hindus and Persians was not the same as modern chess. The Hindus played a four-handed game with four toy armies—elephants, horses, chariots, and foot soldiers. This game was known as *chaturanga* and probably involved the use of dice.

Modern chess, with a chequered board, did not evolve until the 16th Century. Spain and Italy were the first countries to take it up, followed by France and England. The first world chess champion was a Frenchman called Philidor.

KOSHER FOOD

Food is kosher when it has been made fit and clean to eat according to Jewish religious practices.

The food must not come from animals, birds or fish prohibited in the Bibilical books of Leviticus and Deuteronomy.

The meat must be salted to remove the blood after the carcass has been examined for physical defects, and the ischiatic nerve must be removed from the hindquarters, as stated in Genesis.

Meat and milk must not be cooked together and separate utensils must be used.

The *shehita* method of slaughtering is carried out by a specially trained person using a special knife with a smooth, sharp edge. An incision is made across the animal's neck and the knife moved in a fast, uninterrupted sweep without stabbing or pressing. The sweep cuts the main arteries, rendering the animal unconscious and allowing the blood to drip from the body.

was the Identikit invented?

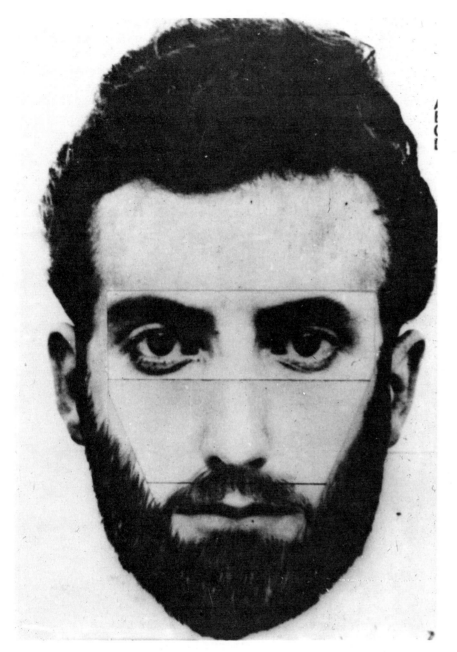

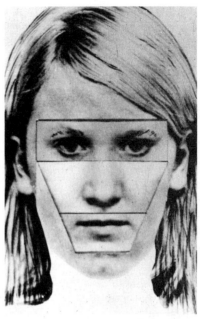

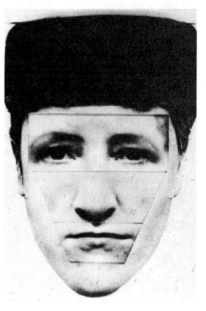

These three pictures have been produced by Photofit.

IDENTIKIT

The Identikit system of building up a picture of someone sought by the police was developed in the United States in 1960 by Hugh Macdonald. It consists of transparent sheets on which are drawn different shapes of faces, eyebrows, noses, mouths and other physical features. These are interchangeable and can be put together according to witnesses' descriptions, thus presenting in one picture their impressions of a wanted person's appearance. A later system called Photofit uses photographs instead of linear drawings.

Both systems are based on ideas similar to those developed in 1879 by Alphonse Bertillon, a French criminologist. Bertillon's system, which was used in many countries until the turn of the century, was founded on three basic principles: that the precise measurements of certain parts of the body can readily be obtained; that these measurements remain constant in a fully grown person; and that no two human beings have exactly the same measurements.

Although most of Bertillon's work involved accurate measurements of the body, an important feature was the *portrait parlé* or descriptive portrait. This was a system of sectional photography introduced to replace the haphazard methods of the time.

WHAT is Baroque? **WHAT** is halva? **WHAT** is a clairvoyant?

BAROQUE

Baroque and post-Baroque are terms used to describe a particular style of art and architecture that flourished in Europe from the close of the 16th Century to the late 18th Century.

This style was much concerned with vivid colours, hidden light sources, luxurious materials, elaborate, contrasting textures, and drama and illusion. But the art of the period was so varied that it is impossible to supply a simple set of rules or criteria for it.

In architecture the buildings were designed to stimulate faith in church and state. Each element in the design contributed to the central culminating feature. Precision and elegance were thought less important than vitality and movement. Unity and harmony were essential.

Carlo Maderno (1556–1629) is known as the father of Baroque. In 1607 he designed the façade of St Peter's Rome. The colonnade was the work of the brilliant Giovanni Lorenzo Bernini (1598–1680).

The Baroque influence soon became international and rapidly developed into two separate forms —free, active architecture in Roman Catholic countries such as Italy, Spain and Portugal, and more restrained but impressive buildings in Protestant areas such as England, The Netherlands and parts of Northern Europe.

During the post-Baroque period (about 1700–1780) a particular style known as Rococo developed which refined the flamboyant Baroque to suit elegant 18th Century tastes.

These two magnificent examples of Baroque are right *the clock window in St Peter's, Rome and* far right *the basilica from the Steinhausen in Bavaria.*

HALVA

Halva is a crumbly sweetmeat. It is usually made in large blocks and consists of crushed sesame seed and sugar, sometimes flavoured with chocolate and almonds. Halva is very cheap in Greece and Turkey where it is made.

If you are not able to visit those countries, you could probably find some in a Greek or Turkish shop in a big city.

CLAIRVOYANT

A clairvoyant is a person who possesses the power to discern or detect objects not present to the usual senses—objects we cannot see, hear, touch, taste or smell. The small number of people with this form of extra-sensory perception (ESP) can be said to own a sixth sense.

Many people sceptical of clairvoyance and telepathy have been

WHAT is a billion?

forced to admit that such phenomena cannot be explained in terms of the laws of normal physics and psychology.

A simple method, often used, of detecting clairvoyancy in a person is to hold a shuffled pack of cards face downward. The person is asked to guess the top card, then the next one and so on. Usually the pack of cards will be in front of the clairvoyant, but sometimes it is not even in the same room. Experiments at various psychic research centres have produced remarkable successes.

A famous clairvoyant is recorded as having seen a crashed car on a road which, to all other observers, was absolutely empty. Only a day later a car did crash on the exact spot forecast.

BILLION

In Britain a billion is a million times a million, or 12 zeros. In France, America and most other countries a billion is only one thousand million, or nine zeros.

The French and American way of counting seems far more practical and is being used more often in Britain. The official British billion is so big that it has become meaningless and is rarely used.

WHERE is the world's largest painting? WHERE did cricket WHERE is radium found?

LARGEST PAINTING

The largest painting ever made was undoubtedly *Panorama of the Mississippi*, completed by the American John Banvard in 1846.

The painting depicted the great river over its 1,200 miles course, on a strip some 5,000 feet long and 12 feet wide. In area it was nearly as big as a field of an acre and a half—an amazing size.

But this painting was destroyed when the barn on Long Island, New York, where it was stored burned down in 1891.

The largest painting now in existence is *The Battle of Gettysburg*, completed in 1883 after two-and-a-half years' work. It took Paul Philippoteaus of France and 16 assistants to paint the 410-foot-long picture. It is 70 feet high and weighs nearly five-and-a-half tons. The painting is now in a private collection in Winston-Salem, North Carolina, United States. Size alone, of course, is no guide to quality.

CRICKET

Pictures belonging to the middle of the 13th Century show a simple team game with bat and ball which bears a marked resemblance to cricket, the national game of England. The first written evidence about the game is possibly to be found in an extract from the accounts of King Edward I of England in 1300. This refers to some money which was spent by the young Prince Edward on a game called "creag".

Cricket was being played by boys of the free school of Guildford, Surrey, in 1550. Oliver Cromwell, Lord Protector of England, was said to have played both cricket and football in his youth, and a kind of cricket club at St Albans, Hertfordshire, was mentioned in 1666. The first regular cricket club was formed in the Hampshire village of Hambledon in 1750.

The game has been played under recognized rules at least since the beginning of the 18th Century. The first definite match recorded was played in 1679 in Sussex—11 a side and for a stake of 50 guineas. In 1719 the "Londoners" met the "Kentish men" in what must have been the first match at county level.

At first the greatest enthusiasm for the game was in the southern counties. The most famous cricket centre was the Artillery Ground, Finsbury. Here was played on June 18, 1744, the famous match between Kent and All England. This was the first game to be recorded in A. Haygarth's *Scores and Biographies 1744–1878*.

The Marylebone Cricket Club, which eventually became the game's ruling authority, was established in 1787. In 1814 it purchased its present ground at St. John's Wood, London, named after the club's founder, Thomas Lord.

Cricket is now widely played in the English-speaking lands.

begin?　WHERE is Britain's money made?
WHERE does the word "barbecue" come from?

RADIUM

Radium is found in the ore of uranium. Two French scientists working in Paris discovered radium in 1890. Professor and Mme. Curie found this rare and precious element in a mineral called pitchblende, a black substance which also contains uranium. During a period of four years they treated six tons of this material and obtained a teaspoonful of a pure radioactive substance which they called radium.

They found that radium had many very unusual properties. It affected ordinary photographic plates, it made certain substances glow when placed in the dark, and it quickly killed off tiny dangerous organisms when placed near them.

Radium gives off powerful radioactive waves—the well-known gamma rays. These are used in the treatment of various diseases, especially in the case of cancer where "deep ray" treatment is given.

Pierre and Marie Curie were awarded the Nobel Prize for physics for their work. Professor Curie was killed in a motor accident in 1906, but Mme. Curie continued the work they had started together and in 1911 was awarded the Nobel Prize for Chemistry.

BARBECUE

The word "barbecue" comes from the Spanish word "barbacoa". Barbacoa was the native Haitian name adopted by the Spanish for a kind of scaffolding. Then the French used it to describe a sort of grid or grill—one, no doubt, often used for cooking. The word came to designate an animal roasted whole, usually out of doors.

In the 19th Century, Americans adopted the name barbacoa and anglicized it to barbecue, which came to mean an open air feast or social gathering, as we know it today.

BRITAIN'S MONEY

Britain's money is made in the Royal Mint on Tower Hill, in London. The word "mint" is used to describe a place where coins are manufactured, usually with the authority of the state.

Gold, Silver and base metal coins were being used by various tribes in Britain before the Roman occupation. In the 3rd Century the Emperor Marcus Aurelius Carausius opened three English mints, one of which was in London. These were soon closed however, and not until the 6th Century was there further definite record of a mint in England.

Seventy mints were in existence in England at the time William the Conqueror landed because the transport of money from one place to another was so risky. As conditions improved, the number of mints declined. Since the 16th Century, all English gold and silver coins, with one or two important exceptions, such as the Great Recoinage of 1696 to 1698, have been struck in the London Mint.

To enable decimal coinage to be produced without interrupting current output, it was announced in 1967 that a mint would open in Llantrisant, South Wales. Queen Elizabeth II struck the first decimal coin on December 17, 1968, when, accompanied by the Duke of **Edinburgh and the Prince of Wales, she opened the new mint. The South Wales mint took over coin production in Britain in 1975.**

WHEN did jazz begin?   WHEN were Christmas cards first

JAZZ

The beginning of jazz cannot be dated with accuracy because it is the secular music of the Negro people of the United States and originates in African folk music.

Prominent in the history of jazz is the fundamental flexible music-poetry form called the blues. Here an interplay of African and European musical traditions has produced a flexible folk music of three rhyming lines. One of the great blues singers was Bessie Smith (1894–1937).

Ragtime is very different from the blues, being formal, melodic and fairly limited in rhythm. Its first major composer was Scott Joplin (1868–1917) whose best-known work was *Maple Leaf Rag*.

Between ragtime and orchestral jazz was W. C. Handy, who harmonized blues themes. Then came the New Orleans style, first played by the Original Dixieland Jazz Band in 1917 and best preserved on records by the 1923 group of Joseph "King" Oliver and by "Jelly Roll" Morton's Red Hot Peppers in 1926–1930.

In the late 1920s Louis Armstrong, shown below, emerged as a great solo artist, and in the 1930s and 1940s Duke Ellington's band produced some of the finest jazz. At this time also appeared the Count Basie orchestra, a product of Kansas City and the Southwest. In the next two decades jazz became "cool", with names like Miles Davis and Thelonious Monk. Today, artists like Ornette Coleman are finding new modes of expression in a musical tradition which has its roots in tribal Africa.

CHRISTMAS CARDS

The first Christmas card was designed in England in 1843 by J. C. Horsley for his friend Sir Henry Cole. A thousand copies of it were placed on sale at Felix Summerley's Home Treasury office in London. The card was printed by lithography on stiff dark-brown cardboard and measured $5\frac{1}{8} \times 3\frac{1}{4}$ inches. Underneath the picture of a family party on the front was the greeting "A Merry Christmas and a Happy New Year to You". Inside were panels, framed in trellis work, showing examples of Christmas giving.

Louis Prang of Boston, Massachusetts, is regarded as the "Father of the American Christmas card". He first produced Christmas cards in 1875. They were beautifully designed and much admired abroad.

SACRED CATS

Cats were regarded as sacred by the ancient Egyptians 3,000 years ago. They were worshipped in the temples and adorned with jewels in their ears and with necklaces. Figures of cats were kept in people's homes and buried in their tombs.

When cats died they were buried with great respect amid public mourning, and their bodies were mummified to preserve them for the day of judgment.

Special reverence was paid to the cat in the temple of Bubastes where Pasht, the local goddess of the city, was represented as a woman with a cat's head. A festival was held in her honour every year.

A curious custom which may have had its origin in pilgrimages to the goddess's shrine survived until recent years among Egyptian Mohammedans. Before starting on a pilgrimage to Mecca, they would set apart a camel for the conveyance of cats.

GUERRILLA

A guerrilla is a member of an independent body of fighters carrying on irregular warfare against authority. This usually involves fighting on a small scale against units of national armies. Guerrillas often use unconventional weapons and equipment, and are extremely mobile. Psychological warfare, including the use of sabotage and terrorism, is also part of their system of fighting.

"Guerrilla" is a Spanish word meaning "little war". The word came into use during the Duke of Wellington's campaigns when the Spanish-Portuguese irregulars or *guerrilleros* helped drive the French from the Iberian peninsula. Lawrence of Arabia, who made great use of guerrillas against the Turks in the First World War, once said: "Guerrilla war is much more intellectual than a bayonet charge".

Che Guevara of Cuba also made his name as a guerrilla. He was eventually shot while fighting in Bolivia for the Communists against the country's government.

SMALL HOURS

The small hours are the early hours of the morning from midnight until daybreak, or in winter until about 5 o'clock.

They are the time when most people are asleep. But others find that, if they can stay awake past their normal bedtime when their bodies get drowsy, they do their best work then.

Winston Churchill, the great British war prime minister, was such a person. He used to sleep for an hour until midnight and hold his councils of war in the small hours, to the annoyance of his advisers who would rather have been asleep.

The end of the small hours in summer is heralded by the dawn chorus when the birds wake each other up with their songs.

Che Guevara: probably the best-known modern guerrilla leader.

PERFECT PITCH

Perfect pitch is the ability to identify by ear, or to sing, any musical note with extreme accuracy and without recourse to an instrument. The gift, possessed by few and impossible to acquire, is not essential to musicians, but is of enormous help to them if they are lucky enough to possess it. Many composers have had this gift, but two who lacked it were Wagner and Schumann.

In ancient Greece, where instruments were mainly stringed, no fixed pitch standard was used. This was the case even in Renaissance times. When large wind and string orchestras were created it became necessary to agree on one constant. The organ was chosen because the standard note it gave was less variable than that of other instruments.

For unaccompanied singing a pitch pipe or tuning fork is often used. If the conductor has perfect pitch, he can give a note or a range of notes himself without the use of an aid. In unaccompanied choral music, therefore, perfect pitch is a particularly valuable accomplishment.

perfect pitch? **WHAT** was Prohibition?

WHAT is a poltergeist?

PROHIBITION

In January 1919, a law was made in the United States forbidding the manufacture, sale or transport of alcohol anywhere in the country. That was the beginning of Prohibition in America.

It was an attempt to make the American people more moral and self-disciplined. Congregationalist and Presbyterian ministers had preached for some time about the evils of drink. Many immigrants were coming to settle in America. Middle-class Protestants, descendants of early settlers, wanted these newcomers to adopt the same Puritan values as themselves.

The law proved appallingly difficult to enforce, and encouraged acts of gangsterism—for instance, Al Capone's massacre of his rivals on St Valentine's Day in Chicago in 1929. Al Capone was a bootlegger, a man who profited from making and selling drink illegally. He made 60,000,000 dollars a year. On that St Valentine's Day—February 14—his gang killed seven members of a rival gang who were trying to make money doing the same thing.

By 1929 many people in America were sick of Prohibition. The Democratic Party became known as the party which wanted to repeal the law. The economic depression of 1930–1933 was another reason for abolishing Prohibition. Millions of men were out of work. It was thought that jobs could be created if the sale and manufacture of alcohol were allowed by law. So in February 1933 Prohibition was repealed.

POLTERGEIST

A poltergeist is an invisible force or alleged spirit said to be responsible for the occasionally mystifying noises in a house and the movement of objects around a room. A poltergeist has no shape. There are recorded cases where for no apparent reason, glasses and plates have flown off shelves and crashed to the ground. These inexplicable movements were said to be the work of poltergeists.

Many people do not believe poltergeists exist. Various theories have been put forward to account for the phenomena, most of which tend to discount the mass of evidence available. Most of this evidence may well be inaccurate or even totally false, but some of it seems to defy explanation.

February 1920—33,100 gallons of wine pumped into the gutter in Los Angeles.

WHY do we use double glazing? WHY are Wellington boots WHY is Confucius so admired?

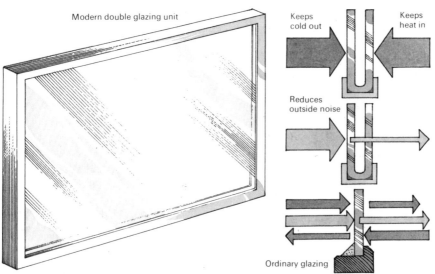

Modern double glazing unit

Keeps cold out

Keeps heat in

Reduces outside noise

Ordinary glazing

Heat and cold pass through the bottom, unglazed window.

DOUBLE GLAZING

Double glazing for windows reduces loss of heat through the glass and cuts down noise from outside. There are many different systems, including some which do not need professional installation, but the principle is the same. Two sheets of glass are fitted together with a constant cushion of air between them.

This glass-air-glass sandwich should, therefore economize on fuel and make the room quieter. It should also reduce condensation, or water on the inside of the window caused by warm air meeting the cold glass. It will make a room more comfortable in winter, especially near the windows, and may even make it more difficult for a burglar to get in.

The efficiency of this insulation (or separation from the cold outside) is effected by the distance between the glass sheets. Heat insulation increases with the air space up to three-quarters of an inch, but a four-inch space is required for effective sound insulation.

Half or even more of the heat that goes out through single windows can be retained by double glazing, but three-quarters of the heat lost from an average house may escape through other outlets.

WELLINGTON BOOTS

Wellington boots take their name from the first Duke of Wellington. The duke had a special pair designed for him to suit the conditions of his campaigns through Spain and Belgium. No doubt the changes in climate and, in, particular the muddy Belgian fields prompted his desire for tougher footwear.

The original boots reached as far as the knee and were impregnated with waterproofing materials, probably with a rubber base. They were equally suited to walking and to riding.

SHOE SOLES

The soles of shoes are worn out by the pressure of the feet on the ground. The harder the ground or the rougher the surface, the sooner the soles will wear through.

Every time you walk, tiny particles are scraped off the soles by the ground. To obtain the maximum degree of durability the leather used for soles is compressed. Nowadays this firmness is achieved through the pressure of heavy rolling machines. Before mechanization cobblers hammered layers of leather together.

CONFUCIUS

Confucius dedicated his life to attempting to relieve the suffering of the people of China, where he lived between 551 and 479 B.C. He was a philosopher and political theorist, whose ideas have deeply influenced the civilization of Eastern Asia.

This great teacher was deeply distressed by the misery he saw on every hand. The Chinese were oppressed by wars, taxes and hunger. Confucius believed the solution must lie in the creation of a form of government which would have as its objective not the pleasure of the rulers, but the happiness of the people.

He advocated such measures as the reduction of taxes, the mitigation of severe punishments and the avoidance of unnecessary war. He tried to secure a position of administrative influence; but in this he failed because the Chinese rulers thought his ideas dangerous. So he taught his beliefs to younger men and sought government posts for these disciples.

Confucius was the first man in China to use teaching as an instrument of reform. But he was not dogmatic or authoritarian. He merely asked questions and insisted that the students found the answers for themselves.

He declared: "If, when I point out one corner of the subject the student cannot work out the other three for himself, I do not go on."

His belief that the state should be a wholly co-operative enterprise was quite different from the ruling ideas of his time. Aristocrats were believed to rule by virtue of the authority and the powerful assistance of their divine ancestors.

The right to govern, Confucius held, depended upon the ability to make the people governed happy.

Right: A large Shibuichi Tsuba, showing Lao-Tse, Buddha and Confucius.

so called? WHY do the soles of shoes wear out?

LITTLE MERMAID

The famous bronze statue of the Little Mermaid, carved by Edvard Eriksen, is posed on a rock near the Langelinie promenade in Copenhagen harbour, Denmark. She is the heroine of Hans Christian Andersen's fairy tale about a mermaid who falls in love with a prince and who sacrifices her tongue to exchange her fish-tail for human legs.

Hans Christian Andersen (1805–75) was born in Odense, Denmark. When he was 14, he went to Copenhagen to try to be an actor or opera singer. He was not successful and turned to writing, but failed in that, too. However, a friend who had faith in his talent persuaded the King of Denmark to grant him a pension, so that he could continue his education and travel to other countries. Soon afterwards he began to write poems, plays, novels and travel books that sold well.

Nowadays these are all forgotten, and the world remembers him for his fairy tales which appeared in 1835. Today they are published in more than 60 languages.

AMERICA'S GOLD

America keeps most of her gold at Fort Knox, a United States Army reservation, about 35 miles south of Louisville in Kentucky. Covering 110,000 acres, the reservation contains the United States Army Armoured Centre and the principal United States bullion depository.

The fort was established in 1918 as Camp Knox and was used as the army's Field Artillery officer training school. In 1932 the name was changed, and the following year the 1st Cavalry Regiment was moved from Texas to Fort Knox, where it was mechanized.

For maximum security, the bullion depository was built at Fort Knox in 1936. By the second half of the 20th Century the gold stocks there were valued at more than 10,000 million dollars. The gold is housed in a solid square bomb-proof building constructed of granite, steel and concrete, enclosing a two-level torch-proof steel and concrete vault. Added security is provided by guards, sentries and an encircling steel fence, as well as by mechanical protective devices, such as the photo-electric eye.

During the Second World War the gold vault was used as a storage place for the original copy of the United States constitution, the Declaration of Independence and England's Magna Carta.

Mermaid? **WHERE** would you use a rouble, yen, rupee, you look for a yard of ale? drachma, guilder?

ROUBLE, YEN, RUPEE, DRACHMA, GUILDER

You would use a rouble in the Soviet Union, a yen in Japan, a rupee in India and Pakistan, a drachma in Greece, and a guilder in Holland. They are all units of the monetary systems of those countries.

The rouble, which is divided into 100 kopeks, was the name for silver bar money which was in use in Russia from the 14th to the 17th Centuries. Peter the Great set up the modern system of coins, and the silver bar money was abolished.

The yen was originally a gold coin, but was changed to silver. A one yen coin is now made of aluminium and the five and ten yen pieces are made of nickel.

The word rupee means "silver coin". It came into use in 1542 when the Sultan of Delhi, Sher Sha, reorganized the currency. It was kept as a monetary unit and is now divided into 100 noye paise (new paisas). Large amounts of rupees have special names: a lakh is 100,000 and a crore is ten million rupees.

The drachma, in Ancient Greece was a silver coin and also a measure of weight. There were 100 drachmae to one mina which weighed about one pound. The modern drachma is divided into 100 lepta.

The guilder, which is the currency of The Netherlands and its overseas territories, is divided into 100 cents. This unit of currency spread to Northern Europe from Florence in Italy and is also used under the name of florin.

KNIVES AND FORKS

Knives were invented a long time before forks. Flint knives for general purposes were used in the Stone Age. The Romans had eating knives. But even in the 16th Century only very rich houses had enough knives for each guest at dinner to have one to himself. This meant that people often carried their own knives with them in a sheath round their waists. Often they were made in pairs so that even before forks were employed you did not have to use your fingers.

The first forks had only two prongs like a carving fork, and there was usually only one in a house. The use of forks at table was probably introduced into Europe from the East through the Venetians in the 11th Century.

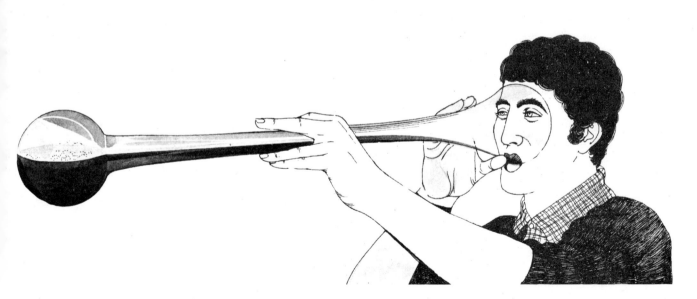

YARD OF ALE

You would look for, and perhaps find, a yard of ale in an old public house or a tavern in England. It is a narrow tube, three feet long, opening out at one end and with a bulb at the other. When filled with ale or beer, it forms one yard of ale. Although now rare, these strange-shaped glasses can still be found hanging on the walls of inns, particularly old or historic ones, as a curiosity.

This odd drinking vessel was an example of the glass-blower's art. But it was never in general use for drinking. Instead it was used either as a joke or as a challenge. When the glass was filled to the brim with ale or beer, the contestant had to drink "the yard" without pausing or taking breath. At a really lively party, every man present would have had to take his turn. When this type of entertainment was popular, the locally brewed ale was probably less strong and intoxicating than it is now. But the feat still required considerable swallowing power and breath control.

WHEN was Big Ben built? WHEN was Stonehenge built?

BIG BEN

Big Ben was cast in 1858. It is the bell that chimes the hours in the Clock Tower of the British Houses of Parliament, London, and is so called because Sir Benjamin Hall, as the Chief Commissioner of Works, was the minister responsible for its installation. The famous deep, resonant boom of the bell is regularly broadcast by the B.B.C. all over the world.

The way to Big Ben is up a spiral staircase of 374 steps. The Roman numerals on the clock face are two feet high and the pendulum is 13 feet long. Big Ben itself weighs $13\frac{1}{2}$ tons. When the clock was installed, two men used to wind it every week. Now it is wound by electricity.

STONEHENGE

Stonehenge was built on Salisbury Plain, Wiltshire, England, apparently in three different stages between 1800 and 1400 B.C.

The first stage consisted of a circular ditch and bank, with a series of circular holes called Aubrey holes after the man who discovered them. It also included the Heel Stone. There may have been a structure of stone or wood

at the centre of the circle.

During the second stage of construction, which probably took place about 200 years later, the entrance of the earthwork was widened on the east side and connected to the River Avon by a processional way marked by parallel banks and ditches. At the same time a number of Blue Stones, which were apparently brought from the Prescelly Mountains in Pembrokeshire, South Wales, were erected in the centre of the site to form two circles.

The third stage of the work is thought to have been begun after 1600 B.C. The entire monument was remodelled, and about 80 large blocks of sarsen were presumably transported from the Marlborough Downs north of the site. These were erected in a circle of 30 uprights, capped by a continuous ring of stone lintels.

It is generally assumed that Stonehenge was constructed as a place of worship, but its exact purpose is unknown. There is an astronomical explanation for the placing of the stones where they are in relation to the rising and the setting sun.

378

WHAT is the Koran?   WHAT is a Red Letter Day?   WHAT is

KORAN

The Koran is the sacred book on which is founded the religion of the Mohammedans, the followers of the Prophet Mohammed (about A.D. 570–632). The name comes from the Arabic *qu'ran* meaning "that should be read". It is used in public worship and is the chief textbook in Mohammedan schools. Upon the Koran are based the Mohammedan laws and way of life.

This sacred book is the word of Allah (God) revealed in a vision to Mohammed by the Archangel Gabriel. Mohammed, who could not write, dictated Gabriel's words to his friends. These were written on dried palm leaves, bits of leather, whitened shoulder-blades of sheep or whatever was to hand. Soon after the prophet's death,

Caliph Abu Bakr (573–634 A.D.) called a conference of those who had heard Mohammed, and ordered the writing of an authentic Koran. All variations on it were destroyed. Because of this, and because of the phenomenal verbal memory Arabs are known to possess, it is almost certain that the Koran is indeed composed of the authentic sayings of Mohammed.

The Koran is about as long as the New Testament. It is written in rhymed prose and is divided into 114 *suras* or chapters, each of which begins with the words "In the name of God, the merciful, the compassionate". It consists of history, legends, prophecies, moral precepts and laws.

The histories are chiefly about Old Testament characters, and

many of the laws are the same as those of Judaism or Christianity. Moses, Jesus and Mohammed are named as the greatest prophets, and the Bible is held in great respect. Mohammedans are told to treat "the peoples of the Book" (i.e. Jews and Christians) with kindness.

The most important teaching is the oneness of God—"There is no God but Allah". Submission to his will (Islam) is the highest virtue. The Last Judgment is stressed. Then everyone shall receive reward or punishment for his deeds. The Mohammedan must pray five times a day, turning towards Mecca, the holy city, which is in Saudi Arabia. He must also make at least one pilgrimage to Mecca, if he can afford it.

RED LETTER DAY

A red letter day has come to mean an important day when some noteworthy event or celebration is taking place. Originally the phrase came from the habit of ecclesiastics of making special saints' days in red ink in their calendars. This custom started very early on in the days of hand-written manuscripts.

There are 29 red letter days in the Anglican Book of Common Prayer. There are also "black letter days" in the ecclesiastical calendar, but these are not days of sadness and repentance as one might imagine from their name. They signify days of lesser feasts and obligations.

It is a little known fact that a devout Anglican could ask for his children to be excused school on red letter days to attend religious services.

ATHEIST

An atheist is a person who denies the existence of God. An agnostic takes a neutral view and says he does not know.

the difference between an atheist and an agnostic?
WHAT is the pony express?

PONY EXPRESS

The pony express provided a fast postal service between two cities in America—St Joseph, Missouri, and Sacramento, California—from April 1860 to October 1861. It was established by a freighting and stagecoach firm called Russell, Majors and Waddell, and was used only for letters. The charge was five dollars for half an ounce.

Expert riders, either small men or boys, were chosen to ride fast horses which were changed six to eight times on the scheduled ride. A specially designed square of leather, called a mochila, was thrown over the saddle and the letters were carried in four leather boxes attached to its corners.

The route covered 1,838 miles and included 157 stations, which lay from seven to 20 miles apart. "Home Stations", providing food and a little rest for riders, were placed at distances of 75 to 100 miles. The time scheduled for the run was 10 days, but this was only occasionally achieved.

The pony express followed the Oregon-California trail and passed through Ft. Kearney, Julesburg, Ft. Laramie, South Pass, Ft. Bridger, Salt Lake City and Carson City. During the Paiute War of 1860, Indians burned stations and killed employees.

Among the best-known riders were William ("Buffalo Bill") Cody (1846–1917) and "Pony Bob" Haslam. Russell, Majors and Waddell introduced the pony express in the hope that it would save them from bankruptcy. But the completion of the transcontinental telegraph line in October 1861 ended its usefulness, and another romantic chapter in American history was over.

380

WHERE does velvet come from? WHERE is the Whispering

VELVET

Velvet comes from silk, but there are many imitations made from cotton and other materials. Real velvet is a closely woven fabric made by weaving loops of silk on to two silk backcloths, one on top of the other. In between the two backcloths the woven silk will form what is called a pile. The pile is the soft, furry hairs characteristic of velvet and many carpets.

The two layers of silk, which have been woven face-to-face, will have long furry pile yarns connecting the two layers. After the cloth is woven, the two layers are sliced apart leaving two separate soft rows of velvet.

Velvet was originally developed in the 15th Century in Italy from where the art spread throughout the world. Turkish velvets were especially successful, and beautiful designs from 16th and 17th Century Turkey survive today.

WHISPERING GALLERY

The Whispering Gallery is one of the most famous features of Sir Christopher Wren's great masterpiece, St Paul's Cathedral in London.

If you speak in this gallery, which runs round the inside of the great dome, the sound waves of your voice will be carried round to the opposite side of the gallery because the waves are prevented from going outwards by the stones lining the circular wall.

The great dome of St Paul's is really two domes—an outer dome with a diameter of 148 feet and an inner dome with a diameter of 103 feet. A hollow cone of brickwork between them supports a steeple-like structure in six diminishing stages culminating in the ball and cross. The top of the cross is 404 feet above the ground.

St Paul's has been acclaimed as the most magnificent domed build-

ing of the Renaissance period. It replaced the Norman cathedral which was destroyed in the Great Fire of London in 1666 and whose tower and spire were 124 feet higher than the present building.

The foundation stone of the new St Paul's was laid in 1675 and 35 years later the final stone of the cupola was put into position.

Great craftsmen were employed on the interior decoration. Francis Bird carved the Conversion of St Paul over the great pediment. Grinling Gibbons, one of England's and the world's finest woodcarvers, worked on the choir stalls, and the wrought iron work was done by Jean Tijou, the renowned ironsmith.

During the Second World War St Paul's was hit three times by bombs, the most serious damage being the destruction of the high altar on the night of October 10, 1940. The new high altar was dedicated as a British Commonwealth war memorial in May, 1958.

The tombs of many famous men—Nelson, Wellington, Roberts, Jellicoe and Beatty—are either in the cathedral or in the crypt beneath. Wren, too, is buried there, and his epitaph is inscribed in Latin over the north door. It is *Si monumentum requiris, circumspice*—If you seek his memorial, look around you.

THE CALENDAR

Early in history man began counting time by days, months and seasons and so had the beginnings of a calendar. When he studied the supposed movement of the sun more closely he began to use the year as a unit of time.

The Greeks dated everything from the Olympic Register, a traditional list of the victors in the Olympic games starting in 776 B.C. The Romans counted time from the founding of their city in 753 B.C. The Mohammedans use the Hejira, or flight of Mohammed from Mecca, A.D. 622. Jewish reckoning dates back to the Creation, calculated as having taken place 3,760 years and three months before Christ's birth-date. The Christian practice of dating events from the birth of Christ did not come into general use until the time of Charlemagne (9th Century), and a mistake was made

which placed the Christ's birth five years too late.

In 46 B.C., acting on the advice of the astronomer Sosigenes, Julius Caesar fixed the year at $365\frac{1}{4}$ days, giving every fourth year, or leap year, an extra day. But the correction by a whole day every four years was too much, and by the 16th Century the Julian calendar was 13 days behind the solar year.

In 1582, Pope Gregory XIII directed that 10 days should be dropped from the calendar. He also directed that three times in every 400 years the leap year arrangement should be omitted, by not counting as leap years the years ending in two noughts unless they are divisible by 400. This arrangement will keep the calendar and solar year together until the year 5,000, when the difference will be one day.

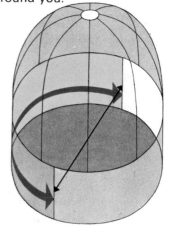

The red arrow shows how sound travels around the walls

Gallery? **WHERE** did calendars begin?

382

WHEN was Braille invented?   WHEN did a nuclear
                                  WHEN was

BRAILLE

Braille was invented by a Frenchman, Louis Braille, in about 1829. It is an alphabet consisting of an arrangement of raised dots, which can be read by blind people using their sense of touch. While Braille was cutting some leather in his father's shop at the age of three, a knife slipped and plunged into an eye causing blindness.

In 1819, when he was 10 years old, the boy went to Paris with a scholarship to study at the National Institution for Blind Children. The institution's founder hit on the idea of providing texts in embossed Roman lettering which the blind could decipher.

Two years after Braille's arrival Charles Barbier exhibited at the institution an apparatus by which a coded message in dots and dashes could be embossed on cardboard. Braille worked on this system and was able to adapt it to meet the need of the sightless. He published expositions of his system in 1829 and 1837.

Braille became a dedicated teacher at his school and also a talented organist. It was through his life's work that thousands of blind people today can read.

submarine make its first passage under the North Pole?
the first game of Mah Jongg? **WHEN** did newspapers begin?

NUCLEAR SUBMARINE

The first voyage under the North Pole was made from August 1 to August 5, 1958, by the United States submarine Nautilus. She crossed from Point Barrow, Alaska to the Greenland Sea, travelling 1,830 miles under the polar ice cap and passing the geographic North Pole on August 3.

The Nautilus could maintain submerged speeds of over 20 knots almost indefinitely.

She was designed to run on direct water heat from an atomic pile. The crew were shielded so well from the pile that in a year's cruise they received less radiation than that set by the American Bureau of Standards as permissible for a single week.

Nuclear submarines are equipped with alternative electrical power for use should the reactor fail.

MAH JONGG

Mah Jongg is probably of 19th Century origin. It is a Western version of a Chinese game and is played with 136 to 144 pieces or tiles, similar to dominoes. These are engraved with Chinese symbols and characters and divided into suits and honours. The object of the four players is to complete combinations or sets of these tiles.

The name Mah Jongg was coined and copyrighted by Joseph P. Babcock, a United States resident of Shanghai, who is credited with introducing the game to the West after the First World War. He wrote a modified set of rules, gave English titles to the tiles and added index letters and numerals familiar to Western card players.

His game became a craze in the United States, Britain and Australia in the mid 1920s. It was revived in 1935 but did not regain its earlier popularity. The words Mah Jongg signify a mythical bird which appears on one of the tiles.

NEWSPAPERS

The earliest regular newspapers of which we have record date back many centuries before the invention of printing to the *Acta Diurna* of the Roman Empire and the gazettes published in China during the first centuries of the Christian era.

The *Acta Diurna* or *Daily Acts* began regular and official publication on the orders of Julius Caesar in 59 B.C. The news was collected by reporters (*actuarii*) employed by the state who posted the *Acta* on a whitened board so that all could read or copy the reports of wars, speeches, legal decisions, political events, marriages, divorces, accidents and deaths.

Pioneers in printing, the Germans were also pioneers in printed newspapers. The first irregular news-sheets began to appear in Cologne, Nürnberg and other cities within 50 years of the invention of modern printing in 1450. By the end of the 17th Century a number of German towns were reading their own daily papers, thus establishing a tradition for local dailies which has been maintained to this day.

In 1562 Venice had a printed monthly newspaper which was sold for a *gazetta*, a small coin with a name which soon became another word for a newspaper. Among the first journals to use the name was the *Gazette de France* of 1631.

The first regular newspaper in the English language was produced in Holland in 1620 by the English Puritans who later sailed to America in the Mayflower. But more than 80 years were to pass before the first English daily, the *Daily Courant* appeared in 1702.

The first American newspaper, called *Public Occurrences*, was published in Boston on September 25, 1690, but was suppressed by the authorities before it could produce a second issue. The first regular American paper was the Boston *News-Letter* which appeared in April 1704 and ran for more than 70 years.

WHAT is a billabong?   WHAT is the America's Cup?

BILLABONG

A billabong is a small island created by a river, usually in a particularly marshy area. This happens when a river, meandering along its course, curves so much that it turns round completely, thus flowing into itself. The land encircled by the river is known as a billabong.

The name originates from the Billabong River in New South Wales, Australia. The river has its source in the foothills west of Canberra and flows into the Murray River.

The billabong immortalized in the song *Waltzing Matilda* has come to represent Australian independence and self-reliance, two qualities that have been evident since the earliest settlers.

Typical billabong country along the Murray River valley in Victoria, Australia.

AMERICA'S CUP

The America's Cup is a gold cup offered originally by the Royal Yacht Squadron in 1851 for a 53-mile race round the Isle of Wight, off the south coast of England. The winner was the United States schooner America.

In 1857 the syndicate that had built the America gave the cup (thereafter known as the America's Cup) to the New York Yacht Club, which then offered the cup to all challengers. Subsequent races have been sailed off the American coast.

The N.Y.Y.C. offer to all still stands, but the British, Canadian and Australian challengers have never succeeded in any of the 22 contests.

The races have exerted great influence on yachting progress, the large sums spent on America's Cup yachts having raised the science and art of design to a high level of refinement.

WHAT is a gargoyle?

GARGOYLE

A gargoyle is a quaintly formed head of an animal, man or devil, carved in stone. It was used by the stonemasons of the Middle Ages as a decorative spout for the rainwater from a roof.

The builders of Gothic churches, where gargoyles were chiefly used, allowed their imaginations to take full flight, unconcerned that their little sculptured masterpieces were to be placed so high that earthbound man could hardly see them.

Perhaps the best example of the use and variety of gargoyles is seen on the top of the cathedral of Notre Dame which was founded in 1163, and stands on the Ile de la Cité, an island on the River Seine, in Paris. Here hundreds of the grotesque and gaping figures reach out from balustrades and towers to spout water clear of the cathedral walls. Victor Hugo, the French author, wrote about the walls of the cathedral in his historical romance, *Notre Dame de Paris*, which was later made into the film, *The Hunchback of Notre Dame*.

Not all churchmen have approved of the gargoyle as a decorative embellishment. A French monk, St Bernard of Clairvaux (1090–1153), one of the most illustrious and eloquent preachers of the Middle Ages, condemned them. He said that people might prefer "to spend the whole day in admiring these things piece by piece rather than meditating on the Law Divine."

WHERE are the Elysian Fields? WHERE was the first book

ELYSIAN FIELDS

The Elysian Fields was a phrase used in Greek mythology to describe what we would call Heaven. Before European navigators sailed far beyond the Mediterranean and found other lands inhabited with people like themselves, people believed the world was flat. In early Greek mythology the souls of those who died went for refuge to the Infernal Regions. This the "afterworld" was said to lie at the extremity of the earth.

At that extremity were the Elysian Fields or the Isles of the Blest. It is thought by some that this land adorned with every beauty might well be the Canary Islands or the Azores in the Atlantic Ocean.

Later when the Greeks learned more of other lands, they changed the location of the Infernal Regions to the centre of the earth. There were two great regions in the Underworld. One was the Elysian Fields, where those who had led a just life in the world above ground joined the children and favourites of the gods of Olympus and where harsh weather was never known and soft breezes forever refreshed the beautiful land.

The other place was Tartarus, the awful region of the damned, who had committed crimes against the gods and were punished by tortures. One inmate was Tantalus, son of Zeus, the father of the gods. He had betrayed his father's secrets and was condemned to stand forever with water all around him and rich fruit just above his head. When he tried to eat and drink, both fruit and water drew away from him.

From this story we get the word "tantalize". Another prisoner was Ixion, father of the Centaurs, who was bound to a rolling, flaming wheel for the rest of time for attempting to win the love of Hera, sister and wife of Zeus.

FIRST PRINTED BOOK

The first known book to be printed from movable type was the Bible, probably in the year 1455. It was certainly on sale by the middle of the year 1456. The book was printed at Mainz in Germany. It is often called the Gutenberg Bible, from the name of the man who is generally supposed to have been the printer, although two other men called Fust and Schoeffer are also associated with the task.

Sometimes this Bible is called The Forty-two Line Bible, because it had forty-two lines to the page. Another name for it is the Mazarin Bible, because a copy was discovered in the Mazarin Library in Paris in the year 1760. A copy of the first volume, in fine condition and with the old binding still on it, was sold for £21,000 at an auction in London in 1947.

The first Bible to be printed in Ireland in 1716 made an error in the Gospel of St John, chapter 5, verse 14. The text should read "Sin no more", but the printer put "Sin on more". A much more costly mistake—for the printers—

printed? **WHERE** is the Bridge of Sighs?
WHERE is the quarter-deck of a ship?

BRIDGE OF SIGHS

The Bridge of Sighs (*Ponte dei Sospiri*) is in Venice and connects the east side of the Doge's Palace with the old state prisons, crossing the Rio di Palazzo. Its name symbolizes the sadness of the prisoners crossing the bridge. The Doge's Palace was begun early in the 14th Century and took several centuries to complete. The Bridge was not built until the 17th Century. It became the path by which prisoners crossed to the "*pozzi*", the prisons on the other side of the canal.

The Bridge of Sighs is one of nearly 400 bridges over some 150 canals which make up the thoroughfares of Venice, a city built on wooden piles driven into the mud of the lagoon. The city became known as the "Mistress of the Adriatic" from the custom carried out each year by the city's rulers, from the 12th to the 18th Century, of throwing a wedding ring into the Adriatic in token of their claim to dominion over that sea.

Lord Byron's famous reference to the Bridge of Sighs appears in his poem, *Childe Harold's Pilgrimage:*
"I stood in Venice, on the Bridge of Sighs;
"A palace and a prison on each hand".

was made in the reign of Charles I. Psalm 44 says: "The fool hath said in his heart, there is no God". But the printer made it read: "The fool hath said in his heart, there is a God". That little slip was punished with a fine of £3,000 and the destruction of all the copies—proving it pays to be careful!

In book-printing history the name of the Englishman William Caxton, called the Father of English Printing, will always be remembered. He set up his press in 1476 close to Westminster Abbey.

QUARTER-DECK

The quarter-deck, as its name implies, is only part of a deck. In a sailing vessel it is that portion of the upper deck between the mainmast and the stern or back of the ship. The upper deck is the highest complete deck having all openings fitted with permanent means for closure against sea and weather.

In naval vessels the quarter-deck is that most glamorous part of the ship, an area of the weather deck—the highest continuous deck exposed to the weather—reserved for the officers of the ship.

Ships' decks serve the same purpose as floors and roofs in a building. They provide living and working surfaces, add strength to the structure of a ship and form a cover to keep bad weather out. Decks may be given numbers or letters to distinguish them from each other, but those which serve a definite purpose have their own distinctive names.

In the British Navy officers are allowed to drink the loyal toast seated since in the old days the deck "ceilings" were so low.

A sea leopard from the Roman floor, Fishbourne, England.

MOSAICS

Mosaics are patterns or pictures produced with closely-set small pieces of stone, mineral, glass, tile or shell. In their earliest forms they were often used in a religious connection. The most primitive examples come from New Guinea —trophy skulls and masks covered with rows of small shells.

In ancient Greece mosaic floors were first made of pebbles. Later small cubes of stone and pieces of glass were introduced. Mosaic floors were discovered in the Roman ruins of Pompeii, destroyed in A.D. 79, and others have been found in all lands which formed part of the Roman Empire in which mosaic work was highly popular.

The next great stage was the development of Christian wall mosaics. A light but firm mortar was introduced and an increasing use was made of gold cubes and

eater?

St John the Evangelist from a mosaic in Venice.

LUCIFER

"Lucifer" is a slang name for a match, made usually of a splint of wood tipped with an inflammable substance which ignites when the match is struck on a prepared surface.

The word comes from Latin and means "light-bringing". It has been used in poetry as a name for the morning star, the planet Venus, when it appears in the sky before sunrise.

It is also found in the Bible, where the fall of the King of Babylon is described in these words:

"How art thou fallen from Heaven, O Lucifer, son of the morning."

Early members of the Christian Church interpreted the words of Jesus—"I saw Satan fall like lightning from heaven"—as a reference to this passage in Isaiah. So Lucifer came to be regarded as the name of Satan before his fall.

John Milton (1608–1674), in his poem *Paradise Lost*, gave the name Lucifer to the rebel arch-angel whose overweening pride made him seek to dethrone God Himself—a sin perpetuated in the phrase "As proud as Lucifer".

LOTUS-EATER

A lotus-eater is someone who is forgetful and careless about responsibility, living only for pleasure. The original lotus-eaters, or Lotophagi, were a people whom Odysseus and his men encountered in Homer's great epic poem, the Odyssey. They lived on a plant called lotus, which they offered to travellers. Those who ate of it forgot home, friends and responsibilities and wanted only to lie in the sun and eat lotus for ever.

The lotus in the poem is Zizyphus lotus, from South Europe. It has large fruits holding a mealy material which can be used for making bread or wine.

brilliantly coloured glass.

The Byzantines of the 11th and 12th Centuries brought the art of mosaic to its full flower. These mosaics are of unparalleled magnificence—a wholly successful attempt to show divinity in human form. Monumental figures are placed against a golden background and can be seen today in churches like that of Daphne, near Athens.

After the fall of the Byzantine empire the Venetians carried on the craft into Renaissance and modern times.

WHEN was the first steamboat built? WHEN was the first tie
WHEN was the first solo circumnavigation

STEAMBOAT

The first boat ever to be moved by steam power was designed by a Frenchman Jacques Périer and tested on the Seine in Paris in 1775. But the first really successful steamboat was built by Périer's fellow countryman, the Marquis Claude de Jouffroy d'Abbans. His craft which was 141 feet long and equipped with straight-paddled sidewheels travelled several hundred yards against the current on the Saône at Lyons on July 25, 1783.

Among early American pioneers was James Rumsey who in 1786 drove a boat at four miles an hour on the Potomac River, propelled by a jet of water pumped out at the stern. Between 1786 and 1790 John Fitch experimented in the Delaware River at Philadelphia with different methods of propulsion, including paddle wheels, a screw propeller and steam-driven oars.

The first to apply successfully the principle of steam to screw propellers was John Stevens whose boat, equipped with two propellers, crossed the Hudson River in 1804. However, his achievement was soon eclipsed by Robert Fulton's 150-foot long paddlewheeler Clermont which in

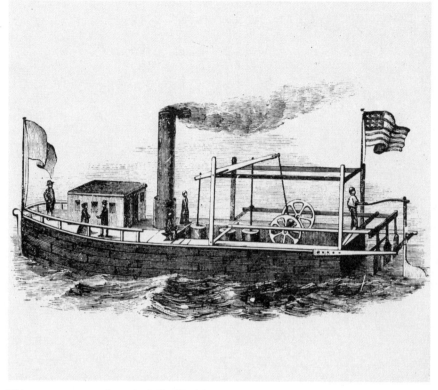

This strange steamboat is John Fitch's second boat.

1807 covered the 150 miles from New York to Albany in 30 hours at a maximum speed of five miles an hour. With Fulton in command on the Hudson, Stevens looked elsewhere, and in 1808 his new boat, the Phoenix, sailed out of New York harbour to become the first steamboat ever to go to sea.

Both Stevens and Fulton were following in the steps of the Scottish inventor William Symington who in 1802 constructed a steamboat in Scotland, the Charlotte Dundas, which was used as a tug on the Forth and Clyde Canal. The Charlotte Dundas was a paddle-wheel steamer. For many years all steamboats used this method of propulsion.

TIE

Today's neckties are the direct descendants of the neckcloths worn by the Croatian troops in the army of the French king Louis XIV (1638–1715). The French called the neckcloth by the same name they called the Croat: *Cravate*. In English it became the cravat, ancestor of the modern tie.

In the mid-1660s men of fashion began to adopt the cravat as a replacement for the large linen collars which were then customary. At first the chosen style consisted of linen strips tied at the throat in a bow with cravat-strings which

were sometimes coloured ribbons. Later the neckcloth was looped at the throat. By the turn of the century it had become wider with tasselled or lace-bordered ends.

Towards the middle of the 18th Century a twist of fashion decreed a stiff, folded neckband called the stock, which fastened at the back of the neck and became higher round the throat as the century progressed. Soon after 1800 the collar of the shirt began to appear above the stock and the neckband was worn almost to the ears.

As collars rose still higher, the

folded stocks gave place to ties. These were sometimes very large, but smaller bow ties with the stocks were quite common. The frilled shirt gave way fast to the plain shirt front visible above the waistcoat. About the year 1840 men about town resorted to turning their collars down.

A Oriental B Mathematical
C Osbaldeston D Napoleon
E American F Mail Coach
G Trone a amour H Irish I Ballroom
J Horse collar K Hunting
L Maharatta M Gordian Knot
N Barrel Knot

worn?

of the world? **WHEN** was the Peace Corps started?

CIRCUMNAVIGATION

The first single-handed voyage round the world was achieved by Joshua Slocum in his sloop Spray, between 1895 and 1898.

He wrote about his experiences in his book, *Sailing Alone Around the World*, published in 1900 Slocum was born in Canada in 1844 and died at sea sometime in 1910.

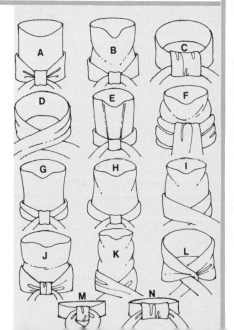

PEACE CORPS

The Peace Corps was established by President John F. Kennedy on March 1, 1961 and became a permanent United States government agency under The Department of State in the following September. Its aim, in the words of President Kennedy, was to create, "a pool of trained American men and women sent overseas by the United States government to help foreign countries meet their need power".

Volunteers for the Peace Corps must be United States citizens and at least 18 years old. An accepted volunteer is assigned to a project requested by a foreign country and prepares for his task by studying for three months at a United States college or university. During this time he learns the language, history, politics and customs of the country to which he is to be sent. When he goes overseas, he works directly with the inhabitants of the country, speaking their language, sharing their lives and receiving a living allowance comparable to that earned by the people among whom he is working.

The normal term of service is two years. In 1961 about 900 volunteers served in 16 different countries of Latin America, Asia and Africa and the number has risen steadily each year. Two years after its foundation the corps won the Ramon Magsaysay Award, the 10,000 dollar prize which is the Asian equivalent to the Nobel Peace Prize. This had never before been won by a non-Asian group.

WHERE did Rugby football begin? WHERE is the highest
WHERE is Constable country?

RUGBY

The highly organized rugby football games of today developed from the crowd game of ancient and medieval Britain in which a round or oval object—usually the inflated bladder of an animal—was kicked, punched or driven towards a goal. The origins of games between two teams, which attempt to kick, carry or otherwise force a ball through a goal or across a goal line defended by their opponents, are lost in antiquity.

When football was taken up by the great English public schools, all agreed that the ball must never be carried or passed by hand in the direction of the opponents' goal. It was a violation of this rule by William Webb Ellis at Rugby School in 1823 which led to the division of modern footballers into those who want to play only with their feet and those who wish to use both feet and hands.

At first, Ellis's behaviour was condemned even at Rugby. But the school soon decided to permit running with the ball by players who received it by a fair catch. Then it was permitted if the ball was caught on the bound. Later other restrictions on running with it were abolished.

Ellis became a great hero and a tablet on one of the boundary walls of Rugby School bears this inscription: "This stone commemorates the exploit of William Webb Ellis who with a fine disregard for the rules of football as played in his time took the ball in his arms and ran with it, thus originating the distinctive feature of the Rugby game. A.D. 1823".

It was some time before rugby football was accepted as a game in its own right, but on January 26, 1871 representatives of 17 clubs and three schools met at the Pall Mall restaurant, Regent Street, London. They formed the Rugby Football Union, drafted by-laws, appointed officers and instructed a committee of 13 to draw up the basis of the code in use at Rugby School.

HIGHEST RAILWAY

The highest railway in the world is in Peru. A branch siding of the track rises to 15,844 feet above sea-level. But the highest point on the main line is 15,688 feet in a tunnel called La Galera.

All the railway lines in Peru belonging to the Central Railway of Peru are of standard gauge (4 feet 8½ inches), like most railways in Europe and North America.

The highest railway station in the world is also in Peru, at La Galera. This station is at an altitude of 15,685 feet above sea-level. Henry Deiggs was the engineer for this extraordinary railway line, which was completed nearly a hundred years ago.

railway in the world?

WHERE does the blue in blue cheese come from?

Detail from "Dedham Vale" by John Constable

BLUE CHEESE

Blue cheeses are all made from cows' milk except for the famous French Roquefort cheese, which comes from ewes' milk.

The blue in blue cheeses is essentially blue mould. But it is extremely good for you. What happens is that an organism similar to penicillin is added to the milk or curd used to make ordinary white cheese. The mould, during three to six months of ripening, grows either in small, irregular, natural openings in the cheese or in machine-made perforations, depending on the type of cheese

The small amounts of mould reproduce or spread to give the typical blue streaks in the white cheese, and, once ripened, the distinctive flavour. Blue cheeses are usually heavily salted to add to the flavour.

CONSTABLE COUNTRY

The neighbourhood of Dedham, in Essex, and Flatford, in Suffolk, England, is often spoken of as "Constable country" because it provided so many subjects for the brush of John Constable (1776–1837), the English landscape painter.

This picture is "Dedham Vale".

It has been said that Constable was the first artist to discover that trees were green. What this really means is that, in the days when Constable began to paint, it was fashionable to represent trees and fields in pictures in a dull brown colour which was considered "harmonious" and also to re-design the landscape to make it more majestic or romantic.

Constable had no use for such notions. He depicted the beauty of the English scene, with its changing seasons, as he saw it. So it was a long time before he was recognized as a great painter. When he tried to reproduce the effect of shimmering light on trees the critics talked contemptuously of "Constable's snow". They thought his use of green vulgar and showy.

However, in 1824 three of his landscapes which he sent for exhibition at the Paris Salon were awarded a gold medal and had considerable influence.

WHY does a trumpet have valves? WHY is glue sticky?
WHY do tennis racquets have strings

TRUMPET VALVES

Valves in a trumpet enable the player to lower, momentarily, the pitch of the note he wishes to to make. What happens when one of the valves is pushed down is that the air is diverted through a small loop of tube thus lowering the pitch or sound of the instrument.

When the first valve is pressed, usually by the first finger, the pitch of the trumpet will be lowered by a whole tone. The second valve, according to the same principle, lowers the sound by a semitone, and the third lowers it by a minor third.

Nearly all trumpets and brass instruments today are made with valves. The mechanism was invented in 1815 by two Germans. Today most valves are of the piston type with springs to return the valves to their original position.

The history of trumpets dates back to 1500 B.C. in Egypt. But until the beginning of the 19th Century all the variations produced by valves had to be made by the player controlling his breath.

LASCAUX

The Lascaux caves in southwestern France contain some of the finest examples of prehistoric art. These are mural paintings dating back about 15,000 years and representing the very beginning of European culture.

The caves were discovered in 1940 in the Dordogne region. Their impressive frescos depict—in a startlingly modern style—ancient hunting expeditions, bulls, horses, deer and wild fowl. It has been suggested that the art had a definite function—that the animal pictures were believed to ensure the success in hunting necessary for the painters.

The limited amount of air in the caves and the humidity generated by the visitors caused the paintings to begin to deteriorate. So the caves have had to be closed to all except archaeologists, and tourists must be satisfied with expert reproductions in caves nearby, where great care has been taken to simulate the colours of the original paintings.

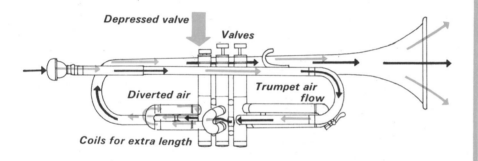

Depressed valve

Valves

Diverted air

Trumpet air flow

Coils for extra length

GLUE

The chemical and physical processes which cause glue to stick are still not completely understood. So the manufacture of adhesives tends to be based largely on experiment rather than on theory.

Usually it is easier to stick together two porous objects such as paper or wood. The glue will enter the tiny pores of the material, then dry and solidify to form a grip.

For metals, synthetic glues are required. It helps to roughen the surface slightly, since there are no natural openings for the adhesive. Synthetic glues were not developed until the 1930s but natural glues such as rubber or beeswax, have been used since prehistoric times. Discoveries in ancient tombs showed the early Egyptians used animal glues to make furniture and attach ornaments to wood surfaces.

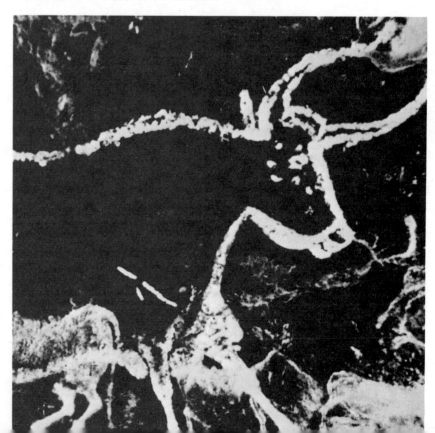

WHY is Lascaux famous?
WHY do some coins have a milled edge?

TENNIS RACQUETS

As long ago as the 11th Century games similar to tennis were being played with racquets. These racquets were already made with strings of plaited catgut to provide a light, strong and springy surface.

Solid racquets, presumably made entirely of wood, were used in ancient Egypt and Persia. But they must have been extremely unwieldy and probably damaged beyond repair after a few games.

Some early racquets were strung diagonally in diamond shapes. The present vertical and horizontal network was adopted because it gave greater resistance.

Several grades of gut are used in modern tennis, varying in thickness, resiliency and adaptability. The tension of the stringing can be adjusted. The lighter the strings the faster the ball leaves the racquet, but the more difficult it is to control. Looser stringing makes it easier to cut the ball.

COINS

The practice of minting coins with a milled or raised edge dates back to the 15th Century. It was introduced to protect the design on both faces of the coins, by leaving them slightly below the edge. Also, this made it easier to stack them.

Any peculiarity of a coin, such as a raised edge, makes forgery more difficult. Only the complicated machinery in the possession of the national mint can produce coins with accurately milled edges.

ROSE OF SHARON

You would find the most famous reference to the rose of Sharon in the Bible. It is chapter 2, verse 1 of the Song of Solomon, the 22nd book of the Old Testament—"I am the rose of Sharon, and the lily of the valleys".

The rose of Sharon is a low bushy plant which originated in the Mediterranean region but is naturalized in Britain and other north European countries. Known also by the name of Aaron's beard, it has evergreen leaves and yellow flowers, and is a member of the St John's wort family.

There are more than 300 species of this family which has a wide distribution in most temperate and tropical countries of the world. Forty species are to be found in the United States, where some are specially cultivated for their bright, showy flowers.

Ever since the plant was immortalised in the "Song of Solomon" it has become a synonym for grace and elegance. The flower is by no means spectacular but it has a shy and delicate quality.

UNCLE SAM

It is thought that the original Uncle Sam was an affable, pleasant man named Samuel Wilson (1766–1854), who lived in Troy, New York State, and supplied beef to the United States Army in the war with Britain in 1812. Wilson was known locally as "Uncle Sam" and, as government purchasers stamped U.S. on the barrels of meat being shipped, local workmen referred to it as "Uncle Sam's beef".

Tradition has it that the name was picked up by soldiers and soon came into familiar usage as a nickname for the United States. A resolution passed by the Congress of the United States in 1961 recognized Wilson as the namesake of the national symbol.

The symbolic Uncle Sam is a tall, thin, angular figure with long white hair and chin whiskers. He is usually dressed in a swallow-tailed coat, waistcoat, top hat and striped trousers. In American stories and tales he is associated with Yankee Doodle, the British-inspired nickname for American colonials during the American Revolution, and with Brother Jonathan, a country folk-hero who always beats his enemies by surprising displays of native intelligence and wit.

Uncle Sam live? WHERE are the world's earliest paintings?

These delicately drawn deer are on the wall of a cave in Lascaux, France. They have a startlingly "modern" look.

EARLIEST PAINTINGS

The earliest paintings of which we have records are on the walls of caves in France and Spain. They are paintings of animals, mostly of horses, bulls and bison.

Those in France are at a place called Lascaux, in the Dordogne area. They are painted in thick black outline. Some of the bodies are filled in with red or brown paint. On the edge of the roof of the cave is a frieze of horses and bulls. It looks as though the cave people were trying to decorate the roof of the cave to a pattern.

Other famous early paintings are at a place called Altamira, in the province of Santander, Spain. Here the walls of the cave are covered with standing and squatting bison, thickly outlined in black and filled in with red.

The people who did the paintings took a lot of trouble to mix the colours properly. The black they used came from soot, and the red and yellow from iron. They stored the colours in bones and skulls, and mixed them with water, then put the paint on the walls with their fingers or brushes.

Some of the paintings were not purely for decoration. At Lascaux there are drawings of oxen and goats about to fall into a pit. Probably the people thought that if they painted the animals they wanted to kill on their cave walls, they would catch them more easily.

The name given to the cave art of this period is palaeolithic art.

WHAT is Maundy money?   WHAT is the longest word in the   WHAT is an ingot?

Queen Elizabeth the Queen Mother distributes Maundy money at Westminster Abbey.

MAUNDY MONEY

Maundy money is the name given to the silver coins distributed to the poor by the sovereign of England on what is called Maundy Thursday—that is, the Thursday before Easter.

The name Maundy is derived from the Latin *mandatum* or commandment, the first word of an anthem sung on this day in Roman Catholic churches. At Mass the priest ceremonially washes the feet of 12 men in memory of the action Christ took in washing the feet of his disciples at the Last Supper.

The Maundy ceremony, the giving of Maundy money, usually held in London's Westminster Abbey, is the relic of the former practice whereby the monarchs of England used to wash the feet of the poor on this day.

If the sovereign is not in the country on Maundy Thursday, the ceremony is carried out by the High Almoner and his assistants. His office dates from the 12th Century and is always held by an important church dignitary. Maundy money is often known as the Royal Maundy.

LONGEST WORD

Webster's International Dictionary lists pneumononoultramicro-scopicsilicovolcanoconiosis. This consists of 47 letters and is the name of a lung disease usually contracted by miners. It is thought that Webster's included this word in their dictionary to satisfy those who wanted to know what was the longest word in the American version of the English language.

The longest word to appear in the Oxford English Dictionary is floccinaucinihilipilification, which has 29 letters. This word, which means "the action of estimating as worthless", was first used in 1741.

FOOL'S GOLD

Fool's Gold is iron pyrites, a compound of iron with sulphur. It is a gold-coloured or pale brassy-yellow mineral often found in coal seams. The colour fooled many miners and prospectors, who thought it was real gold—hence its nickname. The substance has a metallic appearance and is brittle.

The Greek word *pyr* means fire, and iron pyrites produces many sparks when struck against steel. It has a practical use as a source of sulphur in the manufacture of sulphuric acid.

INGOT

Ingots are blocks of cast metal from which other things are made. You have probably heard of cast iron. Casting is the process by which molten metal is passed into a specially made mould. It then hardens into the shape of the mould, like jelly or blancmange does.

Moulds can be for any shape, from enormous sections of railway trains or bridges to small pieces of sculpture. But if it is a plain block shape it is called an ingot mould.

Many different metals can be cast, iron being perhaps the most

English language? WHAT is fool's gold?

WHAT is a concerto? WHAT are pinking shears?

CONCERTO

A concerto is a musical composition for a solo instrument and an orchestra. It often has three separate movements with a small pause between each one, when the audience remains silent. The first movement is quick, the second slow and the last quick.

Often the orchestra begins a movement, the solo instrument joins in, weaving the theme of the music against the background of the other instruments. The solo instrument may have passages on its own, with the orchestra joining in from time to time and then coming together finally to finish the movement.

The concerto style originated in Italy in the 17th Century. Many of the world's most famous composers have written concertos, often with a particular soloist in mind, and designed to show off his special skill.

The piano has been the most popular solo instrument for concertos, but the harpsichord, viola and violin have often been featured. More recently concertos have also been composed for the horn, bassoon, trumpet, 'cello, double-bass, trombone, oboe, flute and the harp.

A concert by the Hungarian State Symphony Orchestra.

important. So can alloys, or metal mixtures, such as bronze which is a combination of copper and tin.

Most casting is done in moulds made of special hard-packed sand, which resists very high temperatures. But metal moulds may be used if their melting point is higher than that of the substance being cast. When a metal mould is used the process is called die-casting. Usually when we use the word ingot we think of gold ingots. This is because gold has for centuries been stored in the form of ingots.

PINKING SHEARS

Pinking shears are large scissors with serrated blades which, when cutting a material, leave a notched edge. This edge does not easily fray and, therefore, it is not necessary to hem or oversew it.

The word "pinking" is of Middle English origin and originally meant making holes in something, piercing, pricking or stabbing. Later it came to mean the action of decorating cloth or leather with holes, perforations or eyelets and, later still, ornamenting edges by cutting into jags, scallops or narrow points and, finally, the regular triangular notching we know today.

Every home dressmaker counts pinking shears among her most useful equipment. Shears should be from seven to eight inches long with a bent shank and one finger hole larger than the other. They should be kept only for cutting material, never paper.

WHY does the tower of Pisa lean? WHY is there a U-bend

TOWER OF PISA

The tower of Pisa is the bell tower of the cathedral of Pisa in Tuscany, Italy. It leans because, when the building was half completed, the soil under one half of the circular structure began to subside and the tower tipped.

Work on the tower was begun in 1173, but was discontinued for a century after the subsidence. However, in 1275 architects devised a plan to compensate for the tilt. Two storeys, the third and the fifth, were built out of line with the others and closer to the vertical in an effort to alter the tower's centre of gravity.

But the leaning has continued to increase gradually throughout the centuries. Pumping to keep water away from the surrounding ground and the injection of cement grout into the foundations and the surrounding subsoil have been tried in recent years, but without success.

The tower, which is one of the most unusual in existence, is Romanesque in style and made of white marble. It is cylindrical in shape and has eight storeys.

The tilt is about 17 feet, or more than five degrees from the perpendicular. The tower continues to increase its tilt by about a quarter of an inch each year.

U-BEND

U-bend pipes are installed under sinks and toilets to provide a water seal against the outside sewer pipes. The U-bend retains a permanent pool of clean water, protects the fixture and prevents any gases, vermin or bacteria from escaping out of the sewers.

The U-bend was invented in the middle of the 18th Century but, for economic reasons, was not widely used until more than 100 years later. Since its introduction the U-bend has been an important factor in preventing infectious illnesses and diseases in large cities.

below a sink or toilet?

WHY is the Ganges considered to be sacred?

GANGES

The River Ganges is considered sacred by more than 200 million people because of its part in the observance of the oldest organized religion existing in the world, the 3,500-year-old religion of Hinduism. For century after century hundreds of thousands of pilgrims have visited its shores every year to wash away their sins in the muddy waters. Brahmans and outcasts, kings and beggars, people of every caste and race of Hindu India have swarmed down stone steps to wade in "Mother Ganga" for spiritual purification and the good of their souls.

Devout Hindus hope to die on its shores and have their ashes strewn on the surface of the holy river. For those unable to make the pilgrimage quantities of the water are widely distributed and preserved to be drunk as the hour of death approaches.

The most sanctified spot of the sacred Ganges is the ancient city of Benares with its 1,500 temples, countless idols, and a four-mile curve of ghats, or steps, leading down to the river.

Apart from the pilgrims, many boats and steamers gather in the Ganges because it is also a great commercial highway. The vast plain which it crosses in a gentle gradient is a maze of life-giving irrigation projects, for more people live there than in any other river valley except the Yangtze in China.

The source of the Ganges is usually given as the Bhagirathi which gushes from an ice cave more than two miles above sea-level. It flows from west to east for 1,540 miles and drains an area of 430,000 square miles. Finally it pours its silt-laden waters into the Bay of Bengal. Here is the most extensive delta in the world, a fan-shaped formation which the Ganges shares with another river, the Brahmaputra, after the latter's southward sweep from Tibet.

WHERE was Valhalla? WHERE is the 'lost continent'?

VALHALLA

In ancient legends about the Norsemen, Valhalla was the place where all the brave warriors went when they died.

The kind of man they most admired was one who had great courage and a spirit of adventure. The warriors who went to Valhalla were supposed to lead a very happy life, eating boar's meat daily and amusing themselves by fighting each other. They were supposed to live in Valhalla till Doomsday, the end of the world. Then, led by Odin, father of the gods, they would march out of the 640 doors of the palace to fight against the giants.

LOST CONTINENT

The lost continent is a legendary island called Atlantis. It was discribed by Plato, a philosopher who lived in ancient Greece, as being in the Atlantic and also as being larger than Asia Minor and Libya put together! The Greek legends claimed that Atlantis had been inhabited by a powerful nation who had offended the gods by their independence and disrespect. The gods took their revenge. Some versions of the story say that it was submerged and others that it was destroyed by an earthquake about 9,000 B.C.

Some people have tried to identify Atlantis with America, some with Scandinavia, the Canaries and even the Palestine region. Many naturalists and philosophers, including Buffon, Montaigne and Voltaire, have theorized about Atlantis. Attempts have been made to prove that the Basques of Spain and France, the original inhabitants of Italy and the Indians of South America were descended from the Atlanteans, who were said to have overrun the entire Mediterranean.

One theory is that the Minoan civilisation was destroyed by the eruption of a volcano on Thera (Santorin) — or "lost Atlantis". Thera's cliffs are shown below.

WHERE is the Winter Palace?
WHERE was the first stamp used?

FIRST STAMP

The first postage "label" or stamp was used in England in May, 1840. Letters had been sent by post since the time of the Egyptians. The Greeks, Romans, Chinese and Arabs all used pigeon-post very effectively. They sent a duplicate letter by a different pigeon in case the first bird met a hawk on the way.

Before this first stamp—the Penny Black of 1840—many marks had been used in Britain to record time and place of receipt, and money paid or owed. Rowland Hill started a movement for Post Office reform. This was founded on pre-payment for letters and a standard charge of one penny, regardless of distance. The idea of a sticky stamp was suggested to Hill by Charles Knight. The design was taken from a medallion showing the head of Queen Victoria, designed by William Wyon.

These first stamps were printed in sheets of 240. Perforations had not been invented, and the first job of the day for post office clerks was to cut rows of stamps out of the sheets. They were backed with what was called "cement" and many people found that they were difficult to stick on their letters.

These Penny Black stamps were in use for 11 months. Of the 68 million printed, six million still survive. They are not rare but collectors like to have a good example of the first stamp issued.

The rarest stamp in the world was in fact issued 16 years later. This is the British Guiana one cent which was discovered in 1873 by a schoolboy who sold it for six shillings. In 1922 it fetched £7,343.

Collectors today make a point of looking for stamps that have been misprinted, since as these, being rarer, have a great deal more value. A common misprint is for the perforation to be omitted.

WINTER PALACE

The Winter Palace is in Leningrad in the Soviet Union. It was built between 1754 and 1761 by the Empress Elizabeth, daughter of Peter the Great. The architect of the palace was Rastrelli and the proportions of the building are so good that its huge size is not immediately apparent.

Leningrad, then called St Petersburg, was the capital of the Russian Empire from 1703 to 1917, when the capital was moved to Moscow. It is the second largest city in the Soviet Union and was built by Peter the Great, against his ministers' advice, on unsuitable terrain and with a terrifying death toll in building labourers. The site at the mouth of the River Neva was marshy. Its great advantage was that it was a vital link with Europe and Russia's only outlet to the Baltic.

The design of the city is magnificent. Its contacts with Europe brought its citizens more freedom of thought. The first blood of the Russian Revolution was shed outside the walls of the Winter Palace, a fact which gives it great symbolic importance to the Russian workers.

WHEN would a person be excommunicated?
WHEN were traffic lights invented?

Detail from Botticelli's Adoration of the Magi.

TWELFTH NIGHT

Twelfth Night is the night of the twelfth day after Christmas. It is one of the oldest festival days of the Christian Church, and was celebrated as long ago as the 3rd Century. Another name for the festival is Epiphany, or the Feast of the Three Kings. It commemorates the showing of the infant Jesus to the three Magi, or holy men, from the East.

According to tradition Twelfth Night is the day Christmas decorations are taken down.

WOOLWORTH'S

Woolworth's began in 1879 when Frank Winfield Woolworth (1852–1919) opened a "five cent" store in Utica, New York with the financial help of W. H. Moore, a former employer. That store was unsuccessful, but later in the year he opened a "five and ten cent" store in Lancaster, Pennsylvania, with a larger selection of goods to sell. His idea of selling a wide variety of merchandise at two fixed prices proves so popular that he was soon opening stores in other cities.

Similar stores were started by Woolworth's brother, C. S. Woolworth, his cousin, Seymour H. Knox, and his friends, F. M. Kirby and E. P. Charlton. All were merged in 1912 into the F. W. Woolworth company.

When Frank Woolworth died at Glen Cove, Long Island on April 8, 1919, his company owned more than 1,000 stores and his personal fortune amounted to many millions of dollars. The great Woolworth empire still operates and expands throughout the world, and the famous 60-storey Woolworth building in New York, designed by Cass Gilbert in 1931, is regarded as one of the most beautiful early skyscrapers.

EXCOMMUNICATION

Excommunication occurs when a person is punished by being officially excluded from a religious community and banned from entering into "communion" with the other members. The later epistles of St Paul show that this exclusion was carried out as a last resort against those who had "made a shipwreck of their faith", either by immorality or by denying what were regarded as the fundamentals of Christian teaching.

The Roman Catholic Church distinguishes between two types of excommunication, that which leaves a person *toleratus*, or tolerated, and that which makes him *vitandus*, or someone who must be avoided.

Both kinds bar the person from the sacraments of the Church, as well as from Church burial. There is a specific list of offences punishable by excommunication. They include heresy, schism, blasphemous treatment of the eucharist, personal violence against the Pope and membership of forbidden societies.

TRAFFIC LIGHTS

Fixed-time traffic lights were invented in the United States and introduced in New York in 1918. Eight years later the United States set up a Committee on Uniform Traffic Control. The purpose of traffic lights is to control the flow of traffic, determine the right of way at intersections and give greater safety to drivers. By linking successive traffic signals together a progressive movement through the streets can be provided.

Traffic lights were used for the first time in Britain at Wolverhampton, Staffordshire, in 1928. Sixty years earlier the London police had introduced a system of traffic control signals based on the swinging arms of the semaphore.

406

WHAT does sterling mean? WHAT is a cat's cradle? WHAT

STERLING

The word sterling refers to metals and coins of a standard value. It is also used, as in "pounds sterling", to distinguish British pounds from other currencies.

Sterling is said to be derived from the Easterlings, who were German coiners and were brought to England by King Henry II to improve the quality of the money. Another suggestion is that the word comes from the star with which some early Norman coins were stamped.

In 1300 King Edward I ordered that all silver worked by silversmiths should be of the same purity as the silver coins. This purity was called the sterling standard. It was introduced to prevent silversmiths from debasing silver with cheap metals. Sterling silver contains 92·5 per cent silver. The other 7·5 per cent is usually copper and is used for hardening.

When fixing this standard, Edward also instituted a system called hallmarking. This meant that every single piece of silver worked by the smiths had to be tested or assayed at the Goldsmiths' Hall. If the article passed the test, it was then stamped with a leopard's head. (A crown was later used for gold.) In 1544 the mark for English silver was changed to a walking lion, or lion passant. This is still used to stamp silver in London.

Modern hall-mark on silver showing Maker's Mark; Sterling Standard Mark (lion); Assay Office Mark (leopard's head for London); and Date Letter (1964).

CAT'S CRADLE

A cat's cradle is not a kitten's bed, but a game played with a piece of string or wool. You loop the wool behind the fingers of each hand, stretching it tight. Then, by moving your fingers in different positions, behind or in front of the wool, you can make the wool form different patterns in the space between your hands. You can make it look like a gate, or a trampoline or tramlines.

It is possible to manipulate the wool by yourself, but then you get only a few patterns. It is better to play cat's cradle with a friend, each trying to produce a new design.

ANEMOMETER

An anemometer is an instrument for measuring the speed of wind. It is very difficult to measure the strength of a small movement of air, so we do it by observing some physical effect caused by the motion. Among these effects are the drift of objects suspended in the moving air; the pressure built up by resisting the moving air; the cooling of heated objects in the air stream and speed changes in sound waves passing through the moving air.

Anemometers have been built which can measure each one of these effects, but the most common is the rotating cup type of instrument which measures the drift of objects in air. The instrument consists of three or four cups placed at the ends of arms like the spokes of a wheel round a rotating central shaft. The wind force is greater on the concave cup face than the convex cup back on the opposite side of the wheel, and it therefore rotates in the direction which allows the concave faces to retreat before the wind. A recording is kept by electrical means and by a magnetically operated pen on a chart attached to a drum.

is an anemometer? **WHAT** do we mean by a plebeian? **WHAT** is a bandolier?

PLEBIAN

When we describe someone as plebian we mean someone of low birth or rank and often someone who is undistinguished, commonplace, lacking in imagination or vulgar. The word comes from the Latin "plebeius" meaning a citizen who did not belong to one of the privileged patrician families.

A clear division between patricians and plebians first developed in the early 5th Century. The patricians were descended from the "patres", a body of advisors who surrounded the early kings of Rome. They gradually excluded plebians from many public offices, while continuous wars and the loss of trade worsened the conditions of the poorest plebians. Some of these became slaves or "followers" (clientes), men who gave service and obedience in exchange for protection. In the years of prosperity the plebians themselves developed a class structure, with their own wealthy élite, who became very influential. Leading families of plebs and patricians intermarried and a new nobility emerged drawn from a limited number of families who were as exclusive as the old patriciate had been.

Nevertheless, the word "plebian" still has a contemptuous ring about it, indicating that a man is plodding, without finer feelings or nobility, dull and uncultured.

Shakespeare's play *Coriolanus* exemplifies this attitude of contempt towards classical plebians. The over-proud Coriolanus refers scathingly to them as the "mutable rank-scented many" and, later, when he is banished from Rome, as "You common cry of curs! whose breath I hate as reek o' the rotten fens, whose loves I prize as the dead carcasses of unburied men that do corrupt my air." It seems not very surprising that he was unpopular.

BANDOLIER

Bandoliers are leather belts formerly worn by musketeers over their shoulders to hold their ammunition. They are provided with a number of cylindrical containers, each holding enough powder for one shot, a little flask for priming powder, and a bag for bullets. The word is derived from the French bandoulière.

This equipment first appeared in the 16th Century, and became popular throughout America and most of Europe. Musketeers, especially those in Mexico, often wore two bandoliers in the shape of a cross against their front and back as an extra protection.

WHERE was Expo '70? WHERE do you find pygmies?

EXPO 70

Expo 70 took place in Osaka, Japan. It was the first world fair to be held on the Asian continent and commemorated the 100th anniversary of the coming of modern Western civilization to Japan. Expo 70 attracted more visitors than any previous world fair. From March 15 to September 13 in 1970 it was visited by more than 64 million people.

Seventy-six nations plus the United Nations Organization took part. The United States built an extraordinary building, elliptical in shape, made out of plastic and supported by air. The Soviet Union built a pavilion to rise like a sharp-edged arrow on top of which shone a huge red star which could be seen for miles around.

The fair also had the 1,100-foot Expo Tower from which the visitors could enjoy a spectacular view of the Kita Settsu mountains to the north-west, and to the south-west a rather less beautiful sight— industrial Osaka.

Six of the buildings have been preserved since the close of the fair, including the splendid Japanese garden which covers over 60 acres.

PYGMIES

The best-known pygmies are a people known as the Bambuti, who live in the African republic of the Congo. They are nomadic hunters and eat wild plants. They seldom stay in any one place for longer than a month, during which time they live in simple huts made of sticks covered with phrynium leaves, in the shape of a beehive.

Pygmies, known as the Bush-men, live in the Kalahari Desert in Botswana, Southern Africa. There are also pygmies called Negrito in some islands of the Malay archipelago. No records have been discovered of pygmies in prehistoric times.

"Pygmy" is the word used to describe *groups* or *races* of people who are less than 59 inches tall. They are found only among primitive peoples. The word is used to describe a racial type. Thus a man from New York, for instance, is not a pygmy if he is only 46 inches tall.

410

WHEN were the first cigarettes made? WHEN did Mark Twain

CIGARETTES

The Spanish conquistadors of 1522 found the Aztec Indians of Mexico smoking a primitive cigarette in the form of tobacco stuffed into a hollow reed or cane tube. Other inhabitants of America at that time crushed shreds of tobacco and wrapped them in corn husks.

However, it was the cigar that the Spaniards brought to Spain as a luxury for the wealthy. The cigarette was improvised early in the 16th Century by the beggars of Seville, who picked up discarded cigar butts, shredded them, rolled them in scraps of paper and called them cigarillos.

It was not until the late 18th Century that they became respectable. The tobacco used for them was of a milder and lighter type, and the French gave them their present name of cigarette or little cigar.

A cigarette factory was set up in Havana in 1853, but the widespread use of the cigarette in the English-speaking world dates from the Crimean War (1854–1856) which introduced British soldiers to Turkish tobacco. Strangely, British taste switched later to straight Virginia tobacco. Americans prefer a blend which includes some of the Turkish variety.

In recent years a connection has been established between cigarette smoking and various diseases of the chest and lungs. There have been many attempts to dissuade the public from smoking and cigarette manufacturers have devoted a great deal of money and research in an attempt to pinpoint and eliminate the harmful elements in tobacco. Filter-tip cigarettes which accounted for only 1·4 per cent of production in 1952, have now risen to more than two-thirds of the total. Many countries have started extensive campaigns to warn of the risks to health.

MARK TWAIN

Mark Twain was the pen-name of the American writer Samuel Langhorne Clemens who was born on November 30, 1835 in the village of Florida, Missouri. He was first apprenticed to a printer and worked on newspapers in New York and Philadelphia. He became apprenticed as a steamboat pilot in 1856 and stayed with the boats until 1861 when he went to Nevada to seek a fortune in mining. In this he was unsuccessful, but he soon obtained a job as a newspaper reporter signing his articles Mark Twain. He took the name from a phrase meaning "two fathoms deep", which he had used to report river soundings during his steamboat career.

The rest of his working life was devoted to writing. He produced books about travel, such as *A Tramp Abroad* and *Roughing It*, but he is best remembered for *Tom Sawyer* (1876) and *The Adventures of Huckleberry Finn* (1884) which tell of the amusing and hair-raising adventures of young boys in the 1830s. The blend of romance, horror and humour in the books has made them favourites with children and adults ever since. Mark Twain was still writing his autobiography when he died on April 21, 1910.

live? **WHEN** was the first pope?

WHEN are people buried at sea?

THE POPE

Between the third and fourth centuries, the title of pope was bestowed on bishops other than the head of the Church and sometimes on ordinary priests. The word comes from Latin *papa* (from the Greek *pappas*) meaning father.

The title has been exclusively reserved since the 9th Century for the Bishop of Rome. From the earliest times the Bishop of Rome's claim to the supreme headship of the Roman Catholic Church has been acknowledged by all within the fold. Among his other titles are Holy Father, Vicar of Christ and Pontifex Maximus, meaning chief bridge-builder.

Roman Catholics believe that the Pope is elected as the direct successor of St Peter to be the visible head of the Church on earth. By virtue of his position, he is the Church's supreme governor, judge and teacher.

The coronation of Pope Paul VI.

BURIAL AT SEA

Although burials at sea are much less common than in the days of sailing ships, they still occur on occasions when people die during a voyage and the boat is still a long way from its destination. A service is held on board and the weighted coffin is lowered into the sea.

Sometimes a burial at sea is carried out in accordance with a dead person's wishes, or the ashes are scattered over the waves after a cremation.

In ancient times sea burial was often practised as a cheap method of disposing of dead slaves, foreigners and people considered of little importance. Today some islands, where land is scarce, reserve parts of the sea near the coast as cemeteries.

Viking chiefs before the 10th Century were cremated on burning ships to symbolize a voyage to the land of the dead.

WHY do we have Easter eggs?

WHY do golfers have

EASTER EGGS

Easter eggs provide one of the many popular traditions that have grown up around the great spring celebration in the Christian calendar of the resurrection of Christ. During the period of Lent preceding Easter eggs were forbidden as part of the fast in preparation for the festival. So it was natural for the end of Lent to be marked by the eating of eggs on Easter Sunday.

As traditional symbols of life and creation eggs suggested the resurrection. The decorations on the eggs can be regarded as symbolizing the end of the penitential season and the beginning of joyful celebration.

Sometimes eggs are blessed in church. Egg-rolling and egg-hunting are two self-descriptive Easter games. An expensive custom developed in Imperial Russia, where the nobility exchanged egg-shaped curios made of precious materials and decorated with jewels. These "eggs" are now extremely valuable.

Many of the folk customs and traditions now associated with Easter may be adaptations of practices connected with pagan spring ceremonies. So eggs coloured like the rays of the sun may have originally symbolized the return of spring.

GOLF CLUBS

Golfers' clubs can be divided into four basic classes: drivers; irons, spoons and putters. All four are shaped for different purposes and are used according to the ground the golfer is playing on and the shot he intends to make.

Wooden drivers are used for the first stroke from the tee. Spoons are designed chiefly to get a ball out of a rut. Various irons are selected for the approach to the green, where the putter is brought into play for the final shots.

Usually a good player's set will include seven to ten irons and three to four wood clubs. The different clubs are known by both number and name. Wood clubs are numbered one to five—the fifth sometimes replacing an iron—and irons from one to ten. No more than 14 clubs should be carried by a player during a round.

Details from above Compotier aux Poires and right Crouching Woman.

PICASSO

Pablo Ruiz Picasso was a Spanish painter, sculptor and engraver who lived from 1881 to 1973. He was a very independent artist and, with another painter called George Braque, founded a whole new movement in art which became known as Cubism.

At a very early age he showed exceptional talent. He went to the School of Fine Art in Barcelona and to the Academy of San Fernando in Madrid. Eventually, in 1905, he established himself in Paris.

Between 1899 and 1905 his first subjects were lively scenes of popular and bourgeois life—cabarets, racecourses, dance halls. Later he changed to depicting the victims of society—prostitutes, beggars, drunkards, the blind and the crippled.

He tried to get closer to what he felt was reality by approaching his subjects from several different angles. He extracted new meanings from them and employed the fullest possible range of expressive techniques.

Eventually he started a new way of pictorial representation based on a shifting viewpoint, a free approach to colour and the right to show what one knows instead of what the eye sees. This was the start of Cubism which was an alternative pictorial language to naturalism.

He went through many changes of style and awareness, and his contribution to the world of art has been immense and revolutionary. His paintings are highly valued throughout the world.

different clubs?

WHY was Picasso considered to be such a great painter?

THE LEVANT

The Levant is the name given to the eastern Mediterranean and the adjoining lands of Turkey, Syria, Lebanon and Israel. Levant means "east". The levanter wind is a strong easterly wind in the Mediterranean.

In English history the Levant was indirectly the cause of the Crown using customs and excise to raise revenue. The Levant Company was in 1581 given the monopoly of trading with Constantinople (now called Istanbul), the meeting place of traders from east and west.

This company claimed that it protected routes and ensured the safe passage of merchant ships. It therefore charged merchants duty on goods arriving in England. The Levant Company continued in being until 1825, but its power to levy duty was taken back by the Crown in the reign of James I. Customs and excise have been an onerous and unpopular method of raising revenue ever since.

SOCCER

Soccer is a corruption of the word "association". Since the rules of Association Football were laid down by the Football Association, formed in England in 1863, it can be said that soccer began in England.

Where football began, on the other hand, is a question impossible to answer. Various forms of a game involving the kicking about of a ball were played by the ancient Chinese, and by the Greeks and Romans. By the early Middle Ages several types of mass football, often with hundreds of people taking part, were very popular. Indeed, football's popularity led to its being banned for a long time in England as it interfered with the practice of archery which was considered necessary for the defence of the country.

The team game, which led to the formation of the Football Association, was born on the playing fields of English public schools.

Soccer is now one of the world's most popular and widely followed sports. It is particularly popular throughout Europe and Central and South America.

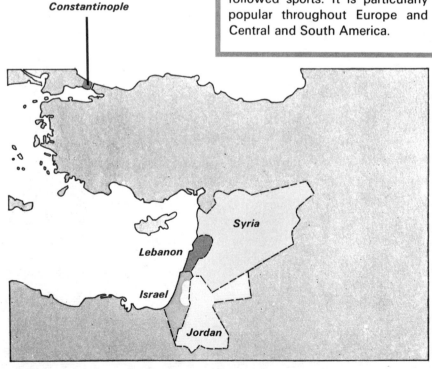

Constantinople

Syria

Lebanon

Israel

Jordan

THE HERMITAGE

The Hermitage Museum, one of the great art museums of the world, was founded in 1764 by Catherine the Great of Russia in Leningrad, then St Petersburg. Leningrad is second only to Moscow in the Soviet Union as a cultural and educational centre. It is the traditional home of Russian ballet, has 13 theatres, one of the largest libraries in the world, a university and many academies.

The city has 48 museums. Of these by far the most famous is the Hermitage, where the collection of art of all countries and

s the Hermitage?

periods, especially that of the French Impressionists and Post-Impressionist painters, is considered one of the finest in the world.

Over the years, acquisitions by the Tsars and the addition of a considerable volume of works gathered over the past half century have contributed to the collection, which now includes more than 2,500,000 works.

The Hermitage was a private, or court, museum for many years until it was opened to the public by Tsar Nicholas I (1825–1855). It is part of the Winter Palace.

This splendid hall has a map of the Soviet Union in semi-precious stones. Above: a magnificent portico.

PAPIER MACHE

The name papier mâché is French and means "chewed paper". Although the art of making articles of papier mâché, beautifully decorated and lacquered, had been known in the East for centuries, the process was first used in the West by the French early in the 18th Century.

Waste paper was torn and shredded, soaked in water and pressed into moulds, glue or paste being applied between each layer. Interest spread to other countries. Papier mâché was used in England as a cheap substitute for carved woodwork, and Frederick the Great established a papier mâché factory in Berlin in 1765.

In 1772, Henry Clay of Birmingham, England, invented a heat-resisting "paper-ware" that could be polished to a glossy surface. The body of his material was made by pasting sheets of specially prepared paper together until a desired thickness was obtained. It could then be pressure-moulded into a number of articles, especially panels for furniture or coaches.

The industry declined during the second half of the 19th Century, but the substance is still used in the manufacture of toys, masks and model scenic materials. Trays are also made from it.

A beautifully painted and laquered Indian jewel casket made of papier mâché in about 1660.

PHOENIX

The phoenix was, according to legend, a bird which died in a fire but came out of the flames alive. In ancient Egypt the phoenix was connected with the worship of the sun.

According to some stories, it was like a large eagle, with red and gold feathers. It lived for hundreds, or even thousands of years. But when its death was near it built a nest of the scented branches of trees, and spices. It then sang a beautiful, haunting and sad song, and fanned the nest until it burst into flames. The phoenix died in the fire it had made, but from the flames and ashes came a new phoenix, which would live for many years.

In other legends the phoenix was like an Egyptian heron called the bennu. It was also associated with the worship of the sun and is found carved on ancient Egyptian monuments as a symbol of the rising sun and life after death. Because the phoenix was regarded as immortal, it was adopted by the Christian Church as a symbol of the Resurrection of Jesus and of eternal life. It has also been used as a sign over chemists' shops from its association with alchemy and the search for immortality.

This brilliantly coloured phoenix is from an illuminated manuscript in the famous Bodleian Library at Oxford, England.

TENNESSEE VALLEY

The Tennessee Valley Authority (T.V.A.) was a United States government agency established in 1933 to control floods, improve navigation and produce electrical power along the Tennessee River and its tributaries. Its jurisdiction is generally limited to the drainage basin of the river which covers parts of seven states—Alabama, Georgia, Kentucky, Mississippi, North Carolina, Tennessee and Virginia.

America's fifth largest river, the Tennessee, was interrupted in its westward flow at Muscle Shoals, Alabama, where it dropped 100 feet in the course of 20 miles. Many schemes for generating hydroelectric power had been put forward, but it was not until 1933 that the decision was made. At that time the United States was experiencing a great depression and President Franklin Delano Roosevelt (1882–1945) strongly favoured development at Muscle Shoals which would stimulate the economy of the region.

The authority eventually operated 32 major dams and river traffic increased from 33 million ton miles in 1933 to more than 2,000 million in the 1960s. The T.V.A. power system possesses a huge generating capacity which is sold in bulk. Nitrate plants at Muscle Shoals have been developed into a vast laboratory for the development and production of experimental fertilizers, and studies of forest conditions have been carried out.

The T.V.A. also played an important part in increasing recreational opportunities in the valley. The "Great Lakes of the South" provide many such facilities.

are there so many skyscrapers in New York?

SKYSCRAPERS

There are so many skyscrapers in New York because these enormous buildings are able to accommodate hundreds of people on their many storeys while taking up only a relatively small amount of land — and New York is short of land.

The skyscrapers are found in the heart of New York City, the centre of its business, financial and entertainment activities, which are all packed into an area of 10 square miles on the lower half of Manhattan Island, between the Hudson and East Rivers. The lack of space makes the value of land tremendously high and therefore the building of tall structures has become a necessity.

Manhattan is shaped rather like a tongue and is made of solid

granite. The skyscrapers are grouped in two great clusters, the lower group standing at the southern tip of the island, looking down across Upper New York Bay towards the Atlantic and making up the famous New York skyline which greets visitors by ship to America. This group includes the Woolworth building (792 feet) and the Bank of Manhattan (900 feet).

The upper cluster of buildings is about halfway up the island, in what is known as the 'midtown' section. Here the enormous Empire State building rises to a height of 102 storeys (1,472 feet) and often has its peak wreathed in cloud. Nearby is the Chrysler building (1,046 feet).

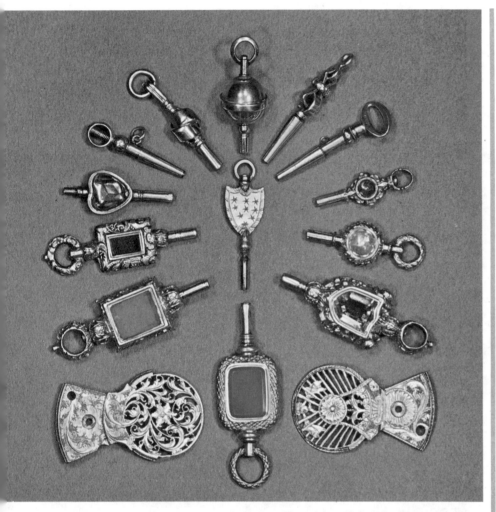

Some beautiful antique watch keys.

KEYS

The first known form of lock and key was used by the Assyrians in the Middle East about 4,000 years ago. This was revealed by the discovery of such a lock in the ruins of the palace of the Assyrian kings at Khorsabad, near the site of the city of Nineveh on the River Tigris in modern Iraq.

The lock was made of wood with the bolt held in a closed position by several loose wooden pins. The lock could be operated by inserting a long wooden key also fitted with pins, which would raise the loose pins enough to allow the bolt to be withdrawn.

This type of lock was apparently known to the Egyptians. It has also been found in Japan, the Faroe Islands and Norway. The long keys were carried on the shoulder, a fact which accounts for the verse in Isaiah 22–22: "And the key of the house of David will I lay upon his shoulder."

Another ancient type of lock known to the Chinese and the ancient Egyptians was the tumbler lock, improved versions of which are still in use today. This lock has small movable levers or "tumblers" and is opened with a key whose indentations will raise each tumbler exactly to the proper height.

Metal locks and keys were invented by the Romans. They designed a lock with a number of ridges or "wards" on the inside. These prevent the turning of the key unless the grooves on it coincide with the wards.

SHAKESPEARE

William Shakespeare (1564–1616), widely regarded as the world's greatest poet and playwright, is believed to have written his 34 plays between 1591 and 1614. His first play is thought to have been *Henry VI* and his last two were probably *The Tempest* and *Henry VIII*.

In 1594 Shakespeare was a member of the Lord Chamberlain's company of players which performed nearly all the time in London. When James I succeeded to the throne in 1603, he took the company under his patronage as the King's Men. They played at the Globe Theatre, Bankside, which was burned down in June 1613 during a performance of *Henry VIII*.

In 1611 Shakespeare left London and lived the life of a retired gentleman in his native Warwickshire town of Stratford-on-Avon.

his plays? WHEN was the first home refrigerator?

REFRIGERATOR

The first home refrigerator was made early in the 19th Century in the United States. It consisted of an insulated cabinet into the top of which a block of ice was lowered.

Modern refrigerators which first appeared in 1918 are automatic. They use one of two methods technically known as absorption and compression—to keep foods at temperatures near freezing point, 0° Centigrade (32° Fahrenheit). The period during which foods can be preserved at this temperature is limited to a few days, but in freezers, at temperatures of −18°C (0°F) and lower, they can be stored indefinitely.

The home refrigerator of today is a double-walled box with a hinged door, the space between the walls being filled with insulating material. The door is also double-walled and insulated. A rubber gasket on the inside of the door frame maintains a seal to stop warm air leaking into the box when the door is closed.

above *Anne Hathaway's cottage where Shakespeare lived in Stratford-on-Avon.* below *The Memorial Theatre at Stratford-on-Avon.*

WHERE would you hunt for the Abominable Snowman?

ABOMINABLE SNOWMAN

The Abominable Snowman or Yeti is a half-human, half-ape figure of legend among the Nepalese of the high Himalayas. Nepalese mothers use the tradition of the Yeti to scare their disobedient children. "The Yeti will get you if you don't watch out" is a popular warning.

No one can say whether the Yeti actually exists. The first apparent confirmation of its existence came with photographs of huge footprints in the snow taken by Eric Shipton, the mountaineer, in 1951. Few people claim to have seen the Yeti and some believe it to be invisible.

Skins which the Nepalese say have been taken from dead Yetis turn out to be those of the serow goat-antelope or of the rare Tibetan blue bear. Tracks in the snow said to be the Yeti's footprints have proved to be those of a snow leopard, a bear, a wolf or a fox, which have melted to form the larger, man-like tracks of the Yeti. Nevertheless, the legend lingers and it may yet be proved to have a basis in fact.

PLIMSOLL LINE

The Plimsoll Line is a mark on the side of a ship to denote its loading capacity. Until a century ago many ships were lost as a result of overloading. These accidents were not only due to greedy shipowners insisting on too quick a return on their investment. Often a ship would be heavily insured, then overloaded to make it lie dangerously low in the water. When the boat sank these speculators collected the insurance money.

Dismayed at this total disregard for human lives, a British member of Parliament, Samuel Plimsoll (1824-1898), agitated for a law to control this abuse. As a result of Plimsoll's efforts, the British Merchant Shipping Act was passed in 1876.

This Act laid down that every ship must have a safety line painted on its side. As long as the line is visible above water, a ship is safely loaded.

The deadweight tonnage of a boat is related to its carrying capacity. This deadweight capacity is marked by the Plimsoll Line, so the weight of the cargo and everything a ship must carry for a voyage is taken into account.

Load line marks according to Lloyd's register. These show the depths to which a ship can be legally loaded in different zones and seasons.

LR	*Lloyd's register*	**T**	*Tropical*
TF	*Tropical fresh*	**S**	*Summer*
F	*Fresh*	**W**	*Winter*
		WNA	*Weather in the North Atlantic*

The draught marks on the bow and stern show the distance in feet from the ship's keel to the water line. The ship's draught is read as the average between stern and bow draughts.

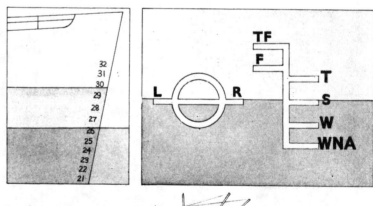

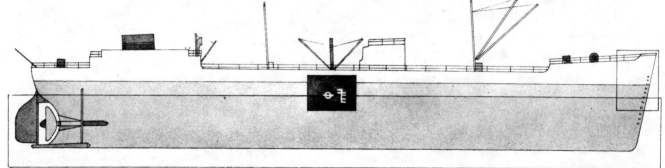

WHERE is the Plimsoll Line? WHERE do raisins come from?

RAISINS

Special varieties of grapes are dried, and are then called "raisins", the French word for grapes. Until the 20th Century they were produced mainly in the Mediterranean regions. Now huge quantities come from California and Australia.

Naturally produced raisins are spread out on trays and dried in the sun to a greyish brown colour. They have a tough skin and sometimes keep the bloom—the bluish powdery coating—found on grapes. But most of the raisins grown commercially are dried quickly in heated sheds and treated with sulphur to preseve them. These are usually small and dry and are used in cakes and puddings.

One type of raisin which is particularly good to eat is called Muscat. These raisins are grown near Malaga in Spain, and are dried in bunches, partly while still on the vine. These are called muscatels.

WHAT are tarot cards?

TAROT CARDS

Tarot cards are the oldest form of playing cards in Europe. They were made in Italy in the late 14th Century.

The name comes from *tarocchi*, a game played with a 78-card pack in which there are four suits. The emblems of these suits symbolized the four "estates" into which society was divided—the church (represented by a chalice), the nobility (by a sword), the merchants (by money) and the peasants (by clubs). Each suit contains 14 cards, the additional card being the valet.

As well as the four suits, there are 21 numbered trump cards and the joker card (il Pazzo), The first five cards are the magician, the high priestess, the empress, the emperor and the pope. These are called the *grands atouts* (big trumps). The last five cards, the star, the moon, the sun, judgment and the world, are the *petits atouts* (little trumps). The remainder of

the *atouts* consists of the lovers, the chariot, justice, the hermit, the wheel of fortune, the hanged man, death, temperance, the devil and the tower.

From this list you can see how tarot cards came to be used not just for a game but also as a way of telling fortunes. In fortune-telling the position of a card is all-important. A death card upright means a need for change, the beginning of a new phase. If the card is reversed, it means that the subject cannot make any change. He has reached an impasse in his affairs. The devil upright means an urge to give way to temptations. Reversed, the card means a repressed character.

A 56-card pack evolved from the tarot pack. Then came the English and French 52-card pack, the Spanish 48-card pack and the German 32-card pack. The tarot symbols are still used in these shortened packs.

SOLO FLIGHT

The first solo flight across the Atlantic was made on May 20–21, 1927, by an American, Charles Lindbergh. He flew from New York to Paris in an aircraft called Spirit of St Louis after the city where the machine was made.

The flight, which took $33\frac{1}{2}$ hours, gained Lindbergh worldwide fame and a prize of 25,000 dollars offered by a man called Raymond Orteig to fly non-stop from New York to Paris. He later made an air tour of the United States, visiting every state and 78 cities.

REAL ROADS

The earliest artificial roads, as distinct from the natural routes, trails and paths of primitive man, were probably built by the city kingdoms of the Tigris-Euphrates Valley in the Middle East where the first wheeled vehicles may have rolled about 5,000 years ago.

Among the first road engineers mentioned in history were those who accompanied the army of the Assyrian empire-builder Tiglath Pileser I about 1100 B.C. and constructed a route to enable the conqueror to pursue his enemies through the mountains to the north of Mesopotamia. The Assyrians set an example to succeeding empires by establishing an elaborate system of roads for the transport of troops and the dispatch of instructions from the central government to local governors.

Before the coming of the Romans, the biggest and best organized road systems were those belonging to the Persians who founded their empire about 500 B.C., and the rulers of northern India whose dominions around 300 B.C. were already served by a well-equipped highway more than 2,500 miles long. A source of great pride to the Persian Empire, which at one time covered the territory now occupied by Iran, Syria, Iraq, Turkey and northern Egypt, was the so-called Royal Road. This stretched some 1,600 miles from Susa, the capital, to the Aegean Sea, and was provided with staging posts which enabled relays of horses to cover the distance in nine to ten days.

Comparatively few of the roads of antiquity were properly surfaced or metalled until the great Roman engineers began to set a standard for reliability, directness, ingenuity and strength which has not been equalled until recent times. The construction of the Appian Way in 312 B.C. from Rome to the important salt deposits of Capua was the start of a network which provided the empire with vital arteries and gave Europe its principal roads for more than 1,000 years. On the main routes the Romans provided fresh horses at regular intervals to carry imperial messages to and from the capital at speeds of up to 150 miles a day.

Before the Spanish conquests in South America, the great Inca empire, which stretched from Ecuador into modern Chile, was sustained by a 3,200-mile road spanning deep gorges and climbing rocky heights to cross one of the world's most mountainous regions. In North America the first big man-made highway was built in Maryland by a British army on its way to fight the French.

In Europe centuries of neglect were ended with a revival led by two Scottish engineers, John Loudon McAdam (1756–1836) and Thomas Telford (1757–1834). But the world knew nothing to rival the old Roman network until the coming of the automobile produced the 20th Century revolution in overland communications.

Charles Lindbergh sets off from New York

were the first real roads made? **WHEN** is an overture played? **WHEN** is a ruby wedding celebration?

'n the "Spirit of St. Louis" on May 20, 1927. Next stop—Europe.

OVERTURE

An overture was originally a piece of music played as an introduction to an opera and suggesting some of the themes that were to follow.

The earliest operas usually opened with a trumpet fanfare or a sung prologue, as in the work of the French composer Luly. This form of the French overture was widely copied by German composers.

A more modern style was established by the German composer Glück who declared that an overture should "prepare the audience for the plot of the play". He meant that the overture should not be brought to a close with the rising of the curtain, but should be merged into the mood of the opening act. Glück's example was followed by Mozart in, for example, his overture to Don Giovanni, and by Beethoven in his overture to Leonore.

Towards the end of the 19th Century the opera overture was frequently replaced by a shorter introductory prelude, notably in Wagner's Lohengrin. This was an entirely new concept which was carried a stage further in Benjamin Britten's overture to Peter Grimes, which consists of only 10 bars.

In the 19th Century the concert overture became established as an independent work, as in the case of Mendelssohn's Hebrides Overture. Some overtures took on the character of symphonic poems. They are now often heard as part of a concert and not merely as introductions to operas or plays.

RUBY WEDDING

A ruby wedding is celebrated after 40 years of married life. Here are some of the other anniversary celebrations used to mark the passing years of matrimony:

One year, cotton; two years, paper; three, leather; four, silk; five, wood; six, iron; seven, wool; eight, bronze; nine, pottery; 10, tin; 12, linen; 15, crystal; 20, china; 25, silver; 30, pearl or ivory; 35, coral; 40, ruby; 45, sapphire; 50, golden; 55, emerald; 60, diamond; 75, more diamonds.

428

WHERE was Robinson Crusoe's Island? WHERE would you

CRUSOE'S ISLAND

Daniel Defoe's famous story of *Robinson Crusoe* (first published in 1719) is based on a real island—Juan Fernández. This island lies off the coast of Chile in South America and is now owned by that country. It was the scene of the true adventures of a Scottish sailor, Alexander Selkirk, who lived from 1676 to 1721.

Selkirk was born at Largo in Fife, became a sailor and, when he was young, took part in privateering expeditions to the South Seas, as the Pacific was then called. In 1704, he was the mate of the English vessel Cinque Ports. But he quarrelled with the captain and was left, at his own request, on the uninhabited island of Juan Fernández.

Before the ship departed, Selkirk begged to be taken on board again, but his request was refused and it was not until four years and four months had passed that he was rescued by the British ship Duke in January 1709. When abandoned Selkirk was left with clothes and bedding, firelock, gunpowder, bullets, tobacco, a hatchet, a Bible, mathematical instruments and books.

His powder soon gave out, but he learned to capture the goats on the island by running them down. He built himself a shelter and made clothes from the goats' skins. Fortunately, Juan Fernández never has very severe weather—only a little frost and hail in June and July (winter in the Southern Hemisphere). It is hot in the summer, but never unbearably so.

Selkirk found his island infested with rats, but kept down their numbers round his shelter by taming the stray cats whose ancestors had been left on the island by visiting ships.

He kept healthy and sane by working hard and by making companions of animals. But when he was rescued, he could scarcely make himself understood by the crew of the Duke, and he had lost all taste for civilized food and drink. He returned to England in 1711 and followed the life of the sea until his death.

CATACOMBS

The most famous catacombs in the world are to be found in Rome. The word catacomb is of unknown origin, and describes subterranean cemeteries composed of galleries or passages with side recesses for tombs. It seems to have been applied first to the catacombs of St Sebastian, on the Appian Way near Rome, which became famous as the supposed temporary resting place of the bodies of Saints Peter and Paul in the last half of the 3rd Century.

Catacombs are by no means confined to Rome. The custom of burying the dead in underground rock chambers goes far back into antiquity, and catacombs are found all over the Mediterranean world.

Most of the Christian catacombs—about 40 of which are known—belong to the 3rd Century and the early part of the 4th. Ruined by the Goths in the 6th Century and later by the Lombards, they were abandoned and their very existence forgotten until they were rediscovered by chance in 1578.

All the catacombs follow roughly the same pattern. Beginning as small private burial areas they finally became vast labyrinths of narrow galleries, usually three to four feet wide, lighted and ventilated by shafts spaced at wide intervals. The galleries led to small rooms called "cubicula" and the bodies lay in grave niches, cut in the wall or floor and sealed by slabs of marble or huge tiles.

The catacombs were used in times of persecution as hiding places, but there seems to be no truth in the widespread belief that early Christians used the catacombs as secret meeting places for worship.

Catacomb paintings provide the chief knowledge about primitive Christian art. They are also rich in early Christian inscriptions.

NUMBERS

The earliest written numbers we know of were used in Egypt and Mesopotamia about 5,000 years ago. At first men reckoned by chipping notches on wood or stone to record the passing of the days. Later the Egyptians wrote on papyrus made from reeds, and the Mesopotamians wrote on soft clay. They used simple strokes for ones, but marks for tens and up.

Three thousand years later the Romans still made strokes for one to four, but they used new signs in the form of letters for tens, fifties and so on. About the same time, the Chinese used a different sign for every number up to ten, but still used strokes for the first three numbers.

The Mayas in Central America invented the most remarkable system. They used only three signs—a dot, a stroke and an oval. With these they could write down any number, however large.

POLICE

Every society, with very few exceptions, has some form of police force. The chief function of the police is to protect society and the individual from the criminal and the criminally insane. Their duty is to ensure the maintenance of public order and the protection of the citizen and his property.

Unfortunately many police forces have existed, throughout history, which have exceeded their basic duties of protection and have persecuted people and organizations on political or racial grounds. A notable example was the Gestapo of Hitler's Germany.

The first recognizably modern police force was established in Britain in 1829 by Sir Robert Peel, whose policemen were given the nickname of Peelers or Bobbies.

WHY do people kiss under the mistletoe?
WHY are monks tonsured?

CHRISTMAS HOLLY

The custom of having holly in the house at Christmas probably comes from the old Germanic races of Europe who used to hang evergreen plants indoors during the winter as a refuge for the spirits of the forest.

Also, holly was considered to be a symbol of survival by the pre-Christian Romans and was much used as a decoration during their Saturnalia festival which was held at the end of December.

The Germanic Yuletide celebrations took place at the same time of the year. So when people began to celebrate Christmas the feast of the Nativity of Christ, many of the older customs were preserved.

Popular superstitions about holly still survive. Some people consider it extremely unlucky to bring holly into the house before Christmas Eve. Another idea depended on the belief that prickly and non-prickly kinds of holly were respectively male and female. So the kind of holly used for decoration decided whether husband or wife would be master of the household over Christmas.

MISTLETOE

From the earliest times mistletoe was regarded as a bestower of life and fertility. The common mistletoe is one of the most "magical" plants of European folklore.

The mistletoe of the sacred oak was especially venerated by the ancient Celtic Druids. The Druid rite of plucking the mistletoe, described by Julius Caesar, adds an aura of mystery to the magical folklore surrounding the plant.

Decorating the house with mistletoe may be a survival of the old Druid oak cult. The custom is also associated with certain primitive marriage rites.

MONKS' TONSURES

Tonsure is the name given to the rite of shaving the crown of the head of a cleric entering certain religious orders. It is particularly associated with monks and is a sign of dedication to religious observance.

In the Eastern Orthodox Church tonsure was practised as early as the 4th Century. Prayers of the 9th Century which accompanied such ceremonies show clearly that tonsure was regarded as an outward manifestation of the casting off of earthly values and vanities to dedicate oneself to the service of God.

There are three kinds of tonsure: the Roman type consists in shaving the whole head, leaving only a fringe of hair supposed to symbolize the crown of thorns. The Eastern or Greek style used to involve shaving the entire head, but is now held to have been observed if the hair is closely shorn. The Celtic tonsure means shaving in front of a line stretching over the top of the head from ear to ear.

Long before Christianity there was a religious practice among the Romans and Semites of cutting some of the hair and offering it to a deity as a sign of dedication.

WHEN was the source of the Nile discovered?

WHEN is Thanksgiving Day?

Detail from a portrait of Speke.

NILE SOURCE

The source of the Nile was finally discovered in 1862 by John Hanning Speke when he reached the Ripon Falls at the northern tip of Lake Victoria in Uganda.

Explorers had searched for the spot for centuries. As far back as the 2nd Century the Greek geographer Ptolemy learned enough from travellers' tales to trace a map of the Nile which was later found to be fairly accurate. It was believed that the waters of the Nile came from high snow-covered mountains in central Africa called the Mountains of the Moon.

Modern exploration of the upper part of the Nile began about 1837 when Mohammed Ali, the Turkish ruler of Egypt, ordered a search to be made for the river's source. Three Turkish-led expeditions were made and two of them got to within about 400 miles of their objective.

The Nile runs over 4,100 miles from its source to the Mediterranean.

THANKSGIVING DAY

Thanksgiving Day is an annual national holiday which takes place in the United States and Canada on the last Thursday in November in celebration of the harvest and other blessings during the year.

The first Thanksgiving Day was observed when the Pilgrim Fathers held a three-day festival after the harvest of 1621. But the day was not celebrated as a regular national holiday until more than two centuries later. Gradually each state adopted the idea until, in 1863,

WHEN were the Lyrical Ballads published?

Detail from "The First Thanksgiving", a painting in the Pilgrim Hall Museum.

President Lincoln proclaimed a national harvest festival on November 26.

The festival is still basically a home celebration, with religious overtones, for families and friends. Turkey is the traditional meat at the feast, and such autumnal dishes as pumkin pie and plum pudding stress the harvest theme.

LYRICAL BALLADS

The Lyrical Ballads—one of the most celebrated book of poems ever published in English—were published anonymously in 1798. The ballads were written by William Wordsworth and his friend Samuel Taylor Coleridge and were mainly composed when the two friends lived in Somerset on the slopes of the Quantock Hills. Although very different both in their poetry and in their life styles—Coleridge took drugs and Wordsworth believed in plain living and high thinking—

they shared a common belief that poetry should be simple in form and words and be close to nature. Both sought to break free from the formalities of poetic expression regarded as "tasteful" at that time.

Coleridge's chief contribution to the Ballads was The Ancient Mariner. Wordsworth's preface to the book expounded his new principles of poetry. Although the book created little interest when it first appeared, it is now recognised as a turning point in English poetry.

WHAT is a Dutch barn? WHAT is the marathon? WHAT does

DUTCH BARN

A Dutch barn is a roof supported on pillars with no walls. It is used for hay or straw storage only, since animals or grain need better protection. The name comes from the shape of the roof, which is similar to that of Dutch houses.

The word barn covers a large number of different structures, fulfilling several different functions—storing grain, fodder, machinery and animals. Older barns also combined a threshing floor where the ears of grain were beaten out by flails.

Barns are built big, with as few internal pillars as possible, so that full use can be made of the space, and carts, trailers and machinery can pass in and out. Often they have lofts where hay is stored.

Runners shortly after the start of the fourth International Marathon race held in 1970 in the German Democratic Republic.

MARATHON

The marathon is a modern road race first staged at the revival of the Olympic Games at Athens, Greece, in 1896. It was founded in honour of the Greek soldier Pheidippides, who is supposed to have run from Marathon to Athens, a distance of 22 miles and 1,470 yards, in 490 B.C. to bring the news of his countrymen's victory over the Persians. Appropriately, the first winner of the marathon race was a Greek, Spyros Louis.

In 1924 the Olympic marathon distance was standardized at 26 miles, 385 yards. But other marathon courses may differ in length, so the International Amateur Athletic Federation does not list a world record time for the event.

It is a fascinating race because neither age nor training seems to play a vital part in winning it. The South African Comrades' Marathon (54 miles and 1,100 yards) was won in 1922 by Arthur Newton at the age of 39. The Boston Athletic Association Marathon was won by a 19-year-old Japanese in 1951.

Long-distance training would seem to be essential for the race.

But in the 1952 Olympic Games, Emil Zatopek of Czechoslovakia, set an Olympic record of 2 hours, 23 minutes, 3·2 seconds, although he had never run the distance before.

Zatopek's record was broken in 1960 by the Ethiopian, Abebe Bikila, who covered the distance, barefooted, in 2 hours, 15 minutes, 16·2 seconds. In the next Olympic Games, four years later, running with shoes that time, he again broke the world record, with a time of 2 hours, 12 minutes, 11·2 seconds.

clinker-built" mean? WHAT is the "Royal" game of tennis?

CLINKER-BUILT

"Clinker-built" or "clincher-built" is a term used about boats which have hulls formed of overlapping planks fastened with clinched copper nails. Clinched nails are nails which are fixed securely, especially by beating back or flattening the ends when they have been driven through.

By the late 8th Century the Scandinavians had developed the well-known Viking "long ship". This was a clinker-built vessel with a high bow and stern. The strength of its construction can be imagined when the extent of Scandinavian travel at that time is considered. For many years this sort of craft dominated the seas.

Of course, smaller boats were built as well, roughly to the design of the larger ones. After the invasion of England by William the Conqueror in 1066, war galleys were adapted for trade and longer trading voyages led to the exchange of ideas between northern and southern ship designers.

The "Grace Dieu", built by Henry V of England at Southampton in 1418 was clinker-built and was more than 125 feet long. Many of the larger vessels of the 14th and 15th Centuries were of two-layer clinker work.

ROYAL TENNIS

Royal, or real, tennis is the distant ancestor of lawn tennis, the game which is now played all over the world.

The old game of Royal tennis was popular with the kings of both England and France in the 16th and 17th Centuries. It is mentioned in Shakespeare's play *Henry V*, when the French Dauphin sent a contemptuous gift of tennis balls to the English king. A famous tennis court at Hampton Court Palace, near London was built for Henry VIII in 1530. But the earliest known rules date from 1599, and those used today were drawn up in 1878.

The game, which can be even more strenuous than lawn tennis, is played by two or four players, with a ball made of tightly-bound cloth strips and rackets made of ash wood, about 27 inches long and weighing 15–17 ounces. The enclosed walled court is usually 96 feet long and 30 feet wide, with galleries and openings which form the scoring points. Scoring is generally similar to lawn tennis, but usually the best of 11 games is played.

WHERE did baseball begin? WHERE is the Sistine Chapel?

BASEBALL

Abner Doubleday, later a general in the United States Army, was supposed to have laid out the first baseball field in Cooperstown, a village in Otsego County, New York State, in the summer of 1839 and there conducted the first game of baseball ever played. So strong was the belief in this story that in 1920 the playing field was established as a permanent memorial with the title Doubleday Field.

Doubts were later cast upon the story, and attempts made to prove that the game had evolved from the English children's game known as rounders. The name "baseball" to describe some popular English game was traced back to Jane Austen, who in *Northanger Abbey* (written about 1798) remarks of her heroine: "It was not very wonderful that Catherine, who had by nature nothing heroic about her, should prefer cricket, baseball, riding on horseback and running around the country at the age of 14, to books."

Then, in their attempt to tie up baseball with rounders, researchers came across *The Boy's Own Book,* published in London in 1828, and so popular that it ran into many editions. The book was about boys' sports and listed all the rules. The second edition includes a chapter entitled "Rounders" with a note that the game was called "feeder" in London and "baseball" in the southern counties.

As the game is described in *The Boy's Own Book* it bears a strong family likeness to modern American baseball. It was played on a diamond with a base at each corner, the goal or fourth base being the same as the plate beside which the batter stood. A batter might run whenever he hit the ball across or over the diamond. If he struck at it and missed it three times, he was out.

Many English immigrants to America in colonial times were from the southern counties, and it seems probable that they took both the name and game with them.

WHERE is the Cresta Run?

SISTINE CHAPEL

The Sistine Chapel is in the Vatican, the centre of the Vatican City (*State della Citta del Vaticano*), which is the official residence of the Pope and the spiritual centre of the Roman Catholic Church. Situated in the heart of Rome, Vatican City covers 109 acres. It was granted absolute independence in 1929 by the Lateran Treaty signed by Pietro, Cardinal Gasparri and Benito Mussolini, then dictator of Italy.

The Sistine Chapel stands on the site of a chapel built by Pope Nicholas III. It was built by Giovanni dei Dolci, under commission from Pope Sixtus IV (1414–1484), who was a great patron of architects, painters, sculptors and scholars, and a great builder and restorer of churches. The frescoes in the Chapel were painted by Perugino, Pinturicchio, Ghirlandaio, Botticelli and Signorelli.

Under Pope Julius II, Michelangelo was commissioned to paint the ceiling of the Sistine Chapel. This magnificent work tells the story of Genesis from the Creation to the time of Noah, and took from May 1508 until August 1511 to complete. This ceiling is one of the world's masterpieces.

The Sistine Chapel is open to the public in the mornings, except on Sundays and Feast Days.

CRESTA RUN

The Cresta Run was built at St Moritz, Switzerland, in 1884 for the sport of toboganning—or sliding down snow-covered slopes and artificial ice-covered chutes on a sled with two runners. The sport dates from prehistoric times and was extremely popular in America and Europe from the late 1800s until the early 1930s, when widespread enthusiasm for skiing caused its decline.

The sport reaches its most advanced form on the 1,320-yard-long Cresta Run. Here the rider lies flat on the skeleton toboggan or "Cresta"—steel runners fastened to a light frame—and hurtles down the three-quarters of a mile of solid ice, full of steeply banked curves with expressive names such as "the horseshoe" and "the shuttlecock". The maximum speed is about 85 m.p.h. and it is a dangerous and difficult though exhilarating art to ride the magnificent Cresta Run.

Annual grand national championships have been contested on the Run since 1885. The sport, which is administered by the St Moritz Tobogganing Club, was included twice in the winter Olympic Games, in 1928 and 1948, each time at St Moritz.

438

WHY do the Japanese have Shinto priests?   WHY are there

SHINTO PRIESTS

Shinto is a complex of ancient Japanese folk beliefs and rituals which form the basis of the religion of Japan. Priesthood is hereditary, and priests of major shrines may be from noble families. The priests perform rites of purification and fertility, and formally present newly married couples and infants to the Kami.

The Kami is the unifying concept of God. It is a kind of spiritual power, general and impersonal. It includes the many deities of the heavens and the earth, spirits, birds, beasts, trees, seas and mountains—even evil and mysterious things if they are extraordinary and dreadful.

Also in the Kami are sacred emperors, persons in authority, thunder, foxes, wolves and peaches (sex symbols). So are ancestral spirits, brave warriors and "magical" objects such as mirrors, paper and hair.

In the 6th Century, Buddhism was imported from Korea and gained a great deal of prestige. The two religions were combined to make one form of worship called Ryobu Shinto (two-aspect Shinto). Buddhist and Shinto shrines were merged and the priests performed rites in both religions. However, in the 17th Century scholars rediscovered ancient documents and laid the foundations of modern Shinto.

OLYMPIC FLAG

The flag used at the Olympic Games has a white background with five interlaced circles representing the five inhabited continents: Africa, America, Asia, Australasia and Europe. Each symbol has a different colour: red, yellow, green, black and blue. But the colours are merely decorative and in no way represent particular continents.

HOLLYWOOD

Hollywood is the centre of the United States motion picture and television industries. Its situation in the north-west of Los Angeles, California, provided many attractions for pioneers of the film industry at the beginning of this century. The climate was ideal with maximum sunshine and mild tempera- ture. The terrain was well suited with ocean, mountains and desert. And a large labour market was available.

One of Hollywood's first movies to tell a story was *The Count of Monte Cristo*, begun in 1908. By the end of 1911 there were more than 15 producing companies in

the area. Among the famous people working in Hollywood at the beginning of the First World War were Charlie Chaplin, Samuel Goldwyn, Douglas Fairbanks and Cecil B. de Mille.

The advent of the talkie forced many famous stars of the silent screen to retire. But the greatest threat to Hollywood came from television after the Second World War. Many production companies disappeared. Others survived and learned to meet the competition by also making television films.

Today Hollywood is not only the centre of the motion picture industry, but also of the television, film and recording industries of America.

The illustration above shows a magnificent scene from D. W. Griffiths epic film *Intolerance*, made in about 1916 and generally accepted by film buffs, and the public, as one of the great classic films of all time.

WHAT was an Aztec?

AZTEC

An Aztec was an Indian who lived on the plains of Mexico from the 11th Century to the beginning of the 16th. The Aztec civilization was one of the most magnificent in the whole of Central American history. although it was not created by the Aztecs themselves. They simply took over and organized what others had already created. They spoke a language called Nahua, which is still used by over a million Mexicans today, although Spanish is their official tongue.

In 1324 the Aztecs settled in an island village called Tenochtitlan, which later grew up into a large town. Mexico City is built on the same spot.

The Aztecs constructed many beautiful palaces and pyramid-shaped temples for the worship of their numerous gods, to whom they offered human sacrifice. They also developed a surprising knowledge of mathematics and astronomy.

The days of their greatest glory were also their last. In 1519 Hernando Cortez, a Spanish explorer landed in Mexico, marched to Tenochtitlan and took the Aztec king Montezuma prisoner. Two years later he finally defeated the Aztecs and destroyed their city.

Fortunately, not everything belonging to the Aztec civilization has disappeared. It is still possible to find many examples of their culture in Mexico today. Apart from ornaments and trinkets, there are many well preserved architectural remains—sacrificial platforms, temples, and a remarkable calendar stone.

The picture on the left shows Aztec platforms perfectly preserved at Teotihuacan in Mexico. Many of these platforms, which were probably used for sacrifices, still exist as well as other remarkable examples of Aztec civilization, as shown both in its architecture and its art.

WHERE do these knives come from: kris, kukri, machete?

KRIS, KUKRI AND MACHETE

The two-edged Malay dagger or kris came from Java in the western Pacific. It was originally a one-piece weapon. By the end of the 13th Century it had become a dagger with a separate hilt of gold, ivory or wood. This hilt was carved to represent Vishnu's bird, the Garuda, the Hindu demon Raksasa, or Hanuman, the monkey-god. The blade became wavy to represent serpents or Nagas (dragons, spirits).

The kukri is used by the Gurkhas, who live in Nepal on the north-eastern frontier of India. Their soldiers are renowned for their bravery in battle, and there have been regiments of Gurkhas in both the British and Indian armies. The kukri is a sword with a doubly curved blade. It can be used to decapitate an ox with one blow, and was used with devastating effect by the Gurkhas on the battlefield, who were experts in hand-to-hand combat.

The machete is a common chopping tool used in tropical regions where the harvesting of such plants as sugar cane, maize stalks or hemp require tools which carry weight as well as sharpness. The blade comes in a variety of forms, but the basic machete is a plain and very workmanlike object.

FIRST OLYMPICS

The first Olympic Games were held in Greece, in a valley between the Rivers Cladeus and Alpheus. According to tradition they were founded in 776 B.C. After that date they were held every four years until they were abolished in A.D. 393 by the Emperor Theodosius I.

At first, the Games lasted for only one day and were for running and wrestling. Later they became a five-day event, and chariot and horse racing were introduced.

Well-trained young men came from all over the Greek world to compete for the prizes—crowns of olive leaves. Originally a religious festival held in honour of the Olympian Zeus, the competitors took an oath of honesty and fairness in front of the god's statue. The athletes took part in a programme of foot racing, boxing, *pancratium* (all-in-wrestling), chariot racing and *pantathlon* (five events of long jumping, running,

javelin and discus throwing, and wrestling).

In the 19th Century, the idea of the Olympic Games was revived. After a break of 1,500 years, they were held again in Greece in 1896. Since then the Games have been celebrated every four years, except for 1916, 1940 and 1944 when the two World Wars were being fought. In 1924 the special sports of the Winter Olympics were introduced.

WHERE were the first Olympic Games held?
WHERE does all the garbage go?

GARBAGE DISPOSAL

Disposing of garbage is an ever-growing problem as populations increase. In country districts garbage is often taken outside a small town or village and dumped on a selected area of waste ground or in a disused quarry. What will burn is set alight.

A safer and much more efficient way of disposing of garbage is by incineration. It is put into huge furnaces, called incinerators, and burnt at a very high temper-

ature. Everything is reduced to ashes, except metals which are collected and may be used again.

In low-lying areas garbage is sometimes used to build up the land to a higher level. It is spread out in even layers by heavy machinery, pressed down, and covered with a layer of soil. This process is repeated until a thick garbage and soil sandwich has been made. It is then covered with a final layer of soil and left to rot

down. The land can later be used for farming.

In some cities newspapers and rags are collected separately from the rest of the rubbish. These can be pulped to make more paper. In other places, waste food is collected from hotels and restaurants, cooked and then fed to pigs. There is a growing tendency to find new ways of recycling raw materials such as plastics glass and metal, so that they may be used again.

WHY was one group of painters called the Impressionists?

Detail from Monet's painting of Rouen Cathedral.

WHY do fashions in clothes change?

IMPRESSIONISTS

The term Impressionist is used to describe a new and revolutionary movement in painting which was developed in Paris in the 1870s. The word was first used derisively by critics of the movement, and was taken from Claude Monet's canvas representing the sun rising over the sea and entitled *Impression*. Monet was a central figure in the development of the Impressionist movement, along with Manet, Degas, Renoir, Pissarro, Sisley, Cezanne, Guillaumin and Berthe Morisot.

What these painters tried to do was to get away from the romanticism and the fetters of the accepted artistic convention. Experiments were made with the use of the pure colours of the prism and the splitting up of "tone" into its component colours.

The Impressionists painted outdoor modern life and chose as their subjects Paris and urban scenes, the coasts of the English Channel and the North Sea, and the little village resorts along the banks of the Seine and Oise which had been made accessible by railway. They aimed to convey the changing rhythm of light.

FASHIONS

Fashions in clothes change for almost as many different reasons as there are fashions. Among the chief causes are changes in the kind of work we do, the cost and availability of the materials used and the invention of new materials, such as man-made fibres.

The attitude of different societies towards the body and how much of it should be displayed is also important. For example, if a girl in the Middle Ages had worn a mini-skirt she would have been regarded as either mad or wicked. Social standards change from age to age and from country to country.

There have been dramatic changes in fashion in our century, partly owing to the availability of new and cheap materials and partly because this generation believes that clothes should be a matter of personal choice, and comfortable as well as attractive.

Many of the fussy clothes of our ancestors, often requiring yards and yards of material, would be too expensive to produce today. They would also be unsuited to modern living—imagine cycling in a crinoline!

Great wars often influence fashions. During the Second World War the style of women's clothes became military. Jackets for instance, had square and padded shoulders. After the war, this fashion changed to the voluminous, more feminine, new look of Dior, the great French designer.

Another big change happened after the First World War. Women who had worked for the first time with men in the factories during the war, began to dress with greater freedom and started to wear short skirts.

Today, what we wear is largely a matter of personal choice, convenience and what we can afford.

N.A.T.O.

The initials stand for the North Atlantic Treaty Organization, which was founded in 1952 with its headquarters in Paris. Its first secretary-general was Lord Ismay.

N.A.T.O. was formed because the Western powers felt that the United Nations Security Council was not sufficiently powerful to keep the peace. Immediately after the Second World War, the Allies (who included the Soviet Union and the eastern European countries) felt the biggest danger to peace was that Germany and Japan might develop again as great military powers, with aggressive policies to secure world markets for their industrial production.

It was soon seen by both East and West that, because of political differences, the dangers to peace came from inside the alliance, not from the defeated enemies. The Socialist countries therefore united to form the Warsaw Pact, which guaranteed action by every country if any member was attacked by the West.

The Western camp was similarly formed by a treaty in 1949 signed by the United States, Britain, Canada, France, Belgium, The Netherlands, Luxembourg, Norway, Denmark, Iceland, Italy and Portugal. Greece and Turkey joined the Treaty countries in 1951 and the Federal German Republic in 1954.

N.A.T.O. is run by a council of the foreign or defence ministers of their respective countries, who also have permanent representatives. There is a communal defence force with a Supreme Allied Commander. Member countries hold joint military, naval and air exercises in various parts of Europe.

A session of the North Atlantic Council meeting at N.A.T.O. headquarters in Brussels, Belgium.

FRENCH CHALK

French chalk is a soft substance which makes a white mark if it is drawn across other materials, such as cloth. It is used in tailoring and dressmaking as a guideline for cutting, pinning or sewing. In fact it is really not chalk but a variety of talc (hydrous magnesium silicate), a common mineral distinguished from nearly all others by its extreme softness.

This talc was supposed to have been used originally in France, and this, together with the white mark it leaves, explains how it got its name.

If talc is compacted or compressed it is known as steatite or soapstone, because of its greasy, soapy feel. Soapstones have been used since ancient times for carvings, ornaments and utensils. Assyrian cylinder seals, Egyptian scarabs and Chinese figure carvings are the most notable examples.

The colour of talc is white, grey, yellow or various shades of green with a pearly or silvery lustre. As well as making French chalk, talc is used for lubricants, leather dressings, toilet and dusting powders. The major industrial uses are in ceramics, paint, rubber, insecticides, roofing and paper.

CAPSTAN

A capstan is a cylindrical or barrel-shaped appliance revolving on an upright axis. It was formerly powered by thrust applied on movable bars placed in horizontal sockets made around the top and pushed by men walking round and round. When operating, the whole capstan revolves and winds in a line which has been wrapped round it. Nowadays the capstan may also be powered by steam or electricity.

A capstan is chiefly used aboard ships or in shipyards to move or lift heavy weights. When ships had anchor cables rather than

CHAMPAGNE

Champagne is made to ferment twice in order to produce its famous bubbling or sparkling quality. It first ferments in wooden casks. But when fermentation stops for a short time in the first winter, it is transferred to strong bottles after being blended by experienced tasters, the artists of Champagne.

The wine then goes through a second fermentation in the bottle, making it naturally sparkling. For the first three months in the bottle the wine is gradually moved and tipped by hand until the bottles are upside down and the impurities have fallen on to the bottom of the cork. The bottles stay in that position for at least six months, sometimes for years. The "bubbly" effect is produced by the yeast introducing carbon dioxide into the wine under pressure caused by the bottles being upside down.

When the wine is mature and ready for market the cork is released and the sediment shot off with it. Then a small amount of syrup dissolved in old champagne is added and the wine quickly recorked.

Other wines are not bottled until fermentation is complete.

anchor chains both the capstan and the windlass could be used to haul in the anchor, but the capstan was more popular since it was much easier to "walk the capstan round" than to "crank over" the horizontally mounted windlass. A recessed drum was developed to fit round the links of the anchor chain when it was brought into use, while auxiliary power in the shape of the "donkey engine" made sailors' lives easier. However, a capstan is designed so that it can always be operated manually in case of a power failure.

DAY OF JUDGMENT

A vivid picture of the Day of Judgment is drawn in the New Testament book of Revelation. The Bible tells us that at some time not yet revealed the end of the world will come and there will be a Universal Day of Judgment. On that day all people will be called from the dead to face the judgment of God.

The Christian Church however has another interpretation of the Day of Judgment as the day of our death. On that day, according to this interpretation, we have to expect to meet our Creator and answer for our sins.

Detail from The Triumph of Death by Peter Breughel the Elder.

BALLPOINT PEN

The first workable ballpoint pen was patented in 1937 by Laszlo Jozsef Biro, a Hungarian living in Argentina, but ideas for ballpoint pens date back to the late 1890s. Biro's pen became popular during 1938 and 1939.

The United States forces welcomed it because the Quartermaster General of the Army had called for a writing instrument which would not leak at high altitudes, would use a quick-drying ink unaffected by changes in climate and would contain enough ink to last a long time.

In this type of pen a ball, housed in a socket at the tip, transfers special ink from a reservoir on to the surface of the writing paper. The inks used have dyes which are soluble in oil or spirit. The first type dries because it is absorbed into the paper, the second because it evaporates.

At one time most of the balls used in high-quality ballpoint pens were made of stainless steel, but now many other metals and plastic are used.

en first come into use?

WHAT is granite?　WHAT is Esperanto?　WHAT is the
WHAT is the Torah?

GRANITE

Granite is a very hard kind of rock made up of small pieces of mica, quartz and felspar and sometimes other rocks as well. There are many kinds of granite and they may be pink, grey or white. But the most striking thing about granite is that the pieces of rock from which it is made are all crystalline and shine like a wall of snowflakes.

One city in Scotland, called Aberdeen, is known as the silver city, because its granite buildings shine in the sun.

This rock is widely used for building, and is especially useful for large engineering jobs such as the making of breakwaters. Not only does it stand up well to the weather but, unlike many other rocks, it can be quarried in huge slabs. It is also used as an ornamental stone after being polished.

Granite is found all over the world and forms part of most of the world's mountain ranges. There is a city in the State of Illinois called Granite City.

TORAH

The first five books of the Bible—Genesis, Exodus, Leviticus, Numbers and Deuteronomy—or the Pentateuch (five books)—are known among the Jews as the Torah, or Law. This is because they contain the Ten Commandments, or Decalogue, which formed the foundation of the civil and religious laws of the Hebrews.

They are also sometimes called the books of Moses because they contain the story of Moses' life and were for many years supposed to be written by him.

According to Biblical narrative, the Ten Commandments were given to Moses by God on Mount Sinai. Contained in these simple commandments are the fundamental elements of all moral law as we understand it.

ESPERANTO

Esperanto is a language created by Ludovic Lazarus Zamenhof (1859–1917), a Jew who was born on the frontier between Russia and Poland. He realized that language barriers helped to maintain and even to aggravate differences and difficulties between nations, and conceived Esperanto as an international language easily learned and spoken by everybody.

The language's name (meaning "a person who hopes") comes from the pseudonym Zamenhof used for his first book *Internacia Lingvo* (1887) which was translated into English as *Dr Esperanto's International Language* in 1889. Generally speaking, learning Esperanto takes from one-twentieth to one-fifth of the time needed to learn a national language.

It is used by the Universala Esperants-Asocio (founded 1908) which has headquarters in Rotterdam, members in 85 countries, 50 national associations and about 20 professional international associations. Numerous people who do not belong to official organizations also speak the language. In 1963 Professor Mario Pei of Columbia University, United States, suggested that Esperanto was spoken by 8,000,000 people.

Esperanto is a phonetic language with no irregularities of grammar. The roots of words were taken from national languages, so many can be recognized on sight. Many great works of literature have been written in the language.

In 1954 the General Conference of the United Nations Educational, Scientific and Cultural Organization (U.N.E.S.C.O) recognized "the results attained by Esperanto in the field of international intellectual relations in the rapprochement of the peoples of the world." Five years later on the occasion of the centenary of Zamenhof's birth, U.N.E.S.C.O. paid tribute to him.

ouch of Midas? **WHAT** is a Bailey bridge?

BAILEY BRIDGE

A Bailey bridge is a type of bridge designed by Sir Donald Bailey, an Englishman, during the Second World War. Built entirely by man-power, it met a great need. The old types of military bridge were un-able to support the rapidly increas-ing weight of armoured vehicles.

The Bailey bridge proved to be the most useful and versatile military bridge of the war. It was built of panels and sections, or trusses, which could be combined to carry loads of up to 100 tons over spans up to 220 feet.

The roadway of the bridge is supported by two main trusses pinned together. Each 10-foot section of bridge consists of two parallel trusses supporting the cross-members on which the sur-face is laid, and is known as a bay.

The capacity of the bridge may be increased by adding one or two extra trusses alongside the first, by adding extra trusses on top of the first two or three to make a second storey, or by both means. Therefore a single-truss, single-storey bridge is a single-single and you can have double-single, double-double and so on.

The Bailey bridge was also adapted to float on a plywood pontoon.

New versions of the Bailey Bridge have been devised. The Mark 3 Bailey with a roadway 13 feet $9\frac{1}{2}$ inches wide is standard in the British Army.

MIDAS

The "touch of Midas" is the ability to turn everything to gold—or, in other words, to success. In ancient Greek mythology, Midas was the son of Gordius, the king of Phrygia, who devised the Gordian Knot, and of Cybele, the goddess of caverns and the Great Mother of the Gods.

Midas succeeded his father on the Phrygian throne and showed himself a wise and pious king. One day, when he was strolling on the banks of the River Sangarius, he came across a drunken man who had been tied up by peasants. Midas released the man and there-by earned the gratitude of Diony-sus, the god of wine, who promised to grant a wish as a reward.

The king wished that everything he touched should be turned into gold. But he soon regretted his choice, for even the food he took in his hand to eat turned to gold. He begged the god to take pity on him and withdraw the gift. Diony-sus did so and sent Midas to the River Pactolus to cleanse himself. From then on the river was said to flow with gold dust.

This ancient legend gave rise to the expression "the Midas touch".

measured in hands?

STATUE OF LIBERTY

The Statue of Liberty was built to celebrate the birth of the United States of America and to commemorate the friendship between that republic and the republic of France.

It stands on Bedloe's Island (now renamed Liberty Island) at the mouth of New York harbour, in accordance with the wishes of the sculptor Frederic Bartholdi.

The plan for the monument originated in France. The cost of the statue was met by the French people, while the money for the 300-foot pedestal was raised in the United States.

Although the monument was not unveiled until 1886, the idea was conceived at the end of the 18th Century when France and the United States were the only big democratic republics in existence.

Under the 150-foot statue, symbol of freedom and equality, is a moving poem, inscribed inside the pedestal. In this poem *The New Colossus*, the writer, Emma Lazarus, invited the tired, poor and homeless to come to America in search of liberty.

HORSES

Before man invented rulers and tape measures he often used his hands and feet to express the size of things. An old book published in 1561 says: "Foure graines of barlye make a fynger; foure fyngers a hande; foure hands a foote".

Today horses are still measured in hands. The measurement is taken from the ground to the withers, which is the highest part of the back lying between the shoulder blades.

A hand is reckoned to be four inches, the assumed width of a man's palm. Formerly it was taken as equal to three inches, when a man's hand was smaller.

Early horses were probably around 12 hands (48 inches) at the withers, and one measuring 14 hands was exceptional. Some modern horses, however, reach 17 hands and occasionally 20 hands. A small horse under 14·2 hands is called a pony.

WHEN were beauty spots in fashion? WHEN did people first WHEN would one exorcise a

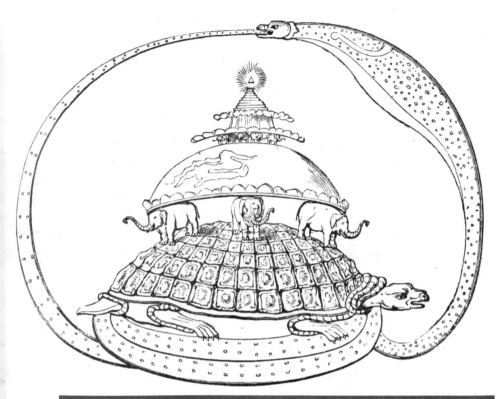

BEAUTY SPOTS

The first women on record as having worn beauty spots on their faces were leaders of fashion in the days of the Roman Empire. These spots were small and round, and evidently worn in great profusion. The poets Ovid (43 B.C.–A.D. 18) and Martial (about A.D. 40–104) were among the classical writers to comment on the habit.

Beauty spots then seem to have gone out of fashion until they reappeared late in the 16th Century. Their return is believed to have started with the use of black velvet or taffeta court-plasters on the temples for the relief of toothache. Women found them more effective in improving their complexion by setting off the whiteness of the skin.

The patches were usually placed near the mouth. As the craze for them developed they became much bigger and were cut to different shapes and patterns.

In London, beauty spots took on political significance. Supporters of the Whig party wore them on the right cheek, those of the Tory party on the left. In 1711 a writer in *The Spectator*, a famous London magazine, noted that women "would be more beautiful than the sun were it not for the little black spots that break out and sometimes rise in very odd figures. I have observed that these little blemishes wear off very soon but, when they disappear in one part of the face, they are very apt to break out in another. I have seen a spot in the forehead in the afternoon which was upon the chin in the morning."

In Paris the fashion produced elaborate variations. One marquise is reported to have appeared at a party wearing 16 patches in the shape of a tree in which perched two love birds. Men also adopted the vogue.

These "little blemishes", cut out of silk, taffeta, velvet and even leather, and stuck on with mastic, continued to wander about the faces of women until the middle of the 19th Century.

ROUND EARTH

Greek scholars had decided by 350 B.C. that the earth must be round. But the earlier belief that it was flat persisted in other countries for many centuries afterwards. Even as late as the time of Christopher Columbus, at the end of the 15th Century, a fear of falling off the edge of the earth existed among seamen.

One theory held by early man was that the sky was a kind of shield which came down to meet the earth on all sides, forming a boxed-in universe. It was the Greeks who hit on the idea that it was a circular slab. A Hindu myth suggested that the slab was supported by four pillars which rested on four elephants, which stood on a gigantic turtle, which, perhaps, swam in a huge ocean.

The Greek philosopher, Anaximander of Miletus (611–546 B.C.) thought man might be living on the surface of a cylinder, which was curved from north to south. He was the first, as far as is known, to suggest any shape for the earth other than that it was flat.

A strange assortment of patches worn in the time of Charles I of England. From Fairholt's "Costume in England".

realize that the earth is round?

house? **WHEN** is eating meat forbidden to certain people?

EXORCISM

A service of exorcising a house is sometimes carried out by a priest when the building is said to be haunted by a spirit. The ceremony involves the performance of a set ritual and, in some cases, the sprinkling of holy water.

The photograph shows the ruins of Borley Rectory near Chelmsford, in Essex, Elgnald. This was once said to be the most haunted house in England and it still has an awesome reputation.

EATING MEAT

Some religions forbid their followers to eat certain kinds of meat. Under the rules for kosher food, Jews must not eat the flesh of pigs and other animals prohibited in the biblical books of Leviticus and Deuteronomy. Hindus are not permitted to eat beef because, in their religion, the cow is a sacred animal. The ancient Celts worshipped Epona, the horse goddess, and were, therefore, not allowed to eat horse flesh.

Until recently Roman Catholics were not supposed to eat meat on Fridays as a gesture of self-sacrifice on the day of the Crucifixion. Fish was substituted. Nowadays some other gesture is often made, such as giving money to charity.

Vegetarians are people who do not eat meat, either for health reasons or on humanitarian grounds, believing that it is wrong to kill animals for food.

456

WHAT is the Red Cross? WHAT is a mandarin? WHAT makes

RED CROSS

The Red Cross organization was established at a conference in Geneva in 1864. It was inspired by a Swiss, Henri Dunant, who had been horrified by the scenes of bloodshed he had witnessed on the battlefield of Solferino in northern Italy after a victory of the French over the Austrians in a war of liberation. His book, *Un Souvenir de Solferino*, aroused the compassion of all who read it.

At the Geneva Convention of 1864, 26 countries were represented. The objects of the International Red Cross were outlined as follows: during wartime prisoners and wounded men were to be respected; military hospitals were to be regarded as neutral; doctors, nurses and medical equipment were to be protected; and the Red Cross was to act as a benevolent intermediary between governments, and to see that suffering was relieved.

In honour of Henri Dunant the Swiss flag with the colours reversed was chosen as the flag of the Red Cross. In 1919 the League of Red Cross Societies was formed with the aim of extending Red Cross activities in times of peace. A relief division was formed to help in natural disasters, such as earthquakes and famines. An international nursing centre was set up in London, which trained hundreds of nurses every year, and Red Cross hospitals were established in countries liable to malaria and tropical diseases.

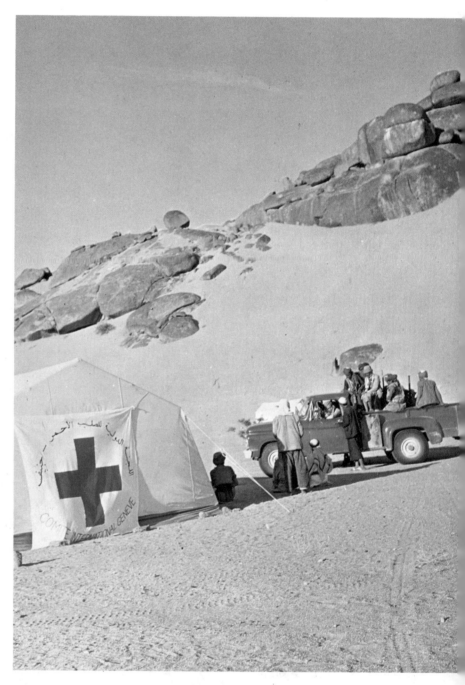

A Red Cross unit on duty during the Yemen civil war.

MANDARIN

The word "mandarin" has several meanings which are all interconnected. Perhaps the most common use of it is as the name for the nine grades of Chinese administrators who were selected by a series of very difficult examinations. In the T'ang dynasty (A.D. 618–906), this system of scholar officials was operating extremely effectively. This administration proved to be the backbone of the great Chinese Empire that persisted through about 20 successive dynasties.

The name mandarin is also given to the language spoken in China by officials and educated people and to a grotesque toy figure in Chinese costume which goes on nodding after it is shaken. The mandarin scholar-official wore yellow silk robes and so a dye obtained from coal tar, a sweet, flattened, easily-skinned orange and a yellow liquor also have the name mandarin.

perfume?

PERFUME

Perfume is made up of vegetable oils, the odours of certain animals and chemical additives. Perfume-making, like cookery, is done from a recipe, a formula. The perfumer takes his list of ingredients and blends them together in a special way. One of the expensive perfumes worn by women on their throats and wrists (the heat from the throbbing at these pulse points brings out the smell) may contain up to two hundred ingredients.

The first smell that reaches you when you open the bottle and dab on the scent is the vegetable oil, a blend of the oils of flowers and herbs varying from lavender, jasmine and rose, to clove and rosemary and even carrot and onion oils. They are extracted by squeezing, or by the use of solvents.

The second category consists of animal odours which give the scent persistence. These include ambergris, which is phlegm coughed up by the sperm whale, a gland secretion of the civet cat, musk from the musk deer and castoreum resin from the beaver.

The third set of ingredients, the chemical ones, are used to set off and fill out the flower and animal products. They are much cheaper.

The blending of these ingredients calls for great skill, and a perfumer takes many years to learn his art.

Not all perfumes are sold in bottles or even in cosmetic products. One of the perfumer's main tasks is to disguise the bad smells in products such as detergents and plastics, and to provide the smells which people have come to associate with certain products. Plastic car seats are given the smell of leather. Restaurants can buy a bottle of bacon and hamburger essence for an appetizing aroma.

Collecting roses for perfume in Bulgaria.

WHEN were wigs first worn? WHEN was ice cream invented

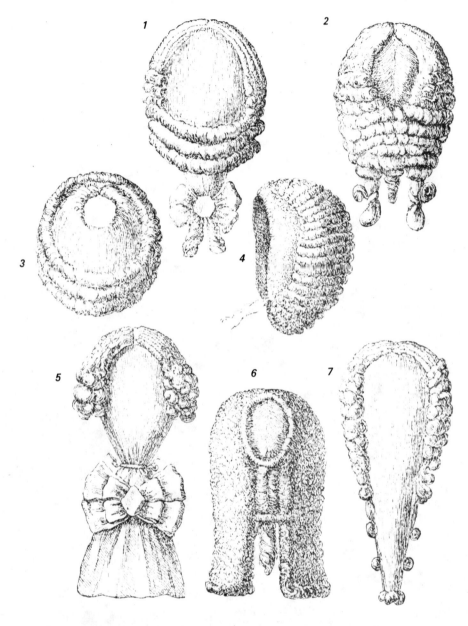

1 Wig a la brigadie 2 Knotted wig 3 Abbe's wig 4 Woman's wig 5 Bag-wig 6 Square-wig 7 Newly growing wig

WIGS

The wearing of wigs by both men and women dates from our earliest recorded history. Wigs have been found on Egyptian mummies, and the appearance of the frizzled-out hair on some of the figures on the frescoes at Knossos suggests that wigs were also familiar to the ancient civilization of Crete. The Medes and Persians also wore artificial hair, and Greek women were using hairpieces by the 4th Century B.C. The Romans began wearing wigs in the early years of the Empire.

The word wig is a shortened version of periwig, which is derived from the French perruque. It was in 17th-Century France that wigs began to assume their greatest glory as features of men's fashion. Louis XIV, who was very proud of his own hair when he was young, did not wear a wig until after 1670 when he was in his 40s. From Versailles, the fashion then spread throughout Europe.

During the first decade of the 18th Century men's wigs reached their maximum size, covering shoulders and back, and floating down over the chest. After that they gradually became smaller until, for normal wear, they disappeared. In recent years wigs have again become popular with women and the wearing of artificial hairpieces has become an accepted device among men.

ICE CREAM

Water ices were known in the Roman Empire, and Marco Polo (1254–1324) is said to have brought back a recipe for milk ices from his travels in the Far East.

Centuries later, chefs for the royal courts of Europe were experimenting with ice cream and trying, without success, to keep the recipes secret. In the 19th Century the commercial production of ice cream was made possible by the discovery that ice mixed with salt produced a lower temperature than ice alone. The industry grew rapidly towards the end of the century because of the introduction of mechanical refrigeration.

About 80 per cent of the liquid mixture for making ice cream is milk and cream, and about 15 per cent is sweetener. Sometimes egg yolk is also used, and fruit, nuts and flavourings are often added to the mixture.

Most commercial ice cream is made in a refrigerated tube with revolving blades or beaters. The partially frozen ice cream is drawn off into containers and sent to a hardening room with a temperature of from −18° to −26° Centigrade (0° to −15° Fahrenheit). It is then delivered in refrigerated trucks to dealers. Strict standards of hygiene have to be maintained.

WHEN was silk first used in Europe?

SILK IN EUROPE

Rome began to import raw silk from the East towards the beginning of the Christian era. When silk first appeared in Europe it was enormously expensive—literally worth its weight in gold—and its use by men was considered effeminate.

The industry of silk weaving began in ancient China. By the 2nd Century, silk weaving flourished in Egypt, Syria and Palestine. By the 4th Century the industry had spread to Constantinople, and **Byzantine silks became world famous. When the moors captured Sicily in the 11th century, they established silk weaving there.** After the Norman conquest of Siciliy in the 11th Century, the industry spread to the cities of Florence, Genoa, Milan and Venice.

Silkworms were introduced to the New World in 1522, by Hernán Cortés in Mexico, but the experiment failed. Since then sericulture, or the making of silk, has been introduced in the United States, but has never become a major industry.

In spite of the progress made in man-made fibres for clothing since the end of the Second World War, silk remains a first choice for luxurious and expensive clothes because of its delicacy, relative strength, elasticity and ability to take colour.

WHAT does a space capsule have a heat-shield for?

SPACE CAPSULE

A space capsule needs a heat-shield to protect it and its occupants from the extremely high temperatures generated by its friction with the earth's atmosphere.

The space capsule starts its return journey to earth at a very high speed. The temperature of the craft's skin rises rapidly as it meets the resistance of the denser air near the earth. The heat turns the colour of the shield red and then bright orange, before the craft is slowed down enough for the final descent to earth.

Without its heat-shield the craft would disintegrate into a long white trail of melting metal—in the same way that meteorites do when they plunge through the atmosphere of the earth.

WHAT happens when things go mouldy?
WHAT makes wrinkles? WHAT happens when we blush?

MOULD

The moulds we find on bread, cheese and other foods are fungi, like the mushroomy substances that grow on the ground and on trees. They appear when certain little organisms in the air find the moist conditions they need in substances such as bread.

Fungi are very important on account of the great good or harm the different kinds can do. One particular green mould has proved of tremendous benefit in medical treatment because Sir Alexander Fleming discovered in 1928 that it stops the growth of certain bacteria. Doctors have used this mould, which is called penicillin, and others like it as "antibiotics" to destroy more serious bacteria which cause disease. Such moulds have been cultivated on a gigantic scale to produce substances of unequalled curative power.

Moulds have many other uses. Some fungi produce the fermentation needed to brew beer or turn grape juice into wine. Others are used in making bread or delicious cheeses. Fungi also perform the important action of turning dead leaves and animal bodies back into soil by the process of rotting.

The picture shows a penicillin mould.

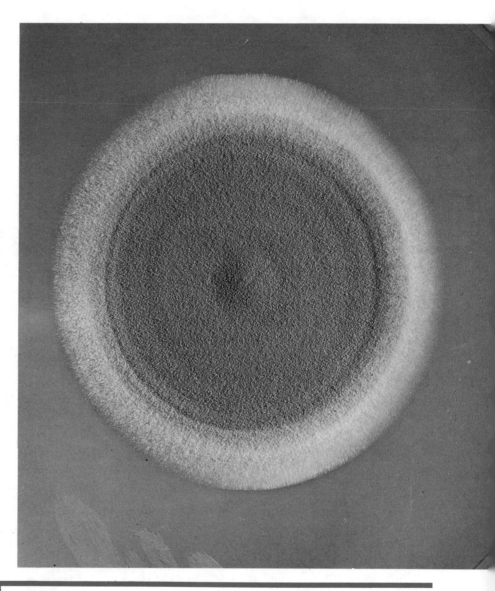

WRINKLES

Just as clothes hang in folds when they are old and have been stretched and washed a lot, so does the skin. The skin ages in five different ways. Some of these begin when you are a child, others at puberty and others after middle age.

The five symptoms of skin ageing are: loss of elasticity; changes in nerve endings which take place from early childhood; a tendency for the apocrine sweat glands which developed at puberty to disappear (old people sweat less); changes in the colouring matter in the skin, causing blotchy patches on the backs of old people's hands and darker freckles; and changes in the skin of the scalp. (This is quite thick when the person is a child, gets thicker and then goes relatively thin with age.)

BLUSH

When we blush we go red in the face, particularly in the cheeks and neck. This is because a sudden emotion, such as embarrassment, a sense of shame or pleasure, causes the very small blood vessels just below the surface of the skin to become larger. As these blood vessels, called capillaries, are full of blood, the skin looks red.

When people blush they usually feel hot and uncomfortable, and imagine that their red faces are very noticeable. This is not always so, because some people's blushes do not show. It depends very much on the colour of the skin. Blushing is most noticeable on a fair-haired, pale-skinned person. Young people, particularly girls in their teens, are supposed to blush more easily than older people. This is true of many girls. As they grow older, they usually blush less easily, because they are embarrassed less often, and learn to cope with sudden emotions.

WHERE is Loch Ness? WHERE is the Wailing Wall?
WHERE would you find the Garden of Eden?

LOCH NESS

Loch Ness is the most famous of all the fresh water lochs in Scotland because of reports that it is inhabited by some kind of aquatic monster.

Since the middle of the 19th Century many local inhabitants and visitors claim to have seen the Loch Ness Monster. In recent years much photographic and documentary evidence has been produced from which some experts have detected a resemblance between the monster and aquatic reptiles that lived more than 50,000 years ago.

Nevertheless, in spite of the stories, official opinion still doubts that such a creature actually exists. Frogmen and submarines have searched in vain for the monster. But it has been pointed out that there are caves and subterranean waterways beneath the surface of Loch Ness leading to other lochs, in which the supposed monster could hide. Perhaps the mystery will never be solved.

WAILING WALL

The Wailing Wall is in Jerusalem. It consists of the surviving portion of the temple built by the Jews on the site of King Solomon's temple. The temple was destroyed in A.D. 70 by the Roman Emperor Titus to punish the rebellious Jews. For centuries the Jews have bewailed the loss of their temple at the western or Wailing Wall.

Jerusalem was divided after the Second World War but Jewish forces regained control of the Old City, which contains the Wailing Wall, in the Six-Day War of 1967.

GARDEN OF EDEN

The short answer is that you would not find it. The Garden of Eden is the place where God is supposed to have created a garden for Adam, the first man. Some people hold it to have been situated in the Mesopotamian region between the Rivers Tigris and Euphrates. The Tree of Knowledge grew in this garden and it was there that man fell from grace in God's eyes because, at the prompting of Eve, the first woman, he ate fruit from this tree.

Because of this act of disobedience, it is said, God devised three punishments. The man was to till the earth, which was cursed; the woman was to experience painful childbirth; and the serpent who prompted the woman to persuade the man to eat the fruit was from that day forth to be hated by mankind. Adam had to be driven out of the Garden of Eden because the Tree of Life also grew there and this would have endowed him with immortality. The inference is that man chose knowledge and death rather than ignorance and eternal life.

The Garden of Eden has been portrayed in many famous paintings and poems. In man's imagination it has always been an ideal to which he longs to return.

WHERE would you find the Hesperides?
WHERE would you find Davy Jones's locker?

THE HESPERIDES

The Hesperides, in Greek mythology, were the maidens who guarded the tree that bore the golden apples given by Mother Earth to the goddess Hera, when she married Zeus. Another version of the myth says the maidens were the daughters of Erelius and Night. Their names are usually given as Aegle, Erytheia and Hesperis, and they lived in Arcadia, which was thought of as a sort of ideal Garden of Eden. Modern Arcadia is in central Greece.

DAVY JONES'S LOCKER

For several centuries men and ships lost at sea have been said to go to Davy Jones's Locker. Davy Jones is the spirit of the sea—the sailors' devil—and his locker is the ocean. A character in *Sir Launcelot Greaves*, a novel by Tobias George Smollett (1721–71) observes: "I have seen Davy Jones in the shape of a blue flame, d'ye see, hopping to and from on the sprit-sail yardarm".

In 1803 the *Naval Chronicles* stated: "The . . . seaman would have met a watery grave; or, to use a seaman's phrase, gone to Davy Jones's locker." In Chamier's *Saucy Arethusa*, written in 1837, we find: "The boat was capsized . . . and . . . all hands are snug enough in Davy Jones's locker."

There have been many explanations as to how Davy Jones came to stand for the sailors' devil. One is that the name Jones evolved from Jonah, the Old Testament prophet, who ended up in the belly of a whale. If that is so, why Davy? For Davy seems to be an essential part of the title as shown by variations—David Jones, Old Davy and, simply, Davy. Another suggestion is that, as Jonah became the Welsh name Jones, a popular Welsh Christian name was added.

ERCOLE ALL'ESPERIDI

WHY do beavers build dams? WHY does the moon shine WHY does smoke go up the chimney

BEAVERS

The beavers of North America build a dam to create an artificial lake in which to construct an island home or lodge. Often the beavers work in colonies. After choosing a narrow place in a shallow stream with a firm bottom, they set to work felling trees by standing on their hind legs and gnawing round the trunks with their large chisel-like teeth. When the tree is down, the beavers lop off the branches and cut the trunk into suitable lengths which they drag into the stream and sink across the current. Sticks, stones and mud are used to keep the dam in position and make it watertight.

In the middle of the lake thus created the beavers use the same materials to build their lodge. When completed this is a dome-shaped, ventilated structure about 8 feet in diameter and rising well clear of the surface of the lake. There are two entrances, both under water. One of these is used for general purposes, the other as an escape route in an emergency or for bringing in food.

The lodge serves as a home, a nursery for the baby beavers and a storehouse for food in winter. The beavers feed chiefly on the bark of trees, of which they keep a plentiful supply at the bottom of the dam, on the bed of the lake and built into the fabric of their home.

In winter, when the lake is frozen over and snow covers the ground, the lodge is virtually an impregnable fortress which the beavers can leave and enter by swimming under the ice. Beavers are experts at keeping the water in the lake at the right level by constructing canals. They work industriously to maintain both dam and lodge — hence the origin of that popular phrase about being "as busy as a beaver".

MOON SHINE

The moon shines by the light it reflects from the sun. It has no light of its own. The sharp definition with which, on a clear night, we see the moon, is due to the absence of any concealing veil of air or cloud on it.

Since there is no atmosphere on the moon to act as a buffer to the sun's rays, temperatures there are extreme and sudden. The maximum is 212° Fahrenheit (100° Centigrade), the temperature of boiling water, and the minimum is −292°F (−180°C). Understandably, it cannot support life.

CHIMNEY SMOKE

Smoke will rise up the chimney or through the nearest opening it can find because it is hotter and, therefore, lighter than the air in the room.

Before the days of chimneys smoke was allowed to escape through vents or open turrets in the roof. Chimneys were introduced to induce a draught, thus providing more air for the fire.

Thus a chimney would not only carry away the smoke and gases from a fire but also act as a ventilator enabling a change of air in the room.

The photograph shows the lunar surface viewed from the orbiting command module of Apollo 15. The light on the surface is reflected from the sun.

WHEN was the United Kingdom formed?
WHEN was the Battle of Hastings?

UNITED KINGDOM

The United Kingdom was formed in 1801 when an Act of Union brought Ireland under the same parliament with England, Scotland and Wales. The official name of the country was changed to the United Kingdom of Great Britain and Ireland. But 26 Irish counties left the Union in 1922 and formed the Irish Free State, now the Republic of Ireland. Five years later the Royal and Parliamentary Titles Act named the union as the United Kingdom of Great Britain and Northern Ireland.

Wales was the first to unite with England, having been subdued by King Edward I in 1282. The heir to the English throne has been known as the Prince of Wales ever since Edward gave the title to his baby son in 1301. But it was not until 1536 when Henry VIII, a Tudor monarch of Welsh descent, was on the throne, that an Act of Union peacefully incorporated the Principality into the kingdom.

The name Great Britain came into use after James VI of Scotland succeeded to the English throne in 1603 as James I and united the two crowns, though not the nations. Another Act of Union brought England and Scotland under one government in 1707.

The Union flag of the present kingdom is composed of the flag of England (white with an upright red cross), the flag of Scotland (blue with a diagonal white cross) and the red diagonal cross of Ireland.

On May 29, 1953, under the Royal Titles Act, a proclamation was issued which gave the Queen the title: Elizabeth the Second, by the Grace of God, of the United Kingdom of Great Britain and Northern Ireland and of her other Realms and Territories Queen, Head of the Commonwealth, Defender of the Faith.

BATTLE OF HASTINGS

The Battle of Hastings was fought on October 14, 1066, on a ridge 10 miles north-west of Hastings in Sussex, England.

The events which led to the battle began when William, Duke of Normandy, in France, extracted a promise from Harold, chief minister of the Saxon king Edward the Confessor, that he would support the Norman's succession to the English throne. When Edward died on January 5, 1066, and Harold was chosen king by an assembly of nobles and citizens, William decided to seize what he claimed was his by right.

In September, while the Normans were still waiting for the wind to change to carry them across the English Channel, Harold had to march northwards into Yorkshire to repulse an invasion led by Harald Hardrada, the seven-foot king of Norway.

The Saxons crushed the invaders in a desperate battle at Stamford Bridge, but Harold was still in York when he received the news that William's army had landed near Hastings. He instantly hurried south, mobilized a new, largely untrained, army of about 7,000 men and led them against the Normans 5,000 strong.

During the battle Harold defended a piece of high ground protected by a barricade. At first the two-handed Saxon battle axes beat back the Norman attacks. But William triumphed with cunning generalship, luring the Saxons from their strong positions by pretended retreats and ordering his archers to aim high in the air so that their arrows fell on heads unprotected by the wall of shields. A chance arrow killed Harold and, as darkness fell, the English survivors scattered.

On December 25 William the Conqueror was crowned king of England in London.

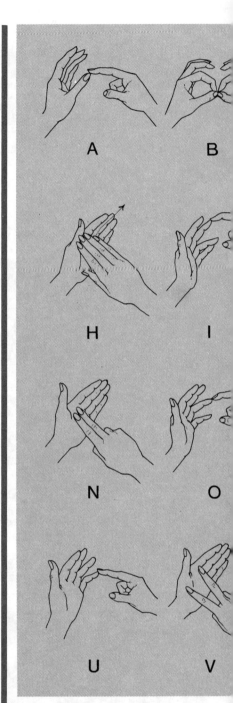

A B

H I

N O

U V

SIGN LANGUAGE

Sign language for people who could not hear or speak was developed in the 18th Century. The Abbé Charles Michel Epée (1712–1789) studied the sign language which had grown up among such people over the centuries and organized it into a systematic language which could be used in education and com-

WHEN was the sign language for deaf-mutes invented?

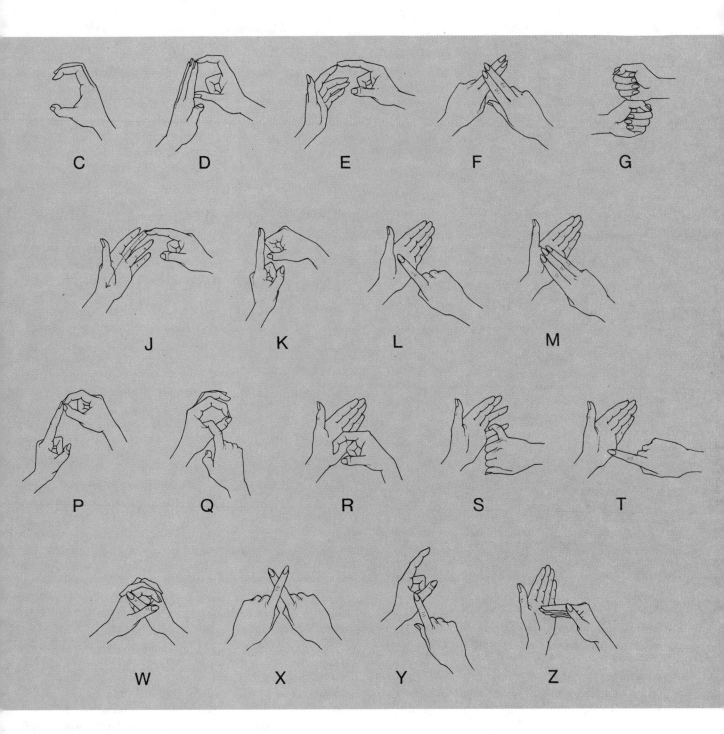

munication. His work was developed by the Abbé Sicard (1742–1822). A code of manual gestures evolved, some representing letters of the alphabet and others symbolizing whole words or phrases.

The Abbé Epée concentrated on gestures in his school for deaf-mutes, but other teachers believed that the deaf should be taught to lip-read and, if possible, to communicate by sounds. One of the greatest teachers of the latter method was the German Moritz Hill (1805–1874). Today many educators use a combination of both methods. The example of Helen Keller (1880–1968), a blind deaf-mute, who was taught to speak by a devoted teacher, Anne Sullivan, made millions of people realize that deaf-mutes failed to develop speech only because they are unable to hear other people speaking.

In the 20th Century tremendous advances have been made in the early recognition of impaired hearing and in the training of teachers and other specialists.

FROST

Frost comes from the atmosphere when the temperature falls below freezing, and invisible water vapour in the air turns into white ice crystals, without first becoming a liquid. It usually occurs when the skies are clear, when there is no wind and when a mass of cold air descends on the land.

This often happens during the night in the spring and autumn of areas with temperate climates. In the morning the fields and roofs are white with what would be dew if the temperature had been above freezing point. It is the most common type of frost and is often called hoar frost.

Sometimes only the leaves of plants are fringed with white rime. This is formed when very small droplets of the moisture from fog have frozen on coming into contact with a cold object.

There is also black frost. This occurs when water vapour turns first into liquid and then freezes into a thin layer of ice instead of white crystals. As it is invisible, it is particularly dangerous when it forms on roads.

The beautiful patterns, looking like trees, ferns or feathers, which are sometimes seen on windows, are made when the water vapour in a cold room condenses.

STALACTITES

Stalactites are the stony deposits hanging like icicles from the roofs of caves. Stalagmites are similar deposits rising in columns and cones from the caves' floors.

Caves occur chiefly in limestone and chalk formations, because water dissolves these rocks. The River Lesse, for example, in its passage through the caves of Han, in Belgium, has been estimated to dissolve some five tons of limestone in a day. It is redeposited as carbonate which builds up the stalactites and stalagmites.

The seepage of water down the cave walls and through the roof produces constant dripping and evaporation. Stone icicles form on the cave roof, slowly growing with the addition of successive layers of calcium carbonate. The word "stalactite" comes from the Greek and means "drop by drop". There is, too, a general term "dripstone" which is used to cover all formations.

Stalactites are at first hollow, for the depositing of the carbonate is fastest at the outer ring of the water drop. As the evaporating water deposits its mineral matter, the cavity slowly fills up and the stalactite becomes solid. When water trickles out of a narrow cleft in the roof, instead of a small hole, a hanging curtain of stone will form in place of a conical stalactite.

If the water flows so quickly that it splashes on the floor of the cave, it deposits its calcium carbonate there and small cones and domes of stone called stalagmites begin to rise. These may grow up to join the stalactites above and form single columns. Some cave floors are covered with stalagmites. They may grow so high that they block the cave entrance.

The stalactites pictured on the right are typical specimens and show how beautiful these formations can be.

across a stalactite ?

WHAT is a caryatid? What is the U.N.? WHAT is Voodoo?

THE U.N.

U.N. stands for United Nations. The Charter of the United Nations was an attempt to establish world peace, drawn up after the Second World War by those countries who had defeated Germany.

The Charter had 111 articles. The 51 countries who belonged to the U.N. in 1945, when the charter was drawn up, included the United States, the United Kingdom, the Soviet Union, Nationalist China, France, India, Egypt, South Africa, Turkey, Greece and Canada. Since then, other countries have joined the U.N., among them Israel, Pakistan, Spain and Uganda. Nationalist China has withdrawn and the Republic of China has taken its place.

One of the main aims of the U.N. is to help underdeveloped countries, such as those in Africa, to become more self-supporting. Sometimes it lends money and sometimes it gives technical help with farming machinery or industrial tools.

The headquarters of the U.N. is in New York, where all member countries meet to discuss world affairs.

CARYATID

The caryatids were the priestesses of Artemis at Karuai or Caryae in Laconia. Representations of draped female figures which are used instead of columns in building are also known as caryatids. Their origin may be traced back to the ivory and bronze mirror handles used in Phoenicia and Ancient Greece which also represented women's bodies.

They first appeared as architectural columns in three small treasuries at Delphi (550–530 B.C.). In Roman times they were used in Asia Minor and North Africa, but the most famous example is the caryatid porch of the Erechtheum, an Ionic temple of Athena on the Acropolis at Athens.

WHAT is a filibuster?

VOODOO

Voodoo, or Vodun, meaning "spirit", is an African name given to rites practised in poverty-stricken rural areas of Haiti. It was developed by African slaves brought to the island by the French during the late 17th Century and has now spread to Cuba, Jamaica and Brazil.

Possessing no doctrine, Voodoo is wonderfully elastic and, as any primitive religion demands, is full of myths and magic. Since most Voodooists are also Roman Catholics, they have introduced many of the church's beliefs into their religion. For instance, they have enthusiastically adopted many saints.

Ritual dances occupy an important part of their lives and usually take place in the presence of a priest or priestess. These dances are rhythmic and are accompanied by drums. Back and forth the dancers shuffle, shoulders shaking and eyes rolling as they chant incomprehensible words. They can become quite unaware of the outside world and, in this state, have often been known to froth at the mouth. When a baby is "baptized", it is thrown through flames to become fortified against danger.

Many Voodoo priests exploit the beliefs and superstitions of their people for their own gain and power. This is bound to happen in any primitive religion, but the situation is beginning to improve as education spreads.

FILIBUSTER

A filibuster was the name originally given to buccaneers, those English French and Dutch adventurers of the sea who haunted the Caribbean and Pacific seaboard of South America during the second half of the 17th Century. The chief bond between them was their hatred of the Spaniards.

The French called their adventurers *flibustiers* (from the Dutch *vrijbuiter*—freebooter) and from this we derive the name filibuster. Its modern use in this sense describes someone who engages in private warfare against any state.

But the word has taken on another meaning—the practice of using delaying tactics or engaging in a prolonged discussion for the purpose of delaying a vote. To frustrate filibusters in parliament, most governments have been forced to introduce some measure of time limit on debates. Nevertheless, filibustering attempts are still made to hinder or prevent votes in legislative bodies. "Talking out" a Bill is often practised.

Index

A

B

See Bicycle *page 330*

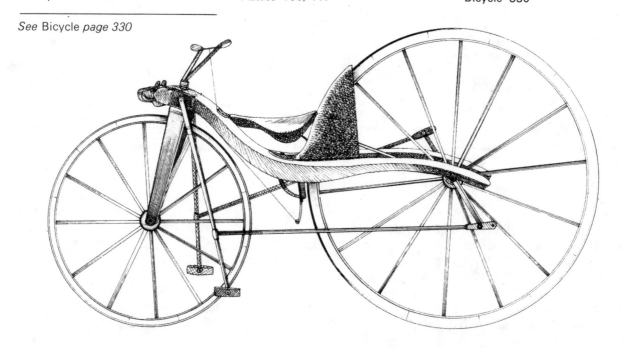

C

See Christopher Columbus *page 119*

See Dodo *page 10*

Q

R

See Bandolier page 407

U

V

W

See Largest Animals *page 10*

X & Y

Z

Acknowledgments

The publishers would like to thank the following individuals and organizations for their kind permission to reproduce the pictures in this book:

A–Z Botanical Collection 50; Ardea 48, 69 left, (I. R. Berches) 16, (K. Fink) 32–33; Australian House 328; Australian News and Information Bureau 71; Barnaby's Picture Library 15 centre, 39, 116–117, 120–121, 158–159, 164 below left, 165, 169, 226, 229, 233, 242–243, 244 below, 251 below, 254, 255, 257 right, 268, 269 above, 273 below left, 279, 280, 283, 292, 304, 306, 316, 317, 333, 337, 340–341, 353, 358, 374, 376, 400, 426–427, 431, 436, 455, (R. Backhard) 41 left, (C. Bernhard) 183, (G. Clyde) 254–255, (J. E. Downward) 30 below, (H. C. Horridge) 31, (D. Huffman) 42, (Courtesy Philips Auctioneers) 347, (Sir George Pollack) 394, (L. Schmitt, Jr.) 277 above right, (W. Thompson) 44 below; B.B.C. 326; Bodleian Library 133, 417; Bulloz 137; Camera Press 91, 103, 123, 129, 151, 152, 153, 170 right, 214, 215 above and below left, 248, 253, 260, 263, 334, 335, 351; Canada House 201 above, 227 above; J. Allan Cash 403; Cinema Bookshop 299, 438–439; City Art Gallery, Bristol 105; Bruce Coleman 37, 41 right, (J. Bartlett) 68, (S. Bisserot) 19, (J. Brownlie) 69 right, (J. Burton) 9, 12, 20, 32, 72, (G. J. Deane) 8 right, (P. Jackson) 60, (J. Markham) 73, (C. Ott) 57, (A. Power) 24, (M. F. Soper) 176 right, (S. Trevor) 26, (J. Van Wormer) 49; Colorsport 324–325, 392; Colour Library International 113, 125, 204–205 below, 217, 240, 241, 273 above, 357; Cooper Bridgeman 85, 115, 393 left, 404–405; Daily Telegraph 208, 384 below; Decca 321; Demag Material Handling Co. Ltd. 285; Dunlop Tyre Co. Ltd. 343; Mary Evans Picture Library 55, 78, 79, 83, 95, 98, 114, 118, 122, 131, 134, 290, 330, 379, 407, 454, 458; Flight Magazine 298; Fox Photos 230, 415; Geological Museum, London 264; Goldsmiths' Hall 406; Hale Observatory/Royal Astronomical Society 315; Sonia Halliday 93, 360 below; Robert Harding 96–97; Michael Holford 80, 94, 100–101, 124–125, 136, 188, 197, 227 below, 369, 373, 388, 416, 429, 432, 445, 448–449, (Charles Dickens House) 144–145; Eric Hosking 30 above; Iceland Information Bureau 215 below right; Institute of Ophthalmology 160; Israeli Government Tourist Office 223; Keystone Press 110, 111, 127, 138, 139 below,
143, 163, 167, 186, 206–207, 234, 235, 238, 246 left, 250, 251 above, 270–271, 272, 302–303, 313, 314, 318, 344 below, 346, 363, 368, 370, 382, 383, 391 right, 395, 398, 399, 418–419, 428, 430, 434, 443, 446, 447, 456, 462; Frank Lane 14, 28, 38 right, 43, 52 left, 53, 59 above, 74, 75, 228 below, (R. L. Cassell) 27 right, (A. Christiansen) 13, (T. Davidson) 11, (P. Kirkpatrick) 301, (W. L. Miller) 38 left, (L. Perkins) 8 left, (H. Schremp) 45, (R. Thompson) 27 left, (Trinkhaus) 18 below, (L. West) 36; The Louvre 356; Mansell Collection 82, 106, 107, 128, 132, 182, 266, 286, 319, 359, 362, 390, 391 left, 410, 435 below, 442, 463; William MacQuitty 196; Ken Moreman 461; N.H.P.A. 18 above, 37 left, 170 left, (A. Bannister) 29, 56, 64–65, (S. Dalton) 25, 35, 46, 62, 459, (D. Dickens) 465, (B. Hawkes) 40; Natural Science Photos 34, 65, 66, 396; Norwegian Embassy 435 above; Novosti Press Agency 308, 414–415; Orbis (Library of Congress) 76–77, (U.S. Naval Academy Museum) 102; Pharmaceutical Society 140–141; Phillips and Co. 88; Picturepoint 17, 21, 84, 104, 112, 164 right and above left, 199, 204–205 above, 216, 224, 228 above, 237, 244 above, 245, 249, 256, 257 left, 264–265, 269 below, 273 below right, 288–289, 303, 305 above, 320, 336 below, 344 above, 361, 365, 376–377, 380, 384 above, 389, 397, 409 right, 420, 421 above, 432–433, 437, 440–441, 452–453, 464, 470 below; Axel Poignant 139 above; The Post Office 311; Popperfoto 63, 90, 130, 154, 198, 201 below, 203, 210, 282, 293, 322, 378, 411, 450, 451, 470 above; PYE of Cambridge 323; Radio Times Hulton Picture Library 50–51, 99, 126, 135, 171, 222, 246 right, 247, 274–275, 307, 349, 366, 367, 371, 386, 471; Rank, Hovis, McDougall Ltd. 325; Rex Features 426; Ronan Picture Library 187, 287, 327; Royal Astronomical Society 278–279; Royal College of Music 354; St. Bartholemew's Hospital 172, 191; Scala 355 right, 385, 424; The Scout Association 352; Seaphot 59 above, 345; Spectrum Colour Library 15 below, 22, 23, 44 above, 52 right, 61, 67, 70, 108–109, 156, 161, 202, 213, 220, 221, 225, 236, 252, 261, 265, 276, 277 above left, 295, 296, 297, 329, 332, 336 above, 348, 355 left, 360 above, 364, 387, 393 right, 401, 402, 408, 409 left, 413, 421 below, 423, 425, 453, 457, 468, 469; Tate Gallery 281; Tourist Photo Library 81; Transworld Feature Syndicate Inc./Nasa 460; Triplex 310; James Webb 149; Joseph Ziolo 412, 444.